HOW TO DO THINGS WITH RULES

LAW IN CONTEXT

Editors: Robert Stevens (Haverford College, Pennsylvania),
William Twining (University of Warwick) and
Christopher McCrudden (Lincoln College, Oxford)

How To Do Things With Rules

A Primer of Interpretation

Second Edition

WILLIAM TWINING
Professor of Law at the University of Warwick

DAVID MIERS
Senior Lecturer in Law at University College, Cardiff

DISTRIBUTED IN U. S. A.
EXCLUSIVELY BY

Fred B. Rothman & Co.

LITTLETON, CO. 80127

WEIDENFELD AND NICOLSON
London

To our parents

Neither this book nor any other can say how a page *should* be *read* – if by that we mean that it can give a recipe for discovering what the page *really* says. All it could do – and that would be much – would be to help us to understand some of the difficulties in the way of such discoveries.

I.A. RICHARDS, *How to Read a Page*

© 1976, 1982 William Twining and David Miers

First published 1976
Reprinted 1978
Second edition 1982

George Weidenfeld and Nicolson Ltd
91 Clapham High Street London SW4

ISBN 0 297 78083 2 cased
ISBN 0 297 78084 0 paperback

Printed by Butler & Tanner Ltd, Frome and London

CONTENTS

CASES AND STATUTES

CASES

Note: This table only includes citations to those cases that are discussed.

STATUTES

ACKNOWLEDGMENTS

In the first edition we acknowledged the help and stimulus of a large number of people. We shall not list them by name again, but our gratitude is as great as ever. Since then our debts have increased. We are particularly grateful to all the students, immediate colleagues and law teachers in other institutions who have helped us to develop our ideas in discussion and who have commented on the first edition in the light of their experience in using it. We are grateful, too, for the friendly criticism of several reviewers. We have not been able to accept all of their advice, for it has often pointed in different directions. But we have carefully considered all the points they raised, and some of the changes in this edition, notably the extension of the range of illustrative material and the more explicit links to contemporary jurisprudential debates, reflect this influence. We should specifically thank Abdul Paliwala for suggesting to us the inclusion of the section on domestic violence and for his valuable comments on it; Alan Page for his comments on Chapters 9 and 10; and Christopher McCrudden, Robert Stevens, Michael Freeman, Robert Summers, Kevin Boyle, Phil Fennell, and Peter Twining for helpful comments and suggestions. Our families have been as patient and understanding as on the first occasion; and we should like to thank Christine Davies, Margaret Wright and Olive Heaton for help with typing, and Susanna Marsh for preparing a new index.

The authors and publishers thank the following for their permission to reproduce copyright material: Aldine Publishing Co. (Laurence Ross, *Settled Out of Court*); the American Sociological Association (Stewart Macaulay, *Non-contractual Relations in Business*); the Aristotelian

Society (William Twining, *Torture and Philosophy*); Jonathan Cape (I. Shah, *Tales of the Dervishes*); the Controller of Her Majesty's Stationery Office (*C.A.S. Occasional Paper No. 13* and *Violence in Marriage*); Douglas Hay (*Albion's Fatal Tree*); (Joseph Heller, Jonathan Cape and A. M. Heath *Catch-22*); P. H. Gulliver, New York University Press and Routledge and Kegan Paul (*Social Control in an African Society*); H. L. A. Hart, *The Concept of Law* © Oxford University Press 1961, by permission of Oxford University Press; Hutchinson & Co. (Joseph Raz, *Practical Reason and Norms*); the Incorporated Council for Law Reporting and Butterworth & Co. (extracts from cases in Chapter 1); Little, Brown & Co. (Karl Llewellyn, *The Common Law Tradition*); Maitland Publications (Julius Stone, *Legal System and Lawyers' Reasonings*); S. F. C. Milsom and the *Yale Law Journal* (Review of Grant Gilmore, *The Death of Contract*); Penguin Books Ltd and Doubleday & Co. (© 1961, Erving Goffman, *Asylums*); Routledge and Kegan Paul (Molly Brearly and Elizabeth Hutchfield, *A Teacher's Guide to Reading Piaget*); Ward, Lock & Co. (Ann Page, *Complete Etiquette for Ladies and Gentlemen*); Weidenfeld and Nicolson (Royston Lambert, *The Hothouse Society* and Patrick Atiyah, *Accidents, Compensation and the Law*) and the West Publishing Co. (Roscoe Pound, *Jurisprudence*).

PREFACE TO SECOND EDITION

All of us are confronted with rules every day of our lives. Most of us make, interpret and apply them, as well as rely on, submit to, avoid, evade them and grouse about them; parents, umpires, teachers, members of committees, businessmen, accountants, trade unionists, administrators, gamesmen, logicians, and moralists are among those who through experience may develop some proficiency in handling rules. Lawyers and law students are, for obvious reasons, specialists in rule-handling, but they do not have a monopoly of the art. A central theme of this book is that most of the basic skills of rule-handling are of very wide application and are not confined to law. There are, of course, certain specific techniques which have traditionally been viewed as 'legal', such as using a law library and handling cases and statutes. But these share the same foundations as rule-handling in general: they are only special in the sense that there are some additional considerations which apply to them and which are either not found at all or are given less emphasis in other contexts.

The purpose of this book is to provide a relatively systematic introduction to one basic aspect of rule-handling: interpretation and application. It is written particularly for students of law and administration, but most of it is directly relevant to problems of rule-handling in non-legal contexts. Within legal education, the focus of attention is orthodox in that it concentrates on certain traditional skills and techniques which have commonly, though misleadingly, been referred to as 'legal method', 'juristic method' or 'thinking like a lawyer'. The approach is mildly unorthodox, in that it questions certain widely held assumptions about the nature of these techniques and about efficient ways of learning to master them. Accordingly, it may be useful to give an indication of some of the juristic and educational assumptions underlying our approach.

The juristic assumptions can be stated in simplified form as follows: specialists in law are characterized as much by their supposed mastery of certain kinds of techniques as by their knowledge of what the law says. This is the core of the notion that law is essentially a practical art. Those who participate in legal processes and transactions, whether or not they are professionally qualified to practise law, are called upon to perform a variety of tasks. Legal practice encompasses such diverse activities as advising on the prudence of a particular course of action, collecting evidence, negotiating, advocacy, other kinds of spokesmanship, drafting statutes, regulations, contracts and other documents, predicting decisions of various types of courts, tribunals and officials, determining questions of fact, making and justifying decisions on questions of law, communicating information about legal rules, devising improvements in the law and so on. To perform these activities intelligently and efficiently requires a wide range of techniques, insights, and abilities. Phrases like 'thinking like a lawyer' or 'legal method' or 'legal reasoning' are misleading in so far as they equate proficiency in handling legal rules and the raw materials of such rules with being a good lawyer. Rule-handling is only one aspect of the crafts of law. Furthermore, interpretation is only one aspect of rule-handling. But it is basic – first, because most rule-handling activities involve or presuppose it, and, secondly, because a clear understanding of what is involved in interpretation inevitably throws light on a number of other matters as well.

Our approach is also based on a number of educational assumptions. First, we think that it is more economical and more efficient to study certain aspects of rule-handling *directly* than to leave the techniques to be picked up during the course of studying something else. This challenges the view, held by many teachers of law, that case-law techniques are best learned in the context of studying subjects such as Contract and Tort and that skill in handling statutory materials can be incidentally acquired in the course of studying such fields as Revenue Law or Commercial Law. Outside the context of law, the analogous view is that skill in rule-handling can only be acquired by experience. Such views are sometimes based on a confusion between laying a foundation for developing a skill and *reinforcing* that foundation through practice. This book proceeds on the premise that a direct approach is both a more economical and a more efficient way of starting off. Reinforcement through practice and experience is essential, but that should come later.

A second assumption is that the art of interpretation is best learned by a combination of theory and practice. A competent interpreter needs to understand the nature of the raw material he is dealing with, in which contexts and under what conditions problems of interpretation arise, how interpreting relates to other activities and what is involved in arguing about competing interpretations; it is also useful for him to have a set of concepts for analysing and discussing these problems, and he needs to be aware of some common fallacies and pitfalls to be avoided. But he also needs practice in handling actual problems. Accordingly this book is a combination of text and exercises. Working through it involves active participation on the part of the reader. If it achieves its objectives we hope that it will help to undermine two other fallacies – that emphasis on 'skills' is inevitably associated with philistine vocationalism and is necessarily illiberal, and that rigorous analysis is incompatible with a contextual approach.

A third assumption is that a subject with such diverse ramifications cannot be mastered by reading a single book. One disappointment with reactions to the first edition has been that relatively few people shared our perception of this book as an introduction to a rich and diverse body of literature in several disciplines. We had hoped that it would not be regarded as a book-in-itself designed to sustain a part, let alone the whole, of a course. Rather we saw it as providing a base from which the reader could sally forth to explore, for example, general books on semantics and reasoning, orthodox treatments of precedent and statutory interpretation, or various themes in jurisprudence, philosophy and social theory. In teaching we have always supplemented it with additional materials; we have been surprised by complaints that it was not self-sufficient and by those who suggested that it is too much to expect a student to use a library to follow up suggestions for further reading or in doing some of the exercises. We have made a few concessions to such reactions – notably by expanding the materials in Chapter 1 – but we still wish to present it as a flexible tool which can be used for a variety of purposes: as an introduction to legal method or to jurisprudence or, more generally, to the study of law; as an attempt to explain, or to demystify, legal ways of thought to non-lawyers, and as a book which may be of practical assistance to anyone whose work involves wrestling with complex laws, regulations and other rules.

Changes in this edition

The first edition was frankly experimental. In substantially revising and expanding the book we have retained the original aims, but have adjusted the means. Apart from updating, the main changes are as follows: Firstly, we have greatly extended the materials in the first chapter by incorporating some of the material from the old Appendix I and by adding new materials, notably on institutional rules, rules and results, bigamy and on protection of human rights. We have also included a substantial case study (one phase of the story of the Domestic Violence and Matrimonial Proceedings Act 1976) which dramatizes some of the main themes in the book.

Secondly, despite frequent expressions of irritation at Johnny, we have retained and, we hardly dare admit it, expanded his role. The *Case of the Legalistic Child* is admittedly artificial, but it is a convenient and easily understood analytical device for illustrating many elementary points. We have, however, tried to produce a better balance by using more illustrations drawn from real life in counterpoint with artificial but analytically neater hypothetical examples.

Thirdly, Chapters 2-6 have been rearranged and slightly expanded to provide a more coherent account of how rules and doubts and disputes about them arise. It is hoped that this will make it clear that Chapter 6 on the conditions of doubt is in some ways the fulcrum of the book – it provides a summary of some of the main factors which give rise to doubt in interpretation and it provides a base from which to start on the process of constructing arguments about competing interpretations, especially in legal contexts. The later chapters can then be seen not only as an exploration of such features of legal interpretation and reasoning about cases and statutes as are special, but also as an application of the general approach in a particular kind of context.

Fourthly, the chapter on algorithms has been shortened and relegated to an appendix because in our experience this particular device is less of a novelty for many modern law students than for their teachers. This has enabled us to strengthen, and lengthen, the treatment of legislation.

Finally, we have tried to bring out more clearly the connections between the analysis presented here and some contemporary debates in jurisprudence, as exemplified by the writings of Hart, Dworkin, Fuller, Llewellyn and others. In the process we may have more clearly revealed our own tendencies or biases, as cautious positivists, qualified relativists, moderate rationalists and committed contextualists. We hope that this will increase the usefulness of the book as an introduction to jurisprudence.

How to use the book

The book has been designed to cater for the needs of several different classes of reader. Accordingly it may be useful to try to provide some guidance on different ways of approaching it. The non-lawyer and the beginning law student who is using it as an introduction to jurisprudence or to the study of law generally should find it sufficient to skim Chapter 1, pausing long enough to become familiar with the range of illustrative material and, in particular, with the *Case of the Legalistic Child* (p. 7), sections (a) and (b) on bigamy (pp. 38–44), the *Buckoke* case (p. 48) and Article 3 of the European Convention (p. 60), and the charts of the Bad Man in Boston (pp. 68–9). These are used as examples throughout the text. From time to time you may wish to refer back to the appropriate point in Chapter 1 to refresh your memory about details or to clarify an allusion, but it is not necessary to grapple with all the details nor to try to answer the questions in the first chapter in order to understand the general thrust of the analysis in the text. Depending on your background and your interests, some of Chapters 3, 7 and 10 may also be skimmed if you find them too complicated or too detailed. Reading the book in this way should be rather like reading a novel or play in order to get a sense of the plot and the main characters.

If the book is being used for the purpose of stimulating thought and developing certain kinds of analytical skill, the recommended order is to try to answer the questions and do the exercises in the first chapter before moving on; to do some of the exercises related to each chapter immediately after reading it, and finally to re-read the text as a whole *and* to follow up at least some of the suggestions for further reading. The subject is a complex one, involving many different levels of understanding: what we have tried to do is provide a starting point for developing some basic skills and for exploring a rich, but scattered, literature in a number of disciplines. The exercises range from quite elementary questions (some of which even have answers) to problems which advanced students, using a library, should find demanding.

In the case of law students our hope is that they will first be exposed to the book before they are swamped with masses of detailed information. The best time for a law student to read this book for the first time may be early in his first year or even at the so-called 'pre-law' stage. As 'deep-enders', we realize that some of our colleagues will jib at this and may prefer to introduce it at a later stage – if at all – for instance as a starting point for a course in Jurisprudence. We have ourselves tried out much of the material in a number of courses: in a first-year course on Juristic Technique at Belfast, in Legal System (first year) and Legal Theory (second year) at Warwick, in first- and third-year courses at Cardiff, and in a post-graduate seminar in Legal Philosophy at Uppsala. Some of it has also been used in one extramural course and in an introductory course for non-lawyers, both at Warwick. For obvious reasons, different aspects have been emphasized, depending on the context. But nothing in our experiences suggests that the basic lessons are beyond the reach of the ordinary beginning law student nor of an interested layman of comparable intelligence, provided that they are willing to struggle with the detailed analysis. If they are not prepared to do this, they cannot expect to become competent interpreters.

W.L.T.
D.R.M.

PART ONE

1 Some Food for Thought

1 Introduction

In this chapter we have collected together some concrete examples that illustrate the main questions and themes that are explored in the book as a whole. The purpose of presenting them at this stage is partly to generate interest and puzzlement, and partly to encourage you to start to think actively about some basic issues.

The materials also indicate some of the varied contexts in which problems of interpretation of rules arise: relationships within the family, in everyday social life, in institutions such as schools, prisons and factories, in commercial relationships as well as in formal legal processes such as prosecutions for bigamy and claims for compensation, whether they are settled out of court or by litigation; one section deals with dispute settlement in a traditional African society, another with provisions protecting human rights under a written constitution and in International Law. This variety of contexts is intended to emphasize the thesis that nearly all of the factors which give rise to difficulties of interpretation – what we shall refer to as the conditions of doubt – are present in a great variety of very different types of social situation, and can cause difficulty in almost any kind of case, whether it is trivial or momentous, simple or complex, legal or non-legal.

Each of the sections is designed to introduce one or more particular topics. The story of Solomon and the baby in section 2 illustrates the difference between questions of interpretation of rules and other aspects of adjudication and problem-solving, and, with the other extracts, introduces the notion of legalistic behaviour. The admittedly artificial example of the legalistic child (3) raises a variety of analytical issues about rules as responses to problems and the relations between rules, processes and roles. Sections 4 and 5 deal with questions about reasons for having rules and the relations between rules and results – especially gaps between what is prescribed by formal rules and the actual outcomes of particular processes. These materials also introduce another central theme of the book: that it is not only officials, adjudicators and judges who are faced with problems of interpretation of rules; any interpreter needs to clarify his situation by asking three preliminary questions: Who am I? At what stage in what process am I? What am I trying to do?

Next comes some specifically legal material. Section 6 contains examples of complex rules in fixed verbal form, taken from statutes and regulations. These seem to be difficult, if not impossible, to understand. Is this difficulty due to the complexity of the subject-matter, or of the rules, or to the way in which they are drafted? Is such complexity and obscurity inevitable? Are there ways of helping the bewildered interpreter to find his way around complex rules? Section 7 deals with the crime of bigamy, including the notoriously problematic section 57 of the Offences Against the Person Act 1861 and *Reg.* v. *Allen*, which will be used throughout the book to illustrate many different points. There follows another bigamy case which highlights further difficulties connected with this section and illustrates the operation of the doctrine and techniques of precedent in a field where there have been recurrent disagreements among the judges. These materials, like some of the others, pose quite sharply the question: how and why do disagreements about interpretation of rules arise?

The case in the next section (8), *Buckoke* v. *G.L.C.*, besides raising some further questions of interpretation, illustrates two classic dilemmas: that of someone who is faced with seemingly conflicting instructions, and that of judges when confronted with a statutory enactment which leads to an undesirable result. Can and should judges mitigate the rigours of the law where Parliament has been unwilling or unable to make an explicit exception covering apparently deserving cases? Underlying this is a more general issue: do officials (and others) ever have a discretion, or even a duty, to disobey the law?

The next section (9) contains some extracts from what is perhaps the most famous single case in the common law, *Donoghue* v. *Stevenson*. It is so well known that we hesitated to include it, because it may be considered hackneyed. We have, however, decided to retain it. First, because it is a remarkably rich example of the operation of judicial techniques of reasoning. Not all the points that it illustrates are obvious or trite. Furthermore, just because the case is so frequently discussed, it provides a useful link with other writings, especially on case law and judicial law-making.

Section 10 introduces some provisions that are found in such documents as the Universal Declaration of Human Rights, the European Convention on Human Rights and Fundamental Freedoms, and domestic Bills of Rights. There are special considerations which affect the styles of drafting and approaches to interpretation of such provisions. The main examples selected here deal with extreme forms of treatment, notably 'torture, inhuman or degrading treatment or punishment' and 'cruel and unusual punishments'. These raise a number of familiar issues: about the connections between moral principles and legal provisions, about the workability and the justification of 'absolute' prohibitions, especially in extreme cases, and about the relationship between ordinary municipal laws and rules which are claimed to be 'fundamental' or 'universal' or 'entrenched'. They also suggest some less obvious questions directly relevant to interpretation. Concepts like 'torture' and 'inhuman treatment' are rather more complex than they seem. It is worth asking questions about the use of highly emotive terms like 'torture' in drafting legal provisions and, as with most other examples in this chapter, about the interaction between appropriate modes of interpretation and the context of interpretation.

Section 11 brings out a theme which has been largely implicit in the earlier material: the crucial importance of differences of standpoint, role and objective in understanding problems of interpretation. We shall stress throughout the book that any particular problem of interpretation needs to be set in the context of some conception of a wider process – a series of events and decisions which have led up to the moment when the interpreter is faced with a choice and which will continue after that moment. Interpretation does not take place in a vacuum. The notion of a total process is just as important in non-legal contexts, where there may be few or no formal procedures, as in the typically formal context of legal processes. There is also a tendency in legal literature to assume, either explicitly or implicitly, 'top down' points of view – exemplified by the standpoint of a legislator, judge or other official making or applying law. There is accordingly a tendency to underplay or to ignore entirely the points of view of those who are subject to the rules – worm's-eye views or 'bottom up' perspectives.

Yet typically (but not universally) the interpreter is someone who is confronted with a pre-existing rule, made by someone else, and which he has no authority to change. His standpoint may be neither that of the eagle nor the worm. The viewpoints of *both* eagles and worms, and of others, are directly relevant to problems of interpretation.

In the final section of this chapter we present a case study which links together in a vivid, and we hope interesting, way some of the main strands which have been illustrated separately by the preceding materials. The study is in essence the story of one phase of the law's response to the problem of domestic violence. This problem is probably as old as the institution of the family, but it was dramatized and brought into public attention in Britain during the early 1970s. To put it in simple terms – the social and public reaction to the publicization of the phenomenon of domestic violence prompted a political initiative which was partly translated into legislative action. This in turn produced a rather complex and unexpected response from the judiciary. Both the case study and the other materials in this chapter touch on issues which might be thought to fall outside the scope of this book because they are not strictly speaking about interpretation. However they are relevant to our purposes because problems of interpretation of rules need to be seen in the context of, and to be differentiated from, other questions relating to rules and social processes.

As was suggested in the Preface, it is not necessary to read the whole of Chapter 1 before proceeding to read the rest of the book. We do, however, recommend that you read the following pages at the outset: 7–9, 38–44, 48–53, 60–61, 68–9. In reading Chapters 2–10, reference will be made from time to time to material in this Chapter which can be read in conjunction with the relevant passages.

2 Legalism

(a) The judgment of Solomon

Then came there two women, that were harlots, unto the king, and stood before him. And the one woman said, O my lord, I and this woman dwell in one house; and I was delivered of a child with her in the house. And it came to pass the third day after that I was delivered, that this woman was delivered also: and we were together; there was no stranger with us in the house, save we two in the house. And this woman's child died in the night; because she overlaid it. And she arose at midnight, and took my son from beside me, while thine handmaid slept, and laid it in her bosom, and laid her dead child in my bosom. And when I rose in the morning to give my child suck, behold, it was dead: but when I had considered it in the morning, behold, it was not my son, which I did bear. And the other woman said, Nay; but the living is my son, and the dead is thy son. And this said, No; but the dead is thy son, and the living is my son. Thus they spake before the king.

Then said the king, The one saith, This is my son that liveth, and thy son is the dead: and the other saith, Nay; but thy son is the dead, and my son is the living. And the king said, Bring me a sword. And they brought a sword before the king. And the king said, Divide the living child in two, and give half to the one, and half to the other. Then spake the woman whose the living child was unto the king, for her bowels yearned upon her son, and she said, O my lord, give her the living child, and in no wise slay it. But the other said, Let it be neither mine or thine, but divide it. Then the king answered and said, Give her the living child, and in no wise slay it: she is the mother thereof. And all Israel heard of the judgment which the king had judged; and they feared the king: for they saw that the wisdom of God was in him, to do judgment.

(1 Kings iv, 16-28.)

QUESTIONS

1. Was the doubt in the case concerned with

   (i) the interpretation of a rule;
   (ii) a dispute about an issue of fact;
   (iii) solving a problem for the future in the best interests of the child;
   (iv) some other matter;
   (v) or a combination of some or all of these?

2. Is it possible to formulate precisely the rule or rules, if any, which were applicable to this case?

3. For what reason(s) is this judgment thought to be wise?

(b)

A man who was troubled in mind once swore that if his problems were solved he would sell his house and give all the money gained from it to the poor.

The time came when he realized that he must redeem his oath. But he did not want to give away so much money. So he thought of a way out.

He put the house on sale at one silver piece. Included with the house, however, was a cat. The price for this animal was ten thousand pieces of silver.

Another man bought the house and cat. The first man gave the single piece of silver to the poor, and pocketed the ten thousand for himself.

Many people's minds work like this. They resolve to follow a teaching; but they interpret their relationship with it to their own advantage. Until they overcome this tendency by special training, they cannot learn at all.

(From I. Shah, *Tales of the Dervishes* (1967), p. 68.)

QUESTIONS
1. Give examples of similar behaviour from legal and non-legal contexts. (See the case *Farrell* v. *Alexander* [1977] A.C. 59.)
2. Why do you think people behave in this kind of way?

(c) *The Merchant of Venice*, Act IV, Scene 1

Tarry a little; there is something else.
This bond doth give thee here no jot of blood;
The words expressly are 'a pound of flesh';
Take then thy bond, take thou thy pound of flesh;
But, in cutting it, if thou dost shed
One drop of Christian blood, thy lands and goods
Are, by the laws of Venice, confiscate
Unto the state of Venice,

QUESTION
Does labelling behaviour as 'legalistic' necessarily involve passing a value judgment on it?

(d)

There was only one catch and that was Catch-22, which specified that a concern for one's own safety in the face of dangers that were real and immediate was the process of a rational mind. Orr was crazy and could be grounded. All he had to do was ask; and as soon as he did, he would no longer be crazy and would have to fly more missions. Orr would be crazy to fly more missions and sane if he didn't, but if he was sane he had to fly them. If he flew them he was crazy and didn't have to; but if he didn't want to he was sane and had to. Yossarian was moved very deeply by the absolute simplicity of this clause of Catch-22 and let out a respectful whistle.

'That's some catch, that Catch-22,' he observed.

'It's the best there is,' Doc Daneeka agreed.

... Yossarian left money in the old woman's lap – it was odd how many wrongs leaving money seemed to right – and strode out of the apartment, cursing Catch-22 vehemently as he descended the stairs, even though he knew there was no such thing. Catch-22 did not exist, he was positive of that, but it made no difference. What did matter was that everyone thought it existed, and that was much worse, for there was no object or text to ridicule or refute, to accuse, criticize, attack, amend, hate, revile, spit at, rip to shreds, trample upon or burn up.

(from J. Heller, *Catch-22* (1964), pp. 54, 432.)

3 The Case of the Legalistic Child

Johnny, aged 7, is an only child. In recent months his mother has been mildly worried because he has developed a craving for sweet things and this has affected his appetite at meal times. She has commented to her husband, a practising lawyer, that Johnny 'seems to be developing a sweet tooth', and that 'he has been eating too much between meals', but until now she has done nothing about the problem. Then one afternoon she finds that Johnny has gone into the larder and helped himself to a half a pot of strawberry jam. Bearing in mind her husband's insistence that discipline in the family should operate in accordance with 'the Rule of Law', she does not punish Johnny on this occasion. Instead she says: 'That's naughty. In future you are never to enter the larder without my permission.' 'What does enter mean, Mummy?' asks Johnny. 'To go into,' says his mother. 'O.K.', says Johnny, relieved that he has got off so lightly.

Four incidents then follow in quick succession.

First, Johnny gets a broom and hooks out the pot of jam from the larder and helps himself. 'I didn't *enter* the larder,' he says.

Next, the cat enters the larder and attacks the salmon which mother has bought for a special meal to celebrate father's birthday. Mother, upstairs, hears Johnny hooting with laughter. She comes down to see him standing outside the larder door watching the cat eating the fish. 'I may not go into the larder,' he says.

The following day, at 5 pm, another pot of strawberry jam is found in the larder – empty. It was half-full at lunchtime. Johnny, who was playing on his own downstairs for much of the afternoon, denies all knowledge of the matter. There is no other evidence.

Finally, without any attempt at concealment, Johnny enters the larder, eats another pot of jam and deliberately knocks down a pile of cans. 'It's as if he were asking to be punished,' sighs Mother.

QUESTIONS

1. In *How Lawyers Think* (1937), Clarence Morris wrote: 'Problems

occur in gross. The unit which appears to be a single problem at first glance is usually a complex of related difficulties, a confluence of more specific problems. Often the initial urge is to dismiss the whole difficulty with some easy, impulsive solution . . .' (p. 5). Explain how this quotation is relevant to the nature of Mother's 'problem' in the story.

2. Consider each of the incidents as an isolated case from the point of view of

(i) Mother in her role as enforcement officer and prosecutor;

(ii) Johnny, defending himself;

(iii) Father as adjudicator;

(iv) a family friend who has the reputation of being a good psychologist.

3. Construct an argument about the appropriate meaning to be attached to the word 'enter', from the point of view of

(i) Mother prosecuting Johnny for a breach of her rule in the first instance;

(ii) Johnny, defending himself.

4. State as many different interpretations as you can of 'That's naughty' in the context in which it was said. Is any one interpretation clearly right or better than the others?

5. Construct an account of the development of a solution to the problem through case-by-case decision, assuming that the sequence of events was (i) creation of the original rule, (ii) the first incident, (iii) adjudication of the first incident, (iv) second incident, and so on. Would this be a more or less satisfactory way of solving this particular problem than by making a rule? Give reasons.

6. Draft a rule to fit Mother's diagnosis that Johnny is 'eating too much between meals'.

7. Do you think that a better approach would have been to give Johnny a clip on the ear immediately after the first incident? Give reasons for your answer. Under what circumstances is it appropriate to deal with problems *before*, rather than after they have arisen?

8. After the episodes concerning the larder, Father decides on a change of strategy. 'From now on', he says, 'there will be only one rule that you must observe in this household: "you must be reasonable at all times".'

(i) Is this a rule, and if so, is it a reasonable one?

(ii) Give examples of practical problems of interpretation which might arise for (*a*) Johnny, and (*b*) his parents, under this provision.

(iii) Does Father's 'rule' leave any outlet for Johnny's legalistic tendencies?

9. Johnny is watching his favourite television programme with Mother's agreement. Father, having just arrived home from work, walks into the room, and without a word to Johnny, switches over to another channel on which a current affairs programme is in progress. Johnny protests, 'You can't do that.'

 (i) Is Johnny invoking a rule? If so, what rule?
(ii) Are there any rules governing (*a*) watching television and (*b*) the distribution of housework where you live? If so, state them. *How do you know whether there are rules about these activities and what they are?*

10. What assumptions about family life and the role of rules within it are to be inferred from the behaviour of Johnny's parents? Is theirs, in your view, a satisfactory way of dealing with discipline in the family?

4 Rules and behaviour

(a) Interpersonal behaviour

(i) SOCIAL ETIQUETTE

The etiquette of games is governed entirely by simplicity, courtesy, and consideration for others. Nowadays girls on the playing field and tennis court learn to 'play the game' and have realized something of that spirit of sportsmanship which rejoices in the victory of the winner, no matter which side he or she represents.

In any sport, two or three outstanding rules should be kept in mind, namely:

(1) Don't lose your temper on any provocation whatever. Nothing is more ill-bred or gives one away more readily than openly to rejoice over a personal triumph or to display annoyance when one's partner makes a bad move.
(2) Don't take any unfair advantage of your opponent and let your scoring be perfectly truthful, giving your opponent the benefit of any doubt.
(3) Don't attract attention to yourself by criticism of the players or their game.
(4) Remember to congratulate the winner, be she partner or opponent.
(5) When congratulated yourself, attribute your performance to good luck; if an opponent wins, assume that is because she played well, but if she loses, that she has been unlucky.
(6) Don't delay the game for deep thought, to study conditions, etc. This is boring for others....

In her social relationships with men, the woman living alone must accept certain conventions.

(7) She should not lunch or dine alone with a married man more than once or twice – unless their relationship is openly a business one that demands it.

(8) She should never allow a man guest to stay on after a party at her flat or room after other guests have gone, or stay on herself at a man's party after the rest have left.

(9) She should not entertain a man alone in her apartment, except for the few brief minutes when he calls for her before an evening out together; nor should she go alone to a man's bachelor flat or room. In most hostels and boarding houses, convention rules that if a man and woman are alone together, which may at times be perfectly permissible and necessary, the door must be left open.

(10) The young woman living on her own will not accept an invitation from a man to visit his country home, unless she knows that his mother or other married relation will be there to act as hostess for him. Preferably, the invitation should come from his mother.

(11) The young woman living alone must be especially discreet about drinking only in strict moderation.

Here again, however innocent her actual life, if she is known not to behave with strict regard for propriety in any one matter, all her other behaviour at once comes under suspicion.

For the same reason she should never accept a valuable present from a man who is not a relation. . . .

'But why bother with rules, if right feeling is the root of the matter?' it may be asked. There are two answers to this. Firstly, as a matter of pure convenience, a rule of etiquette can save endless time-wasting decisions: in the absence of such a rule, one would have to think out afresh each day the problem of where to put the knives and forks on the table.

Secondly, the acceptance by society as a whole of certain conventions of civilized behaviour does impose, even on the more selfish members of the community, some self-discipline, some need for consideration of others, some thought beyond mere self.

(From A. Page, *Complete Etiquette for Ladies and Gentlemen* (1961), pp. 37, 7 and 3.)

(ii) RULES OF THUMB

It may be of some help to examine the sort of reasons usually given for having rules. Our aim in doing this is not to survey comprehensively the possible ways of justifying rules. It is to look at some common ways of doing so in order to gain some insight into the nature of mandatory norms generally. Mill admirably summarizes two very common reasons for having rules: 'By a wise practitioner, therefore, rules of conduct will only be considered as provisional. Being made for the most numerous cases, or for those of most ordinary occurrence, they point out the manner in which it will be least perilous to act, where time or means do not exist for analysing the actual circumstances of the case, or where we cannot trust our judgment in estimating them' (*A System of Logic*, 6, 12, 3). Rules are thus justified as time-saving devices and as devices to reduce the risk of error in deciding what ought to be done. We may add to these features the related justification of rules as labour-saving devices. A rule can be examined in tranquillity on the basis of the best information available concerning the factors likely to be present in the situations to which it applies. The rule states what is to be done in these situations on the balance of foreseeable reasons. When a situation to which it applies actually occurs the norm subjects can rely on the rule, thus saving much time and labour and reducing the risks of a mistaken calculation which is involved in examining afresh every situation on its merits.

(From J. Raz, *Practical Reason and Norms* (1975), p. 59.)

QUESTIONS

1. Many people would consider rules of etiquette old-fashioned and in some instances, absurd. Which of the rules, if any, in extract (i) would you regard as being absurd, and why?
2. Can you give a precise account of the main rules of etiquette which you accept?
3. Page and Raz mention a number of reasons for having rules. Can you think of any other general reasons?
4. On the face of it, the function of the rules in extract (i) is to tell various people what may or may not be done on certain occasions, but rules also have hidden functions. What do you think might be some of the hidden functions of these rules?
5. What values govern the relationships mentioned in extract (i)? Do you think it appropriate to embody them in a relatively specific code?

(b) Institutional behaviour

(i) SCHOOL RULES

Consider the following selection of rules concerning discipline in a school:

1. Paper must be put in dustbin or litter baskets in the playgrounds or into wastepaper baskets in School.
2. Children should not wear outdoor clothing in School. Jewellery may not be worn, this includes rings.
3. Chewing gum is unhygienic and is not allowed.
4. Biro pens spoil writing, use School pens or fountain pens.
5. Classes and individual children must walk in single file on stairs and corridors and always keep to the right.

6. After wash basins have been used, care must be taken to see that dirty water is emptied and the basin is left clean. Keep towels as clean as possible.

7. No bicycles to be ridden through the playground. Only bicycles which satisfy safety regulations will be allowed.

8. Except when staff request it, do not shift or re-arrange any furniture, do not tamper with window poles, windows, thermostats, curtain cords, etc.

9. Pupils may not enter the staff common rooms without hearing permission to do so given (after knocking) from within.

QUESTIONS

1. What can you learn about the school from the above rules?

2. Identify the main values which are promoted by these rules.

3. It is said that rules may impose duties, distribute benefits, or confer power or discretion to act on certain persons. Rules may also be said to confer privileges, liberties, and to impose liabilities. What do the following rules do: nos. 1, 4 and 7?

4. In what institutions other than schools might it be necessary to have rules regulating the discipline and hierarchy of its members? Does this suggest any general lessons about the use of rules as methods for regulating the behaviour of people in societies?

5. Devise a situation in which a legalistic child might avoid the intended effect of any one of the school rules above.

6. Comment on the drafting of the rules nos. 2 and 9. Redraft each rule in the light of any criticisms you have thought of.

Consider the following examples of different attitudes to school rules:

(1) 'I ask myself *why* should I send this boy to his headmaster for being in town at 3.30; *why* should we put 16-year-olds to bed at 10 on Saturday nights; *why* should a boy be on time for every meal, every day; *why* should we force them to sing at compulsory house prayers? Why should we support this artificial state set up by the whims of old governors average age 93, whom you never see?'

Prefect, eighteen, public school
(From R. Lambert, *The Hothouse Society* (1968), p. 174)

(2) 'We must change the rules – they have become an entity in themselves divorced from their original intention. They allow for no original thinking – in their pride they assume themselves equal to any situation.'

Boy, seventeen, public school (ibid., p. 371)

(3) 'At our school they seem to take pride in not having very many

written rules, but there are some people who are walking rule books. Sometimes it seems as if they make up the rules as they go along.'

Karen Twining

(4) 'A study of children's ideas on punishment leads one to re-think the whole question of rules and regulations in schools. The planning of the school and classroom must be such that the children's participation in it leads them to think in terms of the solution to problems rather than obedience or, more commonly perhaps, disobedience.'
(From Molly Brearly and Elizabeth Hutchfield, *A Teacher's Guide to Reading Piaget* (1966), p. 130)

(5) 'I think our school rules are fairly good. Boys are not allowed in class at break in theory. Hair should be kept at a reasonable length, and school uniform worn, but this rule is disobeyed. Many boys wear coloured shirts and trousers. Many also have long hair. Especially Fourth Formers break these rules, coming in 'Crombie' jackets with Manchester Utd or City badges on them instead of blazers.

'Forms one to four are meant to wear caps, nobody does. Boys are meant to walk on the left-hand side of the corridor, the usual practice is a run, but ready to walk if a teacher or prefect appears. Litter is thrown down all over the yard even though enough bins are provided. Chewing is not allowed in class, though many boys do. Soccer with a tennis ball is sometimes played in the washroom when it is not occupied by smokers.'

Andrew Smith, age 13
(From Nan Berger, *Rights* (1974), p. 78)

(6) 'While rules exist they will be broken. While rules exist the University is only encouraging students to start to break these rules on the basis of a principle. The principle being that students are capable and responsible enough to choose who their officers will be. . . .' (Students protesting against university regulations governing elections of Student Union officers.)

QUESTIONS
1. Identify, as precisely as you can, the different attitudes to rules displayed in the quotations.
2. Do any of the quotations indicate that rules and their enforcement may have undesirable side-effects? If so, what might these be?
3. 'Rules are meant to be broken.' Do any of the quotations support

this common attitude to rules? What are the implications of such an attitude?

4. Look carefully at quotation (2). Can you think of any rules which have become divorced from their original intention? What particular problems might this pose for an interpreter?

5. What assumptions about power, authority and discretion in the relevant institution are made in each of the quotations?

(ii) A UNIVERSITY RULE OF DISCIPLINE

Section 1 of the University of Erewhon rules of discipline reads: 'A student must not wilfully or persistently behave in a manner inconsistent with the proper functioning of the University or likely to bring the University into disrepute.'

QUESTIONS

1. (i) What kinds of behaviour do you think this rule is intended to cover?
   (ii) How would you set about determining the intended meaning of 'the proper functioning of the University'?
2. Would a student be in breach of this rule if he:
   (i) cheated in an examination;
   (ii) used the University laboratories throughout his final year to synthesize cocaine;
   (iii) painted defamatory statements about a professor on the factory wall opposite the main entrance to the University;
   (iv) refused to wear a safety helmet in the engineering laboratories because to do so would be contrary to his religious beliefs;
   (v) took drugs to improve his performance and accepted payments inconsistent with his amateur status while representing the University in an international student athletics meeting in France;
   (vi) disrupted a lecture being given by a visiting speaker whom he and many others thought held racist views; and
   (vii) wrote an article making serious allegations about the conduct and standard of examinations at the University, which was published in a national newspaper?

(iii) TOTAL INSTITUTIONS

In institutions such a prisons and hospitals, the individual is submerged in sets of rules which govern and regulate almost every aspect of his life. Stripped of his individuality and treated in the same way as everyone else, the inmate of these 'total institutions' is faced with sets of rules which require constant attention and interpretation, and which can be invoked or waived by the institution's officials as punishments or rewards for his behaviour.

Writing about patients in a mental hospital, the sociologist Erving Goffman draws attention to the way in which these rules provide 'a framework for personal reorganization.'

First, there are the 'house rules', a relatively explicit and formal set of prescriptions and proscriptions that lays out the main requirements of inmate conduct. These rules spell out the austere round of life of the inmate. Admission procedures, which strip the recruit of his past supports, can be seen as the institution's way of getting him ready to start living by house rules.

Secondly, against this stark background, a small number of clearly defined rewards or privileges are held out in exchange for obedience to staff in action and spirit. It is important to see that many of these potential gratifications are carved out of the flow of support that the inmate had previously taken for granted. On the outside, for example, the inmate probably could unthinkingly decide how he wanted his coffee, whether to light a cigarette, or when to talk; on the inside, such rights may become problematic. Held up to the inmate as possibilities, these few recapturings seem to have a reintegrative effect, re-establishing relationships with the whole lost world and assuaging withdrawal symptoms from it and from one's lost self. The inmate's attention, especially at first, comes to be fixed on these supplies and obsessed with them. He can spend the day, like a fanatic, in devoted thoughts about the possibility of acquiring these gratifications or in contemplation of the approaching hour at which they are scheduled to be granted. Melville's report on navy life contains a typical example: ... 'It is one of the most common punishments for very trivial offences in the Navy, to "stop" a seaman's grog for a day or a week. And as most seamen so cling to their grog, the loss of it is generally deemed by them a very serious penalty. You will sometimes hear them say, "I would rather have my wind *stopped* than my grog!"'

The building of a world around these minor privileges is perhaps the most important feature of inmate culture, and yet it is something that cannot easily be appreciated by an outsider, even one who has previously lived through the experience himself. This concern with privileges sometimes leads to generous sharing; it almost always leads to a willingness to beg for such things as cigarettes, candy, and newspapers. Understandably, inmate conversation often revolves around a 'release binge fantasy', namely, a recital of what one will do during leave or upon release from the institution. This fantasy is related to a feeling that civilians do not appreciate how wonderful their life is.

The third element in the privilege system is punishments; these are designated as the consequence of breaking the rules. One set of these punishments consists of the temporary or permanent withdrawal of privileges or the abrogation of the right to try to earn them. In general, the punishments meted out in total institutions are more severe than anything encountered by the inmate in his home world. In any case, conditions in which a few easily controlled privileges are so important are the same conditions in which their withdrawal has a terrible significance.

(From E. Goffman, *Asylums* (1968), pp. 51–3, *reprinted by permission of Penguin Books Ltd.*)

(iv) PRISON RULES

The Prison Rules 1964 as amended to 1976, contain the following provisions concerning prisoners' letters and visits.

33. Letters and visits generally.

(1) The Secretary of State may, with a view to securing discipline and good order or the prevention of crime or in the interests of any persons, impose restrictions, either generally or in a particular case, upon the communications to be permitted between a prisoner and other persons.

(2) Except as provided by statute or these Rules, a prisoner shall not be permitted to communicate with any outside person, or that person with him, without the leave of the Secretary of State.

(3) Except as provided by these Rules, every letter or communication to or from a prisoner [may] be read or examined by the governor or an officer deputed by him, and the governor may, at his discretion, stop any letter or communication on the ground that its contents are objectionable or that it is of inordinate length.

(4) Every visit to a prisoner shall take place within the sight of an officer, unless the Secretary of State otherwise directs.

(5) Except as provided by these Rules, every visit to a prisoner shall take place within the hearing of an officer, unless the Secretary of State otherwise directs.

(6) The Secretary of State may give directions, generally or in relation to any visit or class of visits, concerning the days and times when prisoners may be visited.

34. Personal letters and visits.

(1) An unconvicted prisoner may send and receive as many letters and may receive as many visits as he wishes within such limits and subject to such conditions as the Secretary of State may direct, either generally or in a particular case.

(2) A convicted prisoner shall be entitled—

    (*a*) to send and to receive a letter on his reception into a prison and thereafter once a week; and

    (*b*) to receive a visit once in four weeks....

(3) The governor may allow a prisoner an additional letter or visit where necessary for his welfare or that of his family.

(4) The governor may allow a prisoner entitled to a visit to send and to receive a letter instead.

(5) The governor may defer the right of a prisoner to a visit until the expiration of any period of cellular confinement.

(6) The ... board of visitors may allow a prisoner an additional letter or visit in special circumstances, and may direct that a visit may extend beyond the normal duration.

(7) The Secretary of State may allow additional letters and visits in relation to any prisoner or class of prisoners.

(8) A prisoner shall not be entitled under this Rule to communicate with any person in connection with any legal or other business, or with any person other than a relative or friend, except with the leave of the Secretary of State.

(9) Any letter or visit under the succeeding provisions of these Rules shall not be counted as a letter or visit for the purposes of this Rule.

37. Legal advisers.

(1) The legal adviser of a prisoner in any legal proceedings, civil or criminal, to which the prisoner is a party shall be afforded reasonable facilities for interviewing him in connection with those proceedings, and may do so out of hearing but in the sight of an officer.

(2) A prisoner's legal adviser may, with the leave of the Secretary of State, interview the prisoner in connection with any other legal business in the sight and hearing of an officer.

37A. Further facilities in connection with legal proceedings.

(1) A prisoner who is a party to any legal proceedings may correspond with his legal adviser in connection with the proceedings and unless the Governor has reason to suppose that any such correspondence contains matter not relating to the proceeding it shall not be read or stopped under Rule 33(3) of these Rules.

(2) A prisoner shall on request be provided with any writing materials necessary for the purposes of paragraph (1) of this Rule.

(3) Subject to any directions given in the particular case by the Secretary of State, a registered medical practitioner selected by or on behalf of such a prisoner as aforesaid shall be afforded reasonable facilities for examining him in connection with the proceedings, and may do so out of hearing but in the sight of an officer.

(4) Subject to any directions of the Secretary of State, a prisoner may correspond with a solicitor for the purpose of obtaining legal advice concerning any cause of action in relation to which the prisoner may become a party to civil proceedings or for the purpose of instructing the solicitor to issue such proceedings.

QUESTIONS

1. Are the rules mentioned by Goffman the only ones that apply to inmates of total institutions?

2. What are the limits imposed by the Prison Rules on the discretion of the Secretary of State to restrict (i) the number and content of letters written or received by a prisoner, and (ii) the number of visits

received by a prisoner? Are these limits capable of precise definition?
3. In what ways could the interpretation of the Prison Rules constitute rewards, privileges or punishments?

(c) Public behaviour

(i) NO VEHICLES IN THE PARK

(a) In his will Sir Thomas Cadoggan Bart bequeathed a plot of land to the Mayor and Corporation of Belleville to be converted into a public park, to be called 'Victoria Park' after Queen Victoria. One of the conditions of the bequest was that 'No carriages, broughams, or hansoms should be allowed in the Park, that the ladies and gentlemen of Belleville may the better enjoy the quietude of the scene.' Sir Thomas died in 1871 and his widow opened the Park in 1872. A by-law was passed in that year incorporating the rules governing the use of the park by the public. Regulation 1 reads: 'No carriage, coach, brougham, hansom or other vehicle shall be admitted to the park. The penalty for the infringement of this regulation shall be five shillings.' During the last decade of the century the park was only patronized by members of the upper classes, but since then this conventional barrier has steadily been broken down and today the Park is frequented by all sections of the population of Belleville. It is particularly popular with courting couples and with mothers, who bring their children to play there. The smaller boys of the town also kick footballs about and the place is not as quiet as it used to be.

During 1980 a group of teenagers took to riding round and round the park on motorcycles. Some mothers complained to the park-keeper that their children were frightened and endangered by the motorcycles and he ordered the teenagers to leave. When they argued that they were doing nothing wrong, he informed them of the existence of regulation 1 of the by-law, but after expelling them, took no further action against them. On the following day he caused to be put up a notice saying: 'No vehicles allowed in the Park; penalty £5'. Up to last week no action had been taken against anybody under the regulation.

Consider the following incidents which occurred last week in chronological order. After the determination of (1) it becomes a precedent for (2), and so on.

(1) On Monday Miss Smith rides her pony along the paths of the Park.

(2) On Tuesday Councillor Jones, the Mayor and a practising lawyer, drives his car through the Park gates and parks it unobtrusively under a tree nearby. When asked by the park-keeper to remove the car, he says 'I am the Mayor. Anyway my car is not bothering anybody, it's not being driven in the park, it is not making a noise, it is not endangering anybody. Anyway I have been doing this for years and nobody stopped me. Anyway we have to consider the intention of the Council when they drafted the by-law and they cannot have intended to exclude cars, as cars had not been invented then. Anyway times have changed. Anyway the expression "any other vehicle" has to be read in its context and is limited to things of the same class. Since all the preceding things listed are horse-drawn vehicles, only such vehicles are prohibited by a strict interpretation of the regulation. Anyway I'm the Mayor and you had better mind your step.' Consider this argument (*a*) as a whole, (*b*) point by point. Advise the park-keeper.

(3) Mrs Atkins lives at the top of a steep hill and has baby twins. To help her propel her perambulator up the hill she has ingeniously fitted to it a small petrol-driven motor, similar to that of a motor-mower. On Thursday she 'drives' her children round the park in the pram. Has she broken the regulation? If so, could it make any difference if she switches off the motor before entering the park?

(4) Lord Cutglass, a second-cousin of the late Sir Thomas, is paralysed and can only move about by wheelchair. For the past five years he has been pushed around the park each morning by his faithful housekeeper. Last month he acquired a motor for the chair; on Friday he propels himself into the park, accompanied by his housekeeper. When he is in the middle of the park he suffers a heart attack. The housekeeper telephones for a taxi, which drives into the park, picks up Lord Cutglass and takes him to hospital. This prompt action probably saved his life.

(5) Draft a new regulation to replace regulation 1, bearing in mind particularly present-day social conditions in Belleville, the terms of the Cadoggan bequest, and the events of the past week. Write a short note outlining the difficulties that have to be overcome and how you have tackled the problem.

(b) The following by-laws used to be posted verbatim in Victoria Park, Leamington Spa:

By-laws with respect to Pleasure Grounds made under section 164 of the Public Health Act 1875 for Victoria Park (1958):

5(i) A person shall not except in the exercise of any lawful right or privilege bring or cause to be brought into the pleasure ground any barrow, truck, machine or vehicle other than – (a) a wheeled bicycle, tricycle or other similar machine; (b) a wheelchair, perambulator or chaise drawn or propelled by hand and used solely for the conveyance of a child or children or an invalid.

Provided that where the Council set apart a space in the pleasure ground for the use of any class of vehicle, this by-law shall not be deemed to prohibit the driving in or to that space by a direct route from the entrance to the pleasure ground of any vehicle of the class for which it is set apart.

(ii) A person shall not except in the exercise of any lawful right or privilege ride any bicycle, tricycle or other similar machine in any part of the pleasure ground. Provided that this by-law shall not apply to any person riding a bicycle, tricycle or other similar machine (other than a mechanically propelled bicycle, tricycle or similar machine) along the perimeter road passing through the pleasure ground otherwise than to the obstruction or danger of any other person lawfully using the pleasure ground.

QUESTIONS

1. In theoretical writings the standard example of this kind of prohibition is phrased in some such terms as: 'No vehicles allowed in the park.' Compare and contrast the style of drafting of the Leamington Spa by-law (a) from the point of view of an official called on to decide particular cases under the two provisions; (b) from the point of view of communication of the content of the provisions to those affected by them.

2. Using the Leamington Spa by-law as a model, draft amendments to meet the needs and conditions of Victoria Park, Belleville today.

(ii) SAFETY AT ZEBRA CROSSINGS

Two of the rules which motorists must observe when approaching a zebra crossing are (1) to give precedence to pedestrians, and (2) not to overtake any other vehicles.

(1) In the Highway Code, the first obligation is expressed as follows:

When coming to a Zebra crossing, keep a look-out for pedestrians waiting to cross (particularly children, the elderly, the infirm and people with prams) and be ready to slow down or stop to let them cross. When anyone has stepped onto a crossing, you must give way. Signal to other drivers that you mean to slow down or stop. Allow more time for stopping on wet or icy roads. Do not signal pedestrians to cross: another vehicle may be approaching.

(From *The Highway Code* (1977), provision 55.)
  The corresponding statutory provision reads

Every foot passenger on the carriageway within the limits of an uncontrolled zebra crossing shall have precedence within those limits over any vehicle and the driver of the vehicle shall accord such precedence to the foot passenger, if the foot passenger is on the carriageway within those limits before the vehicle or any part thereof has come on to the carriageway within those limits.

For the purpose of this Regulation, in the case of such a crossing on which there is a street refuge or central reservation the parts of the crossing which are situated on each side of the street refuge or central reservation as the case may be shall each be treated as a separate crossing.

(From the 'Zebra' Pedestrian Crossing Regulations 1971, S.I. 1971/ 1524, regulation 8.)

(2) So far as overtaking is concerned, provision 56 of the Highway Code says:

In the area marked by zig-zag lines on the approach to a Zebra crossing, you must not overtake the moving motor vehicle nearest the crossing, or the leading vehicle which has stopped to give way to a pedestrian on the crossing. Even when there are no zig-zags never overtake just before a crossing.

Regulation 10 of the 1971 Regulations reads:

The driver of a vehicle while it or any part of it is in a zebra controlled area and it is proceeding towards the limits of an uncontrolled zebra crossing in relation to which that area is indicated (which vehicle is in this and the next succeeding Regulation referred to as 'the approaching vehicle') shall not cause the vehicle, or any part of it—

  (a) to pass ahead of the foremost part of another moving motor vehicle, being a vehicle proceeding in the same direction wholly or partly within that area, or

  (b) subject to the next succeeding Regulation, to pass ahead of the foremost part of a stationary vehicle on the same side of the crossing as the approaching vehicle, which stationary vehicle is stopped for the purpose of complying with Regulation 8.

For the purposes of this Regulation—

  (i) the reference to another moving motor vehicle is, in a case where only one other motor vehicle is proceeding in the same direction in a zebra controlled area, a reference to that vehicle, and, in a case where more than one other motor vehicle is so proceeding, a reference to such one of those vehicles as is nearest to the limits of the crossing;

  (ii) the reference to a stationary vehicle is, in a case where only one other vehicle is stopped for the purpose of complying with Regulation 8, a reference to that vehicle and, in a case where more than one other vehicle is stopped for the purpose of complying with that Regulation, a reference to such one of those vehicles as is nearest to the limits of the crossing.

This is supplemented by 'the next succeeding Regulation':

11.(1) For the purposes of this Regulation, in the case of an uncontrolled zebra crossing, which is on a road, being a one-way street, and on which there is a street refuge or central reservation, the parts of the crossing which are situated on each side of the street refuge or central reservation as the case may be shall each be treated as a separate crossing.
(2) Nothing in paragraph (*b*) of the last preceding Regulation shall apply so as to prevent the approaching vehicle from passing ahead of the foremost part of a stationary vehicle within the meaning of that paragraph, if the stationary vehicle is stopped for the purpose of complying with Regulation 8 in relation to an uncontrolled zebra crossing which by virtue of this Regulation is treated as a separate crossing from the uncontrolled zebra crossing towards the limits of which the approaching vehicle is proceeding.

QUESTIONS
1. What are the main differences in style and scope between the formulations in the Highway Code and the regulations?
2. For what purposes were the different formulations intended, and do you think that they succeed?
3. Which formulation do you think is most likely to lead to practical difficulties in interpretation?
4. Can you think of any other ways in which the rules contained in the regulations could be set out so as to help drivers and pedestrians understand how to behave at zebra crossings?

5 Rules and results

'If rules were results there would be little need of lawyers.'
(Karl Llewellyn)

In both legal and non-legal contexts it is commonly assumed that it is unusual for the results of particular cases to diverge significantly from what the applicable rules prescribe and that, where there is not an exact correspondence, something has gone wrong; for example, that the rules are being flouted or manipulated or ignored or that they are not working well. The following extracts suggest that the relationship between rules and results can be more complex than that.

(a) Social control in an African society

Anthropologists have devoted a great deal of attention to modes of dealing with disputes in less-developed societies. The following account by Gulliver concerns the Arusha, a tribe in northern Tanzania, who traditionally had no officials, courts or judges, but who nevertheless had recognized procedures for handling disputes, mainly through negotiation and bargaining. Gulliver shows how a group can have generally accepted rules (norms), which play an important part in the processes of dispute settlement, yet wherein the final outcome of the process more often than not involves some departure from the rules.

DISPUTE SETTLEMENT BETWEEN 'RELATED' PERSONS

The nature of negotiations between the two disputants, each with his supporters, is appreciably affected by the nature of relations existing between them, both in general terms and in respect of the particular matter in dispute. Where the disputants have been in some mutually valuable relationship, then they both have an interest in maintaining or restoring it. Each is inclined to accept compromise for the sake of the relationship; but at the same time each has a measure of bargaining power to use against the other. This is immediately obvious in the case of directly contractual situations, such as a dispute between father-in-law and son-in-law over bride-wealth ..., or between a stock-owner and herdsman.... But a similar situation arises when a dispute lies between members of the same nuclear group – an inner lineage or age-group. Here again, each disputant has something to offer to induce the other to modify his claims or to acquiesce to a settlement. Thus in the first instance the considerations are the maintenance of the marriage and the affinal tie, or of the herding arrangements; and in the second instance, the maintenance of group unity, reciprocal assistance and mutual activity. In both kinds of situation, reconciliation between the disputants is most important, so that a successful resolution of the affair should go beyond the dispute itself.

On the other hand, disputants may have had little or even no significant relationship between them prior to the affair which precipitates their dispute, and they seek no particular relationship thereafter. In that event the bargaining power of each against the other is both weaker and of a different order. The process of reaching a settlement is different in those kinds of situation....

Before beginning this examination, it is necessary to revert to the problem of the connection between pragmatic negotiation and the socially accepted norms of the Arusha. There has been, from time to time, a good deal of debate among anthropologists on the meaning of law in non-centralized, non-literate societies – including the proposition that such societies have no law, but only custom. It is not intended to engage in that argument here, for it is one which is too concerned with semantics and not sufficiently with social realities. Therefore I shall content myself by asserting that among the Arusha there are, as in any society, commonly enunciated and accepted norms of behaviour.

Arusha speak of *embukunoto*, pl. *imbukunot*. These norms are well known, and each is similarly enunciated everywhere in the country. Not all transgressions of norms precipitate disputes, of course; only those which seem to a person to injure his interests or welfare are, or at his volition can be, made subject to regulatory procedures. . . .

Whilst it would be incorrect to say that an agreed settlement of a dispute never wholly conforms with the relevant, socially accepted norms, it is true to say that such precise conformity is the exception. Before I began to understand the general principles of the Arusha dispute process – but often having already recorded some of the norms from informants – I was frequently puzzled by the gap between the details of an agreed settlement and the declared norms. The norms themselves were invariably quoted during dispute discussions, and this confused me further. I noted that the Arusha themselves were not worried by this gap; indeed they seldom commented on it, although it was sometimes large. After beginning to appreciate Arusha concentration on compromise which would provide a mutually acceptable resolution of a dispute, I was almost inclined to describe them as cynical opportunists. If by that is meant 'unprincipled', it is a wrong description of the Arusha in these matters. Clearly they recognize norms, and they hold them in great respect: they are what make Arusha different from other peoples with whom they come into contact. In their modern opposition to outside influences, and their desire and attempt to preserve their distinct way of life, they have in fact come to emphasize these norms, rather than passively take them for granted. They are, then, guided by their principles of right behaviour, and they use them as the bases of claims to rights, but they accept an imperfect world in which an individual does not and should not expect to gain all the ideal rights prescribed by the approved norms. But equally, men hope to be able to avoid some of the obligations implicit in those norms. It is perhaps significant that the Arusha have no word that can be translated as 'justice', nor does any such concept appear in their ideology. It is an irrelevant consideration. They are prepared to agree to something which is as near to their claims as possible in the particular context of the strengths and weaknesses of the two parties to the negotiations. Further, they believe that undue insistence on one's 'rights' under these norms may well conflict with obtaining an effective settlement, and with establishing or maintaining otherwise satisfactory relations. Every dispute begins as the plaintiff contrasts, directly or by implication, the divergence between the defendant's behaviour and the relevant norm. The defendant's reply is usually to attempt to show that no real divergence exists; or, if it does, that some overriding and more general norm necessitates it. The process of negotiation continues from there. . . .

Thus the negotiating-strength of the disputants varies according to the circumstances of each particular case. Sometimes the 'letter of the law' is rigidly applied; sometimes a greater or lesser deviation from it is agreed to. Such variations from the norm of bridewealth are not new in the ethnographic literature, and in themselves would scarcely have been worth comment, had not Arusha often emphasized the specific constitution of a 'proper bridewealth' containing explicitly described items. What is more important for present purposes is, that the possibility of departure from expressed and socially approved norms exists in reference to most, perhaps all norms, the transgression of which may precipitate a formal dispute. It can be said that in the process of discussions and negotiations towards a mutually acceptable resolution of a dispute, there is most usually a departure from the applicable norms in the end result. For the Arusha, one might say that it is what a plaintiff can obtain (after, if necessary, long negotiations) which is important, rather than what he ought to obtain.

(From P. Gulliver, *Social Control in an African Society* (1963), pp. 240-2, 252-3.)

(b) Compensation for accidents

To understand the legal system and the nature of rights and duties, it is not sufficient to know the formal rules; one must know the law in action. The same principle holds for reasonable criticism and proposals for reforming the law. . . . In this book I wish to stress the sociological insight that rules are in part a function of the apparatus that applies them. [T]he term 'law' may have at least three distinct meanings, corresponding to three modes of application:

First, law can be understood as those rules that are enunciated by legislators and by appellate judges. These are the rules that appear in print, in newspapers and law books, and that are learned by rote, plus or minus some comprehension, by law students. This understanding is certainly that of most of my fellow students from law school days, and I dare say of many of my teachers as well.

Second, law can be understood as those rules that arise in the course of applying the first-level laws in the situation of a trial court.

The literature of jurisprudence has less often been concerned with a third meaning of law, which concerns those rules that arise in the course of applying the formal rules in private negotiated settlements. Holmes' revolutionary thought, that law is what the courts will do, did not go far enough. Quantitatively speaking, even trial courts are trivial mechanisms for determining legal relationships. The rules of the third level, the law in action, are not completely independent of the first and second levels, but, being further removed from the appellate courts in time, space, procedure, and personnel, they are more subject to distortions, modifications, and even negations of the formal rules than are the rules of the second level.

Students of trial court law have found it to be bent from the formal law in the direction of a sense of fairness brought to bear by the judge or jury in the individual case. The departure from formal law may be greater in cases decided by a jury, but it occurs as well in disputes decided by a judge. Where the unqualified formal rule strikes the decision-maker as unjust, his application of the rule bends it in the direction of his idea of justice, whether by distorting the facts of the situation so that the rule appears to give good results, or by overriding the rule and hiding behind a screen of rationalization or the silence of the jury room.

Law in action, as exemplified by the situation at hand - the adjustment of claims by representatives of insurance companies – involves additional sources of distortion of formal rules, virtually ignored by the students of courtroom law. These are the formally irrelevant situational pressures on the negotiators. The key role in this situation is that of the adjuster, who is typically a low-level employee of a large formal organization. (Sociologists customarily speak of such large, rule-oriented organizations as 'bureaucracies', following Max Weber; the term as used here in the technical sense is not pejorative.) In addition to his personal views of justice and equity, the adjuster brings to his work the pressures he feels in his role as an employee. Both intended and deliberate company policies on the one hand and unintended and 'accidental' pressures on the other affect the adjuster's performance and modify the outcomes of his negotiation of legal claims.

(From H. L. Ross, *Settled Out of Court* (1970), pp. 6–8.)

The vast majority of tort claims are settled by negotiations and eventual agreement between the claimant and the defendant, or, in practice, the defendant's insurers. Only a very small proportion are ever disposed of by judgment of a court. On the other hand, in a larger number of cases the plaintiff gets as far as commencing proceedings by issuing a writ or summons. From there onwards, cases continue to be settled, so that out of all the cases in which proceedings are commenced, many are settled even before the first serious step in the process is undertaken, i.e. before a statement of claim is delivered; others are settled at later stages of the pre-trial procedures, and a substantial number are settled (more or less literally) at the doors of the court.

The Pearson Commission estimated from its various surveys that 86% of cases are settled without writ or summons being issued; 11% are settled after the issue of writ or summons but before the case is set down for trial, 2% are settled after setting down, and 1% are settled at the door of the court or during the trial, or are actually disposed of by trial. . . .

These figures demonstrate that the administration of the tort system is not what it appears on the face of things. The system is administered very largely by insurance adjustors on one hand, and solicitors on the other hand. The process is not in the hands of the judges in the great majority of cases. On the Pearson Commission figures, it seems that the judges actually handle some 2,000 cases per year, while a further 200,000 are settled without trial. It thus seems that the whole of the tort system could be regarded as an administrative process designed to compensate accident victims, in which a right of 'appeal' is given to the courts of law. Looked at from this point of view, the system may be said to resemble the national insurance system more closely than might be thought at first sight. Here again, the system is run by an administrative process in which there is a right of appeal to various tribunals established under the Acts. But there are important differences; apart from the obvious fact that the 'appellate' tribunals for the tort system are the ordinary courts, and for the national insurance system they are the special statutory tribunals. In particular, the national insurance administration is in the hands of the State and is run by civil servants under the head of a political Minister. On the other hand, the tort administrative machine is in private hands. One consequence of this is that the object of the administrators who run the national insurance system is to see that every claimant gets what he is legally entitled to receive; and the purpose of the appeal procedure is to put right mistakes. But in the tort system, the administrators are not concerned to see that the claimant gets his legal dues: the insurance adjustors who run the tort system are primarily concerned to settle cases for the lowest figure which they can induce the claimant to accept. The Winn Committee acknowledged that the parties do not really want a 'fair' settlement but a 'favourable' one. In these circumstances, the right of 'appeal' to the courts is not so much designed to put right the mistakes of the adjudicators, but to be used as a weapon whereby the administrators may be induced to behave reasonably. This is why such a large proportion of cases in which proceedings are commenced, or even in which preparations are made for trial, never are tried in the result, and this is why a former chief justice of Ontario has said that 'the judicial process is being used for other than judicial purposes.... It is being used as a threat to bring about an adjustment rather than as a means of adjudication.'

(From P. S. Atiyah, *Accidents, Compensation and the Law* (1980, 3rd edition), pp. 296-8.)

(c) Non-contractual relations in business

Disputes are frequently settled without reference to the contract or potential of actual legal sanctions. There is a hesitancy to speak of legal rights or to threaten to sue in these negotiations. Even where the parties have a detailed and carefully planned agreement which indicates what is to happen if, say, the seller fails to deliver on time, often they will never refer to the agreement but will negotiate a solution when the problem arises apparently as if there had never been any original contract. One purchasing agent expressed a common business attitude when he said:

'If something comes up, you get the other man on the telephone and deal with the problem. You don't read legalistic contract clauses at each other if you ever want to do business again. One doesn't run to lawyers if he wants to stay in business because one must behave decently.'

Or as one businessman put it: 'You can settle any dispute if you keep the lawyers and accountants out of it. They just do not understand the give-and-take needed in business.' All of the house counsel interviewed indicated that they are called into the dispute settlement process only after the businessmen have failed to settle matters in their own way. Two indicated that after being called in house counsel at first will only advise the purchasing agent, sales manager or other official involved; not even the house counsel's letterhead is used on communications with the other side until all hope for a peaceful resolution is gone.

Law suits for breach of contract appear to be rare. Only five of the twelve purchasing agents had ever been involved in even a negotiation concerning a contract dispute where both sides were represented by lawyers; only two of ten sales managers had ever gone this far. None had been involved in a case that went through trial. A law firm with more than forty lawyers and a large commercial practise handles in a year only about six trials concerned with contract problems. Less than 10 per cent of the time of this office is devoted to any type of work related to contracts disputes. Corporations big enough to do business in more than one state tend to sue and be sued in the federal courts. Yet only 2,779 out of 58,293 civil actions filed in the United States District Courts in fiscal year 1961 involved private contracts. During the same period only 3,447 of the 61,138 civil cases filed in the principal trial courts of New York State involved private contracts. The same picture emerges from a review of appellate cases. [...]

At times relatively contractual methods are used to make adjustments in ongoing transactions and to settle disputes. Demands of one side which are deemed unreasonable by the other occasionally are blocked by reference to the terms of the agreement between the parties. The legal position of the parties can influence negotiations even though legal rights or litigation are never mentioned in their discussions; it makes a difference if one is demanding what both concede to be a right or begging for a favour. Now and then a firm may threaten to turn matters over to its attorneys, threaten to sue, commence a suit or even litigate and carry an appeal to the highest court which will hear the matter. Thus, legal sanctions, while not an everyday affair, are not unknown in business.

One can conclude that while detailed planning and legal sanctions play a significant role in some exchanges between businesses, in many business exchanges their role is small.

(From S. Macaulay, 'Non-Contractual Relations in Business: A Preliminary Study', 28 *American Sociological Review* (1963), p. 55.)

(d) Working to rule

The following rules are taken from the British Rail Rule Book (1978):

(i) Employees must be prompt, civil and obliging, afford every proper facility for the British Railway Board's business, give correct information, and, when asked, give their names or numbers without hesitation. (1.1.2)

(ii) Employees must make every effort to facilitate the working of trains and prevent any avoidable delay. (5.1.4)

(iii) Employees must not expose themselves or others to danger. They must prevent, as far as possible, such exposure on the part of other persons, and warn those who neglect to take proper care. (5.3.1)

QUESTIONS

1. Do these extracts suggest that rules have little or no influence on results in these contexts? What other factors are influential?

2. Compare the following two definitions of the phrase 'work to rule' taken from the case, *Secretary of State for Employment* v. *A.S.L.E.F.* [1972] 2 All E.R. 949:

(i) '"Work to rule" has a perfectly well-known meaning, namely,

"Give the rules a meaning which no reasonable man could give
them and work to that"' (Sir John Donaldson, p. 959).

(ii) 'Those rules are to be construed reasonably. They must be fitted
in sensibly the one with the other. They must be construed according to the usual course of dealing and to the way they have been
applied in practice. When the rules are so construed the railway
system, as we all know, works efficiently and safely. But if some of
those rules are construed unreasonably, as, for instance, the driver
takes too long examining his engine or seeing that all is in order,
the system may be in danger of being disrupted. It is only when
they are construed unreasonably that the railway system grinds
to a halt' (Lord Denning M.R., p. 965).

What do you think is meant by 'reasonable' in this context?

3. Does the fact that adherence to the rules will result in inconvenience
to a great many people in typical 'go-slow' situations, such as affect
public transport, mean that

(i) there are too many rules?

(ii) adherence to rules is a value that may be displaced for the sake
of convenience?

(iii) whoever first thought of the 'work to rule' was a shrewd interpreter of rules?

Give reasons for whatever you think about (i)–(iii).

4. Give examples of other situations in which the outcome of a dispute
or other process does not conform precisely with the accepted substantive rules (i) in legal contexts, (ii) in non-legal contexts.

5. (i) Comment on the meaning and implications of Gulliver's statement that 'the Arusha have no word that can be translated as
"justice", nor does any such concept appear in their ideology'.

(ii) What implications, if any, do the accounts by Ross, Atiyah
and Macaulay have for an understanding of the notion of legal
rights?

6. Who are the most important interpreters of rules in the contexts
described in the extracts (a) to (d)? In each case would it be accurate
to say that they were (i) applying; (ii) manipulating; (iii) bending;
(iv) waiving; (v) invoking; (vi) ignoring, the relevant rules?

6 Some complex rules

(a) The following rule is taken from the Transport and General Workers' Union Rules Handbook (1971):

Fatal Accident (At Work) Benefit.

On the death of a member resulting directly from an accident at work, such member being of not less than nine months' membership and having made 39 weekly payments prior to the accident, is in compliance at the time of the accident and less than six weeks in arrears (13 weeks in the case of a seafarer), at the time of death, the General Executive Council may in their absolute and final discretion authorize payment of Fatal Accident (At Work) Benefit to his dependants, as follows.

(*a*) In the case of members contributing to Scale 1, the benefit shall be £250, and members contributing to the female or youth's rate, the benefit shall be £125.

(*b*) Members contributing to Scale 2, the benefit shall be £500, and members contributing to the female or youth's rate the benefit shall be £250.

Notwithstanding the provisions at the beginning of this clause, with regard to arrears benefit shall not be payable in the case of a member who has been more than 13 weeks in arrears (26 weeks in the case of a seafarer), during the twelve months prior to death and who has not cleared off the whole of his arrears. The General Executive Council reserve the right to make no payment under this rule.

(b) Section 83 of the Income and Corporation Taxes Act 1979:

(1) Where in relation to any premises (a) tax has become chargeable under the provisions of section 80 ..., 81 or 82 above on any amount (disregarding any reduction in that amount under this subsection) or (b) tax would have become so chargeable on that amount but for the operation of ... this subsection, or but for any exemption from tax, and, in respect of a lease granted out of, or a disposition of, the lease, estate or interest in respect of which tax so became or would have become chargeable on the said amount (hereinafter referred to as 'the amount chargeable on the superior interest'), a person would apart from this sub-section be chargeable under the said provisions on any amount (hereinafter referred to as 'the later chargeable amount'), the amount on which he is so chargeable shall ..., be the excess (if any) of the later chargeable amount over the appropriate fraction of the amount chargeable on the superior interest.

Provided that where a person would, apart from this subsection, be so chargeable in respect of a lease or disposition which extends to a part only of the said premises, the amount on which he is so chargeable shall, ..., be the excess (if any) of the later chargeable amount over so much of the appropriate fraction of the amount chargeable on the superior interest as, on a just apportionment, is attributable to that part of the premises.

(c) Section 6(1) of the Land Compensation Act 1961:

6. – (1) Subject to section 8 of this Act, no account shall be taken of any increase or diminution in the value of the relevant interest which, in the circumstances described in any of the paragraphs in the first column of Part I of the First Schedule to this Act, is attributable to the carrying out or the prospect of so much of the development mentioned in relation thereto in the second column of that Part as would not have been likely to be carried out if –

    (*a*) (where the acquisition is for purposes involving development of any of the land authorized to be acquired) the acquiring authority had not acquired and did not propose to acquire any of that land; and

    (*b*) (where the circumstances are those described in one or more of paragraphs 2 to 4 in the said first column) the area or areas referred to in that paragraph or those paragraphs had not been defined or designated as therein mentioned.

QUESTIONS

1. Why do you think that the provisions in the extracts (*a*)–(*c*) are so complex?

2. In what ways might they be simplified? If they were simplified, would anything be sacrificed as a result?

3. Russell L. J. said of example (c), 'The drafting of this section appears to me calculated to postpone as long as possible comprehension of its purport' (*Camrose* v. *Basingstoke Corporation* [1966] 1 W.L.R. 1100, 1110 (C.A.)). Can you think of any reasons why the draftsman formulated the section the way he did?

(d) Rules for payment of married women's (flat-rate) retirement pension

The earliest age at which a woman can draw a retirement pension is 60. On her own insurance she can get a pension when she reaches that age, if she has then retired from regular employment. Otherwise she has to wait until she retires or reaches age 65. At age 65 a pension can be paid irrespective of retirement. To get a pension on her husband's insurance, however, she must be 60 or over and retired, and her husband must be 65 or over and retired from regular employment, or 70 if he does not retire before reaching that age.

A man over 70 or a woman over 65 is treated as retired whether working or not, and regardless of the amount of work done.

(From DHSS leaflet NI1, reprinted in W. Ryan *et al*., *The Increasing Use of Logical Trees in the Civil Service* (1970), CAS Occasional Paper No. 13 (HMSO), p. 4.)

Algorithm designed to show eligibility for a married woman's retirement pension

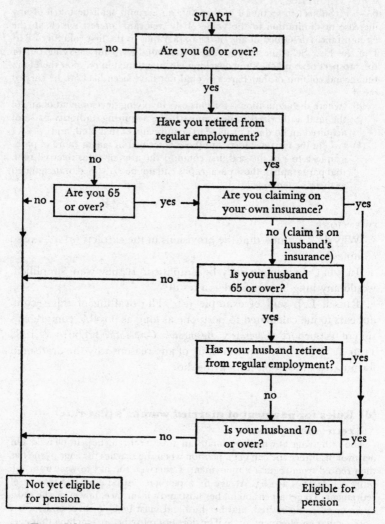

From W. Ryan *et al.*, *op. cit.*, p. 5.

QUESTIONS

1. Read the above section once carefully; and then look carefully at the algorithm and work your way around it for a few moments.

(i) Now keep a record of the time it takes you to determine whether MW is eligible for a pension under this section, by using *only* the algorithm, in the following case.

MW is a married woman who lives at 31 Cedar Street, Piltdown. Although she is 67, she is in good health and has a part-time job with AmCo. Her husband, who is 68, is still working full-time as a watch-repairer. MW is claiming on his insurance.

(ii) Now keep a record of the time it takes you to determine whether MW is eligible for a pension under this section, by using only the section, without looking at the algorithm.

MW is a married woman who lives at 67 Beech Grove, Piltdown. She retired two years ago from her job as a part-time secretary for AmCo. Her husband (aged 71) is in part-time employment (six hours per week) as a gardener. MW is not claiming on her own insurance. MW is 64 and is in poor health.

2. Read the section on algorithms in Appendix I.

Reconstruct the rules in (a)–(c) above in the form of algorithms.

(e)

Another factor which can obscure the comprehensibility of rules and regulations is the way in which they are drafted. The very detailed style which typifies United Kingdom legislation is often said to obscure its comprehensibility. Supporters of this view argue that the adoption of a style which gives a firm and intelligible statement of what the law is and the nature and extent of the rights, duties, powers and liabilities created by it, but without introducing detailed qualifications and conditions, which could be left to be introduced separately, would be preferable. Sir William Dale, who is one of the leading proponents of this view, gives the following example which compares the law of copyright in the United Kingdom, France and West Germany.

(i) THE UNITED KINGDOM: COPYRIGHT ACT 1956, SECTIONS 1 AND 2

Part I

Copyright in Original Works

1. *Nature of copyright under this Act.* (1) In this Act 'copyright' in relation to a work (except where the context otherwise requires) means the exclusive right, by virtue and subject to the provisions of this Act, to do, and to authorize other persons to do, certain acts in relation to that work in the United Kingdom or in any other country to which the relevant provision of this Act extends.

The said acts, in relation to a work of any description, are those acts which, in the relevant provision of this Act, are designated as the acts restricted by the copyright in a work of that description.

(2) In accordance with the preceding subsection, but subject to the following provisions of this Act, the copyright in a work is infringed by any person who, not being the owner of the copyright, and without the licence of the owner thereof, does, or authorizes another person to do, any of the said acts in relation to the work in the United Kingdom or in any other country to which the relevant provision of this Act extends.

(3) In the preceding subsections references to the relevant provision of this Act, in relation to a work of any description, are references to the provision of this Act whereby it is provided that (subject to compliance with the conditions specified therein) copyright shall subsist in works of that description.

(4) The preceding provisions of this section shall apply, in relation to any subject-matter (other than a work) of a description to which any provision of Part II of this Act relates, as they apply in relation to a work.

(5) For the purposes of any provision of this Act which specifies the conditions under which copyright may subsist in any description of work or other subject-matter, 'qualified person' –

(a) in the case of an individual, means a person who is a British subject or British protected person or a citizen of the Republic of Ireland or (not being a British subject or British protected person or a citizen of the Republic of Ireland) is domiciled or resident in the United Kingdom or in another country to which that provision extends, and

(b) in the case of a body corporate, means a body incorporated under the laws of any part of the United Kingdom or of another country to which that provision extends.

In this subsection 'British protected person' has the same meaning as in the British Nationality Act 1948.

2. *Copyright in literary, dramatic and musical works.* (1) Copyright shall subsist, subject to the provisions of this Act, in every original literary, dramatic or musical work which is unpublished, and of which the author was a qualified person at the time when the work was made, or, if the making of the work extended over a period, was a qualified person for a substantial part of that period.

(2) Where an original literary, dramatic or musical work has been published, then, subject to the provisions of this Act, copyright shall subsist in the

work (or, if copyright in the work subsisted immediately before its first publication, shall continue to subsist) if, but only if, –

(a) the first publication of the work took place in the United Kingdom, or in another country to which this section extends, or

(b) the author of the work was a qualified person at the time when the work was first published, or

(c) the author had died before that time, but was a qualified person immediately before his death.

(3) Subject to the last preceding subsection, copyright subsisting in a work by virtue of this section shall continue to subsist until the end of the period of fifty years from the end of the calendar year in which the author died, and shall then expire:

Provided that if before the death of the author none of the following acts had been done, that is to say, –

(a) the publication of the work,

(b) the performance of the work in public,

(c) the offer for sale to the public of records of the work, and

(d) the broadcasting of the work,

the copyright shall continue to subsist until the end of the period of fifty years from the end of the calendar year which includes the earliest occasion on which one of those acts is done.

(4) In the last preceding subsection references to the doing of any act in relation to a work include references to the doing of that act in relation to an adaptation of the work.

(5) The acts restricted by the copyright in a literary, dramatic or musical work are –

(a) reproducing the work in any material form;

(b) publishing the work;

(c) performing the work in public;

(d) broadcasting the work;

(e) causing the work to be transmitted to subscribers to a diffusion service;

(f) making any adaptation of the work;

(g) doing, in relation to an adaptation of the work, any of the acts specified in relation to the work in paragraphs (a) to (e) of this subsection.

(6) In this Act 'adaptation' –

(a) in relation to a literary or dramatic work, means any of the following, that is to say, –

(i) in the case of a non-dramatic work, a version of the work (whether in its original language or a different language) on which it is converted into a dramatic work;

(ii) in the case of a dramatic work, a version of the work (whether in its original language or a different language) in which it is converted into a non-dramatic work;

(iii) a translation of the work;

(iv) a version of the work in which the story or action is conveyed wholly or mainly by means of pictures in a form suitable for reproduction in a book, or in a newspaper, magazine or similar periodical; and (*b*) in relation to a musical work, means an arrangement or transcription of the work,

so however that the mention of any matter in this definition shall not affect the generality of paragraph (*a*) of the last preceding subsection.

(ii) FRANCE: LAW NO. 57–296 ON LITERARY AND ARTISTIC PROPERTY

Title I
Authors' rights

Article 1. The author of an intellectual work shall, by the mere fact of its creation, enjoy an exclusive incorporeal property right in the work, effective against all persons.

This right includes attributes of an intellectual and moral nature as well as attributes of an economic nature, as determined by this law.

The existence, or the conclusion by the author of an intellectual work, of a contract to make a work, or an employment contract, shall imply no exception to the enjoyment of the right recognized in the first paragraph.

Article 2. The provisions of this law shall protect the rights of authors of all intellectual works, regardless of their kind, form of expression, merit or purpose.

Article 3. The following shall in particular be considered intellectual works within the meaning of this law: books, pamphlets, and other literary, artistic and scientific writings; lectures, addresses, sermons, pleadings in court, and other works of the same nature; dramatic or dramatico-musical works; choreographic works, and pantomimes, the acting form of which is fixed writing or otherwise; musical compositions with or without words; cinematographic works and works made by processes analogous to cinematography; works of drawing, painting, architecture, sculpture, engraving, lithography, photographic work of an artistic or documentary character, and other works of the same character produced by processes analogous to photography; works of applied art; illustrations, geographical maps; plans, sketches, and plastic works, relative to geography, topography, architecture, or the sciences.

Article 4. The authors of translations, adaptations, new versions, or arrangements of intellectual works shall enjoy the protection provided by this law, without prejudice to the rights of the author of the original work. This shall also apply to authors of anthologies or collections of various works, which, by reason of the selection and arrangement of their contents, constitute intellectual creations.

(iii) GERMANY: A LAW DEALING WITH COPYRIGHT AND RELATED RIGHTS

Part I: Copyright
Section I: General

Article 1. Authors of works of literature and learning, and of works of art, shall enjoy protection for their works in the manner prescribed by this Law.

Section II: The work

 Article 2. Protected works – (1) The works of literature and learning, and works of art, protected hereunder include, in particular:

1. literary works, such as writings and speeches;
2. musical works;
3. works of pantomime, including choreographic works;
4. artistic works, including architectural works and works of applied art and plans and sketches of such works;
5. photographic works, including works produced by processes analogous to photography;
6. cinematographic works, including works produced by processes analogous to cinematography;
7. illustrations of a scientific or technical nature, such as drawings, plans, maps, sketches, tables and plastic representations.

 (2) 'Works' within the meaning of this Law include only personal intellectual creations.

 Article 3. Adaptations. – Translations and other adaptations of a work which constitute personal intellectual creations of the adapter shall be protected in the same manner as independent works, without prejudice to the copyright in the pre-existing work thus adapted.

 Article 4. Collections. – Collections of works or of other contributions which, by virtue of the selection or arrangement thereof, constitute personal intellectual creations shall be protected in the same manner as independent works, without prejudice to the copyright in the works thus collected.

(From Sir W. Dale, 'Statutory Reform: The Draftsman and the Judge', 30 *International and Comparative Law Quarterly* (1981), 141, 142–5.)

QUESTIONS

1. Can you give precise answers to the following questions concerning the law of copyright in each country:
 (i) what kinds of work may be the subject of copyright?
 (ii) in whom does copyright reside?
 (iii) how long does copyright last?

2. How could the sections 1 and 2 of the Copyright Act be redrafted so as to make them more intelligible?

3. Read the case, *Exxon Corpn.* v. *Exxon Insurance Consultants International Ltd* [1981] 3 All E.R. 241.
 (i) How did the Court of Appeal interpret the phrase 'original literary work' in section 2(1) of the Copyright Act 1956?
 (ii) Would the Court's decision have been (a) easier to arrive at, and (b) different, if the applicable law had been that of the French or West German copyright provisions?

7 Bigamy

In this section we include the statutory provision which makes bigamy an offence and the judgment in *Reg.* v. *Allen* which concerned the interpretation of the first words of that provision, 'Whosoever, being married, shall marry ...'. *Allen* raised a number of different issues to which reference will be made later, in particular in Chapter 7, and you are encouraged to read it closely. Look especially at Cockburn C. J.'s view of the policy behind section 57 and the use which he makes of it in his interpretation of the section. Also consider his reaction to the different interpretations of the words 'shall marry' and to the kinds of argument which were presented to him.

The following case, *Taylor*, shows how decisions in prior cases become established and interpreted to meet the circumstances of subsequent cases, and how the doctrine of precedent, which is discussed in Chapter 8, applies to decisions concerning the criminal law.

(a)   The Offences Against the Person Act 1861, section 57

Whosoever, being married, shall marry any other person during the life of the former husband or wife, whether the second marriage shall have taken place in England or Ireland or elsewhere, shall be guilty of felony, and being convicted thereof shall be liable to be kept in penal servitude for any term not exceeding seven years; and any such offence may be dealt with, inquired of, tried, determined, and punished in any county or place in *England or Ireland* where the Offender shall be apprehended or be in custody, in the same manner in all respects as if the offence had been actually committed in that county or place: Provided, that nothing in this section contained shall extend to any second marriage, contracted elsewhere than in England and Ireland by any other than a subject of Her Majesty, or to any person marrying a second time whose husband or wife shall have been continually absent from such person for the space of seven years then last past, and shall not have been known by such person to be living within that time, or shall extend to any person who, at the time of such second marriage, shall have been divorced from the bond of the first marriage, or to any person whose former marriage shall have been declared void by the sentence of any court of competent jurisdiction.

(b)   R. *v.* Henry Allen (1872) L.R. 1 C.C.R. 367 (Court for Crown Cases Reserved)

The judgment of the Court was delivered by Cockburn C.J.:

This case came before us on a point reserved by Martin B. at the last assizes for the county of Hants. The prisoner was indicted for having married one Harriet Crouch, his first wife being still alive. The indictment was framed upon the statute 24 & 25 Vict. c. 100, s.57, which enacts that 'whosoever being married shall marry any other person during the life of the former husband or wife shall be guilty of felony'. The facts of the case were clear. The prisoner had first married one Sarah Cunningham, and on her death he had married his present wife, Ann Pearson Gutteridge. The second wife being still living, he on the 2nd of December, 1871, married one Harriet Crouch. So far the case would appear to be clearly one of bigamy within the statute, but, it appearing that Harriet Crouch was a niece of the prisoner's first wife, it was objected, on his behalf, that since the passing of 5 & 6 Wm. 4 c. 54, s.2, such a marriage was in itself void, and that to constitute an offence, within 24 & 25 Vict. c. 100, s.57, the second marriage must be one which, independently of its bigamous character, would be valid, and, consequently, that the indictment could not be sustained. For the proposition that, to support an indictment for bigamy, the second marriage must be one which would have been otherwise valid, the case of *R.* v. *Fanning* ((1866) 10 Cox C.C. 411), decided in the Court of Criminal Appeal in Ireland, was cited, and in deference to the authority of the majority of the judges in that Court, Martin B. has stated this case for our decision.

It is clear that, but for the statutory inability of the parties to marry one another if free, the marriage of the prisoner with Harriet Crouch would have been within the 57th section of the Act. The question is, whether that circumstance alters the effect of the prisoner's conduct in going through the ceremony of marriage with Harriet Crouch while his former wife was still living. The same question arose in the case of *R.* v. *Brawn* ((1843) 1 C. & K. 144), which was tried before Lord Denman on the earlier statute of 9 Geo. 4, c. 31, s.22, the language of which was precisely the same as that of the present. In that case the prisoner, a married woman, had, during her husband's lifetime, married a man who had been the husband of her deceased sister. The same point as is now raised being taken on behalf of the prisoner, Lord Denman overruled the objection. 'I am of opinion,' said his Lordship, 'that the validity of ... second marriage does not affect the question. It is the appearing to contract a second marriage, and the going through the ceremony, which constitutes the crime of bigamy, otherwise it could never exist in the ordinary cases, as a previous marriage always renders null and void a marriage that is celebrated afterwards by either of the parties during the lifetime of the other. Whether, therefore, the marriage of the two prisoners' – the male prisoner had been included in the indictment as an accessory – 'was or was not in itself prohibited, and therefore null and void, does not signify; for the woman, having a husband then alive, has committed the crime of bigamy by doing all that in her lay by entering into marriage with another man.' In the earlier and analogous case of *R.* v. *Penson* ((1832) 5 C. & P. 412) a similar objection had been taken, on the ground that the second marriage was invalid, by reason that the woman whom the prisoner was charged with having married whilst his first wife was alive, had for the purpose of concealing her identity been described as Eliza Thick, her true name being Eliza Brown. But Gurney B, who tried the case, overruled the objection, being of opinion 'that the parties could not be allowed to evade the punishment for such an offence by contracting a concertedly invalid marriage'.

We should have acted without hesitation on these authorities had it not been for the case, already referred to, of *R*. v. *Fanning*, decided in the Court of Criminal Appeal in Ireland, a case which, if not on all fours with the present is still closely analogous to it, and which, from the high authority of the Court by which it was decided, was entitled to our most attentive consideration. We therefore took time to consider our judgment.

The facts in *R*. v. *Fanning* were shortly these. The prisoner, being a Protestant, and having within twelve months been a professing Protestant, was married, having a wife then living, to another woman, who was a Roman Catholic, the marriage being solemnized by a Roman Catholic priest.

Independently of the second marriage being bad as bigamous, it would have been void under the unrepealed statute of the 19 Geo. 2, c. 13, which prohibits the solemnization of marriage by a Roman Catholic priest where either of the parties is a Protestant, and declares a marriage so solemnized null and void to all intents and purposes.

On an indictment against the prisoner for bigamy, the invalidity of the second marriage was insisted on as fatal to the prosecution. The point having been reserved, seven judges against four in the Court of Criminal Appeal held the objection to be fatal, and quashed the conviction. After giving our best consideration to the reasoning of the learned judges who constituted the majority of that Court, we find ourselves unable to concur with them, being unanimously of opinion that the view taken by the four dissentient judges was the right one.

The reasoning of the majority of the Court in *R*. v. *Fanning* is founded mainly on the verbal criticism of the language of the 24 & 25 Vict c. 100, s.57; and the words being that 'if any person, being married, shall marry any other person', it was insisted that whatever sense is to be given to the term 'being married', the same must be given to the term 'marry' in the subsequent part of the sentence, and that consequently, it being admitted that the term 'being married' implies a perfect and binding marriage, the second marriage must also be one which, but for the prohibition of the statute, would be – whether as regards capacity to contract marriage or the manner in which the marriage is solemnized – binding on the parties.

Two authorities were relied on in support of this reading of the statute, namely, the language of Tindal C.J., in delivering the opinion of the judges in the House of Lords in the well-known case of *R*. v. *Millis* ((1844) 10 Cl. & F. 534) and the decision of the Judge Ordinary of the Divorce Court in the case of *Burt* v. *Burt* ((1860) 2 Sw. & Tr. 88). In the first of these cases Tindal C.J. undoubtedly says that the words 'being married' in the first part of the sentence, and the words 'marry any other person', in the second, must of necessity point at and denote 'marriage of the same kind and obligation'. But it must be borne in mind that the question before the House of Lords was, whether the first marriage, not the second, was valid, the invalidity of the second not being in question at all. In order to show that the first marriage, which had been solemnized by a Presbyterian minister, at his own house, between a member of the Established Church in Ireland and a Presbyterian, amounted to no more than a contract *per verba de præsenti*, and had failed to constitute a valid marriage, the Chief Justice of the Common Pleas insists that, if such a marriage had occurred in the second instance instead of the first, it would not have been held sufficient to support an indictment for bigamy. The case put by the Chief Justice was not the point to be decided, it was only used for the purpose of argument and illustration. Whether the incapacity of the parties to contract a binding marriage independently of the bigamy would take a case like that of *R.* v. *Fanning* out of the statute, was not present to his mind or involved in the decision of the case before the House. And the Chief Justice expressly states that, though the conclusion he had arrived at was concurred in by the rest of the judges, his reasoning was entirely his own. The language of the learned Chief Justice must therefore be taken as extra-judicial, and cannot bind us in expounding the statute now under consideration. The case of *Burt* v. *Burt*, in like manner, falls altogether short of the question we have now to decide. It was a suit for a divorce instituted by a married woman against her husband on the ground of bigamy, adultery and desertion. To establish the bigamy, evidence was given that the husband had married a woman in Australia according to the form of the Kirk of Scotland, but there was no proof that the form in question was recognized as legal by the local law. Upon this latter ground the Judge Ordinary held that a second marriage was not proved so as to make good the allegation of bigamy. All, therefore, that this case shows is, that a second marriage by a form not recognized by law will not amount to bigamy under the Divorce Act. Admitting, as we are disposed to do, that the construction of the two statutes should be the same, the decision in *Burt* v. *Burt* will not, as will presently appear, be found to conflict with our judgment in the present case, the second marriage having here been celebrated according to a form fully recognized by the law.

We may, therefore, proceed to consider what is the proper construction of the statutory enactment in question, unfettered by these authorities. Before doing so it should, however, be observed, that there is this difference between the case of *R.* v. *Fanning* and the present, that the form of marriage there resorted to was one which, independently of the bigamous character of the marriage, was, by reason of the statutory prohibition, inapplicable to the special circumstances of the parties, and ineffectual to create a valid marriage, whereas, in the case before us, independently of the incapacity, the form would have been good and binding in law. This distinction is expressly adverted to by Christian J., in his judgment as distinguishing the case before the Irish judges from that of *R.* v. *Brawn*, and it may be doubted whether, but for this distinction, the learned judge would not have come to a different conclusion. The other judges, constituting the majority, do not, however, rest their judgment on this distinction, but plainly go the length of overruling the decision of Lord Denman in *R.* v. *Brawn*. Their judgments proceed on the broad intelligible ground, that to come within the statutes against bigamy the second marriage must be such as that, but for its bigamous character, it would have been in all respects, both as to the capacity of the parties and the ceremonial adopted, as binding as the first. Differing altogether from this view, and being prepared to hold that, so long as a form of marriage has been used which the law recognizes as binding, whether applicable to the particular parties or not – and further than this it is not necessary to go – the offence of bigamy is committed, we have only adverted to the distinction referred to in order to point out that our decision in no degree turns upon it, but rests on the broader ground taken by the dissentient judges in the Irish court.

When it is said that, in construing the statute in question, the same effect must be given to the term 'marry' in both parts of the sentence, and that, consequently, as the first marriage must necessarily be a perfect and binding one, the second must be of equal efficacy in order to constitute bigamy, it is at once self-evident that the proposition as thus stated cannot possibly hold good; for if the first marriage be good, the second, entered into while the first is subsisting, must of necessity be bad. It becomes necessary, therefore, to engraft a qualification on the proposition just stated, and to read the words 'shall marry', in the latter part of the sentence, as meaning 'shall marry' under such circumstances as that the second marriage would be good but for the existence of the first. But it is plain that those who so read the statute are introducing into it words which are not to be found in it, and are obviously departing from the sense in which the term 'being married' must be construed in the earlier part of the sentence. But when once it becomes necessary to seek the meaning of a term occurring in a statute, the true rule of construction appears to us to be, not to limit the latitude of departure so as to adhere to the nearest possible approximation to the ordinary meaning of the term, or to the sense in which it may have been used before, but to look to the purpose of the enactment, the mischief to be prevented, and the remedy which the legislature intended to apply. Now, we cannot agree either with Fitzgerald B., in his judgment in *R.* v. *Fanning*, that the purpose of the statutes against bigamy was simply to make polygamous marriages penal, and that, consequently, it was only intended to constitute the offence of bigamy where the second marriage would, but for the existence of the first, be a valid one; or with those judges who, in *R.* v. *Fanning* found their judgments on the assumption that, in applying the statute against bigamy, the second marriage must be one which, but for the first, would be binding. Polygamy, in the sense of having two wives or two husbands, at one and the same time, for the purpose of cohabitation, is a thing altogether foreign to our ideas, and which may be said to be practically unknown; while bigamy, in the modern acceptation of the term, namely, that of a second marriage consequent on an abandonment of the first while the latter still subsists, is unfortunately of too frequent occurrence. It takes place, as we all know, more frequently where one of the married parties has deserted the other; sometimes where both have voluntarily separated. It is always resorted to by one of the parties in fraud of the law; sometimes by both in order to give the colour and pretence of marriage where the reality does not exist. Too often it is resorted to for the purpose of villanous fraud. The ground on which such a marriage is very properly made penal, is that it involves an outrage on public decency and morals, and creates a public scandal by the prostitution of a solemn ceremony, which the law allows to be applied only to a legitimate union, to a marriage at best but colourable and fictitious, and which may be made, and too often is made, the means of the most cruel and wicked deception. It is obvious that the outrage and scandal involved in such a proceeding will not be less, because the parties to the second marriage may be under some special incapacity to contract marriage. The deception will not be the less atrocious, because the one party may have induced the other to go through a form of marriage known to be generally binding, but inapplicable to their particular case. Is the scandal or the villainy the less because the man, having represented to the woman, who is his dupe, and to the priest, that he is a Roman Catholic, turns out afterwards to be a Protestant? Such instances as those we have referred to, thus involving public scandal or deception, being plainly within the mischief which we may reasonably assume it must have been the purpose of the legislature to prevent, we are of opinion that we ought not to frustrate the operation of a very salutary statute, by putting so narrow a construction on it as would exclude such a case as the present, if the words are legitimately capable of such a construction as would embrace it. Now the words 'shall marry another person' may well be taken to mean shall 'go through the form and ceremony of marriage with another person'. The words are fully capable of being so construed, without being forced or strained; and as a narrower construction would have the effect of leaving a portion of the mischief untouched, which it must have been the intention of the legislature to provide against, and thereby, as is fully admitted by those who contend for it, of bringing a grave reproach on the law, we think we are warranted in inferring that the words were used in the sense we have referred to, and that we shall best give effect to the legislative intention by holding such a case as the present to be within their meaning. To assume that the words must have such a construction as would exclude it, because the second marriage must be one which, but for the bigamy, would have been as binding as the first, appears to us to be begging the entire question, and to be running directly counter to the wholesome canon of construction, which prescribes that, where the language will admit of it, a statutory enactment shall be so construed as to make the remedy co-extensive with the mischief it is intended to prevent.

In thus holding it is not at all necessary to say that forms of marriage unknown to the law, as was the case in *Burt* v. *Burt*, would suffice to bring a case within the operation of the statute. We must not be understood to mean that every fantastic form of marriage to which parties might think proper to resort, or that a marriage ceremony performed by an unauthorized person, or in an unauthorized place, would be a marrying within the meaning of the 57th section of 24 & 25 Vict. c. 100. It will be time enough to deal with a case of this description when it arises. It is sufficient for the present purpose to hold, as we do, that where a person already bound by an existing marriage goes through a form of marriage known to and recognized by the law as capable of producing a valid marriage, for the purpose of a pretended and fictitious marriage, the case is not the less within the statute by reason of any special circumstances, which, independently of the bigamous character of the marriage, may constitute a legal disability in the particular parties, or make the form of marriage resorted to specially inapplicable to their individual case.

After giving the case of *R.* v. *Fanning* our best consideration we are unanimous in holding that the conviction in the case before us was right, and that the verdict must stand good.

Conviction affirmed.

QUESTIONS

1. State the facts of *Allen* in chronological order. Was there any question of fact in issue before the Court for Crown Cases Reserved in the case?
2. Formulate as precisely as you can the main question of interpretation (the question of law) that was at issue in this case.
3. Imagine that you were counsel for the defence. What proposition(s) of law would you have had to persuade the court to accept in order to win the case? What reasons might you have advanced in support of the proposition(s)?
4. Why *should* bigamy be an offence? Is the reason that it involves the 'prostitution of a solemn ceremony' the only or the main reason? If so, should it make a difference whether the ceremony took place in a church or a registry office? Should those whose religion permits polygamy, such as Muslims, be subject to the law of bigamy?
5. Do you think, from the point of view of a layman, that it was right that Allen should have been convicted? Give reasons for your answer. What was the source of doubt about interpretation in this case – bad drafting, doubt about policy, doubt about the facts in this case, or what?
6. Redraft the section in words that would leave no doubt as to the application of the law in *Allen*.

(c) R. *v.* Taylor [1950] 2 All E.R. 170 (Court of Criminal Appeal)

LORD GODDARD C.J. delivered the following judgment of the court:
The appellant pleaded Guilty before the recorder at the Central Criminal Court to an indictment containing two counts. In the first count he was charged that on Dec. 18, 1946, he married Lilian Smithers during the lifetime of his wife, Alice Julie Taylor, and in the second count it was alleged that on Dec. 24, 1948, he married Olive Briggs during the lifetime of his said wife.

The appellant was lawfully married to his wife, who is still alive, in 1925. In April, 1927, he went through a form of marriage with another woman. In November, 1942, having left that second woman, he went through another form of marriage. In respect of that marriage he was charged at Maidstone Assizes in November, 1944, with bigamy, but the indictment charged him with committing bigamy during the lifetime of the woman with whom he had gone through the first bigamous marriage, who was then believed to be his lawful wife. When it was shown that she was not, a verdict of Not Guilty was returned. In 1945 he was charged at the Central Criminal Court in respect of the bigamy he had committed in April, 1927, but that charge failed because there was no evidence given by the prosecution that when he went through the second ceremony of marriage in 1927 his first wife was alive. He was, however, convicted on a count in the indictment of making a false declaration for the purpose of the marriage register, and for that offence he was bound over. His habit of contracting marriages continued because he went through another ceremony of marriage in 1946 and a fourth ceremony in 1948, and it was in respect of those two marriages that he was charged at the Central Criminal Court last March and pleaded Guilty.

He appealed against his sentence, and he would not have got leave to appeal against it if he had been properly convicted, but when this court saw the papers with a view to considering whether leave to appeal against sentence should be given, it at once appeared that at the time when he went through the bigamous ceremonies in 1946 and 1948 he had not seen his wife for very many years. The wife had said that the last time she saw him was in 1925, and it was either in 1925 or 1927 that these spouses had last seen each other. We, therefore, inquired how it was that the appellant pleaded Guilty, and his counsel (who had appeared for him at the trial) told us that he felt unable to advise him to take any other course because of the decision of this court in *R. v. Treanor (or McAvoy)*. In that case, in somewhat similar circumstances, the court held that, where more than one bigamous ceremony was shown, in respect of any second or subsequent bigamous ceremony, the prisoner was deprived of the defence that he had not seen his wife for seven years and not known that she was alive. That case seemed to the court to need further consideration, and, accordingly, we gave leave to the appellant to appeal against his conviction so that a full court might assemble to consider the decision in that case.

I should like to say one word about the re-consideration of a case by this court. A court of appeal usually considers itself bound by its own decisions or by decisions of a court of co-ordinate jurisdiction. For instance, the Court of Appeal in civil matters considers itself bound by its own decisions or by the decisions of the Exchequer Chamber, and, as is well known, the House of Lords always considers itself bound by its own decisions. In civil matters it is essential in order to preserve the rule of *stare decisis* that that should be so, but this court has to deal with the liberty of the subject and if, on re-consideration, in the opinion of a full court the law has been either mis-applied or misunderstood and a man has been sentenced for an offence, it will be the duty of the court to consider whether he has been properly convicted. The practice observed in civil cases ought not to be applied in such a case, and in the present case the full court of seven judges is unanimously of opinion that *R. v. Treanor (or McAvoy)* was wrongly decided.

The offence of bigamy, so far as it is a temporal offence, was created in the first place by the statute 1 James 1, c. 11, where it is provided by s. 1:

'... if any person or persons within his Majesty's Dominions of England and Wales, being married, or which hereafter shall marry, do at any time after the end of the session of this present Parliament, marry any person or persons, the former husband or wife being alive ... then every such offence shall be felony ...'

It is clear that what is aimed at there is not merely bigamy, a second illegal ceremony, but what I may call polygamy – any number of marriages, because the words are: 'shall marry any person or persons.' There is a proviso:

'Provided always, that this Act, nor any thing therein contained, shall extend to any person or persons whose husband or wife shall be continually remaining beyond the seas by the space of seven years together, or whose husband or wife shall absent him or herself the one from the other by the space of seven years together, in any parts within his Majesty's Dominions, the one of them not knowing the other to be living within that time.'

It is clear that under that statute the defence of absence for seven years without knowledge of the spouse being alive was a defence however many times the ceremony of marriage had taken place. I need not take up time by reading the next statute, the Offences against the Person Act, 1828, because s. 57 of the Offences against the Person Act, 1861, with which we are immediately concerned, is in substance in the same form. [Lord Goddard C.J. then read section 57.]

It is obvious that the words 'second marriage' in the enacting part of the section must be given the same construction as must be given to those words when they appear in the proviso. It is clear that by limiting the words in the enacting part of the section which constitutes the felony to the second ceremony and not to a third and subsequent ceremonies, a man could be convicted only if he had married twice and not if he had gone through a third, fourth, or fifth subsequent ceremony. In *R.* v. *Treanor (or McAvoy)*, however, it was held that ([1939] 1 All E.R. 332):

'This proviso means precisely what it says, nothing more or less – any second marriage, and not any second or subsequent marriage.'

The court went on to say that the proviso was not to be artificially expanded into applying to a second or subsequent marriage.

The short point on which this court can decide this case, and it seems to me to be the true way of deciding it, is this. A charge of bigamy is an allegation that on a particular day the person charged went through a ceremony of marriage when his lawful wife was alive. The court, therefore, is dealing with two ceremonies of marriage only and no more – the lawful marriage and the polygamous marriage. When the polygamous marriage is proved, it is open to the defendant to show that at the time of that polygamous marriage he had not heard of his wife for seven years, and it does not seem to this court that it is then open to the prosecution to say: 'You cannot avail yourself of that defence because there have been other ceremonies of marriage between the lawful marriage and the ceremony in respect of which you are charged.' The offence committed which is charged is the offence of going through the ceremony alleged at a time when the lawful wife was alive. Therefore, a defendant has a defence if it is shown that at the time he went through the marriage which is charged against him as a felony he had not seen his wife for seven years and had not known her to be living within that time. Any other construction would lead to very astonishing results. If a man went through a form of marriage when he had not seen his wife for seven years and had not known her to be living – in which case he would have a good defence under the proviso – and the woman who he had married secondly died and he went through a third form of marriage, still not having known that his first wife was alive, could it be said that he could not plead absence of knowledge? It is enough to say that, while we do not differ from the opinion the court expressed in *R.* v. *Treanor* (*or McAvoy*) that 'second marriage' must be strictly construed, the second marriage which has to be considered is the second marriage charged in the indictment and no other. Therefore, for those reasons, although we do not differ from the construction put on the section in *R.* v. *Treanor* (*or McAvoy*), we do differ from the result that the court there held followed from that construction. Accordingly, we hold in the present case that, although the appellant might have been charged with other offences, he should not have been convicted of the offence of bigamy, and, therefore, these convictions must be quashed.

Appeal allowed.

QUESTIONS

1. What were the facts in *Taylor*? Were any of them more important than any others? By what criteria could you decide whether a fact is important in a case?

2. What issue(s) arose in this case?

3. Restate the arguments (i) for, and (ii) against, Taylor. Which of them did the Court of Criminal Appeal find convincing?

4. What did Lord Goddard C.J. think that *Allen* had decided?

5. For what propositions of law is *Taylor* an authority?

(d) The American Model Penal Code, Article 230.1

(1) *Bigamy*. A married person is guilty of bigamy, a misdemeanor, if he contracts or purports to contract another marriage, unless at the time of the subsequent marriage:

(a) the actor believes that the prior spouse is dead; or

(b) the actor and the prior spouse have been living apart for five consecutive years throughout which the prior spouse was not known by the actor to be alive; or

(c) a Court has entered a judgment purporting to terminate or annul any prior disqualifying marriage, and the actor does not know that judgment to be invalid; or

(d) the actor reasonably believes that he is legally eligible to remarry.

QUESTION

If this article had been the law in Great Britain, would it have made any difference to the two cases?

(Further exercises concerning bigamy are set out in Appendix II.)

8 Discretion to disobey

(a) **Buckoke** *v.* **Greater London Council** [1971] 2 All E.R. 254
(Court of Appeal, Civil Division)

LORD DENNING M.R.:
The controversy

For many years there has been a controversy in the fire service. It is this: what is the duty of the driver of a fire engine when he comes to traffic lights which are at red? The Fire Brigade Union say that he must obey the law. No matter how urgent the call, he must wait till the lights turn green. Even if it means losing precious seconds, he must wait all the same. The chief officer of the London Fire Brigade says No; he is not going to order the driver to wait. If the road is clear and the driver stops for a second and makes sure that it is safe to cross, he can shoot the lights so as to get to the fire as soon as possible. But, if he thinks it better to wait until the lights go green, he is at perfect liberty to do so. The decision is his, and his alone. The controversy has been considered by the Central Fire Brigade Advisory Council. It has been before the Home Secretary and the Secretary of State for Scotland. They have declined to interfere either by legislation, or otherwise. So the rival views have been brought before us to decide between them.

In accordance with his view, the chief officer of the London Fire Brigade, with the support of the Greater London Council, has issued an instruction. Its formal description is brigade order 144/8, dated 3 February 1967. It states:

> '*Traffic light signals* – Drivers of fire brigade vehicles are under the same obligation at law to obey traffic light signals as the drivers of other vehicles. If however, a Brigade driver responding to an emergency call decides to proceed against the red light, he is (unless signalled to proceed by a police constable in uniform) to stop his appliance, car, or other vehicle at the red light, observe carefully the traffic conditions around him, and to proceed only when he is reasonably sure that there is no risk of a collision; the bell is to be rung vigorously and/or the two-tone horn sounded and the blue flashing light(s) operated. Extreme caution is to be used and the driver is not to cross until it is clear that the drivers of other vehicles appear aware that he is proceeding. The onus of avoiding an accident in such circumstances rests entirely on the Brigade driver, who is to remember that a collision might well prevent his vehicle from reaching its destination and might also block the road for other essential services; no call is so urgent as to justify this risk.'

The Fire Brigades Union take exception to that order. They say that it is unlawful because it is an encouragement to the drivers to break the law. They determined to test the legal position. They told some 20 of their members, the plaintiffs, to refuse to travel with a driver unless he gave them an assurance that he would observe the law and would never cross the lights when they were at red. The drivers refused to give that assurance. Whereupon the plaintiffs refused to travel with the drivers. The chief officer took disciplinary

proceedings against the plaintiffs. They were charged under the Fire Services
(Discipline) Regulations 1948 (S.I. 1948 No. 545, reg. 1 and Schedule) with:

> 'Disobedience to orders, that is to say, if he disobeys, or without sufficient
> cause fails to carry out, any lawful order, whether in writing or not.'

The plaintiffs thereupon brought this action against the Greater London
Council, the defendants. They claimed a declaration that order 144/8 of
3 February 1967 was an unlawful one: and an injunction restraining the defendants from continuing with the disciplinary proceedings.

The issue in the action depends, I think, on this: was the order of the chief
fire officer 144/8 lawful or unlawful? If it was lawful, the plaintiffs had no
possible justification for refusing to travel with the driver. If it was unlawful,
they could justifiably say that they had sufficient cause for their refusal;
because they were not bound to travel with a driver who was under unlawful
orders.

The statutory provisions

There is no doubt that, on a strict reading of the statute, a fireman is bound
to obey the traffic lights just as much as anyone else. If he does not do so, he
may be prosecuted to conviction; his licence may be endorsed; and if it is
endorsed three times he may be disqualified from driving and thus lose his job
– and the fire service would lose a man.

The statutory provisions are as follows. By s. 14 of the Road Traffic Act
1960, as amended (by the Road Traffic Act 1962, s. 8, Sch. I, Part 2):

> '... where a traffic sign ... has been lawfully placed on or near a road, a
> person driving or propelling a vehicle who ... (b) fails to comply with the
> indication given by the sign, shall be liable on summary conviction to a fine
> not exceeding fifty pounds.'

By the Traffic Signs Regulations and General Direction 1964, (S.I. 1964 No.
1857) regs 7 and 34:

> '7. Section 14 of the Road Traffic Act 1960 shall apply ... to the red
> signal when shown by the light signals ...
>
> 34. (1) ... (a) the red signal shall convey the prohibition that vehicular
> traffic shall not proceed beyond the stop line. ...'

as to which see *Ryan* v. *Smith* ([1967] 2 Q.B. 893). By s. 7(1) of the Road Traffic
Act 1962, when a person is convicted of disobeying a traffic light signal:

> '... the court shall order that particulars of the conviction, and, if the
> court orders him to be disqualified, particulars of the disqualification, shall
> be endorsed on any licence held by him. ...'

By s. 7(2):

> 'If the court does not order the said person to be disqualified, the court
> need not order particulars of the conviction to be endorsed as aforesaid if
> for special reasons it thinks fit not to do so.'

By s. 5(3) of the 1962 Act, where a person has already two previous convictions
which have been endorsed:

> '... the court shall order him to be disqualified for ... not less than
> six months ... unless the court is satisfied, having regard to all the

circumstances, that there are grounds for mitigating the normal consequences of the conviction. . . .'

Those provisions, taken in all their strictness, apply to fire engines, ambulances and police cars as much as to anyone else. None of them is exempt from obeying the red lights. But by special permission they are exempt from obeying the speed limit: see s.79 of the Road Traffic Regulations Act 1967.

The defence of necessity

During the argument I raised the question: might not the driver of a fire engine be able to raise the defence of necessity? I put this illustration. A driver of a fire engine with ladders approaches the traffic lights. He sees 200 yards down the road a blazing house with a man at an upstairs window in extreme peril. The road is clear in all directions. At that moment the lights turn red. Is the driver to wait for 60 seconds, or more, for the lights to turn green? If the driver waits for that time, the man's life will be lost. I suggested to both counsel that the driver might be excused in crossing the lights to save the man. He might have the defence of necessity. Both counsel denied it. They would not allow him any defence in law. The circumstances went to mitigation, they said, and did not take away his guilt. If counsel are correct – and I accept that they are – nevertheless such a man should not be prosecuted. He should be congratulated.

Mitigating the rigour of the law

Accepting that the law, according to the strict letter of it, does compel every driver to stop at the red light, no matter how great the emergency, even when there is no danger, then the question arises: can the chief officer of the fire brigade issue an order authorising his men to depart from the letter of the law?

This raises an important question. It is a fundamental principle of our constitution, enshrined in the Bill of Rights (1688), that no one, not even the Crown itself has the 'power of dispensing with laws or the execution of laws'. But this is subject to some qualification. When a law has become a dead letter, the police need not prosecute. Nor need the justices punish. They can give an absolute discharge. So also when there is a technical breach of the law in which it would be unjust to inflict any punishment whatever. The commissioner of police may properly in such a case make a policy decision directing his men not to proceed: *R.* v. *Metropolitan Police, ex parte Blackburn* ([1968] 2 Q.B. 118, at 136) where it was said that a chief officer of police can 'make policy decisions and give effect to them, as for instance, was often done when prosecutions were not brought for attempted suicide'. So in this case, I have no doubt that the commissioner of police could give directions to his men – he may indeed have done so, for aught I know – that they need not prosecute when the driver of a fire engine crosses the lights, so long as he uses all care and there is no danger to others. This would be a justifiable policy decision so as to mitigate the strict rigour of the law. If any police officer, notwithstanding this direction should prosecute for this technical offence, I would expect the justices to give the driver an absolute discharge under s.7 of the Criminal Justice Act 1948. Thus by administrative action, backed by judicial decision, an exemption is grafted on to the law.

We were told that in practice the police do not prosecute the driver of a fire engine for crossing the lights at red except when there has been an accident and they think that he has not taken proper care. They then prosecute him both for crossing the lights at red and also for careless driving. The driver has no defence to crossing the lights and pleads guilty to that charge. He disputes the careless driving, and may or may not be found guilty of it. I would hope that, if he is acquitted of careless driving he would be given absolute discharge on the charge of crossing the lights.

I take it, therefore, that the commissioner of police can give a policy direction to his men saying that they need not prosecute a fireman for crossing the lights at red when there is no danger. If the commissioner of police can do this, I see no reason why the chief officer of the fire brigade should not do likewise. He can say to his men: 'So long as you stop and see that all is clear before crossing the lights, no disciplinary action will be taken against you.' That is a justifiable administrative step taken by him in the public interest. We should, I think, back it by our judicial decision today. I hold therefore, that order 144/8 of 3 February 1967 was a perfectly lawful order.

The disciplinary proceedings

Seeing that order 144/8 was a lawful order, I think that the disciplinary proceedings must go on.

Suppose that a driver were to say to a crewman: 'I am going to break the law and crash the red lights, even when it is dangerous to do so,' I think that the crewman could justifiably refuse to travel with that driver. He would not be bound to submit himself to danger in that way: see *Ottoman Bank* v. *Chakarian* ([1930] A.C. 277). But it is altogether different when the driver says: 'I am not going to crash the lights except when there is no risk of a collision, and then only after taking the precautions laid down in brigade-order 144/8.' If the officer orders the crewman to travel with such a driver, it is a lawful order, and the crewman has no sufficient cause for failing to carry it out.

Plowman J., ([1970] 2 All E.R. 193, at 195 *et seq.*) devoted a considerable part of his judgment to *Ex parte Fry* ([1954] 2 All E.R. 118) but that case was not canvassed before us. It does not warrant the proposition that the rules of natural justice do not apply to disciplinary bodies. They must act fairly just the same as anyone else; and are just as subject to control by the courts. If the firemen's disciplinary tribunal were to hold an order to be a lawful order, when it was not, I am sure that the courts could interfere; or, if it proceeded contrary to the rules of natural justice in a matter of serious import, so also the courts could interfere. But, as in this case, the order was lawful and the tribunal will, I have no doubt, do what is just, there is no ground whatever for interfering.

Conclusion

We have considered here the firemen. Like principles apply to ambulance men and police officers. The law, if taken by the letter of it, says that they are not to shoot the lights when they are at red. But the public interest may demand that, when all is clear, they should follow the precedent set by Lord Nelson. If they should do so, no man should condemn them. Their chief officer says that he will not punish them. Nor should the justices. Now that we in this court support what the chief officer has done, it means that, in point of practice, we have grafted an exception on to the strictness of the law so as to mitigate the rigour of it. It may now truly be said that firemen, ambulance men and police officers are to be excused if they shoot the lights when there is no risk of a collision and the urgency of the case so demands. The courts of the United States have done somewhat similar, but on rather special grounds: *Lilly* v. *State of West Virginia* ((1928) 29 Fed. Rep. (2nd Ser.) 61). We do it on practical grounds but none the worse for that.

Should the law be amended so that there is not even a technical breach? I think that it should. By making it an offence without exceptions, Parliament has opened the way to endless discussion in fire stations which should be brought to a close. I hope that our judgment today will do something to end them. But Parliament can do it better.

I would dismiss this appeal.

QUESTIONS

1. What question(s) of law arose in this case?

2. Is a court the most appropriate body to determine questions of this sort? What other persons or bodies could have taken action which would have had the result that the issue was not left to be settled by a court? Which in your opinion was the most appropriate body for solving the problem? Give reasons for your answers.

3. What did the case decide? Is it authority for the proposition that it is lawful for a fire-engine driver answering an emergency call to shoot the lights?

4. What reasons does Lord Denning M.R. give for his decision?

5. Write a comment on the judgment from the point of view of the Fire Brigades Union.

6. Lord Denning says: 'Thus by administrative action, backed by judicial decision, an exemption is grafted on to the law'; later, he refers to Parliament 'making it an offence without exception'. What, if anything, is the difference between an exception and an exemption in this context?

7. In 1975 the following exception to the normal rule that traffic must stop at a red light was introduced:

on an occasion when a vehicle is being used for fire brigade, ambulance or police purposes and the observance of the prohibition conveyed by the red signal as provided by the last preceding sub-paragraph would be likely to hinder the use of that vehicle for the purpose for which it is being used on that occasion, then the said sub-paragraph shall not apply to that vehicle; but instead the prohibition conveyed to that vehicle by the red signal shall be that that vehicle shall not proceed beyond the stop line, or as the case may be as provided by the said sub-paragraph, beyond the signals in such a manner or at such a time –

    (i) as is likely to cause danger to the driver of any other vehicle proceeding on or from another road or on or from another part of the same road in accordance with the indications of the light signals operating there in association with the said red signal or as to necessitate the driver of any other such vehicle to change its speed or course in order to avoid an accident, or

(ii) in the case of any traffic which is not vehicular, as is likely to cause danger to that traffic proceeding on or from another road or on or from another part of the same road;

(From the Traffic Signs Regulations and General Directions 1975, S.I. 1975/1536, regulation 34(1)(b).)

(i) What considerations do you think were relevant to the decision to allow this exception?

(ii) Do the terms of the exception meet the Union's difficulty as expressed in *Buckoke* v. *G.L.C.*?

(iii) Can you think of any devices other than creating this exception which would achieve the same objectives?

(b) Johnson v. Phillips [1975] 3 All E.R. 682

In this case the appellant had been convicted of obstructing a police constable in the course of his duty, contrary to Section 51(3) of the Police Act 1964. Wien J. said: 'The precise question to be answered in the instant case may be put thus: has a constable in purported exercise of his power to control traffic on a public road the right under common law to disobey a traffic regulation such as going the wrong way along a one-way street? If he himself has that right then it follows that he can oblige others to comply with his instructions to disobey such a regulation.' It was held that the police officer has such a power if such a direction is reasonably necessary for the protection of life or property, even though the situation was not explicitly covered by Parliament. The appeal was dismissed.

QUESTION
Is it paradoxical to talk of lawful departures from legal rules? See M. R. Kadish and S. H. Kadish, *Discretion to Disobey* (1973).

9 **Donoghue** *v.* **Stevenson** [1932] A.C. 562 (House of Lords)

Donoghue v. *Stevenson* is one of the most famous cases in the common law. It is frequently used to illustrate points about matters that fall within the compass of this book. It is thus a useful link with the existing literature on a number of topics. It also provides a good illustration of many other relevant points to which less attention has been paid in the past. Because of pressure of space, we have not been able to reproduce the two speeches of Lord Buckmaster and Lord Atkin in their entirety, so we have selected certain passages from the report, which are extensively referred to, especially in Chapter 8, in order to illustrate at this stage some of the fundamental aspects of rules extracted from judicial decisions, notably the notion of a 'ladder of abstraction' and techniques for handling precedents. It is important that you study the extracts below closely; in particular, compare the level of generality at which the facts, the issue and the decision of the case are stated in the different extracts. Law students are recommended to study the two speeches intact in the law reports.

By an action brought in the Court of Session the appellant, who was a shop assistant, sought to recover damages from the respondent, who was a manufacturer of aerated waters, for injuries she suffered as a result of consuming part of the contents of a bottle of ginger-beer which had been manufactured by the respondent, and which contained the decomposed remains of a snail. The appellant by her condescendence averred that the bottle of ginger-beer was purchased for the appellant by a friend in a café at Paisley, which was occupied by one Minchella, that the bottle was made of dark opaque glass and that the appellant had no reason to suspect that it contained anything but pure ginger-beer; that the said Minchella poured some of the ginger-beer out into a tumbler, and that the appellant drank some of the contents of the tumbler; that her friend was then proceeding to pour the remainder of the contents of the bottle into the tumbler when a snail, which was in a state of decomposition, floated out of the bottle; that as a result of the nauseating sight of the snail in such circumstances, and in consequence of the impurities in the ginger-beer which she had already consumed the appellant suffered from shock and severe gastro-enteritis. The appellant further averred that the ginger-beer was manufactured by the respondent to be sold as a drink to the public (including the appellant); that it was bottled by the respondent and labelled by him with a label bearing his name; and that the bottles were thereafter sealed with a metal cap by the respondent. She further averred that it was the duty of the respondent to provide a system of working his business which would not allow snails to get into his ginger-beer bottles and that it was also his duty to provide an efficient system of inspection of the bottles before the ginger-beer was filled into them, and that he had failed in both these duties and had so caused the accident....

1932. May 26, *Lord Buckmaster* (dissenting). My Lords, the facts of this case are simple. On August 26, 1928, the appellant drank a bottle of ginger-beer, manufactured by the respondent which a friend had brought from a retailer and given to her. The bottle contained the decomposed remains of a snail which were not, and could not be, detected until the greater part of the contents of the bottle had been consumed. As a result she alleged, and at this stage her allegations must be accepted as true, that she suffered from shock and severe gastro-enteritis. She accordingly instituted the proceedings against the manufacturer which have given rise to this appeal.

The foundation of her case is that the respondent, as the manufacturer of an article intended for consumption and contained in a receptacle which prevented inspection, owed a duty to her as consumer of the article to take care that there was no noxious element in the goods, that he neglected such duty and is consequently liable for any damage caused by such neglect. After certain amendments, which are now immaterial, the case came before the Lord Ordinary, who rejected the plea in law of the respondent and allowed a proof. His interlocutor was recalled by the Second Division of the Court of Session, from whose judgment this appeal has been brought.... [1932] A.C. 566.

Now the common law must be sought in law books by writers of authority and in judgments of the judges entrusted with its administration. The law books give no assistance, because the work of living authors however deservedly eminent, cannot be used as authority, though the opinions they express may demand attention; and the ancient books do not assist. I turn, therefore to the decided cases to see if they can be construed so as to support the appellant's case. One of the earliest is the case of *Langridge* v. *Levy* ((1837) 2 M. & W. 519). It is a case often quoted and variously explained. There a man sold a gun which he knew was dangerous for the use of the purchaser's son. The gun exploded in the son's hands, and he was held to have a right of action in tort against the gunmaker. How far it is from the present case can be seen from the judgment of Parke B., who, in delivering the judgment of the Court, used these words: 'We shall pause before we make a precedent by our decision which would be an authority for an action against the vendors, even of such instruments and articles as are dangerous in themselves at the suit of any person whomsoever into whose hands they might happen to pass, and who should be injured thereby'.... [id., p. 567].

The case of *Langridge* v. *Levy* therefore, can be dismissed from consideration with the comment that it is rather surprising it has so often been cited for a proposition it cannot support. [ibid.]

The case of *Winterbottom* v. *Wright* ((1842) 10 M. & W. 109) is on the other hand, an authority that is closely applicable. Owing to negligence in the construction of a carriage it broke down, and a stranger to the manufacture and sale sought to recover damages for injuries which he alleged were due to negligence in the work, and it was held that he had no cause of action either in tort or arising out of contract. This case seems to me to show that the manufacturer of any article is not liable to a third party injured by negligent construction, for there can be nothing in the character of a coach to place it in a special category. It may be noted, also, that in this case Alderson B. said:

'The only safe rule is to confine the right to recover to those who enter into the contract, if we go one step beyond that, there is no reason why we should not go fifty' ... [id., p. 568]

Of the remaining cases, *George* v. *Skivington* ((1869) L.R. 5 Ex. 1) is the one nearest to the present, and without that case, and the statement of Cleasby B. in *Francis* v. *Cockrell* ((1870) L.R. 5 Q.B. 501) and the dicta of Brett M.R., in *Heaven* v. *Pender* ((1883) 11 Q.B.D. 503) the appellant would be destitute of authority. *George* v. *Skivington* related to the sale of a noxious hairwash, and a claim made by a person who had not bought it but who had suffered from its use, based on its having been negligently compounded, was allowed. It is remarkable that *Langridge* v. *Levy* was used in support of the claim and influenced the judgment of all the parties to the decision. Both Kelly C.B. and Pigott B. stressed the fact that the article had been purchased to the knowledge of the defendant for the use of the plaintiff, as in *Langridge* v. *Levy*, and Cleasby B., who, realizing that *Langridge* v. *Levy* was decided on the ground of fraud, said: 'Substitute the word "negligence" for "fraud" and the analogy between *Langridge* v. *Levy* and this case is complete.' It is unnecessary to point out too emphatically that such a substitution cannot possibly be made. No action based on fraud can be supported by mere proof of negligence.

I do not propose to follow the fortunes of *George* v. *Skivington*; few cases can have lived so dangerously and lived so long. Lord Sumner, in the case of *Blacker* v. *Lake & Elliot Ltd* ((1912) 106 L.T. 533) closely examines its history, and I agree with his analysis. He said that he could not presume to say that it was wrong, but he declined to follow it on the ground which is, I think, firm that it was in conflict with *Winterbottom* v. *Wright*. [id., p. 570]

Lord Atkin. My Lords, the sole question for determination in this case is legal: Do the averments made by the pursuer in her pleading, if true, disclose a cause of action? I need not restate the particular facts. The question is whether the manufacturer of an article of drink sold by him to a distributor, in circumstances which prevent the distributor or the ultimate purchaser or consumer from discovering by inspection any defect, is under any legal duty to the ultimate purchaser or consumer to take reasonable care that the article is free from defect likely to cause injury to health. I do not think a more important problem has occupied your Lordships in your judicial capacity: important both because of its bearing on public health and because of the practical test which it applies to the system under which it arises.... [id., p. 579]

At present I content myself with pointing out that in English law there must be, and is, some general conception of relations giving rise to a duty of care, of which the particular cases found in the books are but instances. The liability for negligence, whether you style it such or treat it as in other systems as a species of 'culpa', is no doubt based upon a general public sentiment of moral wrongdoing for which the offender must pay. But acts or omissions which any moral code would censure cannot in a practical world be treated so as to give a right to every person injured by them to demand relief. In this way rules of law arise which limit the range of complainants and the extent of their remedy. The rule that you are to love your neighbour becomes in law, you must not injure your neighbour; and the lawyer's question, Who is my neighbour?

receives a restricted reply. You must take reasonable care to avoid acts or omissions which you can reasonably foresee would be likely to injure your neighbour. Who, then in law is my neighbour? The answer seems to be – persons who are so closely and directly affected by my act that I ought reasonably to have them in contemplation as being so affected when I am directing my mind to the acts or omissions which are called in question.... [id., p. 580.]

There will no doubt arise cases where it will be difficult to determine whether the contemplated relationship is so close that the duty arises. But in the class of case now before the Court I cannot conceive any difficulty to arise. A manufacturer puts up an article of food in a container which he knows will be opened by the actual consumer. There can be no inspection by any purchaser and no reasonable preliminary inspection by the consumer. Negligently, in the course of preparation, he allows the contents to be mixed with poison. It is said that the Law of England and Scotland is that the poisoned consumer has no remedy against the negligent manufacturer. If this were the result of the authorities, I should consider the result a grave defect in the law.... [id., p. 582.]

There are other instances than of articles of food and drink where goods are sold intended to be used immediately by the consumer, such as many forms of goods sold for cleaning purposes, where the same liability must exist. The doctrine supported by the decision below would not only deny a remedy to the consumer who was injured by consuming bottled beer or chocolates poisoned by the negligence of the manufacturer, but also to the user of what should be a harmless proprietary medicine, an ointment, a soap, a cleaning fluid or cleaning powder. I confine myself to articles of common household use, where every one, including the manufacturer knows that the articles will be used by other persons than the actual ultimate purchaser – namely, by members of his family and his servants, and in some cases his guests. I do not think so ill of our jurisprudence as to suppose that its principles are so remote from the ordinary needs of civilized society and the ordinary claims it makes upon its members as to deny a legal remedy where there is so obviously a social wrong. [id., p. 583]

It now becomes necessary to consider the cases which have been referred to in the Courts below as laying down the proposition that no duty to take care is owed to the consumer in such a case as this.

In *Winterbottom* v. *Wright* it is to be observed that no negligence apart from breach of contract was alleged – in other words, no duty was alleged other than the duty arising out of the contract; it is not stated that the defendant knew, or ought to have known, of the latent defect. The argument of the defendant was that, on the face of the declaration, the wrong arose merely out of the breach of a contract, and that only a party to the contract could sue. The Court of Exchequer adopted that view, as clearly appears from the judgments of Alderson and Rolfe BB. There are dicta by Lord Abinger which are too wide as to an action of negligence being confined to cases of breach of a public duty. The actual decision appears to have been manifestly right; no duty to the plaintiff arose out of the contract; and the duty of the defendant under the contract with the Postmaster-General to put the coach in good repair could not have involved such direct relations with the servant of the persons whom the Postmaster-General employed to drive the coach as would give rise to a duty of care owed to such servant.... [id., pp. 587–589]

My Lords, if your Lordships accept the view that this pleading discloses a relevant cause of action you will be affirming the proposition that by Scots and English law alike a manufacturer of products, which he sells in such a form as to show that he intends them to reach the ultimate consumer in the form in which they left him with no reasonable possibility of intermediate examination, and with the knowledge that the absence of reasonable care in the preparation or putting up of the products will result in an injury to the consumer's life or property, owes a duty to the consumer to take that reasonable care.

It is a proposition which I venture to say no one in Scotland or England who was not a lawyer would for one moment doubt. It will be an advantage to make it clear that the law in this matter, as in most others, is in accordance with sound common sense. I think that this appeal should be allowed. [id., p. 599]

Appeal allowed.

QUESTIONS

1. From a non-legal point of view, do you think that the plaintiff should have been able to recover in this case if her allegations were true? Why?

2. Which judge was more 'legalistic' – Lord Atkin or Lord Buckmaster?

3. Which is the most appropriate way of describing the respondent (original defendant) in this case:

  (i)   a Scottish manufacturer of ginger-beer in opaque bottles;
  (ii) a manufacturer of aerated water;
  (iii) a manufacturer of consumable products (food or drink);
  (iv) a manufacturer of products;
  (v)   a person who, in the course of trade, puts goods into circulation;
  (vi) a person who puts into circulation a potentially harmful item;
  (vii) a neighbour, that is to say a person who could reasonably have foreseen that persons in the position of the plaintiff could have been directly affected by any act or omission on his (the defendant's) part which was likely to cause injury?

4. The questions in 3 contain an example of 'a ladder of abstraction', that is to say a continuous sequence of categorizations from a low level of generality up to a high level of generality. Construct a ladder of abstraction in respect of the object that caused the harm in *Donoghue* v. *Stevenson*.

5. Do we know from the report of the case whether the facts alleged by the appellant (pursuer) were historically true?

6. What were the material facts of *Donoghue* v. *Stevenson*? What are the differences between the following formulations? What differences are *material*?

(i) There were two neighbours and one injured the other by negligent conduct.

(ii) A Scottish shop assistant (in Paisley) received as a gift from a male friend an opaque glass bottle, which was closed by a metal cap, and which contained ginger-beer and a decomposing snail. The bottle was manufactured in the factory of a Scottish manufacturer of aerated water. The presence of the snail was attributed to carelessness on the part of the manufacturer or his employees. There was no contractual relationship between the Scottish manufacturer and the shop assistant.

(iii) An article of drink was sold by the manufacturer to a distributor in circumstances which prevented the distributor and the ultimate purchaser and consumer from discovering by inspection, a defect which was likely to and did in fact cause injury to the health of the ultimate consumer. The manufacturer had failed to take reasonable care to prevent the defect.

(iv) A manufacturer of products sold a product in such a form as to show that he intended it to reach the ultimate consumer in the form in which it left him, with the knowledge that the absence of reasonable care in the preparation or putting up of the products would result in injury to the consumer's life or property. The manufacturer failed to take reasonable care, and injury resulted to the ultimate consumer.

Which, if any, did Lord Atkin consider to be the most precise statement of the material facts? Give reasons for your answer.

10 Human rights and freedoms

(a) Universal Declaration of Human Rights

Article 3: Everyone has the right to life, liberty and security of person.

Article 5: No one shall be subjected to torture or to cruel, inhuman or degrading treatment or punishment.

Article 9: No one shall be subjected to arbitrary arrest, detention or exile.

Article 10: Everyone is entitled in full equality to a fair and public hearing by an independent and impartial tribunal, in the determination of his rights and obligations and of any criminal charge against him.

Article 11

1. Everyone charged with a penal offence has the right to be presumed innocent until proved guilty according to law in a public trial at which he has had all the guarantees necessary for his defence.

2. No one shall be held guilty of any penal offence on account of any act or omission which did not constitute a penal offence, under national or international law, at the time when it was committed. Nor shall a heavier penalty be imposed than the one that was applicable at the time the penal offence was committed

(b) Constitution of the United States, 8th Amendment

Excessive bail shall not be required, nor excessive fines imposed, nor cruel and unusual punishments inflicted.

(c) European Convention on Human Rights and Fundamental Freedoms (1950)

Article 3: No one shall be subjected to torture or to inhuman or degrading treatment or punishment.

Article 5

(1) Everyone has the right to liberty and security of person. No one shall be deprived of his liberty save in the following cases and in accordance with a procedure prescribed by law:

   (*a*) the lawful detention of a person after conviction by a competent court;

   (*b*) the lawful arrest or detention of a person for non-compliance with the lawful order of a court or in order to secure the fulfilment of any obligation prescribed by law;

   (*c*) the lawful arrest or detention of a person effected for the purpose of bringing him before the competent legal authority on reasonable suspicion of having committed an offence or when it is reasonably considered necessary to prevent his committing an offence or fleeing after having done so;

   (*d*) the detention of a minor by lawful order for the purpose of bringing him before the competent legal authority;

   (*e*) the lawful detention of persons for the prevention of the spreading of infectious diseases, of persons of unsound mind, alcoholics or drug addicts or vagrants;

   (*f*) the lawful arrest or detention of a person to prevent his effecting an unauthorized entry into the country or of a person against whom action is being taken with a view to deportation or extradition.

(2) Everyone who is arrested shall be informed promptly, in a language which he understands, of the reasons for his arrest and of any charge against him.

(3) Everyone arrested or detained in accordance with the provisions of paragraph 1 (*c*) of this Article shall be brought promptly before a judge or other officer authorized by law to exercise judicial power and shall be entitled to trial within a reasonable time or to release pending trial. Release may be conditioned by guarantees to appear for trial.

(4) Everyone who is deprived of his liberty by arrest or detention shall be entitled to take proceedings by which the lawfulness of his detention shall be decided speedily by a court and his release ordered if the detention is not lawful.

(5) Everyone who has been the victim of arrest or detention in contravention of the provisions of this Article shall have an enforceable right to compensation.

Article 15

(1) In time of war or other public emergency threatening the life of the nation any High Contracting Party may take measures derogating from its obligations under this Convention to the extent strictly required by the exigencies of the situation, provided that such measures are not inconsistent with its other obligations under international law.

(2) No derogation from Article 2, except in respect of deaths resulting from lawful acts of war, or from Article 3, 4 (paragraph 1) and 7 shall be made under this provision.

QUESTIONS

1. Article 3 of the European Convention is said to be an 'absolute prohibition' in that it makes no provision for exceptions and it is not subject to derogation 'in time of war or other public emergency threatening the life of the nation' (Article 15). In what sense is it 'absolute'?

2.(i) Would the *scope* of Article 3 be different if it were amended to read:

    (*a*) 'No one shall be subjected to inhuman or degrading treatment or punishment';

    (*b*) 'No one shall be subjected to inhuman treatment or punishment';

    (*c*) 'No one shall be subjected to inhuman treatment'.

 (ii) Would these amendments alter the *meaning* or the *substance* of Article 3? If so, in what respect(s)?

3. Could Article 3 be expressed without resort to emotive terms?

4. Which of the following do you consider are violations of Article 3:

 (i) In a small jail on an otherwise desert island in the tropics, a prisoner, guarded by a single jailer, is found to have died of thirst. A committee of enquiry established to investigate the reason for the death set out to test four alternative hypotheses (there could, of course, be many others):

    (*a*) that the jailer deliberately withheld water from the prisoner for sadistic reasons;

    (*b*) that the jailer deliberately withheld water in order to coerce the prisoner to do or say something, for example to reveal the whereabouts of a cache of buried treasure;

    (*c*) that the jailer was either reckless or negligent in failing to provide the prisoner with water, for example he went on a binge for three days and forgot all about him;

    (*d*) that the jailer died and no one else was available to bring water to the prisoner.

(ii) As a part of certain kinds of military training, 'volunteers' are subjected to severe and realistic 'interrogation in depth', allegedly in order to teach them how to resist torture if they are captured by the enemy.

(iii)   (*a*) A prisoner or mental patient was so violent that the only feasible means of controlling him was to manhandle him, strip him and keep him in a straitjacket for a substantial period. It was found as a matter of fact that the means used were not disproportionate to the risks of not controlling him and that no other means was available. Is this (1) 'degrading'; (2) 'inhuman' treatment? If (2), does it follow from this that no means is 'inhuman' provided that it is proportionate to the end in question?

    (*b*) An adult mental patient is subjected to electric-shock treatment by doctors who believe that this will be for his own good. What arguments can be advanced for holding that this is not a violation of Article 3, if

        (1) he has freely consented to the treatment?

        (2) his mental condition is such that it is certified by two psychiatrists that he is incapable of making a rational choice about his treatment?

        (3) the patient is a mentally retarded 7-year-old child?

        (4) the patient has refused consent?

        (5) the patient has been certified to be insane because of his deviant political beliefs?

5. The President of Xanadu, a benevolent despot dedicated to rule on utilitarian principles, decides to sign an international convention which contains an absolute prohibition against torture, etc. He signs, on the grounds that (i) the document will generally promote utility; (ii) it is very unlikely that the conditions that he would consider

justifying the use of torture will arise in practice; (iii) any express exception incorporating these conditions would probably be abused by other signatories. Shortly after signing he is confronted with the following situation. The police capture a terrorist who informs them that unless some prisoners are released from jail within twelve hours, his colleagues will cause the explosion of a number of very powerful bombs situated so that the deaths of hundreds of people are virtually guaranteed. The terrorist indicates that he will tell the police of the whereabouts of the bombs, and how they may be defused, once he has a guarantee that the prisoners have been released. Considering this to be an extreme case, the President authorises the police to torture the terrorist so as to extract the information concerning the bombs. Later, terrorism becomes endemic and the President is persuaded 'in the public interest' to set up a torture squad.

Nevertheless, five years later he renews his support for the Convention. Has the President acted consistently as a utilitarian?

6. 'Torture is the systematic and deliberate infliction of acute pain in any form by one person on another, or on a third person, in order to accomplish the purpose of the first against the will or interest of the second.' (B. Paskins, 'Torture and Philosophy', *Proceedings of the Aristotelian Society* (1978), p. 169.)

Is this definition entirely adequate as an elucidation of 'torture' in Article 3?

7. Consider the Eighth Amendment of the US Constitution and Article 3 of the European Convention, with regard to the following:
  (i) capital punishment;
  (ii) corporal punishment of males (*a*) in prison, (*b*) in schools, (*c*) in the home;
  (iii) corporal punishment of females, as above;
  (iv) solitary confinement;
  (v) castration of rapists after conviction for a second offence;
  (vi) imprisonment for life;
  (vii) imprisonment in an overcrowded and insanitary jail.

8. To what extent is it appropriate that such factors as local public opinion, religious tradition or political instability should be taken into account in determining the scope of Article 3 of the European Convention?

11 Standpoint and role

(a) General

A car skids while cornering at a certain point, turns turtle, and bursts into flame. From the car-driver's point of view, the cause of the accident was cornering too fast, and the lesson is that one must drive more carefully. From the county surveyor's point of view, the cause was a defective road surface, and the lesson is that one must make skid-proof roads. From the motor-manufacturer's point of view, the cause was defective design, and the lesson is that one must place the centre of gravity lower.

(From R. G. Collingwood, 'On the So-called Idea of Causation' (1937–8), *Proceedings of the Aristotelian Society*, pp. 85, 96.)

But the different meanings of the term 'law' are not the only source of difficulty in discussions of the 'nature of law'. If we restrict the term to the body of authoritative materials for guidance of judicial and administrative determination, it is possible to look at those materials from more than one standpoint, and the answer to the question, what is law? will depend much upon the standpoint from which it is asked.

There are at least six standpoints from which law in the sense of the body of authoritative precepts may be looked at.

First is the standpoint of the lawmaker. He thinks of something that ought to be done or ought not to be done and so of a command to do it or not to do it....

Second is the standpoint of the individual subject to the legal precept, who would walk in the straight path of social conduct and wishes it charted for him. If, instead he is the bad man of whom Mr Justice Holmes speaks, who has no care for the straight path but wishes to know what path he may take with impunity, he will no doubt think of a legal precept as a threat. But the ordinary man who does not 'wash the idea in cynical acid' has more commonly thought of it as a rule of conduct, a guide telling him what he ought to do at the crisis of action. This is the oldest idea of a law. It goes back to the codified ethical custom of the earlier stages of legal development.

Another standpoint is that of a judge who has a case before him for decision or a ruling to make in the course of a trial; or that of an administrative official called upon to make some determination. Here the significant thing seems to be a body of authoritative grounds or models or patterns of decisions or of administrative determination.

Fourth, there is the standpoint of the counsellor at law or legal adviser, who would advise a client as to what he may do or may not do safely, or how he may act with assurance that courts and administrative officials will back him and further his quest of desired results. From this standpoint law may seem to be a body of threats of official action upon given states of fact, or it may seem to be a body of bases of prediction of official action. Even looked at in this way, however, it must be insisted that a law or a legal precept is not a prediction, as some realists deem it. It is the adviser not the law that does the predicting. As Mr Justice Cardozo pointed out a law or a legal precept is a basis of prediction.

Fifth, there is the standpoint of the jurist or teacher who is called on to put in the order of reason the materials recognised or established as the basis of decision or at hand for the counsellor, or provided for the guidance of the citizen or individual. He may find it hard to say that one of the foregoing aspects, as things are today, is more significant than another, or to find the more inclusive order which will enable him to fit a theory to all of these points of view. From his own special point of view he is likely to regard a law or a legal precept as a basis of development of doctrine.

Finally, there is the standpoint of the entrepreneur or man of business, which was taken at one time by writers on the nature of law but is less heard of today. From this standpoint legal precepts have been thought of as charts and legal conceptions as devices for the carrying out of business plans or carrying on of business enterprises.

It is submitted that the different ideas of a law, reached from these several standpoints, can be unified in terms of the idea from the standpoint of the judge. Judges and benches are expected to and for most practical purposes will follow and decide in accordance with the established precept or established starting point for legal reasoning developed by an authoritative technique. Hence, the precept or developed starting point may serve as a command or threat, or as a rule of conduct, or as a basis of prediction, and the legal conception may serve as a business device.

(Reprinted from R. Pound, *II Jurisprudence* (1959), pp. 129-32, with permission of the West Publishing Company.)

(b) On punishment: utilitarians *v.* retributionists

On the other hand we have the institution of punishment itself and recommend and accept various changes in it because it is thought by the (ideal) legislator and by those to whom the law applies that, as a part of a system of law impartially applied from case to case arising under it, it will have the consequence, in the long run of furthering the interests of society.

One can say, then, that the judge and the legislator stand in different positions and look in different directions; one to the past, the other to the future. The justification of what the judge does, qua judge, sounds like the retributive view; the justification of what the (ideal) legislator does, qua legislator, sounds like the utilitarian view. Thus both views have a point (this is as it should be since intelligent and sensitive persons have been on both sides of the argument); and one's initial confusion disappears once one sees that these views apply to persons holding different offices with different duties, and situated differently with respect to the system of rules that make up the criminal law....

The answer, then, to the confusion engendered by the two views of punishment is quite simple: one distinguishes two offices, that of the judge and that of the legislator, and one distinguishes their different stations with respect to the system of rules which make up the law; and then one notes that the different sorts of considerations which would usually be offered as reasons for what is done under the cover of these offices can be paired off with the competing justifications of punishment. One reconciles the two views by the time-honoured device of making them apply to different situations.

But can it really be this simple? Well, this answer allows for the apparent intent of each side. Does a person who advocates the retributive view necessarily advocate, as an institution, legal machinery whose essential purpose is to set up and preserve a correspondence between moral turpitude and suffering? Surely not. What retributions have rightly insisted upon is that no man can be punished unless he is guilty, that is, unless he has broken the law. Their fundamental criticism of the utilitarian account is that, as they interpret it, it sanctions an innocent person's being punished (if one may call it that) for the benefit of society.

(From J. Rawls, 'Two Concepts of Rules' (1955), 64 *Philosophical Review*, 3, pp. 6–7.)

(c) The counsellor

He is not like the person pressing for legislation, who must often push out to the limit of the feasible and risk pushing beyond; in that area you get what you can get while the legislative getting is good. In sharp contrast, office-counsel can in all but rare circumstances play well inside any penumbra of doubt, he can work, like an engineer, with a substantial margin of safety; he can chart a course which leaves to others the shoal waters and the treacherous channels. For unlike the ordinary advocate, the counsellor need not take the situation as it comes, but can shape and shore it in advance; he can draft documents and set up lasting records against the accidents of memory, death or disappearance of witnesses, even to some extent against the hazard of bad faith – doubly so if he keeps his protective drafting within those bounds of reason which make a court want to give effect to manifest intent; trebly so if he sets a picture of situation and purpose which can appeal even to an outsider as sensible, reasonable, and inherently probable – and it is comforting how much of this last can be gotten by careful counsel into documentary form. Besides (or perhaps first), office-counsel are in a peculiarly good position to study and discriminate among rules and rulings with reference to how strong and solid any of them is, how much weight it will carry, how far the relevant type-situation is already at home in judicial understanding, or is of a character to find a ready welcome. After such discrimination, it is on the rocklike law-stuff that the sane counsellor does his building. Finally, wherever advising counsel can rely on being able to control any relevant litigation, another vital contingency is set to dwindling.

(From K. Llewellyn, *The Common Law Tradition* (1960), p. 383.)

(d) The Bad Man

Take the fundamental question, What constitutes the law? You will find some text writers telling you that it is something different from what is decided by the courts of Massachusetts or England, that it is a system of reason, that it is a deduction from principles of ethics or admitted axioms or what not, which may not coincide with the decisions. But if we take the view of our friend the Bad Man we shall find that he does not care two straws for the axioms or deductions, but that he does want to know what the Massachusetts or English courts are likely to do in fact. I am much of his mind. The prophecies of what the courts will do in fact, and nothing more pretentious, are what I mean by the law.

(From O. W. Holmes Jr, 'The Path of the Law', 10 *Harvard Law Review* (1897), 457, 460–1.)

(e) The Bad Man and legal theory

WHO IS THE BAD MAN?

In the present context, the Bad Man is not a revolutionary nor even a reformer out to change 'the system'. The Bad Man's concern is to secure his personal objectives within the existing order as painlessly as possible; he is not so much alienated from the law as he is indifferent to all aspects which do not affect him personally. Unlike Sartre's Saint Genet, he is not one who has a problem of identity – who defines his being in terms of the system and who is driven to do acts *because* they are criminal or antisocial. Nor is he a subscriber to some perverse ethic which turns conventional morality upon its head. The Bad Man is amoral rather than immoral. He is, like Economic Man and Bentham's 'civilized' actors, a rational calculating creature. In this and in other respects he does not necessarily reflect in a realistic manner the characteristics of actual deviants. Like Dahrendorf's *homo sociologicus*, he 'can neither love nor hate, laugh nor cry. He remains a pale, incomplete, strange, artificial man.' Indeed, there appears to be no reason why the Bad Man should not be an artificial person, such as a corporation. In short, he is a theoretical construct with as yet unexplored potential as a tool of analysis.

Perhaps we can go a little further and suggest that the Bad Man can be defined in terms of prediction. He is the person whose only task is to predict what will happen to him if he embarks on some particular course of action. Here we may anticipate a possible objection. Although it may be granted that prediction is central to the role of the Bad Man, it is admitted that there are others who are similarly concerned – for example, the lawyer who has to decide whether it is worth appealing an adverse decision, the advocate who needs to predict how the personnel of a particular court will react to some line of argument or to the testimony of some witness, the judge who may wish to predict the likelihood of reversal on appeal or the possible effects of sending an offender to jail, the legislator who is concerned with the likely effects of a legal provision on patterns of behaviour. And the scientist – is he not also concerned with prediction?

A simple response is that, although these may all be valid observations, they are not objections to defining the Bad Man in terms of prediction. A comprehensive prediction theory would need to give a comprehensive answer to a question such as 'Who is concerned with predicting what events at what point in time for what purposes using what means?' With the exception of the scientist, whose standpoint raises special difficulties, all the other characters are predicting as part of some other task; for example, the advocate predicts in order to perform the task of persuasion. For some purposes it may be useful to isolate the task of predicting *simpliciter*; for other purposes prediction is more usefully seen as part of a cluster of tasks. In other words, the Bad Man is a device for isolating for special consideration the task of predicting certain kinds of events.

The idea of prediction provides no basis for distinguishing between the standpoints of the Good Citizen and of the Bad Man. It is not incompatible with good citizenship to be concerned with predicting the likely consequences of one's actions. The Bad Man, however, is affected by guidance as to his actions *only* insofar as such guidance predicts the ultimate consequences of those actions. Take, for example, the situation of a law-abiding individual seeking advice on his liability to pay income tax. If his conscience permits him to make a clear distinction between tax avoidance and tax evasion (as far as the law recognizes such a distinction), he may ask what lawful course of action will leave him with the most money. If he has a tender social conscience, he may reject certain kinds of lawful avoidance devices as immoral; nevertheless, he may wish to predict what his net income is likely to be. There may also be occasions when the Good Citizen can be said to have a moral duty to predict the likely consequences of his actions. The difference between the Bad Man and the Good Citizen does not rest on the latter's indifference to prediction, but on the former's indifference to morality....

Thus, the Bad Man has two characteristics: his badness and his citizenship. The distinction between law and morality is related to the former characteristic, the idea of prediction to the latter. When Holmes advised his audience to adopt the standpoint of the Bad Man, he was not seriously urging them to use the Bad Man as an ethical model; rather, he was suggesting that they look at law from the perspective of a citizen who is concerned with predicting the consequences of his actions. He was in effect saying that as intending private practitioners of law they should put themselves in the shoes of the legal adviser of citizens, good or bad. From that standpoint their main concern should be with prediction.

According to Holmes, the Bad Man is anxious to predict what the 'courts will do in fact'. Even if we allow that by 'do', Holmes refers not only to judicial decisions on questions of fact and law, but also to the sanctions courts are likely to impose, this still seems to be an unduly restrictive answer. Such a response reflects, perhaps, a court-centeredness on Holmes' part, with possible overtones of 'appellate court-itis'.

Suppose, for example, that our friend the Bad Man is in Boston (or Cambridge) wondering whether or not to do some specific act. He may ask, 'What

A simple flow-chart: the Bad Man in Boston

Decision to seek professional advice before acting	Decision on what advice to give	Decision whether or not to act	Action; investigation; detection; apprehension	Decision to prosecute; decision on choice of charge (possible plea-bargaining.)	Decision to plead guilty or not guilty	Miscellaneous decisions on tactics and procedure and on conduct of trial	Decisions on facts and law	Decision on sentence	Decision to appeal by losing party	Decision of appellate court	Miscellaneous post-conviction decisions
Bad Man (or Good Citizen)	'Counsellor'	Bad Man (or Good Citizen)	Miscellaneous participants	Prosecutor	Bad Man and professional adviser	Miscellaneous participants	Court (judge and possibly jury)	Court	Losing party and professional advisors	Appellate court	Miscellaneous officials

Note in regard to predictions: differences as to the base line for prediction, the part played by prediction in the various decisions.

are the chances that a Massachusetts court would hold this type of act to be criminal?' But this is only one of a series of questions pertinent to the decision whether or not to do the act. He needs to estimate the likelihood of the authorities discovering the commission of the act; how energetically, if at all, they are likely to investigate it and other matters related to detection and apprehension; if apprehended, whether there will be a decision to prosecute and, if so, the likelihood of conviction; the likely effect of pleading guilty or not guilty; and the probable nature of the sanction if he is convicted. If he wants to follow the total process through, the Bad Man may also need to consider a whole range of possible post-conviction decisions. The decisions of courts are merely a single phase in what Lasswell terms a 'flow of determinative activities' which go to make up the total process which may affect the Bad Man. And, of course, if one is talking about actual people who are in danger of being 'busted', not only do they need to predict a wider range of possible events, but they also need to perform tasks other than prediction. A comprehensive picture of legal process on the Holmesian model would take all of these considerations into account.

(From W. Twining, 'The Bad Man Revisited', 58 *Cornell Law Review* (1973), 275, 280-3.)

An alternative presentation:

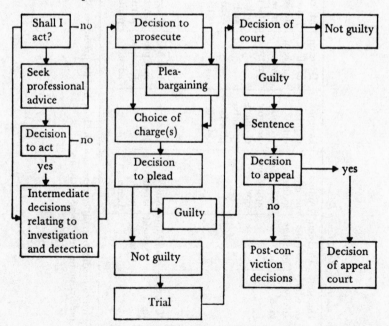

(f) The revolutionary

CONVENTIONAL LEGAL DEFENCE

A conventional legal defense means using the facts and the law – technicalities, rules of evidence, Constitutional rights – to win a case. It can be used alone, or combined with a political defense.

This approach is useful when a good plea bargain has not been offered or when you think you have a very good chance of winning.

Legal technicalities have also been used to delay final judgment on a case until the political situation changed to the defendant's benefit. After the Columbia University busts, the defense lawyers stalled until the new University administration was appointed, which dropped the complaints against five hundred of the students.

Using existing laws does tend to legitimate a legal system which we oppose. Asking the judge to enforce those laws on our behalf reinforces the myth that courts are neutral, and compliance with conventional courtroom procedures may add to the sanctity of the law.

Nevertheless, at the present time, conventional legal defense does keep activists out of jail and free to organize.

(From K. Boudin *et al.*, *The Bust Book: What To Do Till The Lawyer Comes* (1969), pp. 92–3.)

QUESTIONS

1. The word 'standpoint' is ambiguous. It is sometimes used to mean the same as 'role' or 'vantage point' or a special way of looking at things – 'from the standpoint of an economist or an historian'. How is the term used:
   (i) in relation to the Bad Man?
   (ii) in the quotation from Pound?
   (iii) in the phrase 'from the standpoint of Father as Judge'?
2. In the passages from Collingwood and Rawls, are the various persons (e.g. the county surveyor and the manufacturer, the legislator and the judge) *disagreeing*? What do you think of the claim that clarification of standpoint is a useful device for disposing of unnecessary or imagined disagreements?
3. Analyse and differentiate the respective standpoints and roles of Mother, Johnny and Father in the *Case of the Legalistic Child*. Which role is the easiest, and which the hardest, to define?

12   **Domestic violence: a case study**

(a) **Introduction**

The outline of the story is quite simple: largely because of the activities of and controversy surrounding Mrs Erin Pizzey and her associates in Chiswick during the early seventies, problems of domestic violence became a focus of public attention; consequently in 1974–75 a Select Committee on 'Violence in Marriage' was set up by the House of Commons. After only five months it submitted a Report (on violence in marriage), which was followed shortly afterwards by a private member's Bill on Domestic Violence. During its passage through Parliament, the Bill was supported by the government, sections 1 and 2 being redrafted by the government draftsmen and introduced during the Committee stage. It was enacted in 1976 as the Domestic Violence and Matrimonial Proceedings Act 1976. Section 1, one of its important provisions, gave rise to problems of interpretation; it gave county courts jurisdiction, on the application of a spouse or cohabitee, to grant injunctions with respect to molestation and, most significantly, occupation of the matrimonial home. For a time many injunctions were granted to applicants to exclude the spouse or partner from the matrimonial home, notwithstanding that he or she was the owner or tenant.

Then in *B.* v. *B.* the Court of Appeal held that this jurisdiction did not affect rights of property, with the result that this new remedy was only available in the rare case where the complainant, typically the woman, was the sole owner or occupier of the home, i.e. an injunction was not available to prevent the man from exercising his lawful rights to occupy the home. *B.* v. *B.*, in the view of many, including the original supporters of the Bill, defeated the purpose of the Act. The decision in *B.* v. *B.* was followed in *Cantliff* v. *Jenkins* but challenged in *Davis* v. *Johnson*. In this case a majority of the full Court of Appeal (five judges, an unusual occurrence in itself) refused to follow *B.* v. *B.*, citing *inter alia* the report of the Select Committee and Hansard in support of their interpretation of the section. On appeal by the man, the House of Lords upheld the decision of the Court of Appeal on the specific issue but unanimously condemned both their interpretation of the doctrine of precedent and the use of Hansard and the Select Committee Report as aids to interpretation. The story is relevant to our purposes for many reasons, the most important of which are as follows: first, this striking example of a split of opinion (8–8) by senior judges on the interpretation of a recent statute when the mischief that it was intended to remedy seemed clearly to indicate only one inter-pretation. The factors giving rise to this disagreement and the argu-ments which were advanced on each side are of interest, both at the level of technical detail and in respect to more general attitudes to statutory interpretation. Secondly, the Select Committee's Report is a particularly interesting example of some of the difficulties involved in defining, diagnosing and responding to social problems; it also illustrates some uses and limits of law-making in these processes. The particular legal provision which attracted so much attention was, at best, a very modest contribution to the partial alleviation of one aspect of 'the problem'. Yet this narrow remedy illustrates rather neatly how the relationship between narrowly defined 'social problems' and broader social conditions and issues is echoed, but not paralleled, by the relationship between a new piece of legislation and the existing fabric of the law. The problem of 'battered partners' is bound up with alcoholism, poor housing, and various kinds of social deprivation – among other things. The provision of even short-term relief for victims of domestic violence was thought by lawyers to have undesirable implications for the law of property. Thirdly, *Davis* v. *Johnson* is a leading case on the doctrine of precedent and the use of extrinsic aids to interpretation; it is also a dramatic and historically important example of a continuing conflict between the House of Lords, and Lord Denning and some of his brethren in the Court of Appeal.

Thus this small case study illustrates some detailed points about interpretation of cases and statutes in the context of both judicial and legislative processes, which in turn need to be seen within the context of other social and political processes in society.

(b) Extracts from the Select Committee's Report

First Special Report from the Select Committee on Violence in Marriage, 1974–75

The Select Committee appointed to consider the extent, nature and causes of the problems of families where there is violence between the partners or where children suffer non-accidental injury and to make recommendations have made progress in the matter to them referred, and have agreed to the following Report:—

4. Violence in marriage is a wide and difficult subject. It involves a whole range of issues: the general attitudes of men to women and vice versa, the

attitudes of spouses to one another, basic causes of violence in general, alcohol, housing problems, the law and legal services, social services and facilities, psychiatric problems, emergency services, police and other attitudes and facilities, and many more. In five months of work we have not been able to find any easy solutions. They do not exist. We have therefore decided to make a short interim report, referring only to a few of the many aspects of the problems, and leaving the bulk of the evidence which we have received to speak for itself. We have done this simply because shortage of time and resources available to us prevented us from doing otherwise.

5. A general impression must be recorded at the outset. We have been disappointed and alarmed by the ignorance and apparent apathy of some Government Departments and individual Ministers towards the extent of marital violence. Hardly any worthwhile research into either causes or remedies has been financed by the Government. Responsibility is diversified between many Government Departments. No fewer than seven are concerned: the Home Office, the Department of Health and Social Security, the Department of Education and Science, the Department of the Environment, the Lord Chancellor's Office, the Scottish Office and the Welsh Office. Only in a very few of these Departments does the problem of marital violence receive anything other than a very low priority either in terms of manpower or financial resources.

Definition

6. No two cases of violence between the partners in a marriage are the same. We recognize therefore that we are reporting on women in a wide variety of situations but with no single identifiable complaint with a known cure. If a definition is required, that proposed by a Committee of the Royal College of Psychiatrists is probably better than most: 'a battered wife is a woman who has suffered serious or repeated physical injury from the man with whom she lives' (Evidence, p. 100). The definition thus includes women who are cohabiting with men to whom they are not married (see para. 52). In using the word 'battered' in this Report we realize that physical violence is not necessarily any less tolerable than verbal or emotional assault, and that—particularly in the wider sense—men are 'battered' by women as well as vice versa. We will therefore be publishing as an example (as Appendix 5 to our evidence) one short letter from a husband who alleges that he has been battered. We believe, however, that we should concentrate on the problems of women, who form the vast majority of those physically battered. They are often with inadequate means and with dependent children, and in need of shelter or help or advice for themselves and their families.

The scale of the problem

7. Little indeed is known about how much violence in marriage there is, and whether or not it is increasing. What is clear is that the number of battered wives is large - much larger than may be thought - and that the demand for places in the refuges which have been opened reflects the pent up need. Several estimates, all on small samples, with inadequate information and using different definitions, have been made. For what it is worth, the Parliamentary Under-Secretary of State, Welsh Office, using the limited Colchester Study (Evidence, p. 101, para. 15) and other information, thought that there might

be perhaps 5,000 battered wives in Wales each year, out of a figure of 680,000 married women (1971 census). Despite our efforts, we are unable to give any estimates of what the likely numbers are; several witnesses talked in terms of the tip of an iceberg, and this seems to us to be correct. Most witnesses agreed (and this is almost certainly correct) that all strata of society are involved, although the better-off are perhaps less likely to seek outside help in solving their problems (though they may be more ready to seek advice from solicitors). All witnesses were agreed, however, on the need for research on the scale of the problem as well as on causation and remedies (see para. 58).

The nature of the problem

8. Some people, including some in high places, still scorn the thought of a battered wife. Is it not a husband's right to beat her? Is it not her fault? Should she not just leave? Might she even enjoy being beaten? Such people should not forget that a large percentage of all known murders take place within the family setting: home is for many a very violent place. At least some of those murdered were maltreated wives who did not or could not leave in time.

9. We were presented with horrifying evidence of particular cases, and have no doubt that the physical injuries, often inflicted regularly over a period of many years, are very severe in many cases.

10. For example, a Mrs. X gave oral evidence anonymously on 12th March. She was beaten frequently over a period of sixteen years before she left her husband. In her own words 'I have had ten stitches, three stitches, five stitches, seven stitches, where he has cut me'. 'I have had a knife stuck through my stomach; I have had a poker put through my face; I have no teeth where he knocked them all out; I have been burnt with red hot pokers; I have had red hot coals slung all over me; I have been sprayed with petrol and stood there while he has flicked lighted matches at me'. These assaults did not just take place when he was drunk, but 'at any time; early in the morning; late at night; in the middle of the night he would drag me out of bed and start hitting me, he would do it in front of the children. He never bothered if the children were there'. 'I have been to the police. I nicked my husband. He gave me ten stitches, and they held him in the nick over the weekend and he came out on Monday. He was bound over to keep the peace, that was all. On the Tuesday he gave me the hiding of my life'. . . .

12. Perhaps as bad or even worse for the women than the physical violence are the loss of self confidence and self respect that are involved, the inability to understand what is happening, and the moral, emotional and economic problems inherent in a decision to do what appears best for their children, their menfolk and themselves. The evidence of Dr. Gayford, a psychiatrist who is making a special study of the subject, and of those battered women who agreed to appear before us, was particularly moving and persuasive.

13. The practical problems of such women are never identical. Very often they include problems of homelessness, of finance, of the need for support from outside agencies and of protection by the law. What immediate steps can a woman take when she finds herself homeless and perhaps nearly penniless, with young children and perhaps in the middle of the night, as a result of domestic violence? What help and advice should be offered by the police, the local authorities and other agencies to her, to her children, to her husband?

How much liaison should there be between those offering help and advice? What should be done to assist her in legal proceedings, if necessary, and in providing for her longer-term future, either back with her husband or alone in a one parent family? And what, if anything, can be done to reduce the likelihood of violence in the first place? We now attempt to deal with some aspects of these questions.

CAUSATION

14. We have had no evidence that the husband alone is responsible for his violence. The behaviour of the wife is relevant. So, too, is the family's environment, their housing and employment conditions, their physical and mental health, their sexual relationship and many other factors. Very little research has been done and much more is certainly necessary. What has been done has been confined to small samples and usually without the husband's co-operation; it suggests however very clearly that those women who marry (and become pregnant) very young and after short or non-existent periods of courtship are particularly at risk, that drinking of alcohol may well trigger off or accentuate violence, and that children living in an environment of domestic violence may be predisposed to violence in their own adult lives. It is hard to distinguish between cause and effect, and to discover the causal relationship between psychiatric problems, heavy drinking, sexual difficulties, violence, inability to communicate, etc.

PREVENTION

15. The prevention of violence within marriage is as difficult as the prevention of violence in any other situation. Only when the causes of violence are better known and understood will society be in a position to prevent it. Until that Utopia is reached not a great deal can be done to prevent a man from maltreating his wife initially. The law, however it is enforced, is unlikely to stop him, at least the first time (see paras. 42–53). Most violence has a complex origin and therefore attention to only one or two problems is unlikely to be sufficient to make very much impact on the overall problem. Even so we are prepared to recommend a 3-point plan for urgent consideration.

[16–18. The Committee recommends that formal instruction be given in school about the legal aspects of family life, that the Government pursue a vigorous publicity campaign against excessive consumption of alcohol, and that steps be taken to help identify children at risk.]

ALLEVIATION

19. The programme for prevention is inevitably a long term one. However we are convinced that some immediate action can be taken to alleviate the problem. Before turning to the Finer Committee Report and to legal aspects (including police services), we make suggestions and recommendations under the following headings: 24-hour Advisory Services, Refuges, Housing, needs of the children, needs of the husbands, financial and other supporting services, and Medical Services.

24-hour advisory services

20. . . . The crisis centres should have three primary rôles. Firstly, they should provide an emergency service, hence the 24-hour requirement. This means

they will need to develop very close liaison with the local medical, social, legal and police services. A very important link will be with the refuges which we are proposing below, to which they will refer women who need a place of safety. Secondly they should be specially responsible for the co-ordination of the local arrangements already available to women and children in distress. We have been impressed by the fact that one of the prime problems for the family in stress is the need to consult with several different professionals, in different places, employed by different agencies, very often not relating together very effectively. A battered wife needs the advice and help of a police officer, a doctor, a health visitor, a lawyer, a housing department officer, a social security officer, a clergyman, a probation officer, a marriage guidance counsellor, a citizens advice bureau worker and a social worker, just to name the most obvious. The third and non-emergency rôle we see for the family crisis centres is the development of specialist advisory services, education and publicity programmes, group support and meetings for women with similar problems.

THE LAW IN ENGLAND AND WALES

42. We have already referred in para. 41 to the recommendations of the Finer Report on law reform. No laws, however well enforced, can prevent marital assaults. We consider however that improvement of the law can be of material assistance to the problem. If the criminal law of assault could be more uniformly applied to domestic assaults there seems little doubt that it would give some protection to the battered wife. If the enforcement of the civil law could be made more satisfactory a man who had beaten his wife once might well be prevented from repeating his crime. We consider this further in the following paragraphs together with the legal problems associated with the homelessness of one or other partner that often follows assault between them.

Injunctions

45. We accepted the evidence from women and lawyers that civil injunctions restraining husbands from assaulting their wives, or ordering husbands to leave and keep away from the matrimonial home, were on occasions 'not worth the paper they were written on', as the present enforcement procedure of applying for the man to be committed to prison was too slow adequately to protect the woman concerned. We therefore recommend that where a Judge grants an injunction either restraining the husband from assaulting his wife or ordering him to keep away from the matrimonial home, he should have power to grant a power of arrest if, from the evidence before him, he is satisfied that there has been an assault occasioning actual bodily harm and that there seems to be a likelihood that the wife is in continuing danger of assault. When serving the injunction on the man the solicitor would also serve a copy on the Superintendent of the local police station. This would confer power on the police to arrest the man should it appear that he has either entered (or attempted to enter) the matrimonial home when he has been ordered to keep away, or (where the injunction restrains the husband from assault) that he has committed an assault upon his wife or that there is immediate danger of assault. There would be a duty on the police to notify the solicitor of the arrest and the solicitor would be under a duty to find a Judge to deal with the

alleged breach as soon as possible, with a specified time limit. Should the injunction be discharged the solicitor would notify the police concerned. We recognize the arguments against involving the police in civil law but consider this is the only way to make enforcement effective and that the problem of battered women is exceptional enough to require an exceptional remedy.

46. It would also be helpful if there were a general practice whereby solicitors should send copies of injunctions to the local police station so that the police would be aware of the position and more ready to assist should there be further trouble. When solicitors serve any injunction, if it is feared there may be a breach of the peace, it would assist if the police were ready to accompany solicitors and/or process servers.

47. It is not satisfactory that at present women have either to start divorce proceedings or judicial separation proceedings, or undertake to the court to do so, before they may obtain an injunction in the Family Division of the High Court or Divorce County Court. The only other present means of obtaining an injunction is by claiming one in the High Court in an action founded on assault: in the County Court damages must also be claimed for injury or loss occasioned by an assault. This is, to some extent, used by cohabitees who do not have access to the Divorce Courts, but is not used, according to the President of the Family Division, Sir George Baker, by married women (Evidence, 2nd July).

48. We were grateful for the information from Sir George Baker that consideration is being given to the Rules of the Supreme Court being amended to permit a woman, married or unmarried, to apply for an injunction by means of an Originating Summons setting out that she has suffered an assault occasioning actual bodily harm, without having first to start proceedings for divorce or judicial separation. We trust that there will be no delay in making this amendment, since no legislation is involved. We also note that present powers under the Matrimonial Homes Act 1967 to regulate occupation by the spouse do not permit the husband to be even temporarily excluded from the matrimonial home, and we consider it would partly solve this problem if the Act were amended to allow such exclusion.

Magistrate courts

49. We would also wish to see better protection given to married women who apply in matrimonial proceedings to the Magistrates Court. Whereas Divorce County Courts are often up to 20 or 30 miles from the towns which they serve and in many areas Divorce Judges do not sit daily, Magistrates Courts exist in most small towns and there are relatively few houses which are not within 5 miles of a Magistrates Court. Most of these Courts sit frequently, 2 or 3 days weekly at least. Another factor which makes Magistrates Courts more convenient than the County Court is that the procedure in the latter is rather cumbersome usually requiring Affidavits, and documentation in the Court Offices, all of which take some time. Generally it is only in cases where the solicitor is very familiar with this type of proceeding, and the danger has already been marked by actual injury, that injunctions will be made by the Higher Courts, when they can be made within 48 hours. We would wish to see the necessary procedure simplified, and we understand that this is already under consideration. In contrast no such documentation is required in the

Magistrates Court and where the wife is not seeking to end the marriage an immediate remedy, if immediate hearings could be made available, would often be provided more conveniently at the Magistrates Court than in the Divorce County Court or High Court. We therefore also recommend that, as suggested by the Law Commission in its Working Paper No. 53, Magistrates are given power in matrimonial proceedings to make an injunction restraining the husband from assaulting the wife and, when necessary, temporarily excluding him from the matrimonial home. In addition, we recommend bringing the grounds for obtaining a matrimonial order in the Magistrates Court into line with grounds for obtaining a divorce. Such a reform may well save public funds as some legal aid certificates for abortive divorce and solicitors costs in preparing for divorce proceedings would be prevented if adequate relief of this nature was available in the Magistrates Courts where costs are lower.

Cohabitees

52. We have not yet taken evidence relating particularly to the problem of cohabitees or common law wives, but we are aware that such women and their children are in a weaker position when they seek protection and financial relief. If the suggestion of Sir George Baker to amend the Rules of the Supreme Court to permit such women to claim an injunction in the Court is adopted their position would be somewhat improved. In addition we recommend that consideration is given to amending the Guardianship of Minors Act 1971 and 1973 so that when paternity is proved there is power, on application to the County Court or High Court, to settle any property occupied as a home. This power would enable the court to permit the parent caring for the children to have sole occupation of the property during their minority, so that a woman who is caring for the children could continue living with them in their former home, even if she had no legal interest in the property, after the breakdown of the relationship.

Access to the law

53. We consider that if the law as it stands was fully implemented, if police practice was improved as we recommend, if all lawyers advised their clients on all remedies available to matrimonial proceedings and took all necessary steps to obtain injunctions and were on hand to enforce any breach of such injunctions, and if in addition there was liaison between all the different agencies involved, the practical problems facing battered wives would be vastly decreased. We therefore recommend that serious attention be paid by all these agencies to instructing their personnel in the remedies available to battered women, and that in addition a referral list of solicitors willing to deal with such cases in each locality be held by the police and other agencies so that women can be referred to suitable solicitors to help them at an early stage. Women should also be informed of any refuge in their areas. If the system of having a solicitor on hand at Magistrates Courts to help defendants spreads, such a solicitor would be a suitable person to be able to tell women who came to the Court how to obtain the help they need. Many solicitors' offices are both intimidating to most women and inaccessible, not being in the areas in which they live, and usually only receiving clients on appointments days and sometimes weeks ahead. We consider that law centres are potentially

admirably suited to deal with the emergency situation caused by domestic violence, being situated in the community with links with other agencies and flexible working hours, and we recommend that more law centres take on this type of work, if thought advisable transferring cases once the immediate emergency has been dealt with to local solicitors.

SUMMARY OF RECOMMENDATIONS
Our recommendations are, in brief, as follows:—

1. The Committee should be re-established very promptly in the next Session (para. 2);

2. Much more serious attention should be given within our school (and further education) system to the problems of domestic conflict (para. 16);

3. The Government should now introduce a vigorous publicity campaign against the excessive use of alcohol, and should formulate a positive policy on the advertisement of alcohol (para. 17);

4. As much as possible must be done to break the cycle of violence by attention to the welfare and special needs of vulnerable children (para. 18);

5. Each large urban area should have a well publicised family crisis centre open continuously (para. 20);

6. Specialized refuge facilities should be available very readily and rapidly (para. 21);

7. The application for grant from the National Women's Aid Federation should be sympathetically and urgently considered (para. 25);

8. Payments to Chiswick Women's Aid should continue temporarily (para. 25);

9. Legislation, if it is necessary, should be introduced as soon as possible to clarify the duty of local authorities to provide temporary accommodation for battered women who leave home (para. 26);

10. The Finer Report proposals on local authority and private tenancies of homes should be implemented at an early date (para. 28);

11. The Department of the Environment must ensure that more refuges are provided by local authorities and/or voluntary organisations (para. 29);

12. One family place per 10,000 of the population should be the initial target (para. 29);

13. Medical schools and nursing colleges should give special attention to the social dynamics of family life, and to the medical (both physical and psychiatric) correlates of marital disharmony (para. 40);

14. Consultations should continue between the Government and the local authorities to ascertain how far the Finer Committee recommendations can be implemented in the short term without an unacceptably high demand on financial resources (para. 41);

15. Chief Constables should review their policies about the police approach to domestic violence (para. 44);

16. Each police force should keep statistics about incidents of domestic violence, and these should be recorded separately in the National Statistics supplied by the Home Office (para. 44);

17. Where a Judge grants an injunction either restraining the husband from assaulting his wife or ordering him to keep away from the matrimonial

home, he should have power to grant a power of arrest if he is satisfied that there has been an assault occasioning actual bodily harm and that there seems to be a likelihood that the wife is in continuing danger of assault (para. 45);

18. Magistrates should be given power in matrimonial proceedings to make an injunction restraining the husband from assaulting the wife and, when necessary, temporarily excluding him from the matrimonial home (para. 49);

19. The grounds for obtaining a matrimonial order in the Magistrates Court should be brought into line with grounds for obtaining a divorce (para. 49);

20. The principle laid down in the case of Bassett and Bassett should be uniformly applied where wives apply for an order that their husbands be ordered to leave, and, when the wife is in danger, decisions should be reached swiftly to avoid her being homeless (para. 50);

21. Serious attention should be paid by all the agencies involved to instructing their personnel in the remedies available to battered women, and a referral list of solicitors willing to deal with such cases in each locality should be held by the police and other agencies (para. 53);

22. More law centres should deal with the emergency situation caused by domestic violence (para. 53);

23. The Scottish law of evidence should be amended in respect of assaults taking place between husband and wife in the matrimonial home (para. 55);

24. A Scottish divorce bill should be introduced in the next Session by the Government as a Government Bill (para. 57);

25. One or two crisis centres should be set up as action research projects (para. 58);

26. The Government should expedite a decision of principle as to whether to provide the finance recommended in this Report.

27. Conferences should be held up and down the country within the next nine months to consider this Report (and the Evidence to be published as soon as possible after it) and to decide for each area what the best local response to its recommendations should be (para. 64);

28. Shortly after this period of nine months the Government should report to Parliament on the action taken and the further action planned, both at national and at local level (para. 64).

(c) The Private Member's Bill

BILL to amend the law relating to matrimonial injunction; to provide the police with powers of arrest for the breach of injunction in cases of domestic violence; to provide for the obtaining of such injunction in the absence of a claim for damages; and to make further provision for the protection of the rights of victims of domestic violence.

BE IT ENACTED by the Queen's most Excellent Majesty, by and with the advice and consent of the Lords Spiritual and Temporal, and Commons, in this present Parliament assembled, and by the authority of the same, as follows:—

Matrimonial injunction. **1.** Notwithstanding anything to the contrary in any enactment or rule of law relating to the jurisdiction of county courts, a county court may, on the application of a party to a marriage, grant an injunction restraining the use of violence by the other party to the applicant or excluding the other party from the whole or part of the premises occupied by the parties as their home, if satisfied that such an order is necessary for the protection of the applicant.

Powers of arrest. **2.**(1) Where a judge makes an order:

    (*a*) restraining a spouse or co-habitee from using violence towards the other spouse or co-habitee; or

    (*b*) to vacate or not to come within a specified distance of a dwelling house;

or both, he may attach a power of arrest thereto if he is satisfied—

    (i) that the Respondent has assaulted the Applicant occasioning actual bodily harm; and

    (ii) there is a likelihood of further assaults.

(2) A power of arrest attached to an order under subsection (1) above shall authorize any constable to arrest a person whom he reasonably suspects to have disobeyed the order by having committed an assault, or by having entered the area or place specified in the order, as the case may be.

(3) Where a constable arrests a person under subsection (2) above he shall forthwith seek the direction of a judge regarding the time at which and the place to which the arrested person is to be brought before the judge, but shall in any event release the arrested person if he is not brought before a judge within 24 hours of the direction being sought.

(4) Rules of court shall be made for the purposes of this section and to provide for service of the said order duly endorsed as to service on the person to whom it is addressed and on the senior officer of a Police Station in the district where the person who applied for the said injunction resides.

Amendment of Matrimonial Homes Act 1967. 1967 c. 75. **3.** In section 1(2) of the Matrimonial Homes Act 1967 (which provides for applications for orders of the court declaring, enforcing, restricting or terminating rights of occupation under the Act or regulating the exercise by either spouse of the right to occupy the dwelling-house):—

    (*a*) for the word 'regulating' there shall be substituted the words 'prohibiting, suspending or restricting'; and

    (*b*) at the end of the subsection there shall be added the words 'or requiring either spouse to permit the exercise by the other of that right'.

Order restricting occupation of matrimonial home. **4.**(1) Where each of two spouses is entitled, by virtue of a legal estate vested in them jointly, to occupy a dwelling-house in which they have or at any time have had a matrimonial home, either of them may apply to the court, with respect to the exercise during the subsistence of the marriage of the right to occupy the dwelling-house, for an order prohibiting, suspending or restricting its exercise by the other or requiring the other to permit its exercise by the applicant.

(2) In relation to orders under this section, section 1 (3), (4) and (6) of the Matrimonial Homes Act 1967 (which relate to the considerations relevant to and the contents of, and to the jurisdiction to make, orders under that section) shall apply as they apply in relation to orders under that section; and in this section 'dwelling-house' has the same meaning as in that Act.

(3) Where each of two spouses is entitled to occupy a dwelling-house by virtue of a contract, or by virtue of any enactment giving them the right to remain in occupation, this section shall apply as it applies where they are entitled by virtue of a legal estate vested in them jointly.

(4) The occupation of a dwelling-house by one spouse shall for purposes of the Rent Act 1968 (other than Part VI thereof) be treated as possession by both spouses, notwithstanding that the other spouse is excluded from occupation by an order under this section.

5.(1) This Act may be cited as the Domestic Violence Act 1976. Short title and extent.

(2) This Act shall not extend to Northern Ireland or Scotland.

(d) Domestic Violence and Matrimonial Proceedings Act 1976

1976 CHAPTER 50

An Act to amend the law relating to matrimonial injunction; to provide the police with powers of arrest for the breach of injunction in cases of domestic violence; to amend section 1(2) of the Matrimonial Homes Act 1967; to make provision for varying rights of occupation where both spouses have the same rights in the matrimonial home; and for purposes connected therewith. [26th October 1976]

BE IT ENACTED by the Queen's most Excellent Majesty, by and with the advice and consent of the Lords Spiritual and Temporal, and Commons, in this present Parliament assembled, and by the authority of the same, as follows:—

1.(1) Without prejudice to the jurisdiction of the High Court, on an application by a party to a marriage a county court shall have jurisdiction to grant an injunction containing one or more of the following provisions, namely,— Matrimonial injunctions in the county court.

(a) a provision restraining the other party to the marriage from molesting the applicant;

(b) a provision restraining the other party from molesting a child living with the applicant;

(c) a provision excluding the other party from the matrimonial home or a part of the matrimonial home or from a specified area in which the matrimonial home is included;

(d) a provision requiring the other party to permit the applicant to enter and remain in the matrimonial home or a part of the matrimonial home;

whether or not any other relief is sought in the proceedings.

(2) Subsection (1) above shall apply to a man and a woman who are living with each other in the same household as husband and wife as it applies to the parties to a marriage and any reference to the matrimonial home shall be construed accordingly.

2.(1) Where, on an application by a party to a marriage, a judge grants an injunction containing a provision (in whatever terms)— Arrest for breach of injunction.

(*a*) restraining the other party to the marriage from using violence against the applicant, or

(*b*) restraining the other party from using violence against a child living with the applicant, or

(*c*) excluding the other party from the matrimonial home or from a specified area in which the matrimonial home is included,

the judge may, if he is satisfied that the other party has caused actual bodily harm to the applicant or, as the case may be, to the child concerned and considers that he is likely to do so again, attach a power of arrest to the injunction.

(2) References in subsection (1) above to the parties to a marriage include references to a man and a woman who are living with each other in the same household as husband and wife and any reference in that subsection to the matrimonial home shall be construed accordingly.

(3) If, by virtue of subsection (1) above, a power of arrest is attached to an injunction, a constable may arrest without warrant a person whom he has reasonable cause for suspecting of being in breach of such a provision of that injunction as falls within paragraphs (*a*) to (*c*) of subsection (1) above by reason of that person's use of violence or, as the case may be, of his entry into any premises or area.

(4) Where a power of arrest is attached to an injunction and a person to whom the injunction is addressed is arrested under subsection (3) above,—

(*a*) he shall be brought before a judge within the period of 24 hours beginning at the time of his arrest, and

(*b*) he shall not be released within that period except on the direction of the judge,

but nothing in this section shall authorize his detention at any time after the expiry of that period.

(5) Where, by virtue of a power of arrest attached to an injunction, a constable arrests any person under subsection (3) above, the constable shall forthwith seek the directions—

(*a*) in a case where the injunction was granted by the High Court, of that court, and

(*b*) in any other case, of a county court,

as to the time and place at which that person is to be brought before a judge.

Amendment of Matrimonial Homes Act 1967. 1967 c. 75.

3. In section 1(2) of the Matrimonial Homes Act 1967 (which provides for applications for orders of the court declaring, enforcing, restricting or terminating rights of occupation under the Act or regulating the exercise by either spouse of the right to occupy the dwelling-house),

(*a*) for the word 'regulating' there shall be substituted the words 'prohibiting, suspending or restricting'; and

(*b*) at the end of the subsection there shall be added the words 'or requiring either spouse to permit the exercise by the other of that right'.

Order restricting occupation of matrimonial home.

4.(1) Where each of two spouses is entitled, by virtue of a legal estate vested in them jointly, to occupy a dwelling-house in which they have or at any time have had a matrimonial home, either of them may apply to the court, with respect to the exercise during the subsistence of the marriage of the right to occupy the dwelling-house, for an order prohibiting, suspending or restricting its exercise by the other or requiring the other to permit its exercise by the applicant.

(2) In relation to orders under this section, section 1(3), (4) and (6) of the Matrimonial Homes Act 1967 (which relate to the considerations relevant to and the contents of, and to the jurisdiction to make, orders under that section) shall apply as they apply in relation to orders under that section; and in this section 'dwelling-house' has the same meaning as in that Act.

(3) Where each of two spouses is entitled to occupy a dwelling-house by virtue of a contract, or by virtue of any enactment giving them the right to remain in occupation, this section shall apply as it applies where they are entitled by virtue of a legal estate vested in them jointly.

5.(1) This Act may be cited as the Domestic Violence and Matrimonial Proceedings Act 1976.

Short title, commencement and extent.

(2) This Act shall come into force on such day as the Lord Chancellor may appoint by order made by statutory instrument and different days may be so appointed for different provisions of this Act:

Provided that if any provisions of this Act are not in force on 1st April 1977, the Lord Chancellor shall then make an order by statutory instrument bringing such provisions into force.

(3) This Act shall not extend to Northern Ireland or Scotland.

(e) Davis *v.* Johnson

(i) THE FACTS

Jennifer Davis had been living with Nehemiah Johnson for three years, and they had a 2½-year-old daughter. Davis applied for and was granted the tenancy of a council flat in Hackney, but at Johnson's request, the tenancy was put in their joint names. While they lived there, Johnson beat Davis frequently, often very violently. In September 1977 she left the flat, taking their daughter, and went to Erin Pizzey's refuge for battered wives. The refuge was very overcrowded, and in October, Davis applied for an injunction under the 1976 Act to exclude Johnson from the flat, so that she could return to it. The county court judge granted the injunction, but following the Court of Appeal's decision in *Cantliff* v. *Jenkins* shortly afterwards, it was withdrawn by a county court judge upon application by Johnson.

(ii) LORD DENNING M.R.'S JUDGMENT IN THE COURT OF APPEAL
[1979] A.C. 272–283

The Act of 1976

To my mind the Act is perfectly clear. Rejecting words that do not apply, section 1 (1) says that

> 'on an application by a party to a marriage a county court shall have jurisdiction to grant an injunction containing ... (c) a provision excluding the other party from the matrimonial home ...'

Subsection (2) deals with our very case. It says:

> 'Subsection (1) above shall apply to a man and a woman who are living with each other in the same household as husband and wife as it applies to the parties to a marriage ...'

No one, I would have thought, could possibly dispute that those plain words by themselves cover this very case. They authorized the judge in the county court to grant an injunction excluding the man from this flat. So I turn to the reasoning of the two decisions of this court which have said the contrary. I must take each of their reasons in order, although it will take longer than I would have wished.

The comparison with the High Court jurisdiction

The judges in *B.* v. *B.* [1978] Fam. 26 were much influenced by the opening and concluding words of section 1 (1). For myself I think they add nothing and subtract nothing. But this is what they say: 'Without prejudice to the jurisdiction of the High Court, ... whether or not any other relief is sought in the proceedings.'

In *B.* v. *B.* the judges seem to have thought that the High Court had little or no jurisdiction to exclude a husband from the matrimonial home. They said, at p. 34c-d, that if section 1 (1) gave such jurisdiction to a county court,

> 'then it produces the quite astonishing result that the substantive law in the county court is different from the substantive law to be applied in the High Court.'

[Lord Denning then gave a series of examples of the broad jurisdiction of the Family Division of the High Court to grant injunctions to a wife in need of protection from her husband.]

Interference with rights of property

The second reason given by the judges in *B* v. *B* [1978] Fam. 26 was that section 1 should not be so construed as not to interfere with rights of property. It said that there was 'an elaborate legislative code upholding the rights inter se of spouses in relation to the occupation of the matrimonial home' contained in the Matrimonial Homes Act 1967 as now amended by section 3 and 4 of the Act of 1976; and that, in view of that code, section 1 of the Act of 1976 should be regarded as procedural only and not as interfering with the substantive rights of the parties. It did not, therefore, enable the court to exclude Mr. B since he had 'an indefeasible right as against Mrs. B. to continue in occupation in virtue of his tenancy.' Nor did it enable the court in the second case [*Cantliff* v. *Jenkins* [1978] Fam. 47] to oust Mr. Jenkins because he, as joint tenant with Miss Cantliff, had a legal right as a joint tenant to be in possession.

Mr. Joseph Jackson before us placed reliance on that second reason. He urged that there should be no interference with rights of property. But when pressed as to its consequences, it soon became clear that, if this view were correct, it would deprive section 1 of any effect at all. Mr. Jackson said that, as between husband and wife, section 1 (1) did not give the court any power to make an order excluding the husband from the matrimonial home so long as he was the owner or joint owner of the matrimonial home or the tenant or joint tenant. It could only make an order when the wife was the sole owner. But so limited, section 1 (1) was not needed at all: for a wife who is the sole owner can rely on her legal right to exclude him. Then, as between a man and woman living together unmarried, Mr. Jackson said that the woman could never invoke section 1 (2) so long as the man was the owner or joint owner of the home, or the tenant or joint tenant of it: but only when the woman was the sole owner or tenant of it. But in practice the woman never is the sole owner or tenant.

So it seems to me that that second reason must be bad too. In order to give section 1 any effect at all, the court must be allowed to override the property rights of the man: and to exclude him from the matrimonial home, whatever his property rights may be.

The authority of the House of Lords

The third reason given by the court in *B.* v. *B.* [1978] Fam. 26 was that on the authority of the House of Lords in *Tarr* v. *Tarr* [1973] A.C. 254 there was a general principle of construction that an enactment should not be construed so as to affect the rights of property: and that, if 'battered wives' were to be enabled to turn out the men, it would mean 'a very drastic inroad into the common law rights of the property-owning spouse.' Similarly, said Mr. Jackson before us, the personal rights of the deserted wife were not allowed to override the property rights of the husband: and he cited the decision of the House of Lords in *National Provincial Bank Ltd.* v. *Hastings Car Mart Ltd.* [1965] A.C. 1175. I venture to suggest that that concept about rights of property is quite out of date. It is true that in the 19th century the law paid quite high regard to rights of property. But this gave rise to such misgivings that in modern times the law has changed course. Social justice requires that personal rights should, in a proper case, be given priority over rights of property. In this court at least, ever since the war we have acted on that principle. Whenever we have found a husband deserting his wife or being cruel to her, we have not allowed him to turn out his wife and his children and put them on the street. Even though he may have, in point of law, the absolute title to the property as owner, no matter whether it be the freehold of a fine residence or the tenancy of a council house, his property rights have been made in this court to take second place. I know that in those two cases the House of Lords reversed the decisions of this court and gave priority to property rights. But Parliament in each case afterwards passed laws so as to restore the decisions of this court. I prefer to go by the principles underlying the legislative enactments rather than the out-dated notions of the past. In my opinion, therefore, we should reject the suggestion that in this Act of 1976 Parliament intended to give priority to the property rights of the husband or the man. So the third reason, to my mind, fails.

Joint tenancies

I am afraid that I cannot see any possible justification for the decision in *Cantliff* v. *Jenkins* [1978] Fam. 47. The woman there was joint tenant with the man. No joint tenant is entitled to oust the other from the property which they own jointly: see *Jacobs* v. *Seward* (1872) L.R. 5 H.L. 464 and *Bull* v. *Bull* [1955] 1 Q.B. 234. If he does so, the court will not only restore her, but will also order him out. If he were allowed to remain, it would be useless simply to allow her to return: because, as soon as she got in, he would turn her out again. So the court must be able to order him out. That was the very decision of this court in *Gurasz* v. *Gurasz* [1970] P. 11.

The fifth reason—for how long?

In *Cantliff* v. *Jenkins* [1978] Fam. 47 the Court of Appeal were influenced by the thought that an injunction under section 1 would be unlimited in point of time. They asked, at p. 51F–G, the rhetorical question 'For how long?' and answered it by saying that

'As a practical matter, such an injunction, unlimited in point of time, would be equivalent to a transfer of property order, continuing as long as the other party was living.'

That does not frighten me in the least. But in point of practice, I cannot imagine that, in these cases, under section 1 any injunction would last very long. It is essentially a short-term remedy to meet an urgent need. Under the guidance of their legal advisers, the parties will be able to come to a solution between themselves. Thus the council may transfer the tenancy into the woman's name. So may a private landlord. Or there may be divorce proceedings in which the court may make an order transferring the title. Or the parties may come together again. Or one or the other may form a new relationship. And so far as rent and rates are concerned, the judge can easily see to those. If the wife is on social security, she will get an allowance with which to pay these.

The phrase 'are living' in subsection (3)

The judges in *B.* v. *B.* [1978] Fam. 26 felt difficulty with the words 'are living with each other in the same household.' They felt that on the literal meaning of the words they must be living with each other at the time when the woman applies to the court. They realized that in most cases the woman would have already left the house at the time when she makes her application. So the literal meaning would deprive the subsection of much of its effect.

To my mind these words do not present any difficulty. They are used to denote the relationship between the parties before the incident which gives rise to the application. If they were then living together in the same household as husband and wife, that is enough.

The proceedings in Parliament

So, in my opinion, the reasons given by the judges in those two cases were erroneous. But I wish to go further. I notice that in neither case were the judges referred to the Report of the Select Committee, nor to the proceedings in Parliament. If the judges had been referred to those, they would have discovered the intention of Parliament in passing this Act: and they would, I am sure, have given effect to that intention. This shows how important it is that a court should, in a proper case, have power to refer to the report of a select committee or other travaux préparatoires. It will enable the court to avoid an erroneous construction of the Act: and that will be for the good of all. So I will proceed to consider them in this case.

First, the House of Commons appointed a Select Committee on Violence in Marriage. They heard much evidence and presented a very informative report on July 30, 1975. It formed the basis of the Act of 1976. There is clear authority that the court can read it so as to ascertain the 'mischief' which the Act was intending to remedy. Such is plain from the decision of the House of Lords in *Black-Clawson International Ltd.* v. *Papierwerke Waldhof-Aschaffenburg A.G.* [1975] A.C. 591. The House there overruled this court [1974] Q.B. 660. The decisive factor was that they were referred to the report of a committee under the chairmanship of Greer L.J. and we had not been. If we had seen it, we should not have fallen into error. While all the law lords agreed that judges could read the report so as to ascertain the 'mischief' there was a difference of opinion as to whether they could read the 'recommendations' that it contained. I must say that it seems to me the whole of such a report should be open to be read. It is absurd to suggest that the judges are to be selective in their reading of it. As Lord Dilhorne observed: 'Have they to stop reading when they come to a recommendation?'; see [1975] A.C. 591, 622. And as Lord Simon of Glaisdale said, at p. 646:

'Where Parliament is legislating in the light of a public report I can see no reason why a court of construction should deny itself any part of that light and insist on groping for a meaning in darkness or half-light.'

Second, the Parliamentary debates on the Domestic Violence Bill. Some may say—and indeed have said—that judges should not pay any attention to what is said in Parliament. They should grope about in the dark for the meaning of an Act without switching on the light. I do not accede to this view. In some cases Parliament is assured in the most explicit terms what the effect of a statute will be. It is on that footing that members assent to the clause being agreed to. It is on that understanding that an amendment is not pressed. In such cases I think the court should be able to look at the proceedings. And, as I read the observations of Lord Simon of Glaisdale in *Race Relations Board* v. *Dockers' Labour Club and Institute Ltd.* [1976] A.C. 285, 299, he thought so too. I would give an instance. In the debate on the Race Relations Act 1968 there was, I believe, a ministerial assurance given in Parliament about its application to clubs: and I have a feeling that some of their Lordships looked at it privately and were influenced by it: see *Race Relations Board* v. *Charter* [1973] A.C. 868, 899–901. I could wish that in those club cases we had been referred to it. It might have saved us from the error which the House afterwards held we had fallen into. And it is obvious that there is nothing to prevent a judge looking at these debates himself privately and getting some guidance from them. Although it may shock the purists, I may as well confess that I have sometimes done it. I have done it in this very case. It has thrown a flood of light on the position. The statements made in committee disposed completely of Mr. Jackson's argument before us. It is just as well that you should know of them as well as me. So I will give them.

The statements in Parliament

So far as section 1 (1) was concerned, the clause was inserted in the Standing Committee on June 30, 1976. In introducing it, the Member of Parliament in charge (Miss Richardson) proposed a new clause and said:

> 'The position has recently been considered by the Court of Appeal and restated in *Bassett* v. *Bassett* ... The new clause would result in a uniform practice being applied in domestic proceedings of this kind, whether or not matrimonial proceedings were in progress.'

So far as subsection (2) was concerned (dealing with unmarried women), she said:

> 'In these cases, under existing law, an injunction can be obtained only by means of an action of assault which in county courts must include, I understand, a claim for damages. Even an injunction obtained in this way would not extend to the question of the occupation of the home when the applicant is not the sole owner or the official tenant ... the law should be extended to cover these cases. This is what we are seeking to do here.'

She went on to say: 'The words "living with each other in the same household" are intended to avoid a casual relationship, but to indicate a continuing state of affairs.'

It may interest you all to know that she went on to express her gratitude to those who had given her so much assistance in the drafting of the new clause, including the Lord Chancellor and his staff and the parliamentary counsel, and for the Law Commission's suggestions which had been taken into the Bill. 'I hope that now,' she said, 'we really have got it right.' This hope was completely frustrated by *B.* v. *B.* It is surely permissible for us now to get it right.

So it seems to me that on the true construction of this statute, with all the aids that we have at hand, it is plain that the deputy judge in the county court in this case was entitled to make the original order which he made, ordering the man to vacate the house and allowing the woman and her child to return to it: and, in my view, the cases in this court of *B.* v. *B.* and *Cantliff* v. *Jenkins* were wrongly decided.

Departure from previous decisions

I turn to the second important point: Can we depart from those two cases? Although convinced that they are wrong, are we at liberty to depart from them? What is the correct practice for this court to follow?

On principle, it seems to me that, while this court should regard itself as normally bound by a previous decision of the court, nevertheless it should be at liberty to depart from it if it is convinced that the previous decision was wrong. What is the argument to the contrary? It is said that if an error has been made, this court has no option but to continue the error and leave it to be corrected by the House of Lords. The answer is this: the House of Lords may never have an opportunity to correct the error: and thus it may be perpetuated indefinitely, perhaps for ever. That often happened in the old days when there was no legal aid. A poor person had to accept the decision of this court because he had not the means to take it to the House of Lords. It took 60 years before the erroneous decision in *Carlisle and Cumberland Banking Co.* v. *Bragg* [1911] 1 K.B. 489 was overruled by the House of Lords in *Gallie* v. *Lee* [1971] A.C. 1004. Even today a person of moderate means may be outside the legal aid scheme, and not be able to take his case higher: especially with the risk of failure attaching to it. That looked as if it would have been the fate of Mrs. Farrell when the case was decided in this court; see *Farrell* v. *Alexander* [1976] Q.B. 345, 359. But she afterwards did manage to collect enough money together and by means of it to get the decision of this court reversed by the House of Lords: see *Farrell* v. *Alexander* [1977] A.C. 59. Apart from monetary considerations, there have been many instances where cases have been settled pending an appeal to the House of Lords: or, for one reason or another, not taken there, especially with claims against insurance companies or big employers. When such a body has obtained a decision of this court in its favour, it will buy off an appeal to the House of Lords by paying ample compensation to the appellant. By so doing, it will have a legal precedent on its side which it can use with effect in later cases. I fancy that such may have happened in cases following *Oliver* v. *Ashman* [1962] 2 Q.B. 210. By such means an erroneous decision on a point of law can again be perpetuated for ever. Even if all those objections are put on one side and there is an appeal to the House of Lords, it usually takes 12 months or more for the House of Lords to reach its decision. What then is the position of the lower courts meanwhile? They are in a dilemma. Either they have to apply the erroneous decision of the Court of Appeal, or they have to adjourn all fresh cases to await the decision of the House of Lords. That has often happened. So justice is delayed – and often denied – by the lapse of time before the error is corrected. The present case is a crying instance. . . .

So much for principle. But what about our precedents? What about *Young* v. *Bristol Aeroplane Co. Ltd.* [1944] K.B. 718?

The position before 1944

I will first state the position as it was before the year 1944. The Court of Appeal in its present form was established in 1873. It was then the final court of appeal. Appeals to the House of Lords were abolished by that Act and only restored a year or two later. The Court of Appeal inherited the jurisdiction of the previous courts of appeal such as the Exchequer Chamber and the Court of Appeal in Chancery. Those earlier courts had always had power to reconsider and review the law as laid down in previous decisions: and, if that law was found to be wrong, to correct it: but without disturbing the actual decision. I take this from the statements of eminent judges of those days who knew the position. In particular in 1852 Lord St. Leonards L.C. in *Bright* v. *Hutton* (1852) 3 H.L. Cas. 341, 388, said in the House of Lords:

'. . . You are not bound by any rule of law you may lay down, if upon a subsequent occasion, you should find reason to differ from that rule; that is, that this House, *like every court of justice*, possesses an inherent power to correct an error into which it may have fallen.'

Likewise in 1877 Lord Cairns L.C. in *Ridsdale* v. *Clifton* (1877) 2 P.D. 276, 306-307. Then in 1880 the new Court of Appeal on two occasions departed from the earlier decisions of the Court of Appeal in Chancery. It was in the important cases of *In re Hallett's Estate* (1880) 13 Ch.D. 696 and *Mills* v. *Jennings* (1880) 13 Ch.D. 639, given on February 11 and 14, 1880, within four days of one another. In the latter case the Court of Appeal declared in a single reserved judgment (and among their members was James L.J. who had an unrivalled experience of 40 years of the practice of the court) that:

> As a rule, this court ought to treat the decisions of the Court of Appeal in Chancery as binding authorities, but we are at liberty not to do so when there is a sufficient reason for overruling them. As the decision in *Tassell* v. *Smith* (1858) 2 De G. & J. 713 may lead to consequences so serious, we think that we are at liberty to reconsider and review the decision in that case as if it were being re-heard in the old Court of Appeal in Chancery, as was not uncommon (see *Mills* v. *Jennings*, 13 Ch.D. 639, 648–649).

Four years later in *The Vera Cruz* (*No. 2*) (1884) 9 P.D. 96, Brett M.R. with 27 years' experience of the previous practice, said, at p. 98:

> ... there is no statute or common law rule by which one court is bound to abide by the decision of another of equal rank, it does so simply from what may be called the comity among judges. In the same way there is no common law or statutory rule to oblige a court to bow to its own decisions, it does so again on the grounds of judicial comity.

And Fry L.J. said, at p. 101:

> 'Bearing in mind the observations of Lord St. Leonards (he by a slip said Lord Truro) in *Bright* v. *Hutton* (1852) 3 H.L.Cas. 341 and Lord Cairns in *Ridsdale* v. *Clifton* (1877) 2 P.D. 276, I think that we are not concluded from entertaining this case; ...'

Two years later in 1886 in *Ex parte Stanford* (1886) 17 Q.B.D. 259, 269 Lord Esher M.R. [formerly Sir William Brett] called together the full court of six so as to disregard an earlier decision of a court of three. He explained his action quite clearly in *Kelly & Co.* v. *Kellond* (1888) 20 Q.B.D. 569, 572 in a passage very apposite today:

> 'This court is one composed of six members, and if at any time a decision of a lesser number is called in question, and a difficulty arises about the accuracy of it, I think this court is entitled, sitting as a full court, to decide whether we will follow or not the decision arrived at by the smaller number.'

Those were all judges who knew the old practice: and the principles stated by them were accepted without question throughout the next 50 years. In *Wynne-Finch* v. *Chaytor* [1903] 2 Ch. 475 the full court overruled a previous decision of the court. Afterwards Greer L.J. repeatedly said that this court could depart from a previous decision if it thought it right to do so: see *Newsholme Bros.* v. *Road Transport and General Insurance Co. Ltd.* [1929] 2 K.B. 356, 384 and *In re Shoesmith* [1938] 2 K.B. 637, 644. In another case in 1941, *Lancaster Motor Co.* (*London*) *Ltd.* v. *Bremith Ltd.* [1941] 1 K.B. 675, the Court of Appeal again did not follow a previous decision. So much for the practice until 1944.

Young v. *Bristol Aeroplane Co. Ltd.*

The change came about in 1944. In *Young* v. *Bristol Aeroplane Co. Ltd.* [1944] K.B. 718 the court overruled the practice of a century. Lord Greene M.R., sitting with a court of five, laid down that this court is bound to follow its previous decision as well as those of courts of coordinate jurisdiction: subject to only three exceptions: (i) where there are two conflicting decisions, (ii) where a previous decision cannot stand with a decision of the House of Lords, (iii) if a previous decision was given per incuriam.

It is to be noticed that the court laid down that proposition as a rule of law. That was quite the contrary of what Lord Esher had declared in *The Vera Cruz* in 1884. He said it arose only as a matter of judicial comity.

Events have proved that in this respect Lord Esher was right and Lord Greene was wrong. I say this because the House of Lords in 1898 had held itself bound by its own previous decisions as a rule of law: see *London Street Tramways Co. Ltd.* v. *London County Council* [1898] A.C. 375. But yet in 1966 it discarded that rule. In a statement headed *Practice Statement (Judicial Precedent)* it was said:

> 'Their Lordships nevertheless recognize that too rigid adherence to prece-
> dent may lead to injustice in a particular case and also unduly restrict the
> proper development of the law. They propose, therefore, to modify their
> present practice, and, while treating former decisions of this House as
> normally binding, to depart from a previous decision when it appears right
> to do so (see [1966] 1 W.L.R. 1234).'

That shows conclusively that a rule as to precedent (which any court lays down for itself) is not a rule of law at all. It is simply a practice or usage laid down by the court itself for its own guidance: and, as such, the successors of that court can alter that practice or amend it or set up other guide lines, just as the House of Lords did in 1966. Even as the judges in *Young* v. *Bristol Aeroplane Co. Ltd.* [1944] K.B. 718, thought fit to discard the practice of a century and declare a new practice or usage, so we in 1977 can discard the guide lines of 1944 and set up new guide lines of our own or revert to the old practice laid down by Lord Esher. Nothing said in the House of Lords, before or since, can stop us from doing so. Anything said about it there must needs be obiter dicta. This was emphasized by Salmon L.J. in this court in *Gallie* v. *Lee* [1969] 2 Ch. 17, 49:

> The point about the authority of this court has never been decided by the
> House of Lords. In the nature of things it is not a point that could even
> come before the House for decision. Nor does it depend upon any statutory
> or common law rule. This practice of ours apparently rests solely upon a
> concept of judicial comity laid down many years ago and automatically
> followed ever since . . . Surely today judicial comity would be amply satisfied
> if we were to adopt the same principle in relation to our decisions as the
> House of Lords has recently laid down for itself by pronouncement of the
> whole House.

The new guide lines

So I suggest that we are entitled to lay down new guide lines. To my mind, this court should apply similar guide lines to those adopted by the House of Lords in 1966. Whenever it appears to this court that a previous decision was wrong, we should be at liberty to depart from it if we think it right to do so.

Normally-in nearly every case of course – we would adhere to it. But in an exceptional case we are at liberty to depart from it.

Alternatively, in my opinion, we should extend the exceptions in *Young* v. *Bristol Aeroplane Co. Ltd.* [1944] K.B. 718 when it appears to be a proper case to do so. I realize that this comes virtually to the same thing, but such new exceptions have been created since *Young* v. *Bristol Aeroplane Co. Ltd.* For instance, this court can depart from a previous decision of its own when sitting on a criminal cause or matter: see the recent cases of *Reg.* v. *Gould* [1968] 2 Q.B. 65 and *Reg.* v. *Newsome* [1970] 2 Q.B. 711. Likewise by analogy it can depart from a previous decision in regard to contempt of court. Similarly in the numerous cases when this court is sitting as a court of last resort. There are many statutes which make this court the final court of appeal. In every jurisdiction throughout the world a court of last resort has, and always has had, jurisdiction to correct the errors of a previous decision: see *Hadfield's* case (1873) L.R. 8 C.P. 306, 313 and Pollock's *First Book of Jurisprudence* (1896), pp. 333-334. In the recent case of *Tiverton Estates Ltd.* v. *Wearwell Ltd.* [1975] Ch. 146, we extended the exceptions by holding that we could depart from a previous decision where there were conflicting principles – as distinct from conflicting decisions – of this court. Likewise we extended the notion of per incuriam in *Industrial Properties (Barton Hill) Ltd.* v. *Associated Electrical Industries Ltd.* [1977] Q.B. 580. In the more recent cases of *In re K. (Minors) (Children: Care and Control)* [1977] Fam. 179 and *S. (B. D.)* v. *S. (D. J.) (Children: Care and Control)* [1977] Fam. 109, this court in its jurisdiction over children did not follow the earlier decision of *In re L. (Infants)* [1962] 1 W.L.R. 886. I would add also that, when the words of the statute are plain, then it is not open to any decision of any court to contradict the statute: because the statute is the final authority on what the law is. No court can depart from the plain words of a statute. On this ground may be rested the decisions in *W. & J. B. Eastwood* v. *Herrod* [1968] 2 Q.B. 923 and *Hanning* v. *Maitland (No. 2)* [1970] 1 Q.B. 580, where this court departed from previous interpretations of a statute. In *Schorsch Meier G.m.b.H.* v. *Hennin* [1975] Q.B. 416 we introduced another exception on the principle 'cessante ratione legis cessat ipsa lex.' This step of ours was criticised by the House of Lords in *Miliangos* v. *George Frank (Textiles) Ltd.* [1976] A.C. 443: but I venture to suggest that, unless we had done so, the House of Lords would never have had the opportunity to reform the law. Every court would have held that judgments could only be given in sterling. No one would have taken the point to the Lords, believing that it was covered by *In re United Railways of Havana and Regla Warehouses Ltd.* [1961] A.C. 1007. In this present case the appellant, Miss Davis, was at first refused legal aid for an appeal, because the point was covered by the two previous decisions. She was only granted it afterwards when it was realized by the legal aid committee that this court of five had been specially convened to reconsider and review those decisions. So, except for this action of ours, the law would have been regarded as settled by *B.* v. *B.* [1978] Fam. 26 and *Cantliff* v. *Jenkins* [1978] Fam. 47: and the House of Lords would not have had the opportunity of pronouncing on it. So instead of rebuking us, the House of Lords should be grateful to us for giving them the opportunity of considering these decisions.

The truth is that the list of exceptions from *Young* v. *Bristol Aeroplane Co. Ltd.*

[1944] K.B. 718 is now getting so large that they are in process of eating up the rule itself: and we would do well simply to follow the same practice as the House of Lords.

Conclusion

Here we have to consider a jurisdiction newly conferred on the county courts of England for the protection of battered wives. It is most important that all the county courts up and down the country should know at once what their powers are to protect these women: and, if the jurisdiction exists, it is most important that the county courts should exercise it at once so that the law should give these women the protection which Parliament intended they should have. This is a very recent Act: it has only been in force 4½ months. It is almost inevitable in the early stages, with all the urgency attaching to the applications, that some errors may be made. If they are made, and it appears to the Court of Appeal, on further consideration, that a previous decision was clearly wrong, in my opinion we can depart from it. I would prefer to put it on the ground that this court should take for itself guide lines similar to those taken by the House of Lords; but, if this be not acceptable, I am of the opinion that we should regard it as an additional exception to those stated in *Young* v. *Bristol Aeroplane Co. Ltd.* [1944] K.B. 718, especially as by so doing we can better protect the weak and do what Parliament intended.

I would therefore allow the appeal and restore the decision of the original deputy circuit judge who ordered the man to vacate the council flat.

(iii) COUNSEL'S ARGUMENTS BEFORE THE HOUSE OF LORDS [1979] A.C. 317–322

Joseph Jackson Q.C. and *David McIntyre* for Johnson. This appeal raises the question of the ambit of the Domestic Violence and Matrimonial Proceedings Act 1976. Nowhere in the Act is domestic violence defined. Section 1 (1) is not confined to violent behaviour; it would cover harassment, for example, the standing outside the matrimonial home and causing embarrassing situations for the applicant.

The opening words of section 1 are: 'Without prejudice to the jurisdiction of the High Court. . . .' This language supports the appellant's contention that the ambit of section 1 is limited and Bridge L.J.'s construction of those words in *B.* v. *B.* (*Domestic Violence: Jurisdiction*) [1978] Fam. 26, 34B–E, is adopted, namely, that this section contemplates that the jurisdiction which it is conferring on the county court will leave unaffected a parallel jurisdiction to grant the like relief in the High Court, and that the section could not possibly be construed as having an effect on the substantive law to be applied in the High Court in deciding whether or not such relief was appropriate to be granted. For if it were otherwise, and this section alters the substantive law affecting parties' rights to occupy premises, then, as Bridge L.J. observed, it produces the quite astonishing result that the substantive law in the county court is different from the substantive law to be applied in the High Court.

The Court of Appeal both in *B.* v. *B.* and in *Cantliff* v. *Jenkins* (*Note*) [1978] Fam. 47 considered it very significant that a county court 'shall have jurisdiction' to grant an injunction as provided in paragraphs (a)–(d), 'whether or

not any other relief is sought in the proceedings', for before 1976 a county
court could not grant an injunction without other relief sought: see *Halsbury's
Laws of England*, 4th ed., vol. 10, (1975) p. 37, para. 59 and *Rex* v. *Cheshire
County Court Judge and United Society of Boilermakers, Ex parte Malone* [1921] 2
K.B. 694. The word 'jurisdiction' is used in section 1 in its narrow and strict
sense and is being used with reference to the kind of relief sought: see *Garthwaite*
v. *Garthwaite* [1964] P. 356, 387, *per* Diplock L.J. To make a change in the
substantive law so as to make a change in the rights of the parties the following
words would have to be added after the semi-colon in paragraph (*d*) in place
of the words there found, namely, 'whether or not the legal estate is vested in
one of the parties to the marriage or jointly in them or whether or not both of
them are or one of them is entitled to occupy the matrimonial home by virtue
of a contract or by virtue of any enactment giving them or one of them the
right to remain in occupation.' Looking at the statute as it stands, the Court
of Appeal in *B.* v. *B.* [1978] Fam. 26 and in *Cantliff* v. *Jenkins* [1978] Fam. 47,
and Cumming-Bruce L.J. in the present case, were correct in their construction of the ambit of the Act.

It was the deliberate intention of Parliament to limit the powers of the Act
of 1976 and therefore if a power is not given to exclude the appellant from the
house in question in the present circumstances then the court cannot imply
such a power, however desirable it may be.

Previously there were two attempts by the courts to change the law but
both were rejected by this House. The first was the creation of the doctrine of
the equity of the deserted wife. This was rejected in *National Provincial Bank
Ltd.* v. *Hastings Car Mart Ltd.* [1965] A.C. 1175, 1220B, ... It follows, a fortiori,
that a woman who is not a wife cannot be in a better position than a wife. It
was said in the *Hastings Car Mart* case that the law of property in relation to
matrimonial matters was in an unsatisfactory state. This was attempted to be
remedied by the Matrimonial Homes Act 1967: see section 1 (1), (2), and
sections 2, 4 and 5. Section 38 of the Matrimonial Proceedings and Property
Act 1970 added subsection (9) to section 1 of the Act of 1967. The Act of 1967
is to be contrasted with the Act of 1976. The former is very carefully drafted,
nevertheless it requires two amendments. Further, it dealt with all kinds of
practical matters which are not dealt with in the Act of 1976 which makes no
attempt to deal with them.

In *Tarr* v. *Tarr* [1973] A.C. 254 this House reversing the decision of the
Court of Appeal, held that the expression in section 1 (2) of the Matrimonial
Homes Act 1967, 'regulating the exercise by either spouse of the right to
occupy the dwellinghouse,' was not to be construed as empowering a court to
evict from a dwellinghouse of which he was tenant the party to a marriage
against whom the other spouse sought such an order. Reliance is placed on
that decision on the question of pure construction and for the general observations of Lord Pearson at p. 264. If Parliament had intended to over-ride
common law property rights by virtue of section 1 (1) (*c*) of the Act of 1976 it
would have laid down a code or set of guidelines regulating the rights and
obligations of the person remaining in occupation of the home after the other
person had been excluded: see the Matrimonial Causes Act 1973, s. 25 (which
is first to be found in section 5 of the Act of 1970) which lays down guide-

lines which are coupled with specific powers. This is to be contrasted with the Act of 1976 where such powers would have to be 'inferred' to use the expression of Lord Pearson in *Tarr* v. *Tarr* [1973] A.C. 254, 264.

It is emphasized that the Domestic Violence and Matrimonial Proceedings Act 1976 is limited to protecting mistresses who have property rights. The Act does not achieve much and does not seek to achieve much. The appellant's construction of the Act makes sense of its provisions and has no defects. The respondent's construction has defects. If section 1 is to be construed as the Court of Appeal construed it in the present case then as Bridge L.J. observed in *B.* v. *B.* [1978] Fam. 26, 36F, sections 3 and 4 are otiose! As to the oddities which arise on the majority of the Court of Appeal's construction in the instant case: see *per* Cumming-Bruce L.J. ante.

There is no power in the High Court to grant injunctions as between married persons otherwise than in matrimonial causes properly instituted. The only exceptions are not really exceptions: (a) An application for an injunction on the express undertaking that matrimonial proceedings will be instituted; (b) Ancillary proceedings especially those involving children which arise following the matrimonial cause. On the Court of Appeal's construction the Act of 1976 is not confined to domestic violence and is not confined to matrimonial proceedings. It is equating the rights of a mistress to those of a wife. This is such a sweeping change in the law that one would expect to find the most express language in the statute in order to bring it about. This was not the mischief that Parliament was intending to circumvent. Contrast the Inheritance (Family Provision) Act 1975 where in dealing with unmarried persons Parliament has most carefully specifically enacted in relation to the mischief the Act was intended to overcome. See also The Law Reform (Miscellaneous Provisions) Act 1970.

This is the first occasion in the matrimonial field in which it has been held that wide rights have been given by implication. The Act of 1976 should be narrowly construed. There are only two alternatives: either a narrow construction or a very wide construction giving substantial substantive rights. The wide construction is a considerable erosion of the married status.

The Act of 1976 was enacted following the report of the Select Committee on Violence in Marriage, 1975: see paragraphs 4, 6, 7, 13, 47, 48. Paragraph 48 shows that the mischief aimed at in any consequent legislation was limited. Section 1 (1) (a) and (b) does not give to anyone any additional substantive rights; they enable an injunction to be granted coupled with a power of arrest. Both a married woman and a mistress can apply and obtain an injunction to restrain violence and a married woman under section 1 (c) and (d) can obtain an exclusion order from the matrimonial home, but not a mistress. This is consonant with the rights that the *Hastings Car Mart* case [1965] A.C. 1175 declared that a married woman had in relation to the matrimonial home.

Gurasz v. *Gurasz* [1970] P. 11, 16–17D is wrong, for as the *Hastings Car Mart* case declares, there is no power at common law to exclude a husband from the matrimonial home. In *Hall* v. *Hall* [1971] 1 W.L.R. 404, 406C, the middle proposition of Lord Denning M.R.'s statement is also wrong. His Lordship's observation in the present case, 'social justice requires that personal rights should, in a proper case, be given priority over rights of property. In this court at least, ever since the War we have acted on that principle,' are the clue to Lord Denning M.R.'s construction of the Act of 1976. On joint tenancies reliance is placed on *Bull* v. *Bull* [1955] 1 Q.B. 234, 237, which does not support Lord Denning M.R.'s observations, ante.

As to the temporal limits of an injunction granted under section 1 of the Act of 1976, the judgments of Cumming-Bruce and Goff L.JJ. below are adopted. It would be a sad commentary on an Act intended to give short term relief if it was found to give long term relief. Reliance is placed on the observations of Lord Upjohn in the *Hastings Car Mart* case [1965] A.C. 1175, 1231–1232, which highlights the problems that can arise on this question. The present case raises even greater practical difficulties than the *Hastings Car Mart* case. Suppose a man seeks a bank loan, is the bank manager entitled to ask if he is living with a woman and whether he has been violent towards her or not? See the analogous case discussed by Lord Upjohn at p. 1234.

As to the observations of Lord Denning M.R. ante, no court is entitled to look at parliamentary debates. Further, as to the observations of Sir George Baker P., an Act of Parliament must be construed as a whole. This Act deals primarily with occupation. The expression, 'are living with each other in the same household' in section 1 (2) and section 2 (2) of the Act of 1976 is plain beyond peradventure whatever might have been the intention of Parliament by the use of those words. Those sections apply to persons who are living with each other in the same household. The present respondent is not living with the appellant in the same household. Contrast the language of section 1 (2) and section 2 (2) with that used in section 4 (1), where there is a specific reference relating to restricting occupation of the matrimonial home. These latter words should have been used in section 1 and section 2 to achieve the purpose for which the respondent contends was the intention of Parliament. Moreover, it is emphasized that the absence in the Act of any time limit on the length of any injunction which might be made pursuant to it makes it all the more necessary to give a literal construction to its provisions.

[LORD DIPLOCK intimated that their Lordships did not wish to hear argument on the question whether the Court of Appeal bound itself by its own decisions – The House would deal with that question itself.]

Lionel Swift Q.C. and *Judith Parker* for the respondent. There are two principal submissions: (1) Upon a literal interpretation of the Act of 1976 the terms of section 1 are plain and confer jurisdiction on the county court to grant an injunction against a person within the section irrespective of the property rights of the parties.

(2) If it is necessary to consider the mischief rule of construction then it becomes plain that Parliament intended the county court to have jurisdiction to grant an injunction irrespective of the property rights of the parties.

(1) Attention is drawn to the short and long title of the Act. They both refer to domestic violence. The meaning of section 1 (1) is plain if it is read without the opening words, 'without prejudice to the jurisdiction of the High Court', and without concluding words, 'whether or not any other relief is sought in those proceedings'. The words 'without prejudice' are not of themselves restrictive of the power conferred on the county court. Since section 1

(1) is concerned with the parties to a marriage it is quite plain that Parliament recognized that there was an overlapping jurisdiction with that of the High Court. Plainly the subsection was intended to give additional powers. As to the judgment of Bridge L.J. in *B.* v. *B.* [1978] Fam. 26, it is not necessary to imply that the jurisdiction of the High Court is a parallel jurisdiction. It is not co-extensive jurisdiction.

There is no doubt that in the High Court in matrimonial proceedings there is power to grant an injunction which interferes with the property rights of married persons. This power is also to be found in wardship proceedings where a man could be excluded from his own house if it was in the interests of the ward.

As to *Bull* v. *Bull* [1955] 1 Q.B. 234, the court was not there considering an abuse by one joint owner at all but in the present case the court is so concerned. To the argument that it would be astounding if there was a difference in the substantive law in two jurisdictions the answer is that that is already the case, for example, in the realm of cruelty.

As to the expression, 'whether or not other relief is sought,' these are neutral words but they are an indication that an applicant in the county court in order to succeed does not have to have a right of property in the premises in question. Moreover, it has been long established that an injunction could not be obtained in the county court if no other relief was claimed. Parliament is therefore removing that particular obstacle in this limited type of case.

The whole of section 1 (1) contemplates an application where there has been a molestation of a child. But the subsection does not make it a pre-requisite that the wife be living in the premises at the time of the application. This is a further indication that Parliament was not concerned with the proprietary rights of the parties.

As to the argument based on property rights, the appellant's contention is based on *Tarr* v. *Tarr* [1973] A.C. 254 and on a rule of construction that if a statutory provision appears to make inroads on the property rights of a party it must be very clearly expressed. But the relevant provision of the Act of 1976 is plain within the meaning of Lord Pearson's dictum in *Tarr* v. *Tarr* [1973] A.C. 254, 264. In the present Act there is no presumption that Parliament intended to differentiate between the property rights of spouses and that of parties living together. The legislature in this Act did not have to set down rules or guidelines. It might have been desirable so to do to assist the court in exercising its discretion but it was not necessary.

An injunction granted pursuant to this is quite a different 'animal' from an injunction granted under the Act of 1967. In a sense it affects property rights, but in excluding, for example, the man with whom a woman has been living, from the house it is merely extending the licence that the man conferred upon his mistress while she was living in the premises with him. It is emphasized that it is not destructive of the object of this Act that there is no code or guidelines in it. The Matrimonial Homes Act 1967 was the first tentative attempt to deal with property interests. But the Act of 1976 is not concerned with property interests, save incidentally.

As to the duration of an injunction, the county court has the power to exclude the husband even after dissolution of the marriage but this would only be done in very exceptional circumstances. For the protection accorded to a mistress, see Goff L.J. Suppose a girl becomes a man's mistress at the age of 17 and they break up when she is 60. The court might well make an order excluding the man from the premises indefinitely. It is wrong to limit the factors that the judge would take into account but examples are the length of the liaison, the number of children if any, the amount of violence, its duration, and the respective property rights of the parties in the house.

For the mischief at which this Act was aimed, see the Report of the Select Committee on Violence in Marriage July 1975 (H.C. 553/1) which took cognisance of the approach of the Court of Appeal in *Bassett* v. *Bassett* [1975] Fam. 76.

If the interpretation of the Act be adopted as suggested by the appellant then the benefit afforded by section 1 (1) (*c*) and (*d*) is extremely limited indeed. Such a construction would seem to afford very limited relief in respect of a section with such detailed provisions.

On the relationship between sections 1 and 2 and sections 3 and 4, the observations of Goff L.J. are adopted. On the question of jurisdiction, Diplock L.J. was considering a very different situation in *Garthwaite* v. *Garthwaite* [1964] P. 356. His Lordship's observations in that case (p. 387) do not touch the present. The word 'jurisdiction' often means no more than 'power.'

It is plain from the Report of the Select Committee on Violence, para. 50, and *Bassett* v. *Bassett* [1975] Fam. 76, 81c, 87c-d, that throughout the report the committee were not concerned with property rights but with over-riding property rights and protecting women and children from violence. The mischief of this Act is clear beyond a doubt.

In conclusion, on the meaning of the expression 'are living with each other in the same household,' see *per* Goff L.J. It cannot connote physical presence in the premises at the time when the application is made.

(iv) EXTRACTS FROM THE SPEECHES OF LORDS DIPLOCK AND SCAR-
MAN, AND VISCOUNT DILHORNE IN THE HOUSE OF LORDS

LORD DIPLOCK: My Lords, this appeal is from a judgment of the Court of Appeal which, by a majority of three out of five members who sat (Lord Denning M.R., Sir George Baker P. and Shaw L.J.; Goff and Cumming-Bruce L.JJ. dissenting), purported to overrule two recent previous decisions of its own as to the meaning of a statute.

Put in a nutshell, the basic question of statutory construction that has given rise to so acute a conflict of judicial opinion is whether section 1 of the Domestic Violence and Matrimonial Proceedings Act 1976 does no more than provide additional, expeditious and more easily available remedies to prevent threatened invasions of existing legal rights originating from other sources, whether statutory or at common law, or whether it also, of itself, creates new legal rights as well as new remedies for threatened invasion of them. The former I will call the 'narrower,' the latter the 'broader' meaning. In *B.* v. *B.* (*Domestic Violence: Jurisdiction*) [1978] Fam. 26 on October 13, 1977, the Court of Appeal consisting of Megaw, Bridge, and Waller L.JJ. decided unanimously that it bore the narrower meaning: it gave additional remedies but created no new legal rights. In *Cantliff* v. *Jenkins* (*Note*) [1978] Fam. 47 on October 20, 1977, the Court of Appeal then consisting of Stamp, Orr, and Ormrod L.JJ., while holding itself to be bound by the decision in *B.* v. *B.* since it regarded that case as indistinguishable, took occasion, again unanimously, to express its concurrence with the reasoning of Bridge L.J. in *B.* v. *B.* and added, for good measure, an additional reason in support of the narrower meaning placed upon the section in that previous judgment. For my part, I think that *Cantliff* v. *Jenkins* was distinguishable from *B.* v. *B.* but it is conceded that the facts in the instant case are indistinguishable from those held by the Court of Appeal in *Cantliff* v. *Jenkins* to be relevant to its decision in that case. So, when the instant case came before the Court of Appeal, there was a preliminary question which fell to be determined; and that was whether the court was bound by its previous decisions in *B.* v. *B.* and *Cantliff* v. *Jenkins*. The view of a majority of three was that it was not so bound, though their individual reasons for so holding were not identical. This opened the way to a fresh consideration of the meaning of the statute by all five members. On this question they were divided four to one. Cumming-Bruce L.J. sided with the six Lords Justices who in the two previous cases had adopted the narrower meaning of section 1; the remainder were of opinion that it bore the wider meaning and did create new legal rights as well as new remedies for threatened violation of them. So, of the members of the Court of Appeal who sit regularly in civil matters (of whom there are now 17) there were seven who had adopted the narrower meaning of the section, three who, together with the President of the Family Division, had preferred the wider meaning, and a silent minority of seven regular members of the Court of Appeal whose views had not been expressed by the conclusion of the hearing of the instant case in the Court of Appeal.

I draw attention to this arithmetic because if the view expressed by Lord Denning M.R., Sir George Baker P. and Shaw L.J. that the Court of Appeal was not bound by its own previous decisions is correct, this would apply to its decision in the instant case; and had there been no appeal to your Lordships' House to cut the Gordian knot, it would have been open to the Court of Appeal in any subsequent cases to give effect to the wider or the narrower construction of section 1 of the Domestic Violence and Matrimonial Proceedings Act 1976 according to the preference of the majority of the members who happened to be selected to sit on that particular appeal.

My Lords, the difference of judicial opinion as to the true construction of the section has spilled over into this House; for although I agree that on the facts of this case it may be that the order of the Court of Appeal could be upheld, and that the actual decision in *Cantliff* v. *Jenkins* was wrong, I nevertheless find myself regretfully compelled to part company with the rest of your Lordships and to align myself with the seven Lords Justices who have expressed their preference for the narrower meaning. This cannot affect the disposition of the instant appeal nor will it affect the application of the Act in subsequent cases; for the section means what a majority of this House declares it means. But it does make the score of appellate opinions in favour of the broader and the narrower meanings eight all.

Although on the question of the construction of section 1 of the Domestic

Violence and Matrimonial Proceedings Act 1976 this House has not been able
to reach unanimity, nevertheless on what in the instant case was the first
question for the Court of Appeal, viz. whether it was bound by its own
previous decisions, I understand us to be unanimous, so I too will deal with it
first.

So far as civil matters are concerned the law upon this question is now clear
and unassailable. It has been so for more than 30 years. I do not find it
necessary to trace the origin and development of the doctrine of stare decisis
before the present structure of the courts was created in 1875. In that structure
the Court of Appeal in civil actions has always played, save in a few exceptional matters, an intermediate and not a final appellate role. The application
of the doctrine of stare decisis to decisions of the Court of Appeal was the
subject of close examination by a Court of Appeal composed of six of its eight
regular members in *Young* v. *Bristol Aeroplane Co. Ltd.* [1944] K.B. 718. The
judgment of the court was delivered by Lord Greene M.R. Its effect is
summarized accurately in the headnote as being that:

> 'The Court of Appeal is bound to follow its own decisions and those of
> courts of co-ordinate jurisdiction, and the 'full' court is in the same position
> in this respect as a division of the court consisting of three members. The
> only exceptions to this rule are: – (1) The court is entitled and bound to
> decide which of two conflicting decisions of its own it will follow; (2) the
> court is bound to refuse to follow a decision of its own which, though not
> expressly overruled, cannot, in its opinion, stand with a decision of the
> House of Lords; (3) the court is not bound to follow a decision of its own if
> it is satisfied that the decision was given per incuriam, e.g., where a statute
> or a rule having statutory effect which would have affected the decision
> was not brought to the attention of the earlier court.'

The rule as expounded in the *Bristol Aeroplane* case was not new in 1944. It
had been acted upon on numerous occasions and had, as recently as the
previous year, received the express confirmation of this House of Viscount
Simon L.C. with whose speech Lord Atkin agreed: see *Perrin* v. *Morgan* [1943]
A.C. 399, 405. Although prior to 1944 there had been an occasional deviation
from the rule, which was why a court of six was brought together to consider
it, there has been none since. It has been uniformly acted upon by the Court
of Appeal and re-affirmed, notably in a judgment of a Court of Appeal of five,
of which Lord Denning as Denning L.J. was a member, in *Morelle Ltd.* v.
Wakeling [1955] 2 Q.B. 379. This judgment emphasized the limited scope of
the per incuriam exception to the general rule that the Court of Appeal is
bound by its own previous decisions. The rule has also been uniformly
accepted by this House as being correct. Because until recently it has never
been questioned, the acceptance of the rule has generally been tacit in the
course of recounting the circumstances which have rendered necessary an
appeal to your Lordships' House; but occasionally the rule has been expressly
referred to, as by Viscount Simon L.C. in the *Bristol Aeroplane* case itself [1944]
A.C. 163, 169, and by Lord Morton of Henryton and Lord Porter in *Bonsor* v.
Musicians' Union [1956] A.C. 104, 120, 128.

Furthermore, the provisions of the Administration of Justice Act 1969 which authorize 'leap-frog' appeals in civil cases direct from the High Court to this House are based on the tacit assumption that the rule as stated in the *Bristol Aeroplane* case is correct. One of the two grounds on which a High Court judge may authorize a 'leap-frog' appeal is if he is satisfied that a point of law of general importance involved in his decision:

> 'is one in respect of which the judge is bound by a decision of the Court of Appeal or of the House of Lords in previous proceedings, and was fully considered in the judgments given by the Court of Appeal or the House of Lords (as the case may be) in those previous proceedings (section 12 (3) (*b*)).'

The justification for by-passing the Court of Appeal when the decision by which the judge is bound is one given by the Court of Appeal itself in previous proceedings is because that court also is bound by the decision, if the point of law was fully considered and not passed over per incuriam.

So the rule as it had been laid down in the *Bristol Aeroplane* case [1944] K.B. 718 had never been questioned thereafter until, following upon the announcement by Lord Gardiner L.C. in 1966 [*Practice Statement (Judicial Precedent)* [1966] 1 W.L.R. 1234] that the House of Lords would feel free in exceptional cases to depart from a previous decision of its own, Lord Denning M.R. conducted what may be described, I hope without offence, as a one-man crusade with the object of freeing the Court of Appeal from the shackles which the doctrine of stare decisis imposed upon its liberty of decision by the application of the rule laid down in the *Bristol Aeroplane* case to its own previous decisions; or, for that matter, by any decisions of this House itself of which the Court of Appeal disapproved: see *Broome* v. *Cassell & Co. Ltd.* [1971] 2 Q.B. 354 and *Schorsch Meier G.m.b.H.* v. *Hennin* [1975] Q.B. 416. In his judgment in the instant appeal, Lord Denning M.R. refers to a number of cases after 1966 in which he suggests that the Court of Appeal has either refused to apply the rule as laid down in the *Bristol Aeroplane* case or has added so many other exceptions to the three that were stated by Lord Greene M.R. that it no longer operates as a curb on the power of the Court of Appeal to disregard any previous decision of its own which the majority of those members who happen to be selected to sit on a particular appeal think is wrong. Such, however, has not been the view of the other two members of the Court of Appeal who were sitting with the Master of the Rolls in any of those cases to which he refers. Where they felt able to disregard a previous decision of the Court of Appeal this was only because, in their opinion, it fell within the first or second exception stated in the *Bristol Aeroplane* case.

When *Miliangos* v. *George Frank (Textiles) Ltd.* [1975] Q.B. 487 was before the Court of Appeal Lord Denning M.R. appears to have reluctantly recanted. That was a case in which Bristow J. had held that he was bound by a decision of this House in *In re United Railways of Havana and Regla Warehouses Ltd.* [1961] A.C. 1007, despite the fact that the Court of Appeal had purported to overrule it in the *Schorsch Meier* case. On appeal from his decision Lord Denning M.R. disposed of the case by holding that the Court of Appeal was bound by its own previous decision in the *Schorsch Meier* case. He added, at p. 503:

'I have myself often said that this court is not absolutely bound by its own decisions and may depart from them just as the House of Lords from theirs: but my colleagues have not gone so far. So that I am duty bound to defer to their view.'

The reasons why his colleagues had not agreed to follow him are plain enough. In an appellate court of last resort a balance must be struck between the need on the one side for the legal certainty resulting from the binding effect of previous decisions, and, on the other side the avoidance of undue restriction on the proper development of the law. In the case of an intermediate appellate court, however, the second desideratum can be taken care of by appeal to a superior appellate court, if reasonable means of access to it are available; while the risk to the first desideratum, legal certainty, if the court is not bound by its own previous decisions grows even greater with increasing membership and the number of three-judge divisions in which it sits – as the arithmetic which I have earlier mentioned shows. So the balance does not lie in the same place as in the case of a court of last resort. That is why the Lord Chancellor's announcement about the future attitude towards precedent of the House of Lords in its judicial capacity concluded with the words: 'This announcement is not intended to affect the use of precedent elsewhere than in this House.'

Much has been said in the instant case about the delay and expense which would have been involved if the Court of Appeal had treated itself as bound by its previous decision in *B.* v. *B.* [1978] Fam. 26 and *Cantliff* v. *Jenkins* [1978] Fam. 47, so as to make it necessary for the respondent to come to this House to argue that those decisions should be overruled. But a similar reasoning could also be used to justify any High Court or county court judge in refusing to follow a decision of the Court of Appeal which he thought was wrong. It is true that since the appeal in the instant case was from the county court, not the High Court, the 'leap-frog' procedure was not available, but since it was conceded that the instant case was indistinguishable from *Cantliff* v. *Jenkins*, there was no need for anything but the briefest of hearings in the Court of Appeal. The appeal to this House could in that event have been heard before Christmas instead of in January: and at less cost. The decision could have been announced at once and the reasons given later.

Of the various ways in which Lord Denning M.R.'s colleagues had expressed the reasons for continuing to regard the rule laid down in the *Bristol Aeroplane* case [1944] K.B. 718 as salutary in the interest of the administration of justice, I select those given by Scarman L.J. in *Tiverton Estates Ltd.* v. *Wearwell Ltd.* [1975] Ch. 146, 172–173, in the Court of Appeal.

'The Court of Appeal occupies a central, but, save for a few exceptions, an intermediate position in our legal system. To a large extent, the consistency and certainty of the law depend upon it. It sits almost always in divisions of three: more judges can sit to hear a case, but their decision enjoys no greater authority than a court composed of three. If, therefore, throwing aside the restraints of *Young* v. *Bristol Aeroplane Co. Ltd.*, one division of the court should refuse to follow another because it believed the other's decision to be wrong, there would be a risk of confusion and doubt arising where there should be consistency and certainty. The appropriate forum for the correction of the Court of Appeal's errors is the House of Lords, where the decision will at least have the merit of being final and binding – subject only to the House's power to review its own decisions. The House of Lords, as the court of last resort, needs this power of review: it does not follow that an intermediate appellate court needs it and, for the reasons I have given, I believe the Court of Appeal is better without it, save in the exceptional circumstances specified in *Young* v. *Bristol Aeroplane Co. Ltd*.'

My own reason for selecting this passage out of many is because in the following year in *Farrell* v. *Alexander* [1976] Q.B. 345 Scarman L.J. again referred to it in dissociating himself from the view, to which Lord Denning M.R. had by then once again reverted, that the Court of Appeal was not bound by any previous decision of its own that it was satisfied was wrong. What Scarman L.J. there said, at p. 371, was:

'. . . I have immense sympathy with the approach of Lord Denning M.R. I decline to accept his lead only because I think it damaging to the law in the long term – though it would undoubtedly do justice in the present case. To some it will appear that justice is being denied by a timid, conservative, adherence to judicial precedent. They would be wrong. Consistency is necessary to certainty – one of the great objectives of law. The Court of Appeal – at the very centre of our legal system – is responsible for its stability, its consistency, and its predictability: see my comments in *Tiverton Estates Ltd.* v. *Wearwell Ltd.* [1975] Ch. 146, 172. The task of law reform, which calls for wide-ranging techniques of consultation and discussion that cannot be compressed into the forensic medium, is for others. The courts are not to be blamed in a case such as this. If there be blame, it rests elsewhere.'

When *Farrell* v. *Alexander* ([1977] A.C. 59) reached this House Scarman L.J.'s way of putting it was expressly approved by my noble and learned friends Viscount Dilhorne, at p. 81, and Lord Simon of Glaisdale at p. 92, while the other member of this House who adverted to the question of stare decisis, Lord Russell of Killowen, at p. 105, expressed his 'unreserved disapproval' of that part of Lord Denning M.R.'s judgment in which he persisted in his heterodox views on the subject.

In the instant case Lord Denning M.R. in effect reiterated his opinion that the Court of Appeal in relation to its own previous decisions should adopt the same rule as that which the House of Lords since the announcement in 1966 has applied in relation to its previous decisions. Sir George Baker P., on the other hand, preferred to deal with the problem of stare decisis by adding a new exception to the rule in the *Bristol Aeroplane* case [1944] K.B. 718, which he formulated as follows:

'The court is not bound to follow a previous decision of its own if satisfied that that decision was clearly wrong and cannot stand in the face of the will and intention of Parliament expressed in simple language in a recent statute passed to remedy a serious mischief or abuse, and further adherence to the previous decision must lead to injustice in the particular case and unduly restrict proper development of the law with injustice to others.'

Shaw L.J. phrased the exception rather differently. He said:

'It would be in some such terms as that the principle of stare decisis should be relaxed where its application would have the effect of depriving actual and potential victims of violence of a vital protection which an Act of Parliament was plainly designed to afford to them, especially where, as in the context of domestic violence, that deprivation must inevitably give rise to an irremediable detriment to such victims and create in regard to them an injustice irreversible by a later decision of the House of Lords.'

My Lords, the exception as stated by Sir George Baker P. would seem wide enough to cover any previous decision on the construction of a statute which the majority of the court thought was wrong and would have consequences that were regrettable, at any rate if they felt sufficiently strongly about it. As stated by Shaw L.J. the exception would appear to be what might be termed a 'one-off' exception. It is difficult to think of any other statute to which it would apply.

In my opinion, this House should take this occasion to re-affirm expressly, unequivocally and unanimously that the rule laid down in the *Bristol Aeroplane* case [1944] K.B. 718 as to stare decisis is still binding on the Court of Appeal.

I come now to the construction of section 1 of the Domestic Violence and Matrimonial Proceedings Act 1976 under which the applicant, Miss Davis, sought an injunction against the respondent, Mr Johnson, to exclude him from the council flat in Hackney of which they were joint tenants.

I am in agreement with your Lordships that upon the facts that I have summarized the county court judge had jurisdiction to grant an injunction excluding Mr. Johnson temporarily from the flat of which he and Miss Davis were joint tenants. I reach this conclusion notwithstanding that, in disagreement with your Lordships, I remain unpersuaded that section 1 (2) bears the broader meaning rather than the narrower one. As my opinion that the narrower meaning is to be preferred will not prevail I shall resist the temptation to add to or elaborate upon the reasons given by Bridge L.J. in *B.* v. *B.* [1978] Fam. 26 for that preference. There are, however, two initial matters of more general application to the interpretation of statutes that arise out of the judgment of the Court of Appeal. Upon these I wish to comment.

I have had the advantage of reading what my noble and learned friends Viscount Dilhorne and Lord Scarman have to say about the use of Hansard as an aid to the construction of a statute. I agree with them entirely and would add a word of warning against drawing too facile an analogy between proceedings in the Parliament of the United Kingdom and those travaux préparatoires which may be looked at by the courts of some of our fellow member states of the European Economic Community to resolve doubts as to the interpretation of national legislation or by the European Court of Justice, and consequently by English courts themselves, to resolve doubts as to the interpretation of Community legislation. Community legislation viz. Regulations and Directives, are required by the Treaty of Rome to state reasons on which they are based, and when submitted to the Council in the form of a proposal by the Commission the practice is for them to be accompanied by an explanatory memorandum by the Commission expanding the reasons which appear in more summary form in the draft Regulation or Directive itself. The explanatory memoranda are published in the Official Journal together with the proposed Regulations or Directives to which they relate. These are true travaux préparatoires; they are of a very different character from what is said in the passion or lethargy of parliamentary debate; yet a survey of the judgments of the European Court of Justice will show how rarely that court refers even to these explanatory memoranda for the purpose of interpreting Community legislation.

A closer analogy with travaux préparatoires is to be found in reports of such bodies as the Law Commissions and committees or commissions appointed by government or by either House of Parliament to consider reforming particular branches of the law. Where legislation follows upon a published report of this kind the report may be used as an aid to identify the mischief which the legislation is intended to remedy; but not for the purpose of construing the enacting words in such a way as to conform with recommendations made in the report as to the form the remedy should take: *Black-Clawson International Ltd.* v. *Papierwerke Waldhof-Aschaffenburg A.G.* [1975] A.C. 591. This does not mean, of course, that one must shut one's eyes to the recommendations, for a suggestion as to a remedy may throw light on what the mischief itself is thought to be; but it does not follow that Parliament when it legislates to remedy the mischief has adopted in their entirety, or, indeed, at all, the remedies recommended in the report.

This is well illustrated in the instant case. The report on which the Domestic Violence and Matrimonial Proceedings Act 1976 was undoubtedly based is the Report of the Select Committee of the House of Commons on Violence in Marriage published in July 1975 (H.C. 553/1). It deals almost exclusively with the plight of married women exposed to violence by their husbands and resulting homelessness for themselves and their children. In the single paragraph referring to unmarried couples described (regrettably I think) as 'cohabitees,' the members of the committee disclaim any particular knowledge of the problem, on which they had not taken evidence. Nevertheless they recommended that so far as the grant of injunctions against violence by their paramours was concerned mistresses should have the same procedural rights as married women. As regards homelessness of mistresses, however, all the committee recommended was that the Guardianship of Minors Acts should be amended to provide that where there was a child of the illicit union of which paternity could be proved, the court should have power to make orders giving the mistress while she was caring for the children during their minority sole right of occupation of the premises which had been occupied by the unmarried couple as their home. Whatever section 1 (2) of the Act may do it does not do that. ([1979] A.C. 322–331.)

LORD SCARMAN: My Lords, the central question in this appeal is as to the construction of s. 1 of the Domestic Violence and Matrimonial Proceedings Act 1976. ... A layman could be forgiven for thinking that the section was tailor-made to enable a county court judge to make the order that was made in this case. But in three cases reaching the Court of Appeal in the last few months Lords Justices have taken a different view. They found the section difficult and obscure. In *B.* v. *B.* [1978] Fam. 26 the court (Megaw, Bridge and Waller L.JJ.) accepted the submission that the provisions of section 1 of the Act do not alter in any way the substantive law affecting parties' rights to occupy premises and that, in considering the question whether relief can be granted under the section, the court must consider the respective rights and obligations of the parties unaffected by the provisions of the section. In the result, the court in *B.* v. *B.* held that an unmarried woman could not obtain under the section an order excluding from the home the man with whom she was living, unless she could show that she had a right by the law of property to exclusive possession of the premises. In other words, while she could get relief against molestation, as specified in subsection (1) (*a*) and (*b*), she could not get an order enabling her to occupy the home under (*c*) or (*d*) of the subsection.

In *Cantliff* v. *Jenkins* [1978] Fam. 47 another division in the Court of Appeal followed this decision.

In the present case a specially constituted five-judge bench of the Court of Appeal has by a majority (4 to 1) rejected the interpretation put upon the section by the court in *B.* v. *B.* and has held that the full range of relief set out in subsection (1), i.e., orders containing all or any of the relief set out in (*a*), (*b*), (*c*) and (*d*) of the subsection, is available to an unmarried woman, who can bring herself within subsection (2).

For reasons which I shall briefly outline, I have reached the conclusion that the case of *B.* v. *B.* was wrongly decided. In my view the relief specified in (*a*), (*b*), (*c*) and (*d*) of the subsection is available to an unmarried family partner. I would, therefore, dismiss the appeal.

The Act is a short one, its substance being contained in four sections. Section 1 enables the county court to grant the injunctive relief specified in subsection (1), irrespective of whether the applicant is married or unmarried. Section 2 enables a court which grants an injunction in matrimonial proceedings or under section 1 to add to it in certain circumstances a power of arrest. Sections 3 and 4 amend the Matrimonial Homes Act 1967 so as to eliminate two weaknesses in that Act revealed by recent judicial decisions. Section 5 declares the short title, commencement and extent of the Act. That is all there is to it.

Section 1 consists of two subsections. Subsection (1) enables a party to a marriage to make application to a county court. It is without prejudice to the jurisdiction of the High Court and it empowers a county court (any county court, whether or not invested with divorce jurisdiction) to grant an injunction 'whether or not any other relief is sought.' Clearly the subsection provides a new remedy additional to, but not in substitution for, what already exists in the law.

Subsection (2) enables an unmarried woman (or man) who is living with a man (or woman) in the same household as husband and wife to apply to the county court under subsection (1) and expressly provides that reference in subsection (1) to the matrimonial home shall be construed as a reference to the household in which they are living together. This reference indicates to my mind that those provisions of subsection (1), which make available to married people an injunction excluding the other party from the matrimonial home and an injunction requiring the other party to permit the applicant to enter and remain in the matrimonial home, are intended to be available also to unmarried partners.

The availability of paragraphs (*c*) and (*d*) of subsection (1) to unmarried partners without any express restriction to those who have a property right in the house had an important bearing on the answer to the question which I consider to be crucial to a correct understanding of the scope of the section; i.e., what is the mischief for which Parliament has provided the remedies specified in subsection (1)? It suggests strongly that the remedies are intended to protect people, not property: for it is highly unlikely that Parliament could have intended by the sidewind of subsection (2) to have introduced radical changes into the law of property. Nor is it necessary so to construe the section. The personal rights of an unmarried woman living with a man in the same household are very real. She has his licence to be in the home, a right which in appropriate cases the courts can and will protect: see *Winter Garden Theatre (London) Ltd.* v. *Millennium Productions Ltd.* [1948] A.C. 173, *per* Viscount Simon at pp. 188-191; *Binions* v. *Evans* [1972] Ch. 359, *per* Lord Denning M.R. at p. 367 and *Tanner* v. *Tanner* [1975] 1 W.L.R. 1346. She has also her fundamental right to the integrity and safety of her person. And the children living in the same household enjoy the same rights.

Bearing in mind the existence of these rights and the extent to which they are endangered in the event of family breakdown, I conclude that the mischief against which Parliament has legislated by section 1 of the Act may be described in these terms: – conduct by a family partner which puts at risk the security, or sense of security, of the other partner in the home. Physical violence, or the threat of it, is clearly within the mischief. But there is more to it than that. Homelessness can be as great a threat as physical violence to the security of a woman (or man) and her children. Eviction – actual, attempted or threatened – is, therefore, within the mischief: likewise, conduct which makes it impossible or intolerable, as in the present case, for the other partner, or the children, to remain at home.

Where, in my opinion, the seven Lords Justices fell into error, is in their inference that because the section is not intended to give unmarried family partners rights which they do not already enjoy under existing property law it cannot be construed as conferring upon the county court the power to restrict or suspend the right of possession of the partner who does have that right under the property law or to confer for a period a right of occupancy which overrides his right of possession. I find nothing illogical or surprising in Parliament legislating to over-ride a property right, if it be thought to be socially necessary. If in the result a partner with no property right who obtains an injunction under paragraph (*c*) or (*d*) thereby obtains for the period of the injunction a right of occupation, so be it. It is no more than the continuance by court order of a right which previously she had by consent: and it will endure only for so long as the county court thinks necessary. Moreover, the restriction or suspension for a time of property rights is a familiar aspect of much of our social legislation: the Rent Acts are a striking example. So far from being surprised, I would expect Parliament, when dealing with the mischief of domestic violence, to legislate in such a way that property rights would not be allowed to undermine or diminish the protection being afforded.

Accordingly I am unmoved by the arguments which influenced the Court of Appeal in *B.* v. *B.* [1978] Fam. 26 and *Cantliff* v. *Jenkins* [1978] Fam. 47. Nor do I find it surprising that this jurisdiction was given to the county court but not the High Court. The relief has to be available immediately and cheaply from a local and easily accessible court. Nor am I dismayed by the point that the section, while doing no more for married women than strengthen remedies for existing rights, confers upon an unmarried woman protection in her home including a right of occupation which can for a period over-ride the property rights of her family partner.

For these reasons, my conclusion is that section 1 of the Act is concerned to protect not property but human life and limb. But, while the section is not intended to confer, and does not confer upon an unmarried woman property rights in the home, it does enable the county court to suspend or restrict her family partner's property right to possession and to preserve to her a right of occupancy (which owes its origin to her being in the home as his consort and with his consent) for as long as may be thought by the court to be necessary to secure the protection of herself and the children.

How, then does the section fit into the law? First, the purpose of the section is not to create rights but to strengthen remedies. Subsection (2) does, however, confer upon the unmarried woman with no property in the home a new right. Though enjoying no property right to possession of the family home, she can apply to the county court for an order restricting or suspending for a time her family partner's right to possession of the premises and conferring upon her a limited right of occupancy. In most cases the period of suspension or restriction of his right and of her occupancy will prove, I expect, to be brief. But in some cases this period may be a lengthy one. The continuance of the order will, however, be a matter for the discretion of the county court judge to be decided in the light of the circumstances of the particular case.

Secondly, the section is concerned to regulate relations between the two family partners. It does not, for instance, prevent the property owner from disposing of his property. It does not confer upon an unmarried woman any right of occupation of the family home comparable with that which a married woman has and can protect against all the world under the Matrimonial Homes Act 1967.

Thirdly, and most importantly, the grant of the order is in the discretion of the county court judge. It is for him to decide whether, and for how long, it is necessary for the protection of the applicant or her child. Normally he will make the order 'until further order,' each party having the right to apply to the court for its discharge or modification. The remedy is available to deal with an emergency; it is, as my noble and learned friend, Lord Salmon has said, a species of first aid. The order must be discontinued as soon as it is clear, upon the application of either or both family partners, that it is no longer needed.

For these reasons I would dismiss the appeal. I have had the advantage of reading in draft the speeches of my noble and learned friends, Lord Diplock and Viscount Dilhorne. I agree with what my Lord, Lord Diplock, has said on the principle of stare decisis in the Court of Appeal. I also agree with what my Lord, Viscount Dilhorne, has said on the use of Parliamentary material in the interpretation of statutes, and would wish to add only a few observations of my own.

There are two good reasons why the courts should refuse to have regard to what is said in Parliament or by Ministers as aids to the interpretation of a statute. First, such material is an unreliable guide to the meaning of what is enacted. It promotes confusion, not clarity. The cut and thrust of debate and the pressures of executive responsibility, essential features of open and responsible government, are not always conducive to a clear and unbiased explanation of the meaning of statutory language. And the volume of Parliamentary and ministerial utterances can confuse by its very size. Secondly, counsel are not permitted to refer to Hansard in argument. So long as this rule is maintained by Parliament (it is not the creation of the judges), it must be wrong for the judge to make any judicial use of proceedings in Parliament for the purposes of interpreting statutes.

In *Black-Clawson International Ltd.* v. *Papierwerke Waldhof-Aschaffenburg A.G.* [1975] A.C. 591 this House clarified the law on the use by the courts of travaux préparatoires. Reports such as are prepared by the Law Commission, by Royal Commissions, law reform bodies and Select Committees of either House which lead to legislation may be read by the courts to identify the mischief, including the weaknesses in the law, which the legislation is intended to remedy or reduce. The difficulty, however, remains that one cannot always be sure, without reference to proceedings in Parliament which is prohibited, that Parliament has assessed the mischief or understood the law in the same way as the reporting body. It may be that, since membership of the European Communities has introduced into our law a style of legislation (regulations having direct effect) which by means of the lengthy recital (or preamble) identifies material to which resort may be had in construing its provisions, Parliament will consider doing likewise in statutes where it would be appropriate, e.g., those based on a report by the Law Commission, a Royal Commission, a departmental committee, or other law reform body. ([1979] A.C. 345-50.)

VISCOUNT DILHORNE: There is one other matter to which I must refer. It is a well and long established rule that counsel cannot refer to Hansard as an aid to the construction of statute. What is said by a Minister or by a member sponsoring a Bill is not a legitimate aid to the interpretation of an Act: see *Craies on Statute Law*, 7th ed. (1971), pp. 128-129. As Lord Reid said in *Beswick* v. *Beswick* [1968] A.C. 58, 73-74:

'In construing any Act of Parliament we are seeking the intention of Parliament and it is quite true that we must deduce that intention from the words of the Act. ... For purely practical reasons we do not permit debates in either House to be cited: it would add greatly to the time and expense involved in preparing cases involving the construction of a statute if counsel were expected to read all the debates in Hansard, and it would often be impracticable for counsel to get access to at least the older reports of debates in Select Committees of the House of Commons; moreover, in a very large proportion of cases such a search, even if practicable, would throw no light on the question before the court.'

If it was permissible to refer to Hansard, in every case concerning the construction of a statute counsel might regard it as necessary to search through the Hansards of all the proceedings in each House to see if in the course of them anything relevant to the construction had been said. If it was thought that a particular Hansard had anything relevant in it and the attention of the court was drawn to it, the court might also think it desirable to look at the other Hansards. The result might be that attention was devoted to the interpretation of ministerial and other statements in Parliament at the expense of consideration of the language in which Parliament had thought to express its intention.

While, of course, anyone can look at Hansard, I venture to think that it would be improper for a judge to do so before arriving at his decision and before this case I have never known that done. It cannot be right that a judicial decision should be affected by matter which a judge has seen but to which counsel could not refer and on which counsel had no opportunity to comment. ([1979] A.C. 337.)

(f) Postscript on the use of Hansard

In *Hadmor Productions* v. *Hamilton* [1981] 2 All E.R. 724,* Lord Denning M.R. remarked:

Looking at legislative history

In most of the cases in the courts, it is undesirable for the Bar to cite Hansard or for the judges to read it. But in cases of extreme difficulty, I have often dared to do my own research. I have read Hansard just as if I had been present in the House during a debate on the Bill. And I am not the only one to do so. When the House of Lords were discussing Lord Scarman's Bill on the Interpretation of Legislation on 26th March 1981, Lord Hailsham LC made this confession (418 HL Official Report (5th series) col 1346):

'It really is very difficult to understand what they [the Parliamentary draftsmen] mean sometimes. I always look at *Hansard*, I always look at the Blue Books, I always look at everything I can in order to see what is meant and as I was a Member of the House of Commons for a long time of course I never let on for an instant that I had read the stuff. I produced it as an argument of my own, as if I had thought of it myself. I only took the trouble because I could not do the work in any other way. As a matter of fact, I should like to let your Lordships into a secret. If you were to go upstairs and you were a fly on the wall in one of those judicial committees that we have up there, where distinguished members of the Bar ... come to address us, you would be quite surprised how much we read ... The idea that we do not read these things is quite rubbish ... if you think that they did not discuss what was really meant, you are living in a fool's paradise.'

Having sat there for five years, I would only say: 'I entirely agree and have nothing to add.' Thus emboldened, I set about the task of finding out what Parliament meant when it passed s. 17(8) of the Employment Act 1980.

* See now [1982] 1 All E.R. 1042 at 1055-6 (per Lord Diplock).

PART TWO

2 Problems and Mischiefs

In recent years academic law has been dominated by friendly rivalry between two main types of approach. The more traditional one, sometimes known as the 'black letter' or 'expository' approach, treats the systematic exposition and analysis of legal rules ('doctrine') both as the starting point and the almost exclusive focus of the study of law. In this view, sociological, historical, critical and other perspectives are at best ancillary and should only be introduced *after* the student has gained an extensive basic knowledge of the law-as-it-is.

The expository approach has been challenged by some law teachers and others who favour broader approaches to the study of law. A variety of concerns has stimulated this movement, some educational, some scientific, some philosophical and some frankly political or ideological. These differing concerns have stimulated a correspondingly rich, but sometimes confusing, variety of perspectives, ranging from those who maintain that no aspect of law can be understood unless it is seen within the perspective of a grand social theory, such as that of Max Weber or a variant of Marxism, to those who would merely supplement the traditional diet of cases, textbooks, lectures and 'nutshells' with some extracts from policy documents and writings by social scientists – and perhaps an occasional statute.

The approach adopted in this book is sometimes referred to as 'contextualism'. We accept this label if it is taken to mean that law is our primary discipline; that legal rules, institutions, processes, personnel and techniques are the primary subject of study but that, for purposes of understanding, rational criticism or developing basic skills, legal ideas and phenomena are nearly always best viewed in some broader context rather than studied in isolation as if they were things in themselves.[1] Furthermore, we believe that legal concepts, rules and institutions often do not themselves provide the best starting point for study. 'Context first' is a good working rule of thumb, provided that it is not interpreted and applied too rigidly.

One feature of the traditional approach is the way it treats problems of interpreting cases and statutes. The *rules* of statutory interpretation and the *doctrine* of precedent are the main focus of attention. There is a tendency, though by no means universal, to treat both the rules *of* interpretation and the rules *to be* interpreted as things in themselves; when analysis goes beyond the rules to the study of their purposes or rationales or the processes by which they came into existence, there is a tendency to work back from the rules to these 'contextual' aspects.

The approach adopted here diverges from the traditional treatments in three main ways. First, we consider the rules of statutory interpretation and the doctrine of precedent to be relatively minor dimensions of the problems and processes of legal interpretation. They have a place, but it is secondary and it comes near the end of this study. Secondly, as has already been indicated, we believe that problems of interpretation of legal rules share many characteristics of problems of interpreting other kinds of rules: thus this book seeks to set legal interpretation in the context of problems of interpreting rules generally. Thirdly, applying the 'context first' maxim, we propose to begin by looking at the nature of problems before proceeding to consider the nature of rules in general and the use of rules as responses to problems. Diagnosis before prescription is another good rule of thumb.

A problem arises for an individual when he or she is faced with a puzzling question to answer, or a difficult choice to make, or some obstacle in the way of achieving a particular objective. A person is faced with a *theoretical* problem when he or she is confronted by a question calling for an answer that dissolves the puzzlement or solves the problem, without necessarily calling for action. A person is faced with a *practical* problem when there is some doubt about what to do.[2] It is unwise to draw too sharp a line between theoretical and practical problems.

Confronting and solving practical problems is part of everyday living for individuals. When we are confronted with lighting a new

[1] On 'context' see W. Twining, 1 *Brit. Jo. of Law and Society* (1974), 64–8.
[2] D. Gauthier, *Practical Reasoning* (1963), pp. 1–3.

gas cooker, driving an unfamiliar car or moving through a crowd we may have to pause to try to work out, perhaps through trial and error, how to cope with the difficulties and obstacles in the way of achieving the objective. Our responses to this kind of situation often become automatic or semi-automatic, so that we can spot, diagnose and solve the problem without having to pause and analyse the situation and work out a solution. We may proceed by intuition or unreflective imitation, by hunch based on experience or by following precedents. Many of our patterns of behaviour can be interpreted as learned or conditioned responses to problem situations. Indeed, when our response is to some extent automatic, it seems inappropriate to call the process of reasoning and co-ordinating behaviour towards a specific goal 'solving a problem'; for we usually restrict that term to situations in which there is some unresolved difficulty or obstacle that the actor wishes to change, avoid, eliminate or overcome by conscious effort.

Problems arise not only for individuals, but also for groups or classes of people or for whole societies. For example, the *Buckoke* case stemmed from a problem that affected the fire service directly, and indirectly affected society as a whole.[3] Juvenile delinquency, family violence or poverty are examples of what are often referred to as 'social problems'. This term has been defined in a leading sociology textbook as 'some piece of social behaviour that causes public friction and/or private misery and calls for collective action to solve it'.[4] As one moves away from the unique problems of the individual actor to more general problems, analysis tends to become more complex.

One reason for this centres round *who* defines the problem: the problematic aspects of relations between the police and adolescent blacks in England may look very different from the relative perspectives and values of a senior police officer and an unemployed black youth; they may be perceived in a different light again by a Cabinet Minister or a member of an international committee on race relations. It is a widely held view that the 'problem' of abuse of soft drugs represents the imposition of the values of dominant interests on the less powerful, the main 'victims' being young people. Whether or not this is an acceptable interpretation, it is incontrovertible that one could expect a radically different definition of 'the drug problem' from those who support the criminalization of drug abuse and from many

[3] See above, p. 48.
[4] P. Worsley *et al.*, *Introducing Sociology* (1970), p. 51.

young people for whom the attitudes of 'middle-aged, middle class busy-bodies' may constitute 'the problem'.[5]

Furthermore collective decision-making and action tend to be more complex than individual decision and action. So the question arises: who participates with what resources and opportunities through what procedures in producing a 'solution'? Where many persons or several problems are involved it may be unrealistic to expect a pattern of response that will neatly fit a simple rationalistic model of diagnosis, prescription and action. Nevertheless, such a model is a useful starting point for our purposes. In this chapter we shall first explore in an elementary fashion the main ingredients in a rationalistic approach to problem-solving by individuals, in order to identity some of the different points at which things may have happened in a sequence of events with the result that doubts or puzzlements arise for interpreters of rules at a later stage in the process. We shall also examine some of the limitations of this model when applied to individual and to more general problems.

In talking about problems here we shall for the most part be referring to situations in which the actor has to pause to *diagnose* the problem and work out consciously some method of resolving it. However, it is important to recognize from the outset that the process of problem-solving can range from laborious and lengthy rationalistic analysis, perhaps coupled with a process of trial and error, to instantaneous intuitive or semi-automatic response. Similarly, the process preceding the creation of a particular rule could have involved lengthy analysis, debate and deliberation by a large number of people, or it could equally well have involved an intuitive response by a single person or something in between.

A simplified model of problem-solving behaviour by individuals can be characterized in a number of stages as follows:

(i) *clarification* of the actor's *standpoint, role, objectives* and *general position*;

(ii) *perception* by the actor of certain 'facts' constituting a particular situation;

(iii) *evaluation* of one or more elements in the situation as mischievous or undesirable or as presenting an obstacle to the attainment of some objective(s);[6]

---

[5] See D. Farrier, *Drugs and Intoxication* (1980).

[6] Of course, some 'problems' may be both enjoyable and self-imposed, such as climbing a difficult mountain peak or solving a crossword puzzle.

(iv) *identification* of a range of possible courses of action that might be taken in order to solve the problem;

(v) *prediction* of likely obstacles and costs associated with each possible course of action;

(vi) *prescription*, that is to say choice of a general policy and means of effecting that policy for dealing with the problem;

(vii) *implementation* of the prescription.

The first five steps can all be subsumed under the notion of diagnosis, but the fourth step also marks the start of a search for solutions: diagnosis sometimes overlaps with prescription.

There are many ways of analysing problem-solving processes. This characterization is useful for present purposes, because it can form the basis for identifying a number of points at which disagreements may arise or wrong turnings be taken which may create difficulties at a later stage in the process.

Let us apply the model to Mother's behaviour in dealing with Johnny.[7] The story began when Mother saw Johnny eating jam in the kitchen at 3 pm. In the account presented in Chapter 1 the accuracy of Mother's observation was not challenged. But, of course, she might have misperceived the situation. For instance, Johnny may have only been pretending to eat jam; it may have been someone other than Johnny whom she saw; it might in fact have been tea-time, and so on. To put this in general terms, things can go wrong at the very start of a process of problem-solving if facts are misperceived or incompletely perceived or some relevant information was not available.

Secondly, Mother did not like what she saw. In other words, she made a judgment that Johnny's behaviour was *mischievous*. But it could well be the case that Johnny saw nothing wrong with his behaviour. And it is not impossible that Father, on hearing about this, might have agreed with Johnny rather than with Mother about the rightness or wrongness of his action. In other words, when someone says that there is a problem, this involves a value judgment that something is wrong or undesirable or needs to be dealt with, but others might disagree with this evaluation.

Thirdly, in responding Mother made certain implicit assumptions about her standpoint, her role and her objectives. The exact nature of these assumptions could be the subject of elaborate analysis. It is enough to observe here that she took her standpoint as being that of

[7] See above, p. 7.

Johnny's mother; that she conceived of her role as including the promotion of Johnny's health, well-being and moral education; and that in her approach to the problem she took into account such factors as her relationship with Father and the latter's views on how discipline should be administered in the household. Such factors are relevant not only to her response to the situation, but also to her original perception and evaluation of it. For, although it is analytically useful to distinguish between perception of the facts in a situation, evaluation of them and clarification of standpoint, etc., as a matter of psychological fact these elements may be so closely interrelated as to be indistinguishable in practice. For fact, value, role and vantage-point are all intimately bound up in the process of perception.

Mother's *diagnosis* of the mischief was that Johnny was 'eating between meals'. But this was by no means the only way of characterizing the problem, even by someone who agreed with Mother's view of the facts and her judgment that something was wrong. The mischief could have been characterized as stealing, eating things that are bad for his teeth or disobedience. It might even be the case that, although Mother characterized the situation as eating between meals, what really concerned her was the implicit criticism of her cooking. In short, at the stage of diagnosis the principal actors may *misdiagnose*, even by their own standards, by picking on an element other than the one that has disturbed them; or they may produce an incomplete or inappropriate diagnosis, by identifying only one of a number of such elements. Furthermore, other people may disagree about which elements in the situation are mischievous and why. To give a slightly less obvious example: a child psychiatrist might agree with Mother and Father that there was something wrong about Johnny helping himself to half a pot of strawberry jam, but suggest that this was symptomatic of a craving for affection or of some other emotional problem. Similarly, people may confuse symptoms with diseases as well as disagree about the precise nature of a disease. Where people disagree on diagnosis, they are likely also to disagree about the appropriateness of particular prescriptions. A rule prohibiting Johnny from going into the larder is not likely to go far in solving problems arising from lack of affection; it may even make matters worse.

In a rationalistic approach to problems it is not very sensible to talk about solutions until one has agreed on a diagnosis. It is, of course, common in actual life for people to proceed directly to choosing solutions, before they have tried to diagnose the problem. Even where attempts are made to diagnose problems, it may not be possible to introduce appropriate remedies to alleviate their causes; people may agree about the one without agreeing about the other. In addition, the appropriate remedies may be too expensive, long term or difficult to introduce; they may require substantial changes in the behaviour and attitudes of individuals, in the practices of groups and institutions or even in the political and economic ordering of society. Disagreement about both the causes and the nature of the remedies which would be appropriate to deal with such social problems as the inner-city rioting in Britain in 1981, family violence or drug abuse, are ample evidence of these considerations. Such problems often involve conflicting factors which in turn often serve to make some possible remedies inappropriate or unacceptable. Inexpensive, short-term and easily implemented remedies which relieve the symptoms may in many cases be the only practicable options.

Similarly in legal contexts it is hardly surprising to find responses to problems that do not fit a simple rationalistic model of problem-solving. Inertia, delay, diverting attention, buying time by setting up a committee, cosmetic or token measures, placebos, 'knee jerk' calls for new offences or increased penalties, are all familiar features of political and legal life. *Cognoscenti* are also quick to spot somewhat less obvious spectacles such as 'moral panics', the Micawber Response ('It will all come right in the end'), the Way of the Baffled Medic (Prescribe first, Diagnose later – if at all), the Nelson Touch ('I see no problem') and Success ('The problem is now officially solved' or, simply, 'It works').

Let us for the sake of argument accept Mother's characterization of the problem as one of preventing Johnny from eating between meals. Let us also accept her judgment that the problem, so diagnosed, is capable of solution. If she had paused to ponder about the range of possible ways of achieving this object, a number of alternatives might have occurred to her: she could produce such nice meals that he would not be tempted to eat at other times; she could bribe Johnny by offering him rewards or inducements if he disciplined himself; she could reason with him by pointing out the consequences to his health or his character or his relations with his parents if he indulged in this kind of behaviour; she could reduce the opportunities by restricting Johnny's movements, by keeping very little food in the house or by locking the larder door; she could give him a clip on the ear; or she could make a rule or series of rules, and so on. To solve her 'problem' it is not necessary for her to restrict herself to a single device. In the event, she decided to make a rule rather than to tackle the problem by other means.

The next stage was for Mother to design a rule aimed at preventing Johnny eating between meals. It was open to her to formulate a rule co-extensive with the policy – for example, 'Johnny may never eat between meals without Mother's permission'. However, she devised an instrument that was not co-extensive with the mischief – on the one hand, Johnny had opportunities for eating between meals without entering the larder; on the other hand, Johnny interpreted the rule to mean that he was prohibited from entering the larder even to protect his parents' interests. To make matters worse, Mother's formulation of the rule gave Johnny the opportunity to exploit a possible doubt about the meaning of the word 'enter' to secure some jam from the larder.

It is arguable that in her role as rulemaker Mother took not merely one wrong turning, but several. Even if no issue were taken with her original perception of the facts of the first incident, or with her feeling that something was wrong, it could be argued that she inappropriately or incompletely diagnosed the original problem; that her values or her priorities were questionable; that she failed to consider the range of possibilities open to her to solve it; that, having chosen a possibly inappropriate means for solving it, she made matters even worse by establishing a rule that was by no means co-extensive with the mischief,[8] and by leaving a further loophole through her use of the word 'enter' – although in fairness to her, some sacrifice in succinctness would probably have been entailed to cover the broom case.

Up to this point in the story Mother has been the main actor. After the original creation of the rule, some new, complicating factors arise: in particular, Mother acquires other roles, for instance those of prosecutor and advocate, as well as retaining some rule-making power, in that she still has an opportunity to change the rule, at least for the future. Secondly, the fact that a rule has been created has changed her position: from now on the situation will be defined, at least in part, in terms of the rule, which will have created expectations about her future behaviour as well as Johnny's and Father's. And Johnny's response has added some new elements; for instance, it may now be interpreted as a more general challenge to her authority. Mother's 'problem' is no longer a simple one of preventing Johnny from eating between meals; Johnny's attitude to authority, his relations with his

[8] See below, p. 202.

parents and possibly other aspects of Mother's relations with Father are all now relevant. As the story develops, the situation changes, and Mother is confronted with further choices: whether to tell Father about each incident immediately after it has arisen and, if so, how to present it to him; whether to revoke or change the rule and so on. In short, 'Mother's problem' is neither simple nor static; it contains a number of complex elements and changes over time. Moreover, at no stage in this story is Mother's problem identical with Johnny's problem or with Father's problem. Whether it is appropriate to refer to this situation as containing one problem or a series of closely related problems is largely a matter of semantics.

It is worth making two further points at this stage. First, unlike some theoretical problems, practical problems do not typically admit of one single correct solution. A well-defined theoretical problem such as a crossword puzzle or a chess problem may admit of only one correct answer, although this is not necessarily the case. Practical problems tend to be less neat. As we have seen, the relatively specific objective of preventing Johnny eating between meals could be furthered by a number of devices, which could be used as alternatives or in combination. There was not a single correct solution to the problem so defined, but rather a range of possible alternatives of varying degrees of appropriateness to the task in hand. Similarly, 'success' in solving a practical problem is typically a relative matter. Mother's rule, despite its shortcomings, may have been partially successful in reducing the amount Johnny ate between meals, even if it did not entirely eliminate it. Rulemakers usually have to be satisfied with less than 100 per cent success.

Secondly, the story of Johnny illustrates some of the limitations, as well as the uses, of a simple rationalistic model of problem-solving behaviour. There are dangers in seeing problems and solutions as neatly packaged, isolated events. Even a seemingly simple situation can be shown to involve an indefinitely large number of intricately related ingredients in a complex continuing process, in which problems are not necessarily static or well-defined, or perceived or evaluated in identical terms by different actors; similarly 'solutions' may be more or less well-defined, they may be more or less successful in securing particular objectives, and they may also contribute in turn to the generation of new problems. *The Case of the Legalistic Child* reminds us that rules can create problems as well as contribute to their solution and that problems tend to cumulate.

If an apparently simple situation turns out on analysis to be so intricate, we should not be surprised to find the task of analysing more general situations, such as those that confront law-makers in society, to be correspondingly more complex. In the nursery there was initially only one actor who was seeking to diagnose and resolve in a relatively short space of time a situation perceived as problematic; in society as a whole, or in intermediate contexts, a number of complicating factors may be expected: for example, capacity to influence events may be distributed among a variety of people with different vantage points, roles, values, interests and concerns; procedures for decision and action may be slow, arcane, complicated; a policy or rule, once instituted, may be difficult to change or revoke and may, in a sense, take on a life of its own – and so on. Such factors can be used to point to further limitations of the model of problem-solving behaviour outlined above. But this should not be taken as a counsel of despair. For although the model does not claim to be in any sense complete, this does not mean to say that it is useless. Provided its limitations are recognized, the simplicity of the model is an advantage for present purposes, that is to give a broad overview of some of the most common kinds of condition that give rise to puzzlements about interpretation of rules. All the points made about rules as problem-solving devices in relation to the *Case of the Legalistic Child* can be made about laws as problem-solving devices in more complex contexts.

Let us illustrate this briefly by applying the model to the problem that arose in *Buckoke*, taking the standpoint of the Home Secretary. One of the tasks he (and the Secretary of State for Scotland) is called upon to perform is to make recommendations to Parliament for legislation concerning road traffic. As the Court of Appeal emphasized, it was largely due to Parliament's failure to deal with the situation that the various parties in the case, including the Court, were confronted with certain difficulties. The general factual background of the problem, as set out in the report of the case, does not appear to have been disputed. However, the Home Secretary might wish for some more detailed information, such as estimates of the likely consequences to property-owners, fire-crews and other road-users of directives that a driver could, or could not, jump the lights; his basic problem could be stated in such terms as: how to ensure the objective of the speedy arrival of fire engines at fires while minimizing the risk of harm to road-users (including firemen). A range of theoretically possible solutions might be considered: e.g. the provision of police escorts on all fire engines; redirection of traffic by policemen; a change in fire-engine design so that traffic lights can be remotely controlled by the driver; the provision of more fire engines and stations so as to cut down the number of traffic lights to be jumped, particularly in areas of high fire risk; the enactment of an exception, in favour of fire engines, to the general rule; the enactment of an exception in all emergencies; and so on. No doubt some of these ideas are not feasible. Within the fire service, the penultimate was the preferred solution and was introduced by statutory instrument. The grounds for the prior refusal to adopt this expedient are a matter for speculation. There may be a natural reluctance to make special exceptions to the rules governing road traffic; difficult policy choices arise as to what the scope of the exception should be; and in what circumstances it ought to operate. Moreover, the drafting of an exception might possibly be troublesome, for example, in the need for a definition of 'emergency'.[9]

Much of the interest prompted by this case stems from the differences of standpoint of the various actors. To put it simply: Parliament's problem was whether to make a special exception to a generally beneficial rule, while the Chief Fire Officer was concerned to promote the objective of getting to the fires as quickly as possible despite Parliament's refusal to assist. The problem from the Fire Brigade Union's point of view was how to rescue its members from the dilemma of disobeying orders or breaking the law. The Court of Appeal saw its role not only as determining certain technical issues of law, but also in supporting the Chief Fire Officer, and criticizing Parliament and the plaintiffs and going as far as it could to mitigate the rigour of the law without purporting to change an Act of Parliament.

The *Buckoke* case is an example of a problem in which there was a high degree of consensus about the basic facts, the social values, the diagnosis of the original problem and the most desirable way of solving it; but many social problems are not as straightforward as this. Somewhat more complex is the case study of domestic violence.[10] This illustrates changes in the social facts underlying a problem (for example the scale, the forms and the distribution of 'wife-beating'), changes in public awareness of, concern for and categorization of the problem, and changes in official and other responses to it. These range from inertia through merely symbolic or cosmetic reforms, to more determined efforts to tackle it, such as more vigorous enforcement of

[9] See above, p. 48.
[10] See above, pp. 72 ff.

existing laws, creation of new laws, education (e.g. of health visitors to recognize signs of violence or of the public about alcoholism) and through better co-ordination of the efforts of different kinds of functionaries and specialists. It also illustrates some of the complexities and limits of trying to use law to combat what is almost universally and unquestioningly regarded as a social evil in the way that the 'abuse' of certain soft drugs is not.

The Report of the Select Committee on Violence in Marriage illustrates some further points.[11] In many respects this quite modest policy document is a model of what an official report should be: the committee openly acknowledged that neither the scale nor the causes of domestic violence are fully known or understood, and they were sensitive to the difficulties of defining the scope of the problem for their immediate purposes. Should they for example deal only with physical violence to wives, or extend their enquiry to include all women or spouses or partners or children? Should they include threats of physical violence and what might be termed emotional or psychological violence? They recognized the close connections between domestic violence and other social problems such as alcoholism, poor housing and adolescent marriage and pregnancy. They were sensitive to the dangers of over-generalization about many key aspects of the subject. They talked in terms of 'alleviating' rather than 'solving' the problem, and they made reasonably clear distinctions between long-term strategies and short- and medium-term responses. In considering possible uses of law they emphasized that as much might be achieved by more effective implementation of existing laws as by making new ones, that laws are not self-executing and that in this case there were financial and other obstacles to effective law enforcement – for example, the police have traditionally been reluctant to intervene in domestic disputes.

The report makes clear that several different areas of both substantive and procedural law were potentially relevant, but they probably underestimated the difficulty of harmonizing the new remedy of an injunction to protect the battered partner with traditional property concepts, especially where the partners were not married. Account is taken both of the importance and of the practical difficulties of making available speedy, cheap and effective remedies which would in practice be accessible to and used by the victims. There is in particular an unusual sensitivity to the limits of effective legal action, and a clear

[11] See above, pp. 73 ff.

recognition that, at the most, law is only one of a range of social resources available for mitigating this kind of problem and that it is often best used in connection with other strategies such as education, preventive action by social workers and the provision of more crisis centres and refuges. The difficulties of maintaining liaison between different agencies and specialists are emphasized. Finally, the committee, well aware that part of the problem was that the recommendations of two previous reports had not been implemented, went out of their way to emphasize that the report was only a modest contribution to diagnosing and confronting an intractable problem which is not yet fully understood. All in all this provides a far better model of a measured and rational official response to a social problem than many more pretentious and expensive reports. It contrasts even more sharply with the crude simplicities to which we are daily exposed in the media and elsewhere – symbolized by the standard gut reaction to each new alleged crisis: 'There ought to be a law against it.' All of these factors form part of the context of the particular problems of interpretation that arose in *B.* v. *B.* and *Davis* v. *Johnson* which will be considered in Chapter 10.

Many social problems involve wider ramifications and greater potential for disagreement about facts, values, categorization and priorities than do either the *Buckoke* case or domestic violence. As problems aggregate, so do attempted solutions and responses. Also there is a widely held view that holistic solutions tend to be more satisfactory, but less easy to achieve, than fragmented or piecemeal ones. Some of the most acute difficulties in making and interpreting rules concern how they fit in with other rules; similarly there is always potential friction between new reforms and existing institutions, rules, policies and practices. It is beyond the scope of this book to attempt to provide a full treatment of what is involved in analysing social problems.[12] The intellectual procedure outlined in this chapter merely represents the first stage in a relatively systematic approach to diagnosing conditions of doubt in interpretation.

[12] See generally C. Wright Mills, *The Sociological Imagination* (1959, 1970).

3 Of Rules in General

In this chapter we introduce some of the more important general considerations relevant to understanding the nature of rules. After examining the concept of 'rule' and its relation to such notions as principles, policies and values, we consider briefly some standard distinctions concerning the form and structure of rules, and the difference between general exceptions and exemptions in particular cases. We then deal in turn with the variety of rules and the relations between rules within a single aggregation or 'system', between different systems of rules, and between systems of rules and external factors. Next we consider in an elementary way some general theories about the functions of rules, rules as techniques of social management and differences between instrumentalist, formalist and other perspectives on rules, with particular reference to the notion of rules as instruments of power. The purpose of this chapter, then, is to provide a fairly simple theoretical basis from which to proceed to explore what is involved in the interpretation of rules.

1 What is a rule?

In ordinary talk the word 'rule' has many usages. In the present context we are not concerned with 'rule' in the sense of reign, e.g. the rule of Queen Victoria, or in the sense of a habit or empirical generality, as in 'as a rule he catches the 9.55 train to London', or in the sense of a calculating instrument, such as a slide-rule.[1] 'Rule' is used here to

[1] Newton Garver, 'Rules', in P. Edwards (ed.), *Encyclopaedia of Philosophy* (1967), pp. 230-3.

mean a general norm guiding conduct or action in a given type of situation. A typical rule in this sense prescribes that in circumstances X, behaviour of type Y ought, or ought not to be, or may be, indulged in by persons of class Z. Particular attention needs to be paid to three aspects of this formulation:

(a) A rule is normative or *prescriptive*, that is to say it is concerned with ought (not), may (not) or can (not), in relation to behaviour, rather than with factual *description* of behaviour.

(b) A rule is *general* in that it is concerned with *types* of behaviour in *types* of situation or circumstances; a prescription governing a unique event is not a rule.

(c) Rules both guide and serve as standards for *behaviour*, that is to say activities, acts or omissions. In the present context we are concerned solely with *human* behaviour.

The definition of 'rule' adopted here is deliberately broad. As one writer puts it, there are many sorts of action, there are many kinds of guidance, and there are many different ways of prescribing.[2] Some rules impose duties to act or prohibit certain types of behaviour; some confer discretionary powers; others provide for distribution of benefits; yet others specify conditions that need to be satisfied for certain consequences to follow, such as the rules prescribing the method of scoring in Association Football[3] or the rules laying down the requirements of a valid will. Some prescriptions are categorical and specific ('Under no circumstances whatsoever is behaviour of type X permitted'), but others are provisional, or are merely guides, or are subject to numerous unstated exceptions. In this broad sense, 'rule' is a term for the genus of which precepts, regulations, conventions, principles, and guiding standards are species. It is not difficult to produce examples of borderline cases over which people might reasonably disagree, for one reason or another, as to whether or not they deserve to be called 'rules', e.g. (i) 'the neighbour principle'; (ii) 'an advocate should never press an absurd distinction'; (iii) 'promises should be kept'; (iv) 'guidelines'.

Some of the complexities at the borderlines are illustrated by two examples. First, a distinction is sometimes drawn between prudential

---

[2] Ibid.

[3] Raz points out that rules of this type are neither mandatory nor permissive nor power-conferring; because they only guide behaviour indirectly, he maintains that they are not norms. J. Raz, *Practical Reason and Norms* (1975), pp. 117, 186.

and normative prescriptions. A prudential prescription, such as a working rule of thumb, provides guidance as to how to achieve a certain objective. For example, the cricketers' maxim 'never drive against the spin' advises batsmen how to avoid a particular consequence, in this case hitting the ball in the air. Prudential prescriptions may be directed to immoral or illegal ends, such as how to deceive one's spouse or how to evade tax. The relation is solely one of means to ends. A normative prescription, on the other hand, is not merely a recommendation about efficient means or methods of achieving a given end. It involves a judgment about what constitutes good or lawful or valid conduct. Questions about the basis of such judgments are perennial questions of philosophy which form an important part of the background of any study of rules, but are beyond the scope of our immediate enquiry. Here it is pertinent to note that while what is purely prudential or expedient often conflicts with what is considered to be moral or lawful or otherwise right, many examples of actual rules combine both prudential and normative elements: for example, driving under the influence of drink is imprudent, unlawful and immoral, and a particular prescription against such behaviour may reflect all three kinds of concern. This book deals with problems of determining the scope and meaning of normative prescriptions, but much of what we have to say may incidentally be relevant to interpreting purely prudential prescriptions, whether or not they deserve to be called rules.

Another distinction, given prominence in recent years by Professor Ronald Dworkin, is between rules, principles and policies.[4] According to Dworkin, 'rules are applicable in an all-or-nothing fashion'; if the rule is valid it dictates the result; for example, the rule in baseball that provides that if a batter has had three strikes he is out. Dworkin uses 'principle' generically to refer to those standards which guide, but do not *ipso facto* determine, the result, such as the legal maxim that 'no man shall profit from his own wrong'. Legal principles have 'the dimension of weight' and can conflict without being invalid – in a given context the result has to be determined by weighing competing principles. A 'policy' is that kind of standard 'that sets out a goal to be reached, generally an improvement in some economic, political, or social feature of the community', such as the policy of decreasing road accidents. The distinction between principles and policies sometimes collapses, in much the same way as the distinction between prudential

[4] R. Dworkin, *Taking Rights Seriously* (1977), esp. pp. 22 ff.

and normative prescriptions, but for some purposes it is important to distinguish between standards that are to be observed because they advance some goal deemed to be desirable, and standards that are a requirement 'of justice or fairness or some other dimension of morality'.[5]

Dworkin was by no means the first jurist to emphasize distinctions between rules, principles and policies. His account of these notions has been very prominent in recent juristic debate because it is one starting point of his critique of legal positivism, exemplified by H. L. A. Hart's *The Concept of Law*. It may be useful in clarifying some preliminary issues, to explore some differences between Dworkin's approach and that adopted in this book.

The first is mainly a matter of terminology, but also has a direct bearing on some issues of substance. We have deliberately adopted a definition of 'rule' which is broad enough to include Dworkin's notion of 'principles', preferring to use such terms as categorical precepts to cover his rather narrow conception of a rule. But for its rather technical, and perhaps abstruse, associations, the term 'norm' could have been substituted throughout for 'rule' without affecting the substance of the analysis.

We have deliberately adopted a broad, and admittedly vague, definition of rule which emphasizes neither the 'all-or-nothing' nor the 'hard-and-fast' qualities sometimes associated with the notion. One reason for rejecting Dworkin's 'all-or-nothingness' as a necessary element in the notion of 'a rule' is that this obscures three separate ideas: the level of generality or particularity of a prescription; its precision or vagueness; and its status or force in dictating, guiding or influencing a result. In ordinary usage it is quite common to differentiate between rules and principles on the basis that to qualify as a rule a prescription has to be 'precise' or 'specific' – two different ideas. For example, the term 'male persons' is more precise, but less specific (i.e. it is more general) than student. One might say of the maxim 'no man should profit from his own wrong' that it is a principle because it is too general and too vague to count as a 'hard-and-fast' rule. Dworkin's distinction between rules and principles rests on a third ground: for him, a rule *dictates* a particular result; a principle merely points in a particular direction, as a factor to be weighed by the decision-maker. This is an illuminating distinction and a crucial one for Dworkin's purposes. However, as we shall see, levels of generality and the status

[5] Ibid.

of a prescription in influencing a result are both matters of degree, subject to innumerable gradations. Moreover, there is often a correlation in practice between level of generality, precision and prescriptive status: 'no man should profit from his own wrong' is general, vague, subject to numerous exceptions and can at best serve as a guide. But some very general prescriptions – such as the moral principle that no one should be tortured under any circumstances whatsoever, has the status of a categorical precept: for those who accept it, it dictates the result in all situations where a decision whether or not to torture arises – the concept of torture, as we shall see, is neither very precise nor very vague:[6] it is more precise than 'inhuman treatment', but nevertheless there are many borderline cases. Thus an absolute moral prohibition against torture is fairly general, only moderately precise, but quite categorical. For our purposes, it is a matter of indifference whether such a prescription is categorized as a moral principle or a moral rule.

Thus we have stipulated for present purposes a definition of 'a rule' which is somewhat broader than the term is sometimes used in ordinary discussion and much broader than the usage popularized by Dworkin in the context of recent jurisprudential debates. We have deliberately not made any degree of specificity or precision or prescriptive status a necessary condition for the usage of the term. From time to time, it may be useful to differentiate between general and specific rules, between vague and precise rules, between categorical precepts and mere guides or other standards which do not dictate results. Such distinctions have a bearing on problems of interpretation, but to insist on them at the start would introduce an artificial and premature rigidity into the discussion. Levels of generality, precision and prescriptive force are all matters of degree.

This leads on to a second point: in our view Dworkin's distinction between rules and principles is artificially sharp, for there are relatively few clear examples, in law or elsewhere, of norms that have the 'all-or-nothing' characteristic that he ascribes to rules. No prominent legal positivist who has elucidated law in terms of rules, such as Hart, or of norms, such as Kelsen, has been committed to the view that law is made up solely of categorical precepts. To attribute such a view to 'positivism' is to set up an artificial target for attack. The principles of statutory interpretation, the neighbour principle, and perhaps even the maxims of Equity and the notoriously problematic Judges' Rules

[6] Below, pp. 206–8.

can, in our view, all be accommodated in a positivist conception of law.

It is not necessary for present purposes to nail our flag firmly to the mast of some particular legal theory, but we acknowledge that we are more sympathetic to some mild version of positivism (exemplified, perhaps, by Hart's sympathetic critic Neil MacCormick) than to the views of Dworkin. In our view, an adequate account of a legal system in terms of rules or norms would need to include and to differentiate between many different kinds of rules, including precepts, principles, guiding standards, accepted practices, customs, conventions and several types of maxims. The material of law is so rich, so complex and so shot through with fine gradations that we are sceptical of the value of attempting a comprehensive taxonomy of types of rules. It is beyond the scope of this book to attempt a rounded theory of and about law. For the more modest objective of exploring some of the main recurrent problems of interpreting all kinds of rules, some working distinctions between different kinds of rules are especially important and useful, and will be introduced as we proceed. Some of these are fairly standard within the jurisprudence of legal positivism, some of them are suggested by its critics, such as Fuller and Dworkin. For present purposes a comprehensive classification of different kinds of rules is unnecessary, even if it were feasible, but Dworkin's distinction between rules and principles is too rigid and too simple to provide an adequate starting point for an exploration of problems of interpretation.

Thirdly, as will become apparent, we disagree with Dworkin's thesis that there is only one right or correct answer to problems of interpretation in legal contexts even in 'hard cases'. Finally, Dworkin distinguishes between *legal* rules and *legal* principles as part of his critique of *legal* positivism. In this respect our focus is broader, for, as has already been emphasized, one of the central themes of this book is that many of the factors giving rise to difficulties in interpretation of legal rules are not unique to legal contexts. We are more concerned here to present legal interpretation and reasoning as an example of interpretation of rules and practical reasoning generally, than to explore what, if anything, is unique or peculiar about legal ways of thought. In the final chapters on case law, legislation and legal reasoning in interpretation, some special features of interpretation in legal contexts will be identified, for example the existence of developed rules about precedent and the interpretation of statutes, but even there the thrust of our analysis will be that these are rather less important than they are sometimes thought to be when compared to other factors that regularly bear on problems of interpretation.

Most of the examples in this book will be categorical precepts – that is relatively specific and unqualified prescriptions which fall squarely within the definition of 'rule' stipulated above. But it is not necessary to concern ourselves unduly with the borderlines of this definition, because most of what we have to say about interpretation applies, to a greater or lesser extent, to borderline cases as well as to clear examples of rules.

Much attention has been devoted in the literature to elucidating the notion of a rule and disentangling it from other notions such as 'habit', 'prediction', 'practice', 'command' and 'value'.[7] To put the matter very briefly, whereas predictions and statements of habits and practices are capable of verification or falsification, that is to say they are (logically) capable of being tested as to whether they are empirically true or false, statements of rules and commands are propositions of a different logical kind, which are not directly either verifiable or falsifiable. 'Johnny always brushes his teeth' or 'Johnny will probably brush his teeth on Friday next' are potentially capable of being shown to be true or false. But this is not *prima facie* the case with statements of the kind 'Johnny, brush your teeth!' or 'Johnny must always brush his teeth', although such statements are based on assumptions which can be shown to be true or false, such as the assumption that Johnny has teeth.

Rules resemble habits and practices in that all three notions relate to behaviour and are general. Moreover, some kinds of rules, such as customs and conventions, grow out of habits or practices – for instance, what is at first merely habitual may become customary as it gains approval or forms the basis of other people's expectations. Statements of habits or practices are species of *factual generalization*; statements of rules are expressed in the *normative* language of 'ought', 'must', 'may' and 'can'.

The relationship between rule and prediction is of a different kind. Rules are by definition general; predictions may be general or particular. Unlike rules, predictions can turn out to be true or false. Rules have sometimes been confused with predictions because rule-statements are sometimes used as an *aid* to prediction. For example, a solicitor may look up a statute or other legal provision in order to

---

[7] See especially H. L. A. Hart, *The Concept of Law* (1961), *passim*; F. Waismann, *The Principles of Linguistic Philosophy* (1965), Chapter 7.

predict how a court is likely to treat his client in certain circumstances. If the legal provision is clear, the solicitor will be able to make a reasonably confident prediction of how a court will decide, if certain facts are established before it. But the legal provision is not a prediction; it is used as an aid to prediction – and it is a foolish solicitor who always relies on legal rules alone in trying to predict for his client the likely consequences of a course of action, just as the Bad Man in Boston would need to take many factors into account in predicting what would be likely to happen to him if he decided to do some specific act.[8] To confuse rules with predictions is to confuse rules with one of the *uses* of rules.

Similarly, rules and commands are separate but related notions. Both *prescribe* behaviour; but there are important differences. Firstly, some commands are not rules, because they lack the element of *generality* ('Come here immediately'). Secondly, by no means all rules take the form of commands – the notion of command suggests that certain behaviour is *required* ('must') or *prohibited* ('do not'), whereas many rules *permit* or *authorize* behaviour or *confer powers* or *establish* institutions or procedures. They also serve as *standards* for criticizing or evaluating behaviour. Thirdly, the notion of a command suggests that it is the expression of the *will* of a specific source, a *commander*, who is typically human, but who may be divine, etc. While some rules are direct expressions of the will of a person or body that issues them, other rules have different sources. For instance, the rules of English grammar were not laid down by any specific person or body of persons; we are tempted to say they 'just growed', as a way of indicating a much more complicated process of evolution which could not be said to have been willed by anyone in particular. However, some rules can be appropriately expressed in the form of general commands, for example 'Never go into the larder without my permission.' Perhaps because some rules of substantive law, especially in areas such as criminal law, can be fitted more or less into this form, theorists such as John Austin have depicted laws as species of commands (viz. general commands made by authority and backed by threats). While the analogy is quite close in some respects, the theory is now generally discredited; one reason is that, whereas legal rules that impose duties can be made to fit the model fairly easily, the command theory does not give an adequate account of legal rules that confer powers or grant licences or constitute certain activities, such as the making of a valid will.

[8] See above, p. 67.

2 Rules and values

The precise nature of the relationship between rules and values is complex. We may say of a rule that it furthers, embodies or conflicts with some value such as human happiness or the right to life.[9] For example, section 57 of the Offences Against the Person Act may be said to promote such values as the sanctity of monogamous marriage, the solemnity and dignity of religious ceremony, and the protection of potential victims of bigamous unions. On the other hand, some school rules may be considered to conflict with the values of a liberal education, and the rule requiring vehicles to stop at a red traffic light, to conflict with the desirability of fire engines reaching their destination as quickly as possible. Many rules represent a *compromise* between conflicting values: in the case of those governing road traffic, the safety of road-users on the one hand, convenience and traffic progress on the other.

In these instances it is relatively easy to distinguish between the rule and the values it represents. In its simplest form, the relationship is one of means (the rule) and ends (the value(s)). However, the distinction is not always so clear-cut. For example, Article 3 of the European Convention could be said to directly embody absolute moral principles against torture, inhuman and degrading treatment. In this instance we can see that the rule and the values it embodies are co-extensive but distinct, because the rule was created by formal procedures, is expressed in fixed verbal form and is subject to interpretation which may be somewhat narrower than some might like to see, and which may take into account factors other than these moral principles.

In some contexts the distinction between rules and values may collapse. For example, it would be artificial to maintain that in protesting against Father's behaviour in peremptorily switching television channels, Johnny was invoking a 'rule' rather than a 'value', or vice versa. Such situations may be too indeterminate for the distinction between rules and values to be meaningful. However, even where a relatively well-defined rule exists and can be differentiated from the values which it promotes, it does not follow that there will never be

---

[9] 'The term "values" may refer to interests, pleasures, likes, preferences, duties, moral obligations, desires, wants, needs, aversions and attractions, and many other modalities of selective orientation' (*International Encyclopedia of Social Sciences*). A theory of value is concerned with what features of these modalities are good or desirable or right.

any doubt as to the absolute or relative preference to be given to that rule: it may conflict with other rules promoting different values, or with values promoted by the system of which it is part, or it may simply be an inappropriate or inadequate vehicle for promoting those values.

Another important distinction is between values which are held to be intrinsically good, such as the right to life, concern for others, telling the truth, or freedom from racial, sexual, or physical abuse, and values which are good because they promote desirable consequences (extrinsic values) such as brushing one's teeth and keeping fit (health) or doing homework (educational advancement). Some values may be good both intrinsically and extrinsically; for example moral philosophers often argue that keeping one's promises is desirable as a good in itself *and* because it promotes good consequences such as mutual reliability, credibility and the fulfilment of legitimate expectations (all important for successful commercial practice). In addition, the very fact that a proposition is formulated *as a rule* is thought, particularly in legal contexts, to entail the promotion of values intrinsic to the 'enterprise of subjecting human conduct to the governance of rules', such as predictability, consistency, non-retroactivity and order. These intrinsic values have been collectively called 'fidelity to law'[10] and, as we shall see in later chapters, conflict may arise between them and the particular values promoted by the rule at hand.

The distinction between intrinsic and extrinsic values is important in another context, namely the justification of action and of rules prescribing action. The appeal to values in support of actions is a subject which has provoked profound disagreement among moral philosophers. To put the issue very simply, there are three main views as to the criteria which may be adopted to determine the claim of any action (or rule) to be right. The first formulates these criteria in terms of abstract principles such as justice, fairness, equality, liberty, or respect for human life and dignity; values which are held to be intrinsically or self-evidently good. Such a view is technically called deontological, though moralist will do for short. If a moralist were attempting to justify the use of torture in an extreme case, he would have to argue that in this context the values of the right to life of many innocent people and the right of the state to take action to protect its citizens outweigh the individual terrorist's right to freedom from inhuman or degrading treatment. Typically such a moral dilemma

[10] See L. Fuller, *The Morality of Law* (1969).

provokes disagreement both as to the values which are appropriate in the context and the weight that is to be attached to them; and this feature is to be found in other paradigm cases of moral choice such as abortion, capital punishment and the control of pornography.

The second view looks exclusively to the effects or consequences of the action in issue; if it maximizes human happiness or general welfare, it is justifiable. This view is known as utilitarian or consequentialist, which is how we shall refer to it. In the torture example a consequentialist would ask not what moral principles are at stake but what would have the more beneficial effect for everyone? This may yield a different answer than for moralists, some of whom may take the view that torture is *always* wrong. Consequentialists admit no such absolutes – whether it is ever right to torture a person in extreme cases depends on the actual or potential effects. Often, as with torture, consequentialists and moralists may agree as to the wrongness or rightness of a particular action, but the possibility that a consequentialist can come up with a different answer in such a case has given rise to intense debate within moral philosophy.

The third view, sometimes known as ethical pluralism, employs a mixture of consequentialist and moralist arguments; and this is indeed how many people typically argue. When asked why, for example, she is opposed to the easy availability of pornographic books and films, a person might reply that they exploit and degrade women and encourage the commission of sexual offences. In legal contexts, too, it is commonplace to appeal to both types of criteria as supplying tests to determine the rightness of rules and of their interpretation.

3 The form and structure of a rule

It is important to distinguish between rules and *verbal formulations of* rules. Many rules are expressed in words – for instance, the rules of table tennis as adopted by the Table Tennis Federation, the principles of contract as set out in standard textbooks and practitioners' works, and the rule about the larder prescribed for Johnny by his mother. But we are all familiar with unspoken rules. In your family, or within a social circle in which you move, there may be a number of rules which are regularly followed and invoked although they have never been articulated. Similarly, many rules of English grammar and usage had existed for a long time before anyone tried to put them into words, and there are still languages governed by rules that have never been expressed in words. Unspoken rules are not necessarily simple. As Wittgenstein observed: 'The tacit conventions on which the understanding of everyday language depends are enormously complicated.'[11]

Often we can treat the expression or formulation of a rule as being for practical purposes the rule itself; but it is sometimes crucial to distinguish between the notion of a rule and the notion of a formulation of a rule. One reason why this distinction can be important is because some difficulties about interpreting rules arise from the fact that they have no agreed or official verbal formulation or that the rule has only been partly expressed in words. Disagreements may then arise as to what is precisely the 'correct' or 'true' wording of the rule. This particular kind of doubt is absent where there is an agreed official text in which the rule is expressed in a specific form of words.

There is a second, less obvious, reason for distinguishing between the notion of a rule and the notion of the verbal formulation of a rule. The same rule may be expressed in a number of different grammatical forms without any significant change in its substance. For example: 'Johnny, never go into the larder unless I say you may'; 'Johnny may go into the larder only with his mother's permission'; 'Under no circumstances whatsoever may Johnny enter the larder at any time of night or day unless express permission has been given by his mother'; 'You may go into the larder if and only if I say that you may.'

The substance of the rule in all the above examples may be identical for most practical purposes; but the grammar and syntax[12] of the sentences and the grammatical forms (nouns and verbs) used to express the rules are quite varied. In handling rules it can be important to realize that the substance of the rule and the syntax of its formulation are different matters.

One further point needs to be made about the logical structure of rules. For our purposes any rule, however expressed, or even if it has not been expressed, can be analysed and restated as a compound conditional statement of the form 'If X, then Y'. The first part, 'if X', which is known as the *protasis*, is *descriptive* – it indicates the scope of the rule by designating the conditions in which the rule applies. The

---

[11] L. Wittgenstein, *Tractatus Logico-Philosophicus* (1971 edn), p. 37.

[12] 'Syntax' is used here in the sense of 'the arrangement of words (in their appropriate forms) by which their connexion and relation in a sentence are shown' (*Oxford English Dictionary*, Shorter Edition, 2a).

second part, 'then Y', known as the *apodosis*, is *prescriptive* – it states whether the type of behaviour governed by the rule is prohibited ('may not', ought not'), required ('ought' or 'must'), permitted ('may') and so on. Gottlieb puts the matter thus:

> Any utterance which is designed to function as a rule *must* have the potential of being reduced, expanded, analysed or translated into a standard form such as 'in circumstances X, Y is required/permitted.' . . . Normative utterances need not . . . be completely formulated. The crucial question about such an utterance, from a functional viewpoint, is whether it lends itself to a *restatement* in normative form.[13]

Thus the rule about the larder can be restated as follows:

Protasis	*Apodosis*
If Johnny enters the larder without permission from mother . . .	. . . then Johnny is in breach of a duty (not to enter).

This formulation of the rule involves an element of repetition. The agent (Johnny) and the activity prohibited by the rule (entering the larder) appear in both the protasis and the apodosis. It might be more elegant, and certainly would be more succinct, to break the statement up in a different way, for example:

Protasis	*Apodosis*
If and only if Mother gives permission,	may Johnny enter the larder

or

Unless Mother gives permission,	Johnny must not enter the larder.

But for our purposes it is convenient to include in the *protasis* all the ingredients of the rule that could give rise to a question of fact in a particular case governed by the rule: the person or persons whose behaviour is governed by the rule (the agent), the type of behaviour involved (acts, omissions, activities) and the conditions under which the rule applies (e.g. the absence of permission). To put the matter another way: for our purposes, *all ingredients that have a bearing on the scope of the rule should be included in the protasis.*[14]

[13] G. Gottlieb, *The Logic of Choice* (1968), p. 40.
[14] G. von Wright, *Norm and Action* (1963), Chapter 2, distinguishes six ingredients of norms that are prescriptions: the character, the content, the condition of application, the authority, the subject(s) or agent (s) and the occasion. Our recommendation is that

The reason for this recommendation is that, for purposes of analysis and interpretation, it is often important to distinguish between the *scope* of a rule (what fact-situations does it govern?) and its *character* (what kind of prescription?). This will become apparent when we deal with the distinction between questions of fact and questions of interpretation, the problem of the *ratio decidendi* and other topics.

Two problematic aspects of analysing the protasis and apodosis of rules have attracted attention in traditional jurisprudence. First, the elucidation and analysis of the standard normative concepts that typically occur in the apodoses of rules, such as duty ('ought'), privilege/licence ('may'), power ('can') and disability ('cannot'), have been the subject of much discussion and controversy. In order to keep the exposition simple, nearly all of the examples in the text will relate to duties and privileges. But if you are puzzled by any of these concepts or the relationships between them, you might find it helpful to refer to one of the standard discussions cited in the suggestions for further reading.[15]

Another puzzling question is the relationship between rules and sanctions, such as punishments or damages. In our view, some rules are backed by sanctions and others are not. When a rule is backed by a sanction, the question arises whether the sanction is prescribed by the rule, i.e. is prescribed *in* the apodosis, or whether the sanction for the breach of that rule is prescribed by another, independent, but connected, rule.[16] For present purposes it is more satisfactory to treat the prescription of the sanction as a separate rule, for example:

Protasis	*Apodosis*
Rule 1. If Johnny enters the larder without Mother's permission ...	... he is in breach of a duty.
Rule 2. If Johnny is in breach of a duty not to enter the larder ...	... he is liable to be made to stand in the corner for not less than 20 minutes.

---

the content, the condition, the subject and the occasion should all be included in the protasis, even if some are repeated in the apodosis for the sake of clarity. The apodosis is then confined to specifying the *character* of the norm (permission, prohibition, requirement, etc.).

[15] See below, p. 374.

[16] On the question, 'What is *one* rule?' – the problem of individuation – see M. H. James in *Bentham and Legal Theory* (1973), pp. 91 ff.

Note that the apodosis of rule 1 becomes the protasis of rule 2. Complex bodies of rules may on analysis reveal quite long chains of rules connected to each other in this way. However, in ordinary discourse two such connected rules may be run together in a compound proposition which looks like the statement of a single rule:

Protasis	*Apodosis*
If Johnny enters the larder	... he is liable ...
without Mother's permission ...	

Provided this is recognized as a convenient form of shorthand there is no harm in using it. But for the purposes of analysis, for example in constructing algorithms, it may sometimes be necessary to differentiate between a substantive rule and the sanction(s) precribed for its non-observance.

4 Rules, exceptions and exemptions

When Mother said 'in future you are never to enter the larder *without my permission*', she made one *explicit exception* ('without my permission') to a general prohibition against entry. Similarly, the proviso to s. 57 of the Offences Against the Person Act 1861 sets out a number of situations in which the general prohibition against bigamy does not apply.[17] These are straightforward examples of explicit exceptions that accompany the general prescription and are generally considered to form part of the rule.

In law explicit exceptions to a statutory provision may be found in a different place, such as a separate section of the same statute, or in a prior or subsequent statute. Whether or not we choose to say that such provisions are part of the original rule, or that rule B provides an exception to rule A, analytically the function of such explicit exceptions is clear: it is to delimit the scope of the rule.

Even the most detailed and carefully drafted statutory provision does not contain a *complete formulation* of the rule.[18] For there is the possibility that further exceptions may be implied. For instance, some of the general principles of criminal liability may provide the basis for

---

[17] See above, p. 38.

[18] On incomplete formulations, see H. L. A. Hart, 'The Ascription of Responsibility and Rights' in A. Flew (ed.), *Logic and Language* (1st series) (1951), Chapter 8; F. Waismann, 'Verifiability', id., pp. 119-24.

a defence to a charge of bigamy even though they are not explicitly mentioned in the Offences Against the Person Act 1861. Thus a person is not guilty of bigamy in the absence of *mens rea* or if he went through the second ceremony under duress.[19] Thus implied exceptions also delimit the scope of the rule, by indicating conditions under which it does not apply.

If Johnny had entered the larder to rescue the salmon from the cat, the situation is less clear-cut. It would be open to Father to hold that Johnny was not in breach of the rule, because entry in this kind of situation was impliedly permitted; he might hold that Johnny was technically in breach of the rule, but refuse to punish him (on an analogy with an absolute discharge); he might decide to waive the rule in this particular case, thereby granting Johnny an *exemption* on this occasion, but not implying a general *exception* to the rule in this kind of case.[20]

Such distinctions might have no practical consequences for Johnny – for him they might be distinctions without a difference. But it would be wrong to infer from this that such distinctions are unimportant in all contexts. Thus in law there may be practical consequences for a person who has been convicted, but given an absolute discharge rather than acquitted; and the *Buckoke* case is an example of practical consequences of the distinction between an exemption and an exception.[21] If they had been able to graft a general exception on to the road traffic legislation, the Court of Appeal could have put firemen and their superiors in a much more satisfactory position than they were when it was left to the discretion of the police, magistrates and others 'to follow the precedent set by Lord Nelson' when drivers of fire engines were technically in breach of the law. As it turned out, the Court of Appeal was only able to recommend that drivers be exempted from criminal proceedings and exhort Parliament to change the law.

More important for our purposes is the point that such distinctions are analytically important in considering puzzlements about interpretation. Philosophers have debated for a long time whether, as Kant suggested, it is always wrong to make exceptions to a moral rule.[22] The distinction between a general exception and an exemption in a

[19] *D.P.P for N. Ireland* v. *Lynch* [1975] A.C. 653; *R.* v. *Gould*, below, p. 356.
[20] See K. Baier, *The Moral Point of View* (1965), pp. 96–100; cf. the 'absolute' prohibition on torture in the European Convention, above, p. 60.
[21] See above, p. 48.
[22] See Baier, op. cit., p. 100.

particular case is a useful starting point from which to tackle some of the most common sources of doubt about interpretation of rules. But, as we shall see in due course, this distinction is in need of refinement, because it takes for granted a sharp distinction between 'the general' and 'the particular'; whereas generality and particularity are matters of degree and some of the most difficult choices in interpretation relate to choosing an appropriate level of generality.[23]

5 The variety of rules

One reason why the notion of 'rule' is such an important one not only in law, but in fields as varied as linguistics, sociology, anthropology, education, psychology and philosophy, is that there is hardly any aspect of human behaviour that is not in some way governed or at least guided by rules; indeed, there are some kinds of acts, such as pawning in chess, that can be said to be *constituted* by rules, in the sense that the act could not even be conceived of without the rules. Using language, playing games, courting, getting married, reasoning in mathematics, making decisions in committee, buying and selling a house, passing sentence on a person convicted of crime and even fighting a war are all to a large extent rule-governed activities.[24] These are sometimes contrasted with activities such as going for a walk or kissing, but even they are circumscribed by rules, for example legal rules as to *where* you may walk, or tacit conventions as to when you may kiss, after what preliminaries, in what manner. The generality, and attendant vagueness, of the notion of rule reflects the pervasiveness and importance of rules as social phenomena. Sociologists have emphasized the point that rules are one of the main devices used by people to 'define situations' and 'construct reality'. Understanding the nature of rules is important not only for the actors, but also for those who wish to describe or explain social behaviour.

There are, of course, very many different kinds of rules, or to put the matter more precisely, many different ways of classifying rules into types. Rules can be categorized by the kind of activity they govern, e.g. the rules of mathematics, the rules of football, or the rules governing road traffic; by their source, e.g. statutory rules, judge-made rules, rules made by mother, rules laid down by God, customary rules

[23] See above, pp. 58–9 and below, pp. 169–70.
[24] See Baier, op. cit., pp. 68–72; cf. Waismann, op. cit., Chapter 8.

and so on; rules can be categorized by the character of the prescription – permissions, requirements, prohibitions, rules backed by sanctions, rules that define and constitute behaviour, such as the rules for moving a queen in chess or the rules for making a valid will, and so on; rules may be classified by the form in which they appear, such as in officially approved fixed verbal form, informally stated rules (for instance some judicial formulations of rules) or unspoken rules; and rules may be classified by the kinds of people who are subject to them: for example, rules for officials, rules for ordinary people, rules for members of a club or other limited group. Some modes of classifying rules have been the subject of deep philosophical puzzlements and disagreements; for instance the differences and relations between legal and moral rules, social rules and conventions, rules and standards, rules of etiquette and rules of thumb.[25]

It is obviously not possible here to attempt to provide a comprehensive account of all these distinctions and classifications. Nor is it necessary to do so. But it is important for us to be aware of the pervasiveness of rules and of the many variations that are to be found between them. Also, in order to understand what is involved in interpreting rules in legal and non-legal contexts, it may be helpful to grasp a number of distinctions. We have already distinguished between rules and formulations of rules, between rules and uses of rules and between the notion of a rule and other notions such as values, habits, commands, practices and predictions. Later we shall distinguish between rules and reasons for rules,[26] and between problems of interpretation of rules and other problems connected with rules (such as finding facts under a rule or getting rid of a rule).[27] At this point it may be useful to introduce briefly two further distinctions.

First, there are rules expressed in fixed verbal form and rules not expressed in fixed verbal form. Some, such as statutory rules, are expressed in a particular form of words which has official status, so that is is not open to interpreters to change the wording. Thus, one of the cardinal maxims of statutory interpretation is 'Never paraphrase a statute'. Other rules, as we have seen, may have been expressed differently at different times, may have been only partly articulated or may never have been expressed in words at all. From the point of view of the interpreter, each type to some extent presents different

[25] Ibid.
[26] See below, Chapter 6.
[27] See below, Chapter 4.

problems. Rules in fixed verbal form provide a definite text as a starting point and this removes a lot of potential uncertainty. *Prima facie*, the task of the interpreter is to attach a meaning to a particular word or words.[28] To do this he can be helped by an understanding of the nature of language and meaning, and by certain techniques of linguistic analysis. Very often the words help to reduce the scope of possible doubt. But occasionally the wording may be an obstacle to the interpreter or the source of a doubt which would not have occurred if the rule had not been frozen into a form of words.

Conversely, the absence of a definite and clear formulation of the rule opens the gate to many disagreements about its scope, sometimes about its very existence. Problems of interpretation flood in through that gate. Yet it is a mistake to assume that all rules not expressed in fixed verbal form are, by reason of their form, necessarily vague or perplexing. Many unspoken rules are sufficiently precise and sufficiently well understood to serve their functions adequately in most situations. Some of the problems of interpreting rules apply equally to those that are expressed in fixed verbal form and to those that are not. The form of words is an important factor both in limiting and creating problems of interpretation, but it is by no means the only factor that occasions doubt, as we shall see.

Another distinction, which has been given prominence in jurisprudence by Professor H. L. A. Hart, is that between *primary* and *secondary* rules. Hart summed up the difference as follows:

> Under rules of the one type, which may well be considered the basic or primary type, human beings are required to do or abstain from certain actions, whether they wish to or not. Rules of the other type are in a sense parasitic upon or secondary to the first; for they provide that human beings may by doing or saying certain things introduce new rules of the primary type, extinguish or modify old ones, or in various ways determine their incidence or control their operations. Rules of the first type impose duties; rules of the second type confer powers, public or private. Rules of the first type concern actions involving physical movement or changes; rules of the second type provide for operations which lead not merely to physical movement or change, but to the creation or variation of duties or obligations.[29]

The distinction between primary and secondary rules is not uncontroversial, but it is a useful one. Professor Hart claims that it provides the key to understanding some of the most perplexing features of the

[28] See below, pp. 205 ff.
[29] Hart, op. cit., pp. 78–9.

notions of 'law' and 'legal system'.[30] For our purposes, it is useful for a number of reasons. In this book most of our examples relate to problems of interpretation of primary rules, but it is important to bear in mind that secondary rules are also frequently the subject of interpretation. Furthermore, where a rule is part of a complex system of rules, it may be necessary to look not only at the rule itself, but also at its relationship to a network of other primary and secondary rules. In practice many problems of rule-handling arise from the complexity of the interrelationships within a body of rules and between bodies of rules. An introductory work should concentrate on the elementary components of its subject; for most of the time we shall concentrate on analysing problems and puzzlements relating to the interpretation of single primary rules. But from time to time it will be necessary to remind ourselves that legal systems and other systems of rules are not simply like bundles of sticks, or even as simple and straightforward as the traditional symbol of legal complexity – a seamless web – they are even more complicated than that, and one key to unravelling the complexities is the distinction between primary and secondary rules. This leads us on to the notion of a 'system' of rules and to problems arising from the coexistence of separate or loosely related 'systems'.

6 Rules and systems

It is usually artificial, but convenient, to talk of single rules, for most rules belong to some agglomeration. Like problems, rules cumulate and aggregate: unlike problems there are often cogent reasons for treating rules as an integral part of some larger system. However, this may be artificial in that it suggests a greater degree of integration and internal consistency than is warranted by the facts. How systematic, for example, is that complex congeries of rules, institutions, ideas and traditions which has evolved over centuries and which we glibly call 'the English legal system'?

How far it is feasible, sensible or desirable to think and talk in terms of systems of rules is one of the perennial problems of legal theory. To put the matter starkly: on one view, a legal system is an internally consistent, 'gapless' body of rules and it is theoretically impossible for two rules within the same system to be in conflict. In this view the notion of 'system' is taken literally; logical consistency is a prime value and rigorous logical analysis is the main, perhaps the only, tool for

[30] Ibid., Chapter 3.

resolving doubts in interpretation. It is the role of the 'legal scientist' to create and maintain this consistent, systemic quality.

At the other extreme is the view that law is as messy and contradictory as life itself and that the notion of a 'system of rules' is at best a hopelessly optimistic fiction; it is also misguided and dangerous, because it induces unrealizable expectations of order and certainty, it obscures the messy reality and it encourages an approach to interpretation and exposition that is insensitive to the complexities and nuances of social facts, social change and conflicting values.

Few jurists have subscribed unreservedly to either of these extremes. Even Hans Kelsen, who is sometimes depicted as the leading protagonist of the first view, allowed for the possibility of inconsistent norms coexisting within the same system, and for dynamic processes of interpretation which could take account of changing conditions and values. Conversely, even so-called extreme realists did not see law as a wilderness of single instances, totally unpatterned with no concern for internal coherence or consistency.

We need not pursue this fundamental debate very far here, but it is important to note the continuing tension in interpretation between arguments based on consistency and other kinds of arguments. To put the matter very simply: one context is the other rules within the system; another context is factors outside the system – ranging from society at large to the context and objectives of the particular rule and the circumstances of the case under consideration. Every interpreter needs to be aware of the potential for tension between the systemic context and the social context. The relationships between the rule to be interpreted and other rules is almost always a relevant factor in interpretation; but whether it is sufficient to be satisfied with weak terms like 'fit', 'compatibility', 'coherence', and 'gravitational pull' or whether one should be reaching for strict logical consistency, is a regular source of doubt and disagreement.

Another potential source of tension is between alternative, coexisting or competing bodies of rules. Conflicts between legal and moral rules or principles are familiar enough; the relationship between legal and moral rule-systems is another standard battleground of jurisprudence. In ordinary life most of us have to cope with a variety of sets of rules which may impinge simultaneously – the law of the land, social conventions, institutional regulations, and our own moral and perhaps religious values. Some of these may be treated as sub-systems of a single system; others may be seen as more or less independent rule-systems; the extent of their mutual compatibility may vary tremendously.

In some social contexts 'rule density' may take extreme forms: the 'total institutions' depicted by Erving Goffman, such as prisons, hospitals, barracks and boarding schools are examples.[31] The short passage quoted in Chapter 1 deals with only part of the matter: the relatively formal house-rules and the less formal systems of rewards, privileges and punishments imposed by the staff. In a prison, for example, the inmate is typically subject to other bodies of rules, ranging from international and municipal law (in theory at least, a prisoner can claim rights under the European Convention or sue a prison officer for assault, for example), to the codes of conduct imposed by his fellow inmates or small groups of them. Similarly, the proprietor or manager of a small business, such as a garage or a factory employing forty or fifty people, will find that his relations with his employees, with manufacturers and suppliers, with consumers and other clients, with different departments of local and central government, with his insurers, landlord and others, are all governed by a bewildering, often frightening, number of rules. He may find that rules of contract, tort, company law, employment law, landlord and tenant law, planning, public health, trading standards, consumer protection, VAT, weights and measures, health and safety at work, and many other branches of municipal law impinge on his daily activities. Even finding out about the existence of such rules, let alone interpreting and applying them may be a continuous source of worry, expense and effort. This may be only part of the story. He may also be governed by Local Authority by-laws, EEC directives, Trade Association rules, codes of practice, business usage, accounting procedures, custom and practice on the shopfloor and other informal norms within his own organization, local social conventions and the ways of local officials. The extent to which all of these are or seem to be compatible with each other will naturally vary considerably; even when he can break through the Kafkaesque uncertainty to discern what is governed by rule and what by discretion, he may find himself facing acute dilemmas, posed by competing or conflicting rules from different 'systems'.

Rule density is a familiar feature of modern industrial societies. It often leads to complaints that there is 'too much law'. It is often thought to be closely associated with interventionist or paternalistic government. However, as we shall see, the relationship between

[31] Above, pp. 15–16.

prevailing ideology and the amount of legislation is more complex than that. In the present context our concern is not to arouse sympathy for the poor inmate or businessman, beset by a multitude of demanding and potentially conflicting rule-systems. It is rather to make the point that when confronted with a particular rule an interpreter may not merely be concerned to interpret it in the light of other rules in the same system; he may also be concerned to reconcile it with rules which form part of other systems as well as with factors other than rules. A single-system model of interpretation may prove to be too simple in some contexts.

7 Reifying rules: a note of warning

When we talk of a situation, an event or an act we are normally not tempted to think of them as 'things' even though we use the grammatical form of a noun and often qualify them with adjectives, attach predicates to them or make them the subjects or objects of transitive verbs. Similarly when we talk of reasons having 'weight' or 'strength', of breaking 'the chain' of causation, or of links in 'a chain' of reasoning, we may not need to be reminded that we are talking metaphorically. Words like 'rule', 'norm' and 'standard' are also abstract nouns, but there seems to be a greater temptation in ordinary discourse to 'thingify' (or 'reify' or 'hypostatize') them, that is to talk about them *as if* they are objects in the real world which we can see or touch or measure or examine for their characteristics. This is partly due to the fact that rules are sometimes expressed in a form which does have a physical embodiment: the laws of Moses were engraved on tablets of stone; British Rail has a rule book; school rules may be posted on a noticeboard. We talk quite naturally of reading, drafting, breaking or writing down rules. Normally it is clear that it is not the tablet of stone or the notice or the book which is the actual object of such actions, but sometimes we may fall into the trap of confusing the rule with its physical expression. Often this is quite harmless, but there are hidden dangers, not least that we may be tempted to speak more confidently about the existence or the identity of a rule than is warranted by the context. Accordingly it is important to recognize that talking about the 'scope' of rules involves a spatial concept that is no less metaphorical than talking about the weight of reasons, just as talking in terms of making, waiving, evading, manipulating, handling or doing 'things' with rules or words is a convenient, but metaphorical, way of talking.

Let us illustrate the point by considering some of the difficulties of determining the existence and identity of an alleged rule in a fairly indeterminate situation. When Father entered the room where Johnny was watching television and peremptorily switched to another channel without saying a word,[32] suppose that the following exchange ensued:

J (outraged): 'Hey, you can't do that!'
F: 'Why not?'
J: 'There is a rule against it.'
F: 'We don't have any rules for watching TV.'
J: 'But there are rules of good manners against this sort of thing.'
F: 'Show me!'

Johnny's protest is couched in terms of appealing to a rule and is likely to win more sympathy from readers than some of his other claims. At a commonsense level, it does seem that Father has violated some standard, but how can it be shown that such a standard exists, and what is it exactly – a rule concerning television-watching, some principle of justice, or some convention of polite or civilized behaviour? How can Johnny demonstrate the existence of a particular rule that Father has violated? To put the matter in more general terms: under what circumstances is it true to say that a rule exists? and on what grounds can one identify a particular rule as *the* one that has been broken?

It is not necessary here to attempt to answer these general questions, which raise important and difficult philosophical issues. In this relatively straightforward case, it is not difficult to suggest some ways in which Johnny might take up Father's challenge. He might hoist Father with his own petard by pointing out that he had reprimanded Johnny for exactly the same behaviour on some previous occasion; or he might claim that Mother had told him that he should always ask permission before switching channels; or he might invoke an analogy: 'It's like not interrupting when other people are talking'. Given his precociousness and lawyer-like qualities he might boldly assert a general principle: 'It is unreasonable to change channels in the middle of a programme without at least obtaining the consent of those who are watching.' Father might or might not accept any or all of these as satisfying his demand for a demonstration that there was some rule

[32] Above, p. 9.

that he had violated on this occasion. But even in this rather clear case, in which nearly everyone would agree that some standard has been violated, there is considerable indeterminacy about how precisely the situation is to be interpreted. If the reasonableness or appropriateness or unacceptability of Father's behaviour, when in conflict with Johnny, were less clear-cut, the interpretation of the situation would be even more problematic.

Consider now a variation on this episode: Father enters the room and switches channels without saying a word. Johnny is very angry and glares at him, but says nothing. Father, noticing Johnny's reaction, switches back to the original channel and smiles apologetically. We might be able to give a plausible account of this interaction without invoking notions such as rules or standards. But it would be much simpler to say that Johnny tacitly invoked a rule, which Father recognized and acknowledged that he had violated. In interpreting a situation in this way we typically use words like 'rule' and 'standard' as a shorthand for describing what are essentially very complex processes and interactions, which may be fraught with ambiguities.

Many of the standard examples with which we are concerned in this book posit a situation in which an interpreter is confronted with a pre-existing rule. The rule is taken as given, it is a datum: the problem for the interpreter is to explore and determine the scope (and possibly the meaning and rationale) of the rule. In many contexts it is quite reasonable to assert or to assume that a rule exists and can be identified. In the larder episode Johnny's ploys for dealing with his parents did not include doubting the existence or identity of the rule prohibiting entry to the larder or Mother's capacity, in the sense of authority and power, to make such a rule. The disagreement was about the scope of a particular rule which was acknowledged by both sides to exist, to be identified and to be valid. Similarly, in the convoluted history of disagreements about the scope of the English offence of bigamy, no one has seriously questioned the existence of a law against bigamy, the identity of the primary rule (s. 57 of the Offences Against the Person Act) or its validity.

However, such doubts can and do arise in both legal and non-legal contexts. In non-legal contexts it is often far from clear whether a particular situation can appropriately be interpreted in terms of rules at all and, if so, how to identify what the rules are. Doubts about the very existence of a legal rule may be relatively rare; but disputes about the validity of a rule are frequent, for example in respect of delegated

legislation under the *ultra vires* doctrine, or in determining the constitutionality of acts of state legislatures in the United States and like
jurisdictions. Doubts about the identity of an alleged rule or principle
are, as we shall see, commonplace in the context of case law.

For the purpose of examining what is involved in interpreting rules,
it is often necessary to take for granted the existence, the identity and
the validity of a given rule – to treat the rule to be interpreted as a
given. If doubts of this kind arise, they are often best viewed as
preliminaries to interpretation rather than as problems of interpretation. It is, however, important to recognize that in some contexts there
is considerable indeterminacy about such matters and that they are a
frequent source of puzzlement, confusion and disagreement. In order
to discuss interpretation of rules we have to postulate the existence of
particular rules to interpret, but we should always be on our guard
against being more confident about such assumptions than the situation may warrant. And one useful precept is always to bear in mind
that rules are not things, we merely talk *as if* they are.

In the preceding analysis we have by implication introduced a
distinction between interpreting a situation and interpreting a rule; it
has also been suggested that it is useful to distinguish between doubts
arising prior to interpretation and doubts arising in the process of
interpretation. These can be useful working distinctions, but we must
be careful not to place much weight on them, for in some contexts they
collapse.

In dealing with rules in fixed verbal form, whether written or
unwritten, we can generally use these distinctions with some confidence. Once the rule is identified, and its validity confirmed, we have
a reasonably clear starting point from which to proceed to the task of
determining its scope. Moreover, as we shall suggest later, interpreting
rules is a rather more straightforward matter than interpreting situations. A rule in fixed verbal form is much more like a thing than a rule
not in fixed verbal form, and it is correspondingly easier to take its
existence and its identity for granted and to proceed from there.

Unfortunately this is not the case with rules not in fixed verbal form,
such as rules derived from cases. For here we are concerned with a
much more elusive kind of subject-matter, and to talk of 'determining
the existence' of such rules or of 'identifying' them is much closer to
the language of metaphor. There is no firm text or foundation on
which to anchor. The raw materials from which to extract, formulate
and interpret such rules can be more elusive than shifting sands.

Moreover, like problems, rules and situations are rarely static. As Fuller argues, many rules are in a continual state of development. In order to interpret the rules we will often have to interpret the situation. In order to proceed we need concepts such as rules and standards, and even codes, but we need to be aware of the artificiality of talking in such terms – it is as if we are forced to talk with more confidence and more precision than the situation warrants. How, for example, can we be *sure* that the silent exchange between Father and Johnny involved the tacit invocation and acknowledgement of a rule?

In particular contexts, of course, there may be factors to bolster our confidence: settled ways of thought, accepted conventions of communication, even manuals of interpretation. Thus in interpreting any particular area of legal doctrine based on case law there are many institutionalized and relatively settled 'steadying factors', as Karl Llewellyn called them,[33] to assist in the process of determining the scope of particular rules. On many points of common law we *can* talk with confidence and the same is true of many rules not in fixed verbal form in non-legal contexts. Nevertheless, in such contexts, a very great strain may be put on artificially precise distinctions. To take but one example: in the context of case-law interpretation, the main focus for the interpreter is nothing so concrete as particular rules nor so elusive as a total situation, rather it is judicial opinions or judgments, the raw material from which formulations of doctrine are extracted. It is only in a loose, metaphorical sense that common law rules 'exist' and are interpreted; it is more exact to say that formulations of common law doctrine are extracted or constructed from judicial opinions. The ways in which cases – the raw material of common law rules – are transformed into settled 'doctrine' are complex, varied and elusive; this is a topic about which there is little consensus among jurists.[34]

8 The functions of rules[35]

Why have rules? What are they for? In view of the enormous variety of kinds of rules, and the many different contexts in which they

[33] K. N. Llewellyn, *The Common Law Tradition* (1960), pp. 19ff.
[34] See A. W. B. Simpson, 'The Common Law and Legal Theory' in *Oxford Essays in Jurisprudence* (2nd series) (1973), Chapter 4.
[35] See Waismann, op. cit., pp. 132ff; on 'function', see R. Merton, *Social Theory and Social Structure* (1967).

operate, it is difficult to give very general answers to questions like this. It is sometimes said that the main function of rules is to guide behaviour. But this is not very informative. For instance, it does not tell us when it is helpful or necessary to have general guides to behaviour and when attempts to provide general guidance are useless or even counter-productive. Nor is guidance the only function of rules. Rules may be introduced, for example, in order to communicate information or values, in order to make a public declaration of support for a moral principle or a particular policy, in order to economize effort, or as a form of window-dressing – perhaps as a lazy way of avoiding coming to grips with an intractable problem. The functions of rules are almost as varied as the types of rules. The functions of rules of grammar are not identical with the functions of rules in social relations. And in addition to the obvious functions of a rule in a particular context, there may be secondary or hidden functions, which can easily be overlooked.

We can be a little more specific, although still operating at a very general level, if we examine some of the functions of rules in human groups. And this may also help to bring out a point that many functions performed by rules could also be performed without them. For instance, Mother might have been more successful in keeping Johnny out of the larder by locking the door instead of making a rule.

The American jurist, Karl Llewellyn, developed a theory about the functions of rules in social groups, popularly known as the 'Law Jobs Theory'.[36] This can be briefly restated as follows: All of us are members of groups, such as a family, a club, a teenage gang, a school or commercial organization, a trade union, a political party, a nation state, the world community. In order to survive and to achieve its aims, in so far as it has aims, *any* human group has to meet certain needs or ensure that certain jobs are done. The first, perhaps the most important, of these jobs is to channel behaviour and expectations of members of the group in order to avoid conflicts or disputes within it. Secondly, when disputes arise, they have to be resolved or, at least, be kept at a tolerably low level, or else the group will disintegrate or its objectives will be frustrated or impaired. Thirdly, as the circumstances of the group change, so the behaviour and expectations of members of the group have to be adjusted to such changes in order to avoid conflicts and disappointments. Fourthly, decision-making in the group needs to be regulated both in respect of who has power and authority

[36] K. Llewellyn, *Jurisprudence* (1962), Chapter 15, and references below at p. 374.

to participate in decisions and in respect of the procedures by which decisions are arrived at. This allocation of authority and power is typically the primary function of a 'constitution' of, for example, a club or a nation state. Fifthly, in any group, but especially in complex groups, techniques, skills and devices need to be developed for satisfactorily meeting the first four needs. Channelling behaviour, settling disputes, making smooth adjustments to change and providing for acceptable ways of reaching decisions can often be difficult tasks, involving high levels of skill or quite refined or sophisticated devices. Rules are one type of device for doing the law jobs. Skill in making rules suited to their purposes, and skill in interpreting rules or handling them in other ways, are part of the general job that Llewellyn called 'The Job of Juristic Method'. Some of these skills are highly specialized and may become the province of a few individuals with narrowly defined roles such as legislative draftsmen; but others are basic to many aspects of rule-handling.

It is important to grasp two points about this theory. First, although it is called the 'Law Jobs Theory', it is not restricted to the role of official law in a national legal system. It is very much wider than that. It concerns the regulation and operation of *all* human groups and it emphasizes problems that are common to them. It is accordingly very useful for our purposes, in that, just as we emphasize problems concerning the interpretation of rules in many different types of social context, so Llewellyn emphasizes the universality of the conditions that give rise to the need for rules.

Secondly, Llewellyn stresses the point that rules are one of the main devices for performing the law jobs, but they are not the only ones. For example, within the family perfectly satisfactory patterns of behaviour regarding the watching of television may develop without any resort either to consciously created rules or even to the development of tacit conventions (although it would be an unusual situation in a family of several people in which there were absolutely *no* rules or conventions relating to such matters as how to determine which television programme to watch when different members of the family want to watch different programmes). Or, to take an example from a legal context, let us look at the problem of promoting harmonious race relations in a plural society; among those who desire to promote harmonious relations, some people believe that legislation, such as that embodied in race relations laws, is useless or worse than useless. 'You cannot legislate harmony,' they might argue. On the other hand, many people believe that race relations legislation is important, perhaps even necessary, for controlling and reducing racial conflict. Some would argue that the existing race relations legislation in Britain is too narrow and too timid and should be greatly extended. But few people would argue that all the problems of racial harmony could be resolved by law alone. These are just two examples of situations in which questions arise about the value of resorting to rules at all in order to resolve problems.

Llewellyn's theory is useful as a starting point for our analysis. But it needs elaboration in a number of ways. In particular it is important to emphasize that the functions he lists are not the only functions that rules may perform. Llewellyn's account is concerned mainly with *direct* regulation of behaviour and expectations by rules and other devices. In this view, an ineffective rule is useless or worse than useless. But rules are sometimes introduced in order to educate or to communicate approval or disapproval, even if there is very little chance of getting the bulk of those who are subject to them to conform immediately. For example, during the Prohibition era in the United States there came a time when it was clear to many people that the Prohibition laws were not effective in reducing the consumption of alcohol; and it was even arguable that, by driving the distribution of spirits into the hands of the criminal world, the net result may have been to *increase* rather than decrease the total consumption of alcohol by certain classes of people.[37] It is generally acknowledged that Prohibition gave a boost to organized crime, by giving it a profitable economic base. Some supporters of Prohibition would have no doubt accepted these as good reasons for giving up trying to control this form of social behaviour by means of law; but others could argue that, whether or not Prohibition legislation was effective, it performed a valuable function by expressing *disapproval* of a particular form of social behaviour, even though the state was not in practice able to enforce conformity.

It is sometimes said that the main function of some school rules and certain kinds of safety regulation is to inculcate people into acceptance of certain values or standards. Similarly, in Soviet Russia one of the primary functions of law is seen to be *educative*.[38] And this is seen by some as a secondary function of legislation on race relations.[39]

---

[37] A. Sinclair, *Prohibition: The Era of Excess* (1962).

[38] See, for example, D. Lloyd, *Introduction to Jurisprudence* (1979 edn), pp. 748–50, 797 *et seq.*

[39] See A. Lester and G. Bindman, *Race and Law* (1972), pp. 85–9.

An approach to rules, in both legal and other contexts, that presents them as deliberate instruments designed to further in a direct fashion clear policies is really too simple. Indeed, if 'function' were equated with 'purpose', the picture painted by the 'Law Jobs Theory' would be misleading. For not every group, or every rule, has clear 'purposes'. Some rules may have been created unthinkingly, as an instinctive response without any clear purpose or policy behind them; some may have 'growed' in some obscure and complex way; and some may have survived to be dysfunctional, even if originally they had some useful purpose. Similarly, some rules that developed in response to one kind of need may have survived to perform some quite different kind of function. Many legislative rules represent a compromise between competing interests or values. Moreover, a single rule or set of rules may have a complex set of functions, not all of which are concerned with directly influencing the behaviour they purport to regulate. A good example again is to be found in the following statement on the purposes of race relations legislation:

(1) A law is an unequivocal declaration of public policy.
(2) A law gives support to those who do not wish to discriminate, but who feel compelled to do so by social pressure.
(3) A law gives protection and redress to minority groups.
(4) A law thus provides for the peaceful and orderly adjustment of grievances and the release of tensions.
(5) A law reduces prejudice by discouraging the behaviour in which prejudice finds expression.[40]

Not everyone will agree with this statement, but it clearly illustrates the variety of claims that can be made about the purposes of a law.

In interpreting rules it is of paramount importance to try to ascribe clear and coherent purposes or policies or principles behind them, but it is equally important to realize that such efforts may be wholly or partly unsuccessful. A model of a legal rule as an instrument of policy is very useful. But in using this model, we need to be aware that the problem may be rather more complex and subtle than appears on the surface. In particular, we need to be aware that rules may have *latent* as well as *manifest* functions,[41] that they often have unforeseen consequences, that a rule may be serving a different function from that which was originally intended when it was created, and that some rules are, as judged by the standards of the moment, pointless or positively dysfunctional or counter-productive. Moreover, there may

[40] Race Relations Board, *First Annual Report* (1967), para. 65.
[41] Merton, op. cit., n. 24.

be no clear consensus about one or more of these matters and this too may be a source of perplexity.

9 Rules as techniques of social management

Some of the main examples of rules used so far have been 'primary' rules, which impose duties directly on those who are subject to them, such as the rule about the larder or the prohibition against bigamy in s. 57 of the Offences Against the Person Act 1861. But it is important that such penal rules should not be regarded as providing a simple prototype to be used on all, or even a majority of, occasions on which rules are to be introduced to deal with a given problem. A useful corrective is contained in Professor Robert Summers' account of what he terms the basic techniques of law.[42] Adopting the standpoint of the legislator or other 'societal manager', Summers distinguishes five basic techniques that are available to be used, as alternatives or in combination, to give effect to given policies:

(i) law as a grievance-remedial instrument (recognition of claims to enforceable remedies for grievances, actual or threatened);

(ii) law as a penal instrument (prohibition, prosecution and punishment of bad conduct);

(iii) law as an administrative-regulatory instrument (regulation of generally wholesome activity, business or otherwise);

(iv) law as an instrument for ordering governmental (or other authoritative) conferral of public benefits (governmental conferral of substantive benefits such as education, welfare and highways);

(v) law as an instrument for facilitating and effectuating private arrangements (facilitation and protection of private voluntary arrangements, economic and otherwise).

Each of these techniques may be illustrated by reference to two general areas of social policy which we encountered in Chapter 1 – the protection of individuals from the production of unwholesome food and drink, and the facilitation and preservation of monogamous family life. Thus, in the former case, manufacturers, sellers and others may be liable to pay compensation by way of damages in contract or

[42] R. Summers and C. Howard, *Law, its Nature, Functions and Limits* (1972, 2nd edn), pp. 21ff; R. Summers, 'The Technique Element in Law', 59 *California Law Review* (1971), 733.

tort for loss or injury suffered by an individual customer or consumer (grievance-remedial); in addition, they may be subject to criminal sanctions under food and drugs legislation (penal); the method of manufacturing, processing and distribution may be regulated by a system of licensing and inspection (administrative-regulatory); positive steps towards the provision of a healthy diet may be taken through such devices as the provision of free or cheap milk in schools or dietary counselling of pregnant mothers (benefit-conferring); and some aspects of relations between manufacturers, consumers and others may be left to be determined by the parties concerned, by contract or otherwise, with the law playing a facilitative role, for example by giving recognition to agreements for the servicing of food-processing equipment (private arrangements).

Similarly, all five techniques are used in many societies to support the institution of monogamous marriage. The choice of partner is left largely to private arrangement; the formation and regulation of marriage is primarily dealt with by administrative-regulatory provisions, some of which are backed by penal laws; the grievance-remedial technique can be used to protect monogamous marriages, for example by providing remedies for adultery or loss of consortium (but in England and America, at least, there has been a marked trend away from employing this technique in recent years). Various kinds of tax relief, children's allowances (if confined to legitimate children) and widows' pensions are examples of benefit-conferral devices that can be used, *inter alia*, to encourage or discourage certain patterns of family arrangement.

Summers' analysis is useful for our purposes for two main reasons. First, it underlines the variety of ways in which rules can be employed by the rulemaker; in particular, it warns against over-emphasis on the *pathological* aspects of law, that is the prosecution and punishment of acts considered to be antisocial and the provision of remedies when things have gone wrong. Law is also introduced to regulate, to facilitate and to confer and distribute benefits. Broken contracts and broken marriages represent only a small proportion of all contracts and marriages, and the law has at least as important a role to play in the creation, definition and facilitation of these relationships as in the clearing up of the mess after things have gone wrong.

When a troublesome problem arises in society, such as hijacking or urban terrorism, one instinctive response, typified by the phrase 'there ought to be a law', is to think in terms of creating new offences or imposing harsher sanctions. Summers' theory is a salutary corrective to this tendency to think solely or mainly in terms of the penal, and to a lesser extent grievance-remedial, techniques. For example, recent experience suggests that hijacking can be combated effectively only by deploying a wide range of methods and devices, with regulatory techniques (through such means as efficient systems of surveillance at airports) having a potentially much greater role to play than penal sanctions (such as capital punishment), the main function of which may be more symbolic than deterrent.

Second, Summers' analysis is concerned specifically with the basic techniques of *law*; but, as with Llewellyn's 'Law Jobs Theory', it can be applied with little or no modification in non-legal contexts, and can be used to illustrate certain basic lessons about rules as problem-solving devices.[43] Thus, had Mother employed a similar analysis when deciding how to prevent Johnny eating between meals, she would have been in a position to consider more systematically the range of techniques open to her in securing this objective. By requiring Johnny to seek permission before entering the larder, and implicitly threatening punishment if he did not, she resorted to a combination of the regulatory and penal techniques; but she might equally have considered such devices as requiring Johnny to pay for any food he takes (grievance-remedial), or providing him with more satisfying and attractive meals, possibly as part of a bargain with him (benefit-conferring). Because Mother is in a position of authority over him, a bargain between her and Johnny does not fit neatly into the 'private-arranging' category. But it is not difficult to envisage situations within the nuclear family that fit the category; for example, in a family with several children competing for various scarce commodities, a parent may lay down explicit rules for distribution, or may make *ad hoc* distributions as occasions arise, or may leave it to the children to sort out such conflicts by private arrangement between themselves.[44]

10 Two views of rules

Implicit in the 'Law Jobs Theory' and in Summers' analysis is a view of rules as instruments of policies aimed at solving problems, that is to

[43] What Summers includes under 'law' encompasses much more than legal rules.

[44] One way of looking at Summers' theory is as an extension and elaboration of Llewellyn's 'Job of Juristic Method'.

say as means to ends in problem situations. One of the most famous statements of this view is to be found in the 'Mischief Rule' for the interpretation of statutes, as expounded by the Barons of the Exchequer in *Heydon's case* in 1584:

> That for the sure and true interpretation of all statutes in general (be they penal or beneficial, restrictive or enlarging of the common law) four things are to be discerned and considered: 1st. What was the common law before the making of the Act. 2nd. What was the mischief and defect for which the common law did not provide. 3rd. What remedy the parliament hath resolved and appointed to cure the disease of the commonwealth. And 4th. The true reason of the remedy. And then the office of all the Judges is always to make such construction as shall suppress the mischief, and advance the remedy, and to suppress subtle inventions and evasions for continuance of the mischief and *pro privato commodo*, and to add force and life to the cure and remedy, according to the true intent of the makers of the Act *pro bono publico*.[45]

A similar view of rules as instruments directed against problems and mischiefs underlies the seductive common law maxim, '*cessante ratione, cessat ipsa lex*', which, freely translated, means: 'Reason is the soul of the law, and when the reason of any particular law ceases, so does the law itself.' Both *Heydon's case* and the *cessante* maxim concern interpretation; they both assume that the role of the interpreter is to further the intention of the legislator. Where there is an element of discretion or choice in interpretation, the role of the judge may be seen as that of a junior partner in the enterprise of law-making; translated to the context of rule-making in general this involves a view of rules as problem-solving devices, as attempted remedies for mischiefs.

There are, of course, ways of looking at rules other than as means to ends. It is also common for rules to be seen as things in themselves, which have an existence independent of any motive, reason, purpose or policy that may have originally inspired them. This view implies that, for the person subject to it, the rule is there to be followed; for the interpreter the task is to ascertain the true meaning of the rule and apply it without regard to the original purposes or the consequences. Consider the following statements:

---

[45] (1584) 3 Co. Rep. 8. *Heydon's case* can be interpreted as taking mischiefs of the law, rather than social problems, as the starting point and, as Lord Scarman observes: 'The Barons by their resolution illustrate neatly the relationship in English eyes, between the common law and statute law. The common law is the seamless fabric covering all the activities of man; the statute is the tailor's stitch in time, to patch the fabric where gaps or other defects appear in the course of wear' (*Law Reform: The New Pattern* (1968), p. 46).

That is the rule and we must stick to it.

Their's not to reason why.

If the precise words used are plain and unambiguous, in our judgment we are bound to construe them in their ordinary sense, even though it do lead, in our view of the case, to an absurdity or manifest injustice.[46]

These two views of rules are commonly found opposed to each other in a variety of contexts. The attitude exemplified by *Heydon's case* is commonly referred to by such terms as 'liberal', 'functional', 'the Grand Style of judging';[47] where it is appropriate to generalize about this attitude, we shall refer to it as 'instrumentalism'. The contrasting view is commonly associated with such epithets as 'legalistic', 'literal', 'formalistic' and 'conformist'. We shall use 'formalism' as a general term to refer to the second view.

It is necessary to enter two caveats at this point: first, although instrumentalist and formalist approaches are regularly found opposed to each other, there is need for caution in generalizing about them, especially without reference to some particular context. Not only are there different versions of instrumentalism and formalism, but also the appropriateness of one or other kind of attitude varies considerably from context to context. For example, it is difficult to conceive of a rational approach to rule-making in which rules are viewed as things in themselves rather than as means to ends; from a rule-maker's point of view, making purposeless rules is a pointless activity. On the other hand, there are circumstances in which unquestioning adherence to rules by a person subject to them or by an official charged with administering them is considered a duty to be carried out however unpleasant the consequences, and powerful reasons can sometimes be advanced for such a posture.

Secondly, it is easy to be seduced, by emotive associations of some words commonly used in connection with each of the two views, into prejudging the appropriateness of a particular posture in a particular context. Statements like 'he interprets the law in accordance with the letter rather than the spirit' leave little doubt about the speaker's sympathies; a value judgment is implied. Terms like 'Grand Style', 'creative' and 'liberal' on the one hand, and 'literal', 'legalistic', 'strict' and 'formalistic' on the other, may suggest that the instrumentalist is always to be supported and formalism is always to be opposed. In particular, there is a natural tendency in the literature to assume that

[46] *Per* Jervis C.J., *Abley* v. *Dale* (1851) 11 C.B. 378, 391.
[47] K. Llewellyn, *The Common Law Tradition* (1960), *passim.*

an instrumentalist approach is always more 'rational' than a formalistic one. This tendency is endemic in the academic discussions of 'judicial law-making' in which 'creative', 'liberal', 'bold' judges are regularly cast as heroes and 'timorous', 'literal-minded', 'blinkered' strict constructionists are presented, if not as villains, at least as obstructionists. We are anxious to avoid this kind of naïve romanticism which oversimplifies and obfuscates a number of complex questions.[48]

In this book we shall try to steer a course between naïve instrumentalism and dogmatic formalism, but we acknowledge a bias in favour of a view of rules as instruments for solving problems. However, in later chapters we shall develop a number of themes that will serve to bring out both the limitations of a simple model of rules as means to ends, and some of the main reasons that may be advanced to justify a formalist posture in some contexts. In particular we shall at least touch on the following general topics:

(*a*) adherence to rules as a value, especially when the scope of the rule is clear;

(*b*) the distinction between a rule and reasons for a rule, and the variety of relationships between rules and reasons for rules;

(*c*) the relationship between rule-makers and rule-interpreters and the fallacy involved in assuming that an interpreter will necessarily view his role as partner, agent or subject of the rule-maker;

(*d*) the error of assuming that a word can have only one meaning attached to it – the 'proper meaning fallacy' – and the core of sense in literal approaches to interpretation of rules in fixed verbal form;

(*e*) the relationship between 'lawyer-like' and 'legalistic' approaches to interpretation.

To conclude: instrumentalist and formalist views of rules are regularly found in opposition to each other. Whether an individual in a particular situation is likely to adopt an instrumentalist or a formalist posture or something in between may depend on a variety of factors, such as his personality, his conception of his role, his immediate purposes, other variables in the immediate situation and so on. The same person adopts one attitude to rules in one situation and a quite different one in another, without necessarily being inconsistent. It is accordingly dangerous to generalize about attitudes to rules, but it

[48] On 'legalism' in interpretation, see below, pp. 183-6.

does not follow from this that no patterns are to be discerned – for example, some judges have marked formalistic tendencies, while others do not.

11 Other perspectives on rules

A comprehensive theory of rules would have to give an account of such matters as the validity of rules, the value of adherence to rules, the relationship between rules and the exercise of power and authority, and variations in attitudes to rules; all of which ultimately affect interpretation, but which are generally separable from an analysis of it, and are beyond the scope of this book.

Thus questions of interpretation may be part of a process of determining the validity of a rule, for example in deciding whether a regulation is inconsistent with an Act of Parliament, or even in resolving the very profound issues raised when an interpreter is confronted with a rule that is apparently formally valid but which he regards as fundamentally immoral; but doubts about interpretation normally arise in respect of rules that are assumed to be valid. Similarly, not all interpreters feel themselves under an obligation to adhere to rules: the Bad Man, a revolutionary or a tax consultant may not like the result indicated by a seemingly clear rule, and one way of avoiding the result may be through 'interpretation'; in this situation the value of adherence to rules is directly relevant to an analysis of interpretation and it would be misleading to ignore it; but wider issues which are of central concern to, among others, political and moral philosophers, such as what is the basis of an obligation to obey or observe laws or other rules, or the circumstances under which disobedience (or other forms of non-observance) is morally justifiable, are too complex to be pursued here.

Many rules are instruments for the exercise of power. A friend with mild anarchist sympathies suggested that this book should have been called *How To Do Things to People*. His point was that problems are usually defined and rules are often used as weapons, sometimes as instruments of repression, by those who have power, and that we had too readily accepted official or other 'top-down' definitions of problems and perspectives on rules and had taken inadequate account of those who are subject to them. We do not accept this as fair criticism, for several reasons. Firstly, not all rules are instruments of control or repression; they can also serve to guide, to facilitate, to constitute activities, to confer benefits, to ensure fair procedures and even to protect those subject to them. Secondly, Johnny, the Bad Man, the Unhappy Interpreter and others represent 'bottom-up' perspectives that feature prominently in our analysis. Thirdly, in so far as rules are made, interpreted and enforced by governments and other powerful agencies, it is their definitions of the problems and their responses or 'solutions' which are typically the subject of interpretation; they are aspects of the situation confronting the interpreter. Even those who are fundamentally opposed to the structure of power in a given system may still need to become proficient at handling rules within it, like the authors of the passage from *The Bust Book*, quoted in Chapter 1. Nevertheless our friend's criticism may serve as a reminder of the significance of power as a dimension of rule-handling and of the danger of unthinkingly accepting 'official' definitions of problems and situations.[49] Analysis of power relations may sometimes have a direct bearing on diagnosis of particular instances of doubt in interpretation. However, in our view, questions about power relations are generally severable from questions about interpretation, and should be treated as conceptually distinct.

[49] For a criticism of the tendency of lawyers to transform and to define unduly narrowly many problems that are presented to them, see Z. Bankowski and G. Mungham, *Images of Law* (1976), pp. 32ff.

4 Interpretation and Application

'[T]he interpretive function may be said to be the central function of a legal system.' (Talcott Parsons)

In Chapter 1 we illustrated some points about Holmes's Bad Man by presenting a simplified model of Anglo-American criminal process in the form of a 'flowchart' entitled 'The Bad Man in Boston'. This chart depicted criminal process as a series of decisions and events, involving a variety of participants with different roles to perform at different stages in the process. When the Bad Man is viewed in the context of this process, it is easy to see that he is only one of a number of participants, and that his concern with predicting future events is only one aspect of a complex cluster of tasks that occur at different points in the process, in which other tasks are involved, such as detection, determining what has happened in the past, and sentencing.

In Chapter 2 we focused mainly, but not entirely, on the standpoint of the rule-maker, that is to say on actors who are in a position to introduce, change or adjust a rule in the process of tackling a problem. From now on our attention will shift to a different standpoint, to that of a person confronted with a pre-existing rule who is in one way or another puzzled about how to interpret or to apply it. We shall call this the standpoint of the puzzled interpreter[1]; the central question addressed in this and the next three chapters is, what are the main conditions that give rise to puzzlements about interpreting rules?

To answer this question, we shall first explore what might be meant

[1] The puzzled interpreter includes both those people who have power and authority to change the rule in the course of interpretation and those who do not. See below, p. 172.

by terms such as 'interpretation' and 'application' of rules, how interpretation relates to other rule-handling activities and *who* is typically called on to interpret rules, in what contexts and for what purposes. In the next chapter we shall consider some standard imperfections of rules and rule-statements that tend to give rise to difficulties. Then, in Chapter 6 we propose to adapt and broaden the flowchart in order to present some of the main conditions of doubt in the context of a more general model of typical processes involving the creation and handling of rules up to the point where a participant is called on to interpret a pre-existing rule.

1 Interpretation: what?

Theologians interpret the Bible; producers, actors and critics interpret plays; historians interpret past events; and lawyers, as part of their professional work, are regularly called on to interpret statutes, regulations, cases, contracts, wills and other types of document.

The word 'interpretation' has various shades of meaning; in respect of rules, 'to interpret' is generally used in the sense of 'to clarify the scope of' or 'to attribute a meaning to' a rule or part thereof. In some contexts it can be treated as being synonymous with such words as 'elucidate', 'explain' or 'construe', all of which suggest that the subject-matter has an established or settled meaning which it is the role of the interpreter to search for, discover and bring to light, as in a hunt for buried treasure. But often the word 'interpret' is used to suggest a wider role for the interpreter, one that involves an element of elaboration or choice or even of creation. Typically it calls for exercise of the elusive quality of 'judgment'. Thus the buried treasure analogy is inappropriate in the context of Olivier's interpretation of Hamlet, or Brendel's interpretation of a Beethoven sonata, or a Muslim theologian's 'free' interpretation of the Koran (*ijtihād*).[2] In such contexts it would seem odd to treat interpretation as solely a matter of explanation or discovery; the interpreter is working with material that offers a greater or lesser degree of scope for choice and intervention on his part.

[2] This term refers to the right of individual interpretation on points on which no general agreement has yet been reached; see H. Gibb, *Mohammedanism* (2nd edn, 1953), p. 66. On the relationship between statutory and literary interpretations, see K. Abraham in [1979] *Rutgers Law Review*, 676.

The scope for choice and creativity in interpretation depends in part on the malleability of the raw material to be interpreted, in part on the interpreter's situation and conception of his role, and in part on a variety of other factors. In this book we are concerned with the interpretation of rules, of formulations of rules, and in later chapters of sources of law, that is to say the raw materials of rules of law, such as cases and statutes. In rule-handling contexts it is common to contrast approaches to interpretation by such terms as 'strict', 'literal', 'liberal' and 'free'; such adjectives can be taken to represent various points along a continuum, which ranges from simple search and discovery of a clear settled meaning, to activity that is nearer to relatively unfettered creation of something new.

In theology a distinction is drawn between exegesis (the strict linguistic interpretation of biblical texts) and hermeneutics (the search for the spiritual truth behind the texts). The term 'hermeneutics' was introduced into social science, by Dilthey and others, and has become established in that context as characterizing the view that human actions are to be explained through the internal meanings they have for the actors themselves. It has been suggested that Hart, with his emphasis on the internal view of rules, adopts a hermeneutic approach to law.[3]

There is an affinity between hermeneutics in theology and social science and liberal approaches to interpretation in law, in that they all emphasize intention and purpose as central features of the search for 'meanings'. In the present context we shall from time to time extend the term 'interpretation' to include both determining 'the scope' of rules – the precise circumstances which they cover – and their 'meaning'. These are two separate, but closely related, ideas: a soldier or bureaucrat, for example, may have a precise conception of the scope of a rule or regulation and apply it 'woodenly' without understanding its meaning; in doubtful cases, the meaning of a rule (explicated in terms of intention, purpose and context) may be a valuable aid to determining its scope; but one may be interested in 'the meaning' of a relatively clear rule for other reasons, for example in order to criticize it or merely out of interest. The distinction is summed up in the statement: 'It is one thing to know the law, it is another to understand it.'

We are now sailing near some very deep waters. What is involved in 'understanding' a situation, a rule, or the law is a central, and

[3] D. N. MacCormick, *H. L. A. Hart* (1981), p. 29.

extremely problematic, question of social theory. In studying interpretation of rules we are here faced with a dilemma: we cannot reasonably expect to plumb the depths of fundamental philosophical questions about the nature of understanding social phenomena, but neither can we pretend that such questions are irrelevant. Our strategy will be to concentrate on the difficulties of determining the scope of particular rules – the narrow aspect of interpretation – for these are sufficiently complex to warrant special attention; but we shall argue that it is nearly always useful, and often necessary, to search for, probe, ascribe or construct the meaning of a rule (the nature of the enterprise is another matter of contention) in order to determine its scope and that this is an inherently problematic task.

This leads on to a second warning: it is tempting to treat exegesis and literal interpretation as superficial, and liberal and hermeneutic approaches as profound. After all, the words and the text look like the surface, while exploring meaning, purpose and context involves plunging into those murky depths; 'the letter killeth, but the spirit giveth life'. This is an attractive view, but it involves assumptions that are both superficial and dangerous. It assumes, for example, that textual analysis is *easier* than ascribing or constructing purposes; it assumes that liberal interpretation is always to be preferred to literal; it makes no allowance for purposeless, irrational or meaningless rules; and, most dangerous of all, it sets up rigorous analysis of texts *in opposition* to the exploration of meaning, intention, purpose and context. As we proceed we shall challenge each of these assumptions, without concealing our general preference for a liberal and contextual approach. The skilful interpreter pays attention to both text and context.

Interpretation of rules initially must be distinguished from fact-finding under a rule. Lawyers regularly distinguish between 'questions of fact', 'questions of law' and 'mixed questions of fact and law'. There is an extensive literature discussing these distinctions and the difficulties surrounding them.[4] Much the same considerations apply to the distinction between interpreting rules and finding facts under a rule in the broader context of rule-handling. It is not difficult to provide clear examples of the distinction. For instance, the question 'Was it Johnny who ate the jam?' is a question of fact, while the question of whether Johnny's use of the broom constituted an 'entry' is a question involving the scope of the word 'entry' and is a question of interpre-

[4] See, generally, R. Pound, *V Jurisprudence* (1959), pp. 545ff, and references there.

tation; if Johnny were to be discovered at the larder entrance, with the door open, and if there was some doubt whether his arm was extended over the threshold, then there would be a question of fact whether his arm was within the confines of the larder, and a question of interpretation as to whether, even if it were, that constituted an 'entry' within the meaning of the rule. In this case, if the issue were posed in the form of a single question: 'Did Johnny enter the larder?' this question would be one of mixed fact and interpretation.

In almost all of the examples used in this book, actual and hypothetical, the facts are not in dispute. This eliminates one difficulty which is central both to legal practice and to many problems in real life involving rules in non-legal contexts. For in many problem situations there is a doubt or dispute about what actually happened. Such questions fall outside the scope of this work, but that is not to suggest that they are unimportant.

It is useful to distinguish between the notions of *interpreting* and *applying* a rule, although in practice this distinction is often blurred. Strictly construed, 'interpretation' refers to clarification of the *general* scope or meaning of a rule. Sometimes interpretation of a rule may be called for without reference to any particular situation or event, in much the same way as a compiler of a dictionary sets out to elucidate the meanings of a word without necessarily referring to any particular occasion on which it has been used. Similarly, a statute may have an interpretation section which provides definitions or elucidations of words used in the statute. These give general guidance for future applications of the rule. However, doubts about interpretation very commonly arise with reference to some particular event or case that may allegedly have occurred or may be hypothetical. In such contexts it is not always easy to distinguish between interpreting a rule (general) and applying it to the facts of the case (particular).

It is important to realize why the distinction often breaks down: whenever a rule is applied to a particular case to produce a particular result, interpretation of the rule is involved; but how the rule was interpreted may be left unstated or implicit. If there was some doubt about what the result in a given case should be, it does not follow that it will be clear whether the doubt was one of interpretation or application or both; nor will it necessarily be the case that the doubt was resolved either by moving from the general to the particular or by moving from the particular to the general; moreover, terms like 'general' and 'particular' are relative matters, and some of the most difficult choices to be made in interpretation and application relate to choosing appropriate levels of generality.[5]

2 Rule-handling

Consider the following sets of verbs, all of which are commonly used with 'rule' or 'rules' as their object:

- (*a*) draft, make, amend, adapt, adopt;
- (*b*) promulgate, announce, communicate;
- (*c*) find, identify;
- (*d*) state, expound, elucidate, analyse, explain, restate, paraphrase;
- (*e*) interpret, apply, distinguish, invoke;
- (*f*) obey, conform to, observe, work to, stick to, act on;
- (*g*) disobey, break, flout, ignore, avoid, evade;
- (*h*) twist, stretch, manipulate, restrict, bend, emasculate, waive, make an exception to;
- (*i*) enforce, uphold, defend, criticize, attack, disapprove;
- (*j*) repeal, nullify, render nugatory, abrogate.

This list, which is far from exhaustive, gives some indication of the range of activities involved in 'handling rules'. The groupings suggest a rough and ready way of differentiating various types of rule-handling activities. A whole book could be devoted to elucidating and exploring the relationships between these and other connected activities. A comprehensive theory of rule-handling in general would need an elaborate apparatus of concepts and distinctions – consider, for example, some of the nuances involved in differentiating between 'disapproving' and 'criticizing' a rule, or between 'obeying' rules and 'working to rule'. For the purpose of indicating in a very general way the relationship between interpretation and other rule-handling activities, such refinements are unnecessary, although they may be illuminating. We shall confine ourselves to emphasizing three points at this stage.

First, some of the verbs in the list are clear instances of activity that is commonly understood as 'interpretation', while others, such as 'to bend', 'to twist' or 'to emasculate', are arguably on the borderline; in the context of rule-handling, in so far as such words imply some

---

[5] See Chapters 7 and 8 below.

determination of the scope of a rule, they are justifiably treated as examples of interpreting. Secondly, some of the activities are a *precondition* of interpretation, though independent of it. Generally speaking, interpreting a rule presupposes that it is in existence and has been identified and is probably accepted as valid.[6] One can find, announce or promulgate a rule without interpreting it, but it would usually be odd to say that one can interpret a rule that has yet to come into existence, or be discovered. It is not inconceivable that such a statement could make sense in some contexts; for example, there is an intimate relationship between interpreting a rule and drafting a rule in fixed verbal form. A draftsman will typically try to anticipate possible meanings that might be attached to his formulation and will try to use words in such a way as to exclude interpretations that will defeat the rule's objective(s). Of the draftsman, it may be said that he interprets in anticipation of the existence of the rule. And in respect of rules not in fixed verbal form, stating the rule in a particular way may be a way of interpreting it, or of disguising the fact that creative interpretation is taking place. For formulation of a rule typically involves an element of choice.

Thirdly, some of the verbs *presuppose* interpretation. Thus, 'to obey', 'to disobey', 'to flout', 'to work to', 'to evade' and 'to criticize' typically presuppose that some meaning has been attached to the rule by the actor, whether implicitly or explicitly. It is possible also to use terms like 'disobey' or 'comply with' to describe the behaviour of an actor who is unaware of the rule in question; but such a description itself presupposes some interpretation of the rule.

The point that interpretation may be presupposed by, or may form part of, some other activity deserves emphasis for two reasons: first it is because so many rule-handling activities presuppose or involve interpretation that we are justified in calling skill in interpretation a basic skill; and second, whenever interpretation forms part of another activity, that activity is part of the overall context that provides standards for judging the appropriateness of a particular interpretation. For example, an advocate may advance a particular interpretation of a statute as part of the task of trying to persuade a court to decide the outcome in favour of his client; this role and this objective

---

[6] Of course, questions concerning the validity of a rule may involve issues of interpretation: for example, determining whether a particular regulation is *intra vires* a statute or, in the United States, whether a legislative provision is constitutional may involve interpretation of several provisions. See further Chapter 10, below.

provide a basis for evaluating the appropriateness of his interpretation. Interpretation is typically an element in some more complex activity or task involving rule-handling; some rule-handling activities do not necessarily involve interpretation, for example promulgating or repealing a rule; but many rule-handling activities involve or presuppose interpretation and in such circumstances the task of interpretation needs to be viewed in the context of the activity as a whole.

3 Who interprets?

In considering the functions of rules and problem-solving by rules we were concerned mainly, but not exclusively, with questions about what difference it makes to have or not to have rules. These questions are particularly important for one kind of participant, the actor who is in a position to influence events by introducing, abolishing or otherwise changing a rule[7] – in other words the legislator or rule-maker, whether this be Parliament, a local authority, a university senate, the officers of a club drafting a constitution, a judge interpreting a statute, a parent or Auntie making up or 'remembering' 'house-rules' to suit her convenience during a tense game of croquet.

But this kind of option is not open to all participants. Many problems concerning rules arise in a situation where the rule exists; it is a datum confronting the actor. To him it may be an obstacle or a threat or a guide or an aid or a support or a tool or a puzzle or many other things. Depending on who he is and what he is trying to do, he may wish to conform with, obey, invoke, apply, rely on, wield, manipulate, avoid, evade, twist, flout or ignore it. He may use it as a guide to decision or to action, as an aid to prediction, as a reason justifying a particular course of action or in persuading someone else to come to a particular decision, as a bargaining counter and so on. In the almost infinite number of social processes and social transactions in which rules are an element, there is a corresponding variety of uses of rules. As we have seen, many of these activities presuppose or involve inter-

[7] Typically such a person has both authority and power to introduce, modify, change or abrogate the rule. But it is worth remembering that the effectiveness of a rule may be influenced by people who have no authority to change it – for instance, a police policy not to try to enforce a law relating to gambling or not to prosecute certain kinds of bigamists. See *R.* v. *Commissioner of Police, Ex Parte Blackburn* [1968] 2 W.L.R. 893, *C.E.G.B.* v. *Alderson* (*The Times*, 20 and 21 October 1981) and Kadish and Kadish, *Discretion to Disobey* (1973), pp. 72ff., cf. *Buckoke*, Chapter 1 above.

pretation. If I am a citizen trying to avoid paying unnecessary taxes, yet keeping within the confines of the law, I need to have some conception of what the relevant rules mean. Similarly, if I am setting out to disobey some law as a protest, I need to have a reasonably clear idea of the scope and meaning of the law in question, if only because I shall look rather foolish if it turns out that my purported act of 'disobedience' involved no infraction of any rule.

The distinction between persons in a position to change rules and persons confronted by a pre-existing rule is neither simple not clear-cut. It is a truism that rules often change in the process of interpretation by official interpreters, such as judges. The most obvious example is of rules not in fixed verbal form, such as case law based rules in the common law; but one could also say that the scope of the 'due process' clause in the Fifth Amendment to the Constitution of the United States has expanded over the years, even though the text has remained unchanged. In informal contexts, customary and other rules not in fixed verbal form emerge, evolve, change, fade away and die, often through the acts and choices of unidentified people who have no clearly recognized authority or power. But the distinction is none the less worth preserving, for there are many cases where a person confronted with a rule is not in a position to change it for the future. There is a difference, for example, between a judge who in coming up with an unlikely interpretation of a statute is said to have 'stretched' or 'extended' it, thereby creating a precedent for the future, and someone, perhaps a junior official, who may purport to 'bend a rule', but whose interpretation none the less leaves the rule unchanged afterwards.

It is not possible here to give a comprehensive account of all the different types of actor who need to interpret rules as part of performing some role or task. But it is useful to look at some of the standard situations in which questions of interpretation arise and to see the relationship of various kinds of actor to each other within the context of a single process. To start with a legal example: the sequence of decisions and other events that constitutes what we call 'criminal process' fall into a fairly standard pattern, as illustrated by the flow-chart of 'the Bad Man in Boston'. As that chart shows, in legal processes there are a great many types of participant, but the main ones apart from the parties themselves are usually taken to be the legislator (rule-maker), the counsellor (adviser), the advocate, the judge (or other decider) and the law-enforcer (who features at various points in the process from investigation and detection to execution of the decisions of the court). Each of these categories of participant can be defined in terms of notional *roles*: rule-making, advising, persuading, fact-finding, rule-interpreting and applying, justifying decisions, enforcing and so on.

These roles overlap; for instance, persuading a judge (advocacy) and justifying a decision on a point of law (as in a reported judgment in a case) both involve giving *valid reasons* of an almost identical kind – an advocate in persuading a judge often seeks to promote a result in a case by 'selling' a good justification. Similarly, the judge in particular may sometimes be involved in legislating, in the sense of making or changing rules. Not only do the roles of participants in legal processes overlap, sometimes in quite complex ways, but often a single participant may have more than one role – for instance, the same person may be involved in fact-finding, rule interpretation and application and determining the sanction, if any, to be imposed on the losing party.

This analysis of some of the basic tasks of rule-handling applies in non-legal as well as in legal contexts. Of course, in practice there will often be less differentiation between roles of participants in simpler kinds of social processes than there are in typical legal processes. This is one reason why there is an element of artificiality in talking of Mother as the 'legislator', law enforcer and prosecutor and of Father as the judge. But the tasks of rule-making, advocacy, fact-finding, rule-applying and so on are identifiable in the family situation, even if they are not clearly differentiated in the minds of the participants or if they are all allocated to one or two persons.

This differentiation of different roles and standpoints is a key element in the method of diagnosis of puzzlements about rules which is developed below. The model of criminal process illustrates some of the main roles involved in rule-handling in a highly structured process in which some of the participants have authority to change or modify the rules and some do not. But it does not give a comprehensive account of all the conceivable roles involved in rule-handling and all the possible uses of rules that may be encountered in different kinds of social interaction. For example, rules may be invoked in bargaining as arguments, as we saw in the Arusha examples,[8] or as threats, for instance in crude blackmail or more subtle kinds of pressuring; they are often invoked as justifications for past or future behaviour; similarly,

[8] See Chapter 1 above.

we shall come across situations where the rule-maker may be embarrassed or frustrated or defeated in an argument by having his own rule quoted against him, an example of being 'hoist with one's own petard'. To analyse such examples it is often useful to identify the standpoint and role of the relevant participants, and to explain their use of one or more rules in the particular context in terms of who they are, what their situation is and what they are trying to do.

Some of these points can be illustrated briefly by returning to the *Case of the Legalistic Child*. Assume that Mother has reported the broom-handle episode to Father and he has decided to hold a hearing with Mother as the prosecutor, Johnny conducting his own defence and himself in the role of impartial adjudicator.

From Johnny's standpoint, his perception and evaluation of the situation may be different from Mother's, but the situation is defined to some extent by the existence of the rule, which provides an important criterion for determining what facts or allegations are relevant or irrelevant. Johnny's role is also dictated largely by the context; if his primary object is to avoid punishment (there might of course be others), he has a number of tactical choices open to him. Thus, he may dispute the facts, advance one or more interpretations of 'enter' consistent with his having committed no offence, or admit that an offence has been committed but plead in mitigation. These are the obvious lawyer-like moves.[9] But if he is a good advocate, he will try to anticipate the likely response of the 'court' to any particular argument and this may lead him to choose to adopt some quite different tactic, such as persuading his Father to treat the whole episode as a joke. Johnny in the role of advocate may have a problem with regard to what tactics to adopt, but his role and aims are clear: he has to persuade Father to reach an acceptable result.

Father's position on the other hand is quite different. One reason for this is that the standpoint of the 'impartial adjudicator' is less well defined. There are a number of elements in the situation that might be relevant to diagnosis of Father's problem: for example, his loyalty to Mother and his concern to uphold her authority; his own decree, which might be viewed as eccentric, that discipline in the family

---

[9] Cf. the familiar tale in *Punch* of the lawyer's son who was charged with having broken the schoolroom window: 'In the first place, sir, the schoolroom has no window; in the second place, the schoolroom window is not broken; in the third place, if it is broken, I did not do it; in the fourth place it was an accident.' Cited by Glanville Williams in *Learning the Law* (9th edn, 1973), p. 21.

should operate in accordance with the Rule of Law; his concern to be fair to Johnny; perhaps a feeling that Johnny's behaviour is reprehensible but that Mother has mishandled the situation by inept rule-making and possibly also by deciding to 'prosecute' in an inappropriate case; and he may wish to take into account the likely effect on Johnny and on relations within the family of any action that he decides on in this situation.

In diagnosing his problem and deciding how to act, Father may place considerable emphasis on some of the above factors and may give little or no weight to others, and his choices are likely to be influenced, *inter alia*, by his conception of his role. To take two extreme examples: if he considers his role to be essentially that of the 'impartial judge', he might define the problem very narrowly as being concerned solely with the interpretation of Mother's rule, and he might deliver judgment along the following lines: 'The only question for determination in this case is: did Johnny enter the larder? Since neither Johnny's body, nor any part of it, crossed the threshold of the larder, he is not guilty under the rule. I leave open the question whether, if only part of his person, such as a hand, had crossed the threshold, this would have constituted an entry.'

On the other hand, if Father chooses to cast himself in the role of 'the wise Father', he might well see this as an opportunity for trying to change Johnny's relationship with his Mother or for teaching him some general lessons about relationships within the family or about rule-handling and advocacy. Here Father would have to emphasize a number of elements in this situation in addition to the rule and would define the problem much more broadly than he would if he considered his role to be that of impartial adjudicator. Thus, what is an appropriate method of approach for a puzzled interpreter depends to a large extent upon his standpoint and his conception of his role; and in the archetypal situation of judge or impartial adjudicator, there is typically a lack of precise definition of that role, which creates a corresponding lack of precision about what constitutes the best way to proceed. Thus, as with problem-solving, clarification of standpoint and role is an important preliminary to interpretation.

One of the weaknesses of many traditional accounts of legal interpretation is that they concentrate, explicitly or implicitly, on a single standpoint – typically that of the impartial judge or of a neutral expositor. This is inadequate for two main reasons. First, such allegedly 'neutral' or 'impartial' roles are notoriously problematic. An extraordinary amount of attention has been paid in jurisprudence to questions about the proper role of judges. Do they and should they make law or only apply it? Do they make policy? How far can a judge be impartial in doubtful cases? All too often doubts about the proper role of judges have been conflated with puzzlements about interpretation. We shall suggest later that discussions of one of the central problems of interpreting cases – the traditional problem of determining the *ratio decidendi* – have been made unnecessarily complicated because puzzlements about role have been confused with puzzlements about interpreting precedents.[10] If one looks at what is involved in interpreting a prior case from a standpoint in which the role is relatively clear, for example that of an advocate, it is very much easier to give an account of the matter because doubts about role and doubts about interpretation are then clearly differentiated.

An even more important objection to the traditional concentration on the standpoints of judges and expositors is that little or nothing is said about what constitutes appropriate interpretation by other actors and what difficulties confront them. This leads to a radical impoverishment of most discussions of legal interpretation, sometimes to the point that they are seriously misleading. Sir Rupert Cross in his interesting work on *Statutory Interpretation* laid great stress on the fact that 'the vast majority of statutes never come before the courts for interpretation'[11]; but he then proceeded to an analysis which is seemingly based on the assumption that those who draft or interpret such statutes behave as if they anticipate that they will be interpreted judicially. This is, at best, a tremendous oversimplification. Civil servants, the police, businessmen, accountants, insurance claim adjustors, practising lawyers and ordinary citizens may all be concerned to predict or to speculate about likely judicial interpretations of particular rules – and past or potential future, authoritative rulings have special significance from the internal point of view of anyone who wishes to adhere to a rule – but in the course of conducting their affairs such people inevitably take many other factors into account, some of which are intimately tied up with their respective standpoints and roles.

In order to hammer this point home, let us postulate three characters: a cautious solicitor, an adventurous barrister and an unhappy interpreter. When a client, whether good citizen or Bad Man, consults

---

[10] See below, Chapter 8.

[11] R. Cross, *Statutory Interpretation* (1976), p. 1.

a solicitor (or other professional adviser) he may pose the question: 'If I do X, what will happen to me?' He is in effect asking his adviser to predict some of the consequences of his proposed course of action. Suppose that the solicitor feels that there is some doubt about the scope of some potentially relevant rule, which will form part of the basis for his advice. What would be an appropriate interpretation in the circumstances? He may, of course, explain his doubts to his client, but if pressed for a definite answer the cautious solicitor will probably place a *pessimistic* interpretation on the rule – he will in a sense interpret against his client in order to allow a margin of error. When drafting documents most solicitors typically indulge in such pessimistic or cautious interpretations, for sound reasons – it is part of their job to anticipate contingencies, including adverse interpretations. In our hypothetical situation it would be a rather narrow and unhelpful solicitor who would base his advice solely on a prediction of how the applicable substantive law would be interpreted in the courts, especially if the rule is part of one of Cross's 'vast majority' which are rarely if ever litigated in practice.

Suppose then that the client, in spite of the cautious solicitor's advice, does X, and is unfortunate enough to be sued or prosecuted as a result. Suppose that he decides to contest the case on a point of law and the adventurous barrister is briefed to represent him: how will the latter interpret the applicable rule(s)? Clearly it would be inappropriate in preparing his argument to adopt the solicitor's interpretation. Instead he may behave as if he is optimistic and consider possible interpretations that would produce a result in his client's interests and, if this is a test case, in the interests of other persons in similar situations. In actually arguing the point in court he may concentrate on the most plausible of several possible interpretations, any one of which would be consistent with winning. Thus in respect of the same act a client's legal representatives may give different interpretations of a doubtful rule – one pessimistic, the other optimistic – and *they will both be right* given their respective roles and situations. This, in simplified form, is part of the daily experience of legal practice. It is obvious, but it is forgotten or glossed over by nearly all traditional accounts of legal interpretation.

Finally, let us consider another fictitious character whom we shall call the unhappy interpreter. This is a person who is confronted by a rule which, at least at first sight, seems to be in conflict with what he wants or what he believes to be right. If we revert for a moment to the mechanistic model of decision-making, then to say that an interpreter has a doubt in the particular case would be to say that he was in doubt about the scope of the rule, or its application to the facts, or both, so that the result was in doubt. However, such a model is too simple as a description of most decision-making processes, and it is not uncommon for interpreters to be in doubt about the result for some reason unconnected with either of the premises. The paradigm case of the puzzled interpreter who, though he wishes to conform to the rule, is genuinely puzzled about its scope or application may be usefully contrasted with that of the interpreter who is confronted with a rule about whose scope he has little or no doubt, but who, *for that reason*, is faced with a problem. There are various reasons why an interpreter in this situation may be dissatisfied: he may be in general disagreement with the policy behind the rule; he may sympathize with the policy but dislike the particular rule as an instrument for furthering it; he may be in general sympathy with both rule and policy, but for some other reason wish to avoid the result that would be produced by a straightforward application of the rule in this class of case; or there may be some feature of the particular case that leads him to desire a result other than that suggested by the most obvious interpretation of the rule. Put simply, he wants something despite the rule.

The unhappy interpreter's problem then is that, although the scope of the rule may be clear, at least on the surface, it is an obstacle to his securing the result he desires. Faced with this type of situation, an interpreter may be in a position to secure the desired result by some means other than interpretation, for example by flouting, waiving or avoiding the rule; but where he is not, the temptation to interpret the rule by bending, stretching or straining it, frequently arises. We should not be lured by the emotive associations of such terms as 'manipulative' or 'legalistic' into thinking that such activities are indulged in only by villains. Portia's interpretation of Shylock's contract with Antonio was a classic example of legalistic interpretation; Portia is generally considered to be a heroine, and her objectives honourable; yet the means she used is generally regarded as a clear example of 'legalism'.[12]

In these situations a conflict may arise between the wish to manipulate a clear rule in order to achieve the desired result, and the value of adherence to rules; faced with this conflict the unhappy interpreter may choose to uphold a straightforward interpretation of the rule.

[12] See above, p. 6.

This is often the case where the unhappy interpreter is a judge. The law reports abound with judicial regrets that testify to the acute nature of this conflict; though the value of adherence to the rule and the ultimate obtaining of a change may both be secured by perverse interpretation, as Coleridge J. pointed out: 'Perhaps the most efficacious mode of procuring good laws, certainly the only one allowable to a Court of Justice, is to act fully up to the spirit and language of bad ones, and to let their inconvenience be fully felt by giving them full effect.'[13]

The possible manipulation of the rule does not exhaust the unhappy interpreter's alternatives in dealing with his problem. Words like 'bend', 'stretch' and 'strain' suggest some settled or established meaning that is being altered or departed from in the course of interpretation. But it is important to emphasize that doubt is a relative matter. It is not uncommon in both legal and non-legal contexts for some participants to express doubts about the interpretation or application of a rule, while others maintain that it is clear. Accordingly, the unhappy interpreter may be able to pave the way for a less obvious interpretation, by creating or establishing a doubt that then needs to be resolved. It may be the job of an advocate or other interpreter to engineer doubts in order to achieve his objective. Indeed, some, like the fictional judge in Fuller's *The Case of the Speluncean Explorers*, may positively relish doing so:

My brother Foster's penchant for finding holes in statutes reminds one of the story told by an ancient author about the man who ate a pair of shoes. Asked how he liked them, he replied that the part he liked best was the holes. That is the way my brother feels about statutes; the more holes they have in them the better he likes them. In short he doesn't like statutes.[14]

Doubt and unhappiness are both relative matters. There is no sharp line to be drawn between genuine puzzlement about the scope and meaning of a rule, exploiting possible ambiguities or uncertainties and setting out deliberately to sow the seeds of doubt about what previously was assumed to be clear. In this context we need not take the notion of unhappiness too seriously: the trade unionist working to rule, Johnny sparring with his parents and the advocate involved in

[13] *Per* Coleridge J. in *Pocock* v. *Pickering* (1852) 18 Q.B. 789, 798. For some more complex examples, see Douglas Hay's account of eighteenth-century judges administering the death penalty, in D. Hay *et al.*, *Albion's Fatal Tree* (1975), especially pp. 29 and 33.

[14] L. Fuller, 'The Case of the Speluncean Explorers', 62 *Harvard Law Review* (1949), 616, 634.

the cut and thrust of the adversary process may or may not be enjoying themselves in pursuing their objectives through exploiting available leeways. What is clear is that some kind of conflict is involved, and the unhappy interpreter at least seems to be fighting against the spirit, the purpose or the intention, or what has hitherto been assumed to be the settled meaning of the rule. This leads on to questions about the relationship betweem rule-makers and rule-interpreters.

4 Rule-makers and rule-interpreters

With all its subtleties, the problem of interpretation occupies a sensitive central position in the internal morality of the law. It reveals as no other problem can, the co-operative nature of the task of maintaining legality. If the interpreting agent is to preserve a sense of useful mission, the legislature must not impose on him senseless tasks. If the legislative draftsman is to discharge his responsibilities he, in turn, must be able to anticipate rational and relatively stable modes of interpretation. This reciprocal dependence permeates in less immediately obvious ways the whole legal order. No single concentration of intelligence, insight and good will, however strategically located, can insure the success of the enterprise of subjecting human conduct to the governance of rules.[15]

This passage is a relatively sophisticated example of the view that the relationship between rule-maker and interpreter is essentially one of *co-operation*. Thus judges are spoken of as agents or junior partners of rule-makers; the role of officials is to carry out, enforce, apply or uphold the will of the legislator. While this represents a conception of the interpreter's role that would, for example, be subscribed to by many official interpreters, it is important to recognize that co-operation is not the only possible relationship between rule-makers and interpreters. When the interpreter is not an official, the relationship can range from complete co-operation to outright hostility. Antonio in *The Merchant of Venice* reminds us that the 'devil can cite Scripture for his purpose';[16] Johnny is hardly in a co-operative relationship with Mother, nor is this a realistic way of describing the attitude of the Bad Man, a revolutionary or a tax consultant.

The attitudes of potential interpreters may have important implications for the style of drafting of rules in fixed verbal form. Karl Llewellyn, who was prepared to rely on the good faith of most

---

[15] L. Fuller, *The Morality of Law* (1969), p. 91.
[16] W. Shakespeare, *The Merchant of Venice*, Act I, scene 3.

businessmen and the good sense of most judges, justified the 'open' style
of drafting of the Uniform Commercial Code in the following terms:
'Technical language and complex statement cannot be wholly
avoided. But they can be reduced to a minimum. The essential pre-
supposition of so reducing them is faith in the courts to give reasonable
effect to reasonable intention of language.'[17] Contrast this statement
with the task of the draftsman of a revenue statute: '[I]t is not enough
to attain to a degree of precision which a person reading [the statute]
in good faith can understand; but it is necessary to attain if possible to
a degree of precision which a person reading in bad faith cannot
misunderstand. It is all the better if he cannot pretend to misunderstand it.'[18]

Co-operation between rule-makers and officials is no doubt a more
natural relationship, but it cannot be taken for granted. At the general
level of political theory the relationship between the legislature and
other branches of government is not necessarily to be viewed as that
of partnership in a single joint enterprise. The notion of checks and
balances, the doctrine of judicial review, the concept of judges as
watchdogs are all reminders that such a monolithic view of a polity is
too simple. Legal history can provide many examples of judges acting
in ways that suggested that their role was to frustrate rather than to
further the will of the legislature. Fuller's statement of the ideal is not
one that is universally accepted even as an ideal, still less as a realistic
description.

Moreover, even where an official interpreter sees his role to be
essentially one of co-operation, he may in particular instances be faced
with difficult choices as to how to perform that role. A rule may have
proved to have been an imperfect instrument of its policy; it may have
been overtaken by social change, technological innovation or a shift
in public opinion; the way in which the rule-maker actually behaved
at the time of the making of the instrument and the way he might have
been expected to behave in the circumstances actually confronting a
court at a later date are not necessarily identical. Judges placed in this
kind of situation do not respond in a uniform fashion: some try to
mitigate the situation, as in *Buckoke*; some see their role as being to
interpret and apply the statute without regard for the supervening
events; others may go even further and seek to provoke legis-

---

[17] Memorandum on the Uniform Commercial Code (1940), quoted in W. Twining,
Karl Llewellyn and the Realist Movement (1973), p. 526.
[18] *Per* Stephen J. in *Re Castioni* [1891] 1 Q.B. 149, 167.

lative action by underlining the absurdity of the existing provision, as did Darling J. when confronted with s. 3 of the Sunday Observance Act 1679: 'In my opinion the best way to attain that object is to construe it strictly, in the way the Puritans who procured it would have construed it; if that is done it will very soon be repealed.'[19]

These examples should be sufficient to show that the relationship of rule-makers and interpreters is a complex one and that the co-operative model, however attractive, is an over-simplification.

5 Legalism

We have already encountered several examples of interpretation or other behaviour that might be labelled 'legalistic' and we shall come across more in later chapters. In the nursery example, Johnny is called 'the legalistic child', but it might also be said that Father's notion of ordering the family according to 'the Rule of Law' or of holding formal hearings, and Mother's insistence on trying to enforce her rules in trivial or doubtful cases are also 'legalistic'. Portia, tax consultants, the unhappy interpreter, working to rule and 'Catch 22' provide further standard instances. 'Literal' interpretation by judges and others is also sometimes referred to in such terms as 'literalistic', 'legalistic' or 'formalistic'.

Such concepts are elusive and require quite elaborate elucidation. Here we shall merely make a few elementary observations on different kinds of legalism, on the emotive associations of the term, and on some motives and functions of legalistic behaviour.

The adjective 'legalistic' is variously applied to behaviour, to attitudes, to persons, to judicial styles, and even to whole legal systems and cultures. In respect of behaviour and attitudes, it is important to distinguish between at least three primary uses, which reflect different standpoints: liking to have lots of rules or complex formal procedures; insisting on adhering closely to existing rules, for instance by enforcing clear, but petty, infractions; and interpreting rules in a literal, strict or rigid way. Each of these is closely associated with a different standpoint or role: thus the first relates to *rule-making*, the second to *enforcement* or *observance*; and the third to *interpretation*. There is no necessary correlation between 'legalistic' behaviour in respect of each standpoint. The same person may favour having a lot of rules, but be prepared to waive or ignore existing rules in certain circumstances and he may

[19] *Per* Darling J. in *Slater* v. *Evans* [1916] 2 K.B. 403, 405.

generally favour either liberal or literal interpretation, without being inconsistent. Similarly a rule-maker may oppose the creation of formal rules and procedures *because* he believes that, once created, they should or will be rigorously enforced or strictly interpreted. For example, a university teacher may quite consistently oppose the drawing-up of very detailed regulations governing marking and classifying examination scripts, because if such regulations exist he will feel bound to apply them strictly or to interpret them in a literal or rigid fashion. Similarly a trade unionist may increase the impact of a work-to-rule by interpreting some rules very broadly or liberally and then insisting on adhering rigidly to them as interpreted, even though he may dislike or disapprove of their content. Thus, the prolific rule-maker, the stickler for rules and the strict or literal interpreter have different characteristics, which may or may not coincide in the same person.

In regard to interpretation of existing rules, some further differentiations are required. Whereas the unhappy interpreter may see some rule (if interpreted in a particular way) as an *obstacle* to achieving his particular ends, a judge or administrator may adopt a literal or strict interpretation for different reasons, for example in order to avoid being seen to be 'making rules' or to advance (or frustrate) the intention of the rule-maker. As we shall see later, it is sometimes the case that 'creative' or 'liberal' judges, such as Lord Denning or Lord Atkin, are driven to resort to 'legalistic' interpretation in order to get rid of prior adverse precedents, for it is the bold or innovative judge rather than his more cautious colleague who tends to be troubled by such precedents.[20]

These elementary observations should at least be enough to expose two common assumptions as being at best dubious and possibly fallacious: *viz.* the idea that 'legalism' is necessarily bad and the idea that legalistic behaviour is to be explained solely or even mainly in terms of individual psychology.

In many contexts terms like 'legalism' and 'formalism' are emotive, carrying with them the suggestion of disapproval. For example, lawyers sometimes contrast 'lawyerlike' and 'legalistic' behaviour, perhaps implying that the former is 'professional' and involves good judgment, and that the latter is dishonest, narrow-minded or immature. However, choosing to have few or many rules, to stick closely to existing rules or to ignore, waive or only partially enforce them, to interpret them broadly or narrowly, strictly or liberally are not choices

[20] See below, Chapter 8.

which can sensibly be evaluated generally, *in abstracto*. To put the matter very briefly: the functions and dysfunctions of formalism (including legalism as one of its manifestations) are very varied, especially if one includes making, enforcing, observing and interpreting rules within its ambit. Literal interpretation may be prompted by a desire to do justice in a particular case or to reveal the absurdity of a particular rule, or by a policy of judicial restraint or in order to give effect to some presumption – for example, the presumption of innocence or a presumption in favour of preserving existing property rights. Legalistic interpretation, in this sense, is not in itself either good or bad.

A second doubtful assumption is that legalistic behaviour is primarily a function of individual psychology, to be explained in terms of the personality and attitudes of people as individuals. We have ourselves talked of 'the legalistic child', of formal-style judges, of literalists and rigorists and sticklers for rules. No doubt individuals do exhibit tendencies or patterns of behaviour which can be explained, at least partly, in terms of psychological variables. It should, however, be clear from what has been said that such behaviour might also plausibly be explained in terms of a variety of other factors, such as context, role and immediate purpose. Thus the same judge may adopt a literal approach to one statute and a liberal approach to another for reasons which have little or nothing to do with his personality or general attitudes. Many judges do just this. The moral is that one should be wary of over-generalizing about the behaviour of individual interpreters from a limited number of examples.

It is not possible here to explore in detail or in depth the nature, forms and functions of formalism and legalism. It is an important and neglected subject. It may help to give an intimation of one aspect of its wider significance by ending with a quotation from Douglas Hay's interpretation of one example of legalism:

(M)ost penal statutes were interpreted by the judges in an extremely narrow and formalistic fashion. In part this was based on seventeenth-century practice, but as more capital statutes were passed in the eighteenth century the bench reacted with an increasingly narrow interpretation. Many prosecutions founded on excellent evidence and conducted at considerable expense failed on minor errors of form in the indictment.... If a name or date was incorrect, or if the accused was described as a 'farmer' rather than the approved term 'yeoman', the prosecution could fail. The courts held that such defects were conclusive, and gentlemen attending trials as spectators sometimes stood up in court and brought errors to the attention of the judge. These formalisms in the criminal law seemed ridiculous to contemporary critics, and to many later historians. Their argument was (and is) that the criminal law, to be effective, must be known and determinate, instead of capricious and obscure. Prosecutors resented the waste of their time and money lost on a technicality; thieves were said to mock courts which allowed them to escape through so many verbal loopholes. But it seems likely that the mass of Englishmen drew other conclusions from the practice. The punctilious attention to forms, the dispassionate and legalistic exchanges between counsel and the judge, argued that those administering and using the laws submitted to its rules. The law thereby became something more than the creature of a ruling class – it became a power with its own claims, higher than those of prosecutor, lawyers, and even the great scarlet-robed assize judge himself. To them, too, of course, the law was The Law. The fact that they reified it, that they shut their eyes to its daily enactment in Parliament by men of their own class, heightened the illusion. When the ruling class acquitted men on technicalities they helped instil a belief in the disembodied justice of the law in the minds of all who watched. In short, its very inefficiency, its absurd formalism, was part of its strength as ideology.[21]

6 Leeways for interpretation and application

In a mechanistic model of decision-making the relationship between rule, facts and results can be expressed in the form of a syllogism. The adjudicator discovers and states the rule as the major premise, he discovers and states the material facts as the minor premise, and the result follows as a necessary conclusion. A question of interpretation arises when the interpreter has a *choice* either as to the scope of the major premise or as to how it is to be applied to the facts (which are given). How is it possible for such questions to arise? A brief answer, which will be elaborated in due course, is as follows.

First, rule-makers often deliberately confer a discretion on rule-interpreters, such as judges or civil servants, to determine borderline or otherwise difficult cases; or they may establish a general policy but make a deliberately vague instrument of the policy and leave the working out of detail to the point of application.

Secondly, rule-makers may fail to foresee all possible contingencies, with the result that doubts may arise as to whether the rule was intended to apply in circumstances that the rule-maker seems not to have anticipated; and, closely related to this, rule-makers' aims are prone to vagueness and questions may arise about the precise effect that might have been intended in a particular case.

[21] D. Hay *et al.*, op. cit., p. 33.

Thirdly, in respect of rules in fixed verbal form, even if the draftsman wishes to anticipate every contingency, language is too imprecise and malleable an instrument to foreclose every possibility.

Fourthly, in the case of rules not in fixed verbal form, additional uncertainties may arise at the stage of formulation of the rule (if that stage is ever reached) and because there may be no generally agreed starting point for discussion about its scope and application.

Fifthly, there is the factor of consistency. A major task of interpretation is reconciling rules (and sources of rules, such as cases), for typically a single rule belongs to some larger agglomeration or system. How far internal logical consistency within a body of rules should be treated as one, or even *the*, cardinal value for interpreters is, as we have seen, one of the perennial questions of jurisprudence.[22] The relevant point is that, in so far as consistency is a value, it forms a basis both for creating problems for interpreters and for helping to resolve them. A doubt about interpretation may be resolved by looking to other rules, but doubts about interpretation of a seemingly straightforward and clear rule can be *raised* by pointing to another rule that is arguably inconsistent with it.

Deliberate delegation of discretion, ignorance of fact, indeterminacy of aim, the limitations of language, the fluidity of rules not in fixed verbal form, conflicts between the value of internal consistency within a system and other values, and divergencies of aim or role or situation between the rule-maker and the interpreter, are merely some of the most common conditions that give rise to problems of interpretation and application of rules. Later we shall elaborate and expand this list. At this point it is worth emphasizing that while factors such as these create leeways for interpretation, the leeways are not limitless. The puzzled or unhappy interpreter is presented with some choice, but the range of possible or plausible or otherwise appropriate interpretations is in practice subject to constraints. The nature and force of such constraints will vary from context to context. For example in discussing the leeways open to advocates and judges in American state appellate courts, Karl Llewellyn identified fourteen 'major steadying factors'[23] which tended to reduce doubts and limit the range of choice in practice, such as the mental conditioning of lawyers, the prior identification and sharpening of the issues, accepted ways of handling authoritative sources of law and of presenting arguments in

---

[22] See pp. 145ff. above and Chapter 7 below.
[23] K. N. Llewellyn, *The Common Law Tradition* (1960), esp. pp. 19ff.

court, and the constraints of group decision-making and of publicity. His list could no doubt be greatly extended. Such 'steadying factors' vary according to the context and the participants involved. Typically they operate as a counterweight to conditions which occasion or give opportunities for doubts and disagreement. In a given context it is often a matter of delicate judgment to determine the extent and the limits of choice in interpretation.

5 Imperfect Rules

Someone asked to describe his model of a technically perfect rule might reply: A rule is perfect if (*a*) it has a single clear and acceptable aim; (*b*) it is so clearly and precisely expressed that it leaves no room for doubt about its application in any possible case, and no loopholes for those who might wish to escape its effects; (*c*) its scope is co-extensive with its purpose; and (*d*) it is certain to achieve its purpose without undesirable side-effects.

In a famous passage in *The Concept of Law*, Hart outlined some of the reasons why this is not only unattainable, but also undesirable as a model for all legal rules:

Whichever device, precedent or legislation, is chosen for the communication of standards of behaviour, these, however smoothly they work over the great mass of ordinary cases, will, at some point where their application is in question, prove indeterminate; they will have what has been termed an *open texture*. So far we have presented this, in the case of legislation, as a general feature of human language; uncertainty at the borderline is the price to be paid for the use of general classifying terms in any form of communication concerning matters of fact. Natural languages like English are when so used irreducibly open textured. It is, however, important to appreciate why, apart from this dependence on language as it actually is, with its characteristics of open texture, we should not cherish, even as an ideal, the conception of a rule so detailed that the question whether it applied or not to a particular case was always settled in advance, and never involved, at the point of actual application, a fresh choice between open alternatives. Put shortly, the reason is that the necessity for such choice is thrust upon us because we are men, not gods. It is a feature of the human predicament (and so of the legislative one) that we labour under two connected handicaps whenever we seek to regulate, unambiguously and in advance, some sphere of conduct by means of general standards to be used without further official direction on particular occasions. The first handicap is our relative ignorance of fact: the second is our relative indeterminacy of aim. If the world in which we live were characterised only by a finite number of features, and these together with all the modes in which they could combine were known to us, then provision could be made in advance for every possibility. We could make rules, the application of which to particular cases never called for a further choice. Everything could be known, and for everything, since it could be known, something could be done and specified in advance by rule. This would be a world fit for 'mechanical' jurisprudence.[1]

In the last chapter we set out to give an account of what is meant by interpreting, how it is related to other rule-handling activities and who are typically the actors in the process of interpretation. We now propose to look a little more closely at some of the most important conditions of doubt, in the form of a commentary on, and elaboration of, this quotation. We are in general agreement with Hart's view that a system of rules that left no room for choice in interpretation is neither feasible nor desirable, but in the course of the argument we shall suggest that the reasons for this are rather more complex than this passage suggests. We shall consider the argument under five heads:

(1) the factual context of rules;
(2) intentions, reasons and purposes;
(3) the role of purposes and other reasons in interpretation;
(4) rules and language;
(5) the open texture of rules.

1 The factual context of rules

Hart suggests that the first handicap of a human rule-maker who wishes to regulate conduct 'unambiguously and in advance' is 'our relative ignorance of fact'. Except in regard to closed systems, such as noughts and crosses, few rule-makers can anticipate all the possible combinations of circumstance to which their rules might be applicable, and so they cannot anticipate all the contingencies that might arise to be determined. But the relationship of good rule-making to the world of fact is very much more complicated than that. The omniscient rule-maker would need to know not merely all the possible permutations and combinations of fact-situations that might fall

[1] H. L. A. Hart, *The Concept of Law* (1961), pp. 124-5.

within the scope of the rule; if his purpose in introducing the rule is to influence certain kinds of behaviour in a particular way, he needs to have knowledge of the situation he is trying to influence, the likely effects any particular rule or group of rules will have on the situation and how the situation is likely to develop. Rule-makers in the role of problem-solvers are not merely concerned with anticipating possibilities, they are also concerned to influence events in changing situations. Actual rule-makers are more or less well informed about the situation confronting them, more or less well placed to foretell how the overall situation will change over time, and more or less well placed to predict the likely consequences of introducing a particular measure.

There is a further dimension to the factual context of rule-making. Every event in life is unique and infinitely complex. Rules are blunt instruments which lump together fact-situations into classes to be treated alike; they generalize and they simplify. Every decision to resort to rules involves a decision to treat certain differences as immaterial and to treat complex events as if they were simple. Perhaps the most difficult problems facing rule-makers concern choices as to the level of generality at which to frame the rule, with what degree of precision and with what provision for exceptions: at one extreme is the very precisely worded, very general, purportedly absolute rule which makes few or no concessions to the complexity and particularity of actual events; at the other extreme is the instrument that is so vague and so open-ended as to raise doubts as to whether it can be appropriately referred to as a 'rule' at all.

Thus the perfect rule-maker needs more than omniscience, in the sense of a complete knowledge of existing circumstances and of all possible combinations of factual circumstances; he also needs a capacity accurately to predict consequences and future, causally unconnected, developments, and an infallible judgment about what constitutes an appropriate level of generality in a given context. While the development of an empirical social science of law may help understanding of the present and the past and, to some extent, prediction of future likelihoods, judgments about levels of generality inevitably involve other considerations, to which we now turn.

2 Intentions, reasons and purposes

In the passage quoted above, Hart refers to 'our relative indeterminacy of aim' as one of the features of the human predicament that handicaps attempts to regulate conduct in advance by means of rules. This brings us to the important topic of the role of intentions, aims, purposes and other reasons in the interpretation of rules. A good deal of confusion attends these notions both in the literature and in practice, perhaps for two main reasons: first, terms like 'legislative intent', 'the aim of the rule', 'the purpose of the statute' and 'the reason of/for the rule' (*ratio legis*) are commonly used to cover a wide range of situations and factors that need to be differentiated. There is a tendency to use such terms too simply or too confidently or in ways which take too much for granted. In this area a precise and discriminating vocabulary is especially important. Secondly, the subject is complex. The mental processes of rule-makers are varied and often complicated; they may be difficult to discover or fathom; there is room for disagreement about how much weight should be given to the intentions, purposes and reasons of rule-makers, when they are clear, as against other factors; and, as we shall see, terms like intention and aim are often *attributed* or *ascribed* to rules even when there is no determinate or ascertainable rule-maker.

In order to pick our way through some of these complexities we shall postulate a seemingly simple model of rationalistic rule-making and interpretation, and explore first some potential complications within it and then further difficulties arising through deviations from the model. Let us, therefore, start with the following situation: some years ago a single rule-maker, Lionel (L), made a rule. L was an almost ideal candidate for the job: he was intelligent, well-informed, honest, rational and a skilled draftsman. Furthermore he gave his full attention to the task and he consistently sought to promote values which were generally accepted in the relevant community. He made rules only after he had been through a careful and rational procedure for problem-solving. Suppose that we adopt the standpoint of a co-operative interpreter (C) confronted, shortly after L's death, by one of L's rules made five years previously. C is puzzled by a point of interpretation of this rule and he wishes to interpret it in accordance with L's intentions, purposes and reasons. In order to do this, C sets out to ascertain what these were or, failing that, to try to reconstruct as best he can what they would have been had L addressed himself to the problem.

Even in this very simple situation, some questions need to be clarified. First, *what* precisely is being referred to by L's 'intention', 'purpose' and 'other reasons'? Secondly, *how* should C set about trying to discover or ascribe L's intentions and purposes? Thirdly, what *weight* should C give to them, once they have been clarified, in comparison with other considerations? For example, the social context or the community's values may have changed, some other relevant event may have occurred since the original rule was made or there may be some special features in the particular case under consideration.[2]

The first question can be approached by differentiating several matters which might be encompassed by the term L's 'intent'. Adapting a useful analysis by Gerald MacCallum, we can distinguish several cases and possible deviations from them[3]:

Object of intent	Some possible deviations	Term
1. L intended to make *a* rule.	L did not intend to make a rule; e.g. he merely ventured an opinion.	(un)intended rule (A).
2. L intended to make *this* rule Y.	L intended to make rule Z rather than rule Y.	(un)intended rule (B).
3. L intended to make this rule as an instrument for dealing with a specific problem.	L only made this rule in order to further some ulterior purpose unconnected with the substance or scope of the rule (e.g. because he was bribed or for political gain).	(irrelevant) motive.
4. L intended to use the words that were in fact used in the text of the rule.	The rule was not in fixed verbal form or L intended to use some word(s) other than those that were in fact used.	(un)intended words.
5. L intended that the words should be understood according to some settled convention or technical usage.	The words to be interpreted had no settled meaning or L did not know what the words meant or had no clear intent as to meaning.	intended meaning of words.
6. (*a*) L intended that the rule should cover situations of type O but not situations of type P.	L had no clear intention as to scope.	intended scope.

[2] See below, Chapter 6.
[3] G. MacCallum, 'Legislative Intent', 75 *Yale Law Jo.* (1966), 754.

Object of intent	*Some possible deviations*	*Term*
6. (*b*) L intended that this rule should/should not repeal, make an exception to or otherwise change other rule(s).	L had no clear intention as to possible effects on other rules; the rule had affected other rules in ways not contemplated by the rule-maker.	(un)intended effects.
7. L intended that this rule should have a particular (direct or indirect) impact on behaviour or attitudes or have other consequences.	L had no clear intent as to consequences of the rule or the rule did not have the consequences intended or it had other unintended consequences.	purpose/ (un)intended consequences.
8. L made this rule for some clear reason(s) other than or in addition to its consequences, e.g. to embody a moral principle.	L had no clear reasons for making the rule; the rule represented a compromise between several conflicting reasons.	reasons for a rule.

It should not be necessary to explain and illustrate all of these categories. However, it is worth making a few points about them. First, it should be clear that phrases like 'legislative intent' or 'the intention of the rule-maker' are systematically ambiguous. In this context confusion is more likely to arise from uncertainty about the object (intention as to what?) than from doubts about the meaning of 'intention', which is a notoriously elusive concept in other contexts. We are not much concerned here with reckless, negligent or accidental rule-making, although we may be concerned with inadvertence on the part of the rule-maker.

Secondly, when confronted by a rule made by a determinate rule-maker we normally take it for granted that L (1) intended to make a rule, (2) intended to make *this* rule, (3) had some conception of its scope and meaning, and (4) at least in the case of rules in fixed verbal form, intended to use the words that were in fact used in the text. Usually these are fairly safe assumptions although unintended rules and unintended words are not unknown.[4] Similarly, even where L had some purely incidental motive for making the rule (e.g. he was

---

[4] For example, section 3 (1) (b) (v) of the Child Care Act 1980 specifies that one of the grounds on which a local authority may assume parental rights over a child in its care is where his parents have 'consistently' failed to take proper care of him or her. This Act is a consolidating Act, but in the equivalent provision in the earlier Act the adverb used was 'persistently'. There is no explanation for this change, which is thought to be a drafting error; see the commentary in Current Law Statutes 1980.

bribed), he may nonetheless have had some conceptions about its scope, the meaning of the words used and its likely consequences. Clear deviations from any of these assumptions can be treated as special cases which share the characteristic that the interpreter is not likely to gain much help from trying to ascertain L's actual 'intention' as an aid to interpretation, for L had no relevant intentions.

Thirdly, the relationships between 'intention', 'purpose' and 'reasons' need to be clarified. As used here, L's 'intention' refers to his intention as to *making a* rule and *this* rule; his intention as to the *words* used to express the rule and as to the *meanings* to be attached to the words; his intention as to the *scope* of the rule and its relationship to other rules (its *effects*). In ordinary usage, L's 'intention' may also be extended to cover intended consequences (purposes), his motives and possibly his reasons for making this rule in the way he did. But such extensions give too much work to the concept of 'intention' and may cause confusion. Rather we would suggest that so far as is feasible, distinctions should be made between *intention*, incidental *motives*, *purposes* and other *reasons*.

In this context clarity is served by confining 'purpose' to intended consequences – the hoped-for impact of the rule on external matters such as conduct, attitudes and events, but excluding its 'effects' on other rules within the same system. Of course consequences may be direct or indirect; so may purposes. For example the direct purpose of a rule making rape or hijacking an offence may be to reduce the incidence of such conduct. However, many rules have *ulterior* purposes: for example, regulations requiring searches of passengers before boarding have as a *direct* purpose, reducing the number of weapons taken aboard the aircraft; the main *ulterior* purpose is to reduce the incidence of hijacking. There can be a progression of means to ends in which the intermediate stages are both means and ends – a person does A in order to secure B, which is a means to secure C in order to secure D, and so on.

We refer to 'purposes and other reasons', for under the notion of 'reasons for rules' are included both intended consequences and non-consequential reasons, such as principles embodying values which are not directed towards the future. For example, an important reason for a rule entitling a person to be represented in disciplinary proceedings is that this represents a principle of natural justice. The rule may or may not have good consequences in practice, but the reason is independent of the consequences, for such principles of justice are non-consequentialist, as exemplified in extreme form by the maxim: 'Let justice prevail though the heavens fall' (*fiat justitia ruat caelum*). Similarly much of the European Convention and many statutory provisions are based on non-consequentialist or on mixed reasons.

Finally, it is worth noting that intentions, purposes and other reasons may be more or less precise and may operate at different levels of generality. For example, L may have had a clear intention as to scope but only rather vague purposes; again, he may have had a clear idea as to the general purpose of the relevant measure, but have been relatively unconcerned with the details. Most rule-makers pay more attention to some aspects of their task than to others. As with other aspects of rule-making, inadvertence is a relative matter.

So far we have concentrated on a simple model of a single rule-maker and a co-operative interpreter. In the chart some possible complications were noted when L's performance fell below some ideal standard of good and rational rule-making. It is not difficult to imagine other deviations: for example, L may be under very heavy pressure of work; he may be corrupt or incompetent; there may be no consensus in the community about the relevant values; the interpreter may be unhappy rather than co-operative, and so on. Some of these have already been considered, others will be discussed later. At this stage we need to pause to consider the situation where L is not a single identified person but is either indeterminate or collegiate.

Indeterminate and collegiate rule-makers

A sharp contrast to the model of a single actor consciously setting out to diagnose a problem and designing a rule as a means of solving or mitigating it, is provided by William Graham Sumner's account of the growth of 'folkways':

> ... from the first acts by which men try to satisfy needs, each act stands by itself, and looks no further than the immediate satisfaction. From recurrent needs arise habits for the individual and customs for the group, but these results are consequences which were never conscious, and never foreseen or intended. They are not noticed until they have long existed ... [and a] long time must pass ... before they can be used as a basis from which to deduce rules for meeting, in the future, problems whose pressure can be foreseen. The folkways, therefore, are not creations of human purpose and wit. They are like products of natural forces which men unconsciously set in operation ... which reach a final form of maximum adaptation to an interest, which are handed

down by tradition and admit of no exception or variation, yet change to meet new conditions, still within the same limited methods, and without rational reflection or purpose.[5]

This account of how folkways come into existence contains elements of exaggeration and over-simplification. It serves as a useful reminder that rules not in fixed verbal form tend not to be the intentional and conscious creations of a single person at an identifiable point in time. But the ways such rules come into existence are many and various: conscious factors may have a greater role to play in many cases than Sumner suggests; new rules and adaptations of old ones may arise in response to particular dramatic crises[6] or events rather than to recurrent needs, or they may develop through a series of conscious *ad hoc* decisions, as in case law, and so on. Thus notions such as intention and purpose may not apply to many rules not in fixed verbal form, yet the situation out of which they grew, the needs or mischiefs to which they were a response and the values or policies underlying them may all be of concern to the interpreter. If the relevant information is not available to him, he may nevertheless have to *attribute* some mischief and values to the rule in order to make sense of it; and the speculative nature of such attribution may be another condition of indeterminacy and hence of doubt.

The topic of the intention of collegiate rule-makers has attracted much attention, especially in the specific context of judicial interpretation of statutes. This is an extremely difficult and controversial area, with an extensive and sophisticated literature. Some of the difficulties can be illustrated by postulating a simple case. A committee of twelve persons has voted by a majority of 9–3 to introduce a new rule, which had been drafted and introduced by two of the majority. A doubt later arises as to the intended meaning of one of the words in the rule. Several questions need to be differentiated:

(1) Can two or more people have shared or common intentions?
(2) If so, is it meaningful to talk of a group of two or more people having 'an intention'?
(3) If so, does a group have 'an intention' in the same sense as an individual?
(4) In the case of collegiate rule-making and, in particular, in the case of the committee, with whose intentions are we concerned: the

[5] W. G. Sumner, *Folkways* (1906, 1960), pp. 19–20.
[6] See, for example, K. Llewellyn and E. Hoebel, *The Cheyenne Way* (1941), pp. 29–30.

whole committee; the majority; the proponents; or someone else?

(5) In interpreting rules made by collegiate rule-makers, are we concerned with *ascertaining* or merely with *imputing* or *ascribing* the relevant intention?

(6) What procedures and resources are typically available to the interpreter in ascertaining or imputing intention in this kind of context?

There seems to be no consensus in the literature, or in practice, in respect of *any* of these questions. This can be shown by considering two of many possible reactions – one sceptical, the other claiming to represent common sense. The general attitude of the sceptic is that talk of 'the intention' of a collegiate rule-maker is at best a crude fiction and is potentially highly misleading. He might deal with the example of the committee along the following lines: 'No two persons have identical intentions; even where two persons might have similar intentions, it will in practice be impossible to ascertain with precision how similar they were in fact; accordingly, to talk of a group of two or more people having 'an intention' is to employ a simplifying fiction, which will at best be a rough and speculative approximation of the actual intentions of the individuals involved; but *whose* intentions are in issue? It was the committee, not the proponents, who made the rule; but could those members who voted against it be said to have had an intention about the meaning of the relevant words? Perhaps one or more of them voted against it because they felt that these words were ambiguous or because their meaning was all too clear and was objectionable. Are their intentions irrelevant? Those who voted for the rule may have each interpreted the words differently, if they had considered the matter at all. Suppose one of those who voted for the rule, had not even read the draft and had no intention about the disputed point? Suppose one or more of the majority had voted for the rule because they interpreted the rule differently from the proponents? Suppose the draft was a *verbatim* copy of a rule made by some other body – are we seriously expected to try to ascertain the intention of the draftsmen of the original rule, even if that were feasible? Surely such considerations (and I could add many more) indicate that there is no possibility of *discovering* the intention of the rule-maker. Accordingly all we can do is *impute* an intention to the committee by way of fiction. But *how* are we to set about this? There is no agreed method of doing so; therefore, the interpreter is free to impute whatever intention he pleases. But why bother, if the purpose of ascertaining or imputing intention is to help the interpreter to resolve genuine puzzlements? Talk of 'intention' in this kind of context is purely figurative or fictitious, and conceals the true nature of what is involved in interpretation.'

To which an upholder of a common-sense view, let us call him Earthy, might reply: 'Sceptic has identified some genuine and some spurious difficulties, but he has greatly exaggerated the extent and significance of the genuine ones. The plain fact is that we all regularly talk of 'the intention' of groups of people without any danger of being misunderstood; even some alleged sceptics, such as Gray and Payne[7], have acknowledged that the intention of the legislature is often perfectly clear and obvious; and legislatures are much more complex bodies than committees. It may be the case that no two people have absolutely identical intentions about anything, but we do not need such a high degree of conformity for talk of collective intentions to be meaningful and helpful in interpretation. If I say 'my team intends to score a goal', you know perfectly well what I mean. So with committees and legislatures. Of course, what is meant by 'the intention' of a group is not exactly the same as what is meant by 'the intention' of an individual but, as all lawyers know and ordinary usage acknowledges, they are similar enough for most practical purposes. There may be occasions when it is difficult to decide exactly whose intentions to take into account, but these difficulties can be greatly exaggerated. In the present example we may be able to infer the intended meaning from the text by careful reading and, if there is any doubt, we can consider other evidence such as what was said in committee or in an explanatory memorandum drafted by the proponents. Because what the text of the rule and what they said about it are *evidence* of their intent, it is appropriate to talk of trying to discover or ascertain intention. Of course, the evidence may be meagre and the inferences that we can draw from it may be weak and we may have to rely to some extent on guesswork, but this is true in other factual enquiries. Sometimes, too, sifting and enquiring about the evidence may be more trouble that it is worth – which is one reason for excluding policy documents and Hansard from formal legal arguments about statutory interpretation.[8] Whether we talk of ascertaining

[7] J. C. Gray, *The Nature and Sources of the Law* (2nd edn, 1921), pp. 170–89; D. J. Payne, 9 *Current Legal Problems*, 96 (1956).

[8] See below, pp. 339ff.

or more weakly of imputing or ascribing intentions, this is not a purely subjective matter, as Sceptic suggests. It can involve research, careful exegesis and rigorous argument. "Interpret according to intent" may not resolve all problems, but is a cardinal principle of sound interpretation.'

The arguments of Sceptic and Earthy are only samples of the many differing views to be found in the literature. We cannot pursue the matter further here; nor do we intend to take sides here on these complex issues. Suffice to say that sceptical arguments should be taken as a warning against glib or over-confident use of terms like 'legislative intent', but the common-sense view at least suggests that as a practical matter some of the difficulties have been exaggerated in the literature.

The arguments of Sceptic and Earthy at least raise some relevant considerations bearing on questions about what constitute appropriate methods and resources for ascertaining or ascribing intentions and purposes to rule-makers and to rules. In non-legal contexts there is no agreed or proper method but, as Earthy suggested, insofar as evidence of intention is available, the problem of drawing inferences from that evidence is not in principle different from the problem of trying to ascertain or ascribe intention in other factual enquiries. In the context of statutory interpretation, however, some special policy considerations have given rise to controversy about the range of material that should be allowed to be explicitly referred to in legal arguments in court when there is doubt about the intention (or purposes or other reasons) behind a particular legislative provision. This issue, which was debated in *Davis* v. *Johnson*, will be considered in Chapter 10. We turn now to the uses and limits of purposes, and other reasons for rules, as aids to interpretation.

3 The role of purposes and other reasons in interpretation

We have already seen that a simple view of rules as means to ends is at once dangerous and necessary.[9] From the standpoint of a rule-maker the concept of purpose is indispensable: it is pointless to make purposeless rules. We have also seen that people are often called on to interpret rules that appear to them to have no discernible purpose or to have outlived their original purpose or to be purposeless for some other reason; and that there is an approach that favours treating rules

[9] See pp. 159-63.

as things in themselves, without regard to, perhaps even in spite of, their purposes, however clear and attractive these may be. Thus, notions such as purpose and goal are not an absolutely essential precondition for interpreting a given rule. Yet it is also a widely held view, which we share, that careful examination of the purpose(s) of a rule is one of the most important aids to resolving doubts in interpretation.

At this point it is useful to look more closely at relations between rules and purposes (and other reasons for rules) in order to identify some further aspects of the conditions that give rise to doubts in interpretation.

The classic statement of the Mischief Rule in *Heydon's Case* is echoed in the Latin maxim, *'cessante ratione, cessat ipsa lex'*.[10] The literal translation of this maxim suggests a potential ambiguity: 'The reason of the law ceasing, the law itself ceases'. Normally this is interpreted to refer to the *scope* of a law – the gist of the maxim being that as far as possible common law rules should be interpreted to be co-extensive with their purposes or policies; it could be taken to mean that the scope of a rule extends up to the limits of its reason, but no further. But the maxim is sometimes invoked to justify ignoring or refusing to follow a rule on the ground that the original reason for it no longer exists. Sometimes the claim is that the rule no longer exists: in this latter view the maxim means *when* the reason ceases, the law ceases. This is a proposition that has clearly not been generally accepted by English law.[11]

Even when the maxim is interpreted as referring to the *scope* of a law rather than to its continued existence, it is best taken as an example of a general maxim that is subject to an indefinite number of exceptions. It is relevant here to spell out some of the reasons for treating with caution such a simple rationalistic view of law and of rules in general.

First, it is important not to confuse the notion of a rule with the notion of the reason(s) for a rule, for there are many clear examples where they are not co-extensive. When a relatively precise rule is introduced to deal with a clearly defined mischief, there are at least five possible relations between them:

[10] Ibid. See also *Miliangos* v. *George Frank* [1976] A.C. 443.
[11] On desuetude see C. K. Allen, *Law in the Making* (7th edn, 1964), pp. 478–82; A. L. Diamond, 28 *Current Legal Problems* (1975), 107.

(*a*) the rule may be coextensive with the mischief:

$$\ldots\ldots\ldots\ldots\ldots\ldots \quad \text{mischief}$$
$$\underline{\hspace{3cm}} \quad \text{rule}$$

(*b*) the rule may be wider than the mischief:

$$\ldots\ldots\ldots \quad \text{mischief}$$
$$\underline{\hspace{3cm}} \quad \text{rule}$$

(*c*) the rule may be narrower than the mischief:

$$\ldots\ldots\ldots\ldots \quad \text{mischief}$$
$$\underline{\hspace{2cm}} \quad \text{rule}$$

or

$$\ldots\ldots\ldots\ldots \quad \text{mischief}$$
$$\underline{\hspace{2cm}} \quad \text{rule}$$

(*d*) the rule and the mischief may overlap, but cover different areas:

$$\ldots\ldots\ldots \quad \text{mischief}$$
$$\underline{\hspace{3cm}} \quad \text{rule}$$

(*e*) the rule and the mischief may not even overlap at all:

$$\ldots\ldots\ldots \quad \text{mischief}$$
$$\underline{\hspace{3cm}} \quad \text{rule}$$

This can be simply seen from the *Case of the Legalistic Child*. Assuming that any consumption of food or drink by Johnny between meals would indeed be a mischief, the following examples illustrate the first four relationships.

(*a*) Johnny may not consume any food or drink between meals.

(*b*) Only if he has Mother's express permission may Johnny consume food or drink, or enter the larder.

(*c*) Johnny may not eat food from the larder between meals.

(*d*) Johnny may not enter the larder without Mother's permission.

The rather less likely example (*e*) is illustrated by the example of the child psychiatrist who diagnosed the mischief as being a craving for affection; from this point of view the larder rule is at best irrelevant and has virtually nothing to do with the mischief.

Only in (*a*) is the rule co-extensive with the mischief, but even there the rule should not be confused with its purpose – for instance, if the household has a written set of rules, formally promulgated, the rule may officially survive long after the reason for it has disappeared. As a child grows older some rules will fit less and less well unless they are adjusted or abrogated. In some contexts rules often outlive their original purposes, but sometimes they acquire new ones.

Many doubts and dissatisfactions on the part of interpreters relate to situations where the rule and the mischief are not co-extensive. If the interpreter favours the policy behind the rule, he may be distressed because there is a 'loophole' or 'gap' by means of which the policy has been frustrated. Or the situation may be that the rule blocks harmless or socially desirable behaviour that does not offend against the policy, for instance Johnny entering the larder not to help himself to food, but to save his father's dinner. In so far as the interpreter is concerned to further the policy, he may wish to interpret the rule so that its scope is as close as possible to the scope of the mischief. But how far it will be possible for him to do this will depend on a number of factors, some of which may be quite outside his control. Thus it cannot be taken for granted that a rule can always be interpreted so as to be co-extensive with its purposes.

Secondly, the *cessante* maxim, literally interpreted, assumes that every law has a single clear reason. But a rule may have no reasons, or may have outlived its original reasons, it may have been the result of a compromise or it may have several reasons which could conflict with each other in certain contexts. There is anyway an element of artificiality in treating single rules in isolation. Moreover, reasons for rule-making are not all of one type and the relationship between them can be quite complex.[12]

Thirdly, the maxim encourages, though it does not compel, a dangerous assumption that the purpose(s) of a rule, once identified, will be precise enough to determine its scope. But purposes and reasons are at least as subject to indeterminacy as rules. Indeed, 'the policy of a statute' often shares many of the characteristics of rules not in fixed verbal form, and there is a widely held view among legislative draftsmen that precise statements of purpose may create more problems than they resolve.[13] It is often the case that a rule is more precise than its purposes – for instance, the overall purpose of a taxing statute may be to raise revenue, but the instruments for achieving this often are extremely complex, technical and precise. Reasons and purposes may be helpful in giving a general sense of direction, but they are often not very helpful in drawing precise boundaries and determining border-line cases.

Finally, the *cessante* maxim assumes that the role of the interpreter

[12] See above, pp. 134ff.
[13] See the comments in the report of the Renton Committee, *The Preparation of Legislation* (1975, Cmnd. 6053), paras. 11.6–11.8.

is to further the reasons for the rule. But, as we have seen, it cannot always be taken for granted that the relationship between rule-maker and interpreter is simply one of partners in a shared enterprise. A consensus about values cannot be taken for granted, the situation may have changed since the creation of the rule, and the role and objectives of the interpreter may differ to a greater or larger extent from that of the rule-maker.

The *cessante* maxim, literally interpreted, illustrates a simple model of rules as instruments of policies, purposes or other reasons. This model assumes that every law (and, in the present context, every rule) has a single, precise, ascertainable and acceptable reason which is co-extensive with its rule and which can determine its scope. None of these is a necessary attribute of reasons for rules; indeed, the interpreter for whom all five conditions are satisfied is fortunate. Thus indeterminacy of aim is only one aspect of why reasons for rules may give rise to conditions of doubt or may be of limited utility in resolving such doubts.

So far the analysis of the *cessante* maxim has been largely negative. It is important to restore the balance, for emphasis on some of the limitations of naïve instrumentalism might give the impression that there is no merit in viewing rules as instruments of policies, as means to ends or as remedies for mischiefs. Two points may serve as correctives at this stage.

Firstly, our analysis of the various possible relations between a mischief and a rule designed to remedy it postulated a relatively precise rule designed to deal with a clearly defined mischief. But, in so far as the rule is incomplete or its scope is unclear in some other way, the distinction between a rule and the reason(s) for it begins to break down. Yet, generally speaking, the incomplete rule provides the standard case of doubt in interpretation.

It is picturesque to depict the relationship between a rule and the reason(s) for it in such terms as these: 'reason seeps in to fill the gaps'; 'reason is a compass which points the general direction of the rule'; 'rule and reason are fused at the point of indeterminacy'; 'the reason is part of the rule'. Such metaphors if not overused can be illuminating, but we should not let them tempt us into confusing rules with their reasons. We have seen that in some contexts rules and reasons can be differentiated and are not necessarily co-extensive. There are examples, for instance in the Uniform Commercial Code, where the reasons are expressly stated in the legislative text and could be said to be *part of the rule*.[14] There are examples of vague and other-wise incomplete rules. But in the context of interpretation the distinction is important because, in the process of determining the scope of a rule, the reason(s) for the rule may be only one of a number of aids to interpretation, although often one of the most important. To talk of the reason for a rule as being *part* of the rule obscures this.

A second corrective to the sceptical view of the *cessante* maxim is that, because purposes or other reasons are often vague or indetermi-nate, it does not follow that they are unhelpful or useless. As aids to interpretation they may not on their own resolve all of an interpreter's problems (for example in drawing a precise line on a continuously varying continuum),[15] but where elucidation of purpose can provide a general sense of direction it provides a broad context or frame-work within which detailed consideration of other kinds of factor may be fitted. Purposes and reasons can still be an interpreter's best aid.

Thus the exploration and attribution of purposes and other reasons to rules is, in our view, a vital ingredient in a rational approach to interpretation. Even the unhappy interpreter, confronted with what seems to him to be an obstacle, may benefit from a clear understanding of how and why that obstacle came into existence. To abandon pur-poses and reasons as aids is to give up the best hope of achieving an acceptable degree of rationality in approaching problems of interpre-tation. Such defeatism leads to the Way of the Baffled Medic – pre-scription without diagnosis, concentration on cures without any understanding of diseases.[16]

4 Rules and language

Suppose that a park in your home town has a sign at its entrance gate that reads: 'No vehicles allowed in the park',[17] it would be obvious in the context that motorcars, buses and motorcycles are clear examples

---

[14] See, for example, Uniform Commercial Code S. 4–107 (1) and, more generally, S. 1–102; cf. preambles to statutes.

[15] See below, pp. 213–16.

[16] See W. Twining, 'The Way of the Baffled Medic', 12 *Jo. Society of Public Teachers of Law* (N.S., 1973), 348, 353–4.

[17] This is a standard example used in juristic discussions of open texture; e.g. Hart, op. cit., pp. 125ff, G. Gottlieb, *The Logic of Choice*, Chapter 8; and above, pp. 18–20.

of prohibited 'vehicles'. Similarly, if someone suggested that handbags or trouser pockets or shopping baskets were excluded, you could confidently dismiss the idea as absurd. But would you be so sure about an ice-cream van, an invalid carriage, a child's tricycle, a donkey-cart, a skateboard or a pair of rollerskates? It is said that the word 'vehicle', like all general classifying words, has both a core of settled meaning and a surrounding area in which its meaning is not clear, sometimes called 'a penumbra of uncertainty'. Typically, those cases that fall within the penumbra share some attributes with the standard instances but will lack some others, and may be accompanied by further attributes not to be found in the core cases. Thus a child's tricycle shares attributes with a standard instance of a 'vehicle', the motorcycle, but obviously lacks others, and this discrepancy or divergence from the standard instance creates doubt as to whether the tricycle should be designated 'a vehicle'. Vague words like 'vehicle' provide a standard example of what Hart refers to as an irreducible feature of language – its open texture.

Even talking in terms of a single core of meaning may be too simple; as Ludwig Wittgenstein shows with the word 'game',[18] its ordinary usage cannot be adequately elucidated either in terms of a core and a penumbra or in terms of a set of necessary conditions for its use, or even in terms of a jointly sufficient set of conditions. Rather 'game' seems to cover a range of interconnected activities which are related to one another in that they all share some characteristics with some other activities, some of which are typically thought of as games and some not, but they do not all share all of the same characteristics. Thus patience is like bridge because it involves equipment and is governed by rules; but it is unlike it because there are no teams; bridge is like football because there are teams and a system of scoring, but unlike it because no special clothing is worn; football is like war because there is typically special clothing, sides, equipment, physical exertion and rules governing its conduct, but war is not usually thought of as a game, except ironically or metaphorically.

The complexities on the borderline of a concept are further illustrated by the following analysis of a paradigm case of torture and some variations upon it[19]:

---

[18] See below, pp. 360–61.
[19] From W. L. Twining, 'Torture and Philosophy', *Proceedings of the Aristotelian Society*, vol. LII (1978), at pp. 151–2.

Paradigm	*Some Variations*
1. The intentional	1. Reckless, careless, accidental *etc.*
2. application	2. threats, hints, pretences
3. of 'acute' (i.e., (a) intense and (b) of short duration)	3. 'temporal': gradations of duration and intensity
4. corporal (i.e., directly affect in active or passive capacities including deprivation of sleep, stress, anxiety, mental anguish)	4. privative (e.g., sensory or social isolation; deprivation of liberty or privileges etc.)
5. pain	5. 'painless', or even pleasurable, conditioning or treatment; hallucination; trickery, manipulation of unconscious or unaware victim; education?
6. by officials	6. by others (e.g., freedom fighters, kidnappers, individuals)
7. acting under express authority	7. acting without authority; (gradations of tolerance or condonation by superiors)
8. on a captive	8. unconfined
9. and non-consenting	9. consenting – e.g., human experimentation, military training, electric shock treatment, aversion therapy, masochist. Degrees of voluntariness
10. person	10. other sentient beings (e.g., dogs, lobsters, trees?)
11. against his/her interest	11. for the good of the victim (e.g., to save his/her soul; to cure or educate)
12. for the purpose	12. for no clear or rational purpose; gradations of clarity of purpose; unconscious motives
13. of coercing	13. some other purpose (e.g., disabling, breaking the will, terrorizing)

Paradigm	*Some Variations*
14. that person	14. other person(s)
15. to do an act (typically to give truthful information or to make a true confession)	15. to desist or refrain from other types of act (e.g., political activity; statement irrespective of its truth)
16. which it is (probably) in his/her power to do	16. which is not in his/her power to do
17. immediately	17. at some future time (e.g., to broadcast for the enemy); revenge or punishment for past acts
18. in the public interest (i.e., preponderant utility)	18. for some sectional interest; counter-productively[19]

How many of the elements in the paradigm case are *necessary* conditions for the usage of the word 'torture'? What combinations of them would be *jointly sufficient* for its use?

The use of the word 'torture' in the European Convention is interesting in a number of respects. At first sight it is superfluous, for are not all examples of torture also examples of 'inhuman treatment'? It has been suggested that 'torture' is an aggravated form of inhuman treatment and to find that a particular activity is torture is considered to involve a more serious violation of Article 3, although the main sanctions are the strength of condemnation and the adverse publicity. However, it is probably the case that some of the most objectionable features of particular instances of torture – for example sexual humiliation, long-term psychological damage or the purely sadistic infliction of pain – are themselves aggravating features rather than necessary conditions for the use of the word 'torture'.

Words like 'game' and 'torture' illustrate the point that what is involved in clarifying the scope and meaning of a term – in interpreting rules as in other contexts – can be a rather more complex matter than merely seeking for, or stipulating, a *definition*; rather, modern conceptual analysis stresses the value of *elucidating* words in the context of their ordinary usage, by such techniques as considering standard or paradigm cases and deviations from them and by considering words and phrases in the context of standard sentences in which they occur.[20]

It is not news to lawyers that language is an imperfect instrument

[20] H. L. A. Hart, 'Definition and Theory in Jurisprudence', 70 *Law Quarterly Review* (1953), 37.

which is often imperfectly used. Advances in analytical philosophy, semantics and linguistics in recent years have greatly increased general understanding of the nature and uses of language and its inherent limitations as a precise and efficient instrument of communication. Clearly, one of the most important conditions of doubt in interpretation arises either from the faulty use of language in formulating rules, such as inappropriate vagueness or inadvertent ambiguity, or from the inescapable indeterminacy of language, especially of general classifying terms like 'vehicle', which are commonly used in formulations of rules. 'No definition of an empirical term will cover all possibilities', wrote Waismann;[21] nor will any formulation of a rule.

It is also a truism that a good command of language is one of the most important of lawyer-like qualities. Language is the main medium of legal discourse; words and concepts are basic tools in the performance of such common tasks as drafting, interpreting, analysing, arguing and communicating; similarly, the acquisition of linguistic skills and awareness is central to the development of skill in interpreting rules. At the risk of belabouring the obvious, it is worth spelling out what is involved in a good command of language, why it is important for interpreters of rules, and how to set about achieving it.

Language is important as it is the main, but not the only, medium for communicators of rules. The choice of apposite words is crucial for the draftsman of rules in fixed verbal form, while from the interpreter's point of view problems of language are often the most important single condition of doubt. But rules not in fixed verbal form are also often expressed in words, although they may be communicated in other ways, commonly by examples.[22] The process of arriving at a formulation of such a rule is closely analogous to drafting a rule in fixed verbal form, but with two important differences. Whereas opportunity for the formulation of rules in fixed verbal form is virtually monopolized by one type of actor, the draftsman, this is not so for the other kind of rule. Here other actors may participate, as for example in an English appellate case concerned with a non-statutory rule, where it is possible for counsel for each side to suggest competing formulations of the rule, and for each of the judges to formulate, perhaps more than once, a statement of the rule. Each relevant

[21] F. Waismann, 'Verifiability' in A. Flew (ed.), *Logic and Language* (1st series, 1960), pp. 117, 123; see further F. Waismann, *The Principles of Linguistic Philosophy* (1965), pp. 221–5.

[22] Hart, op. cit., pp. 121–4.

participant has the opportunity to perform a role similar to that of a draftsman; but, and this is the other point of difference between the two types of rule, while one of the formulations may subsequently become authoritative, no participant's formulation of a rule not in fixed verbal form has the status of a frozen, binding text.

From the point of view of the addressee of a formulation of a rule, its language and syntax are of critical importance. Linguistic skills such as ability to spot ambiguities, to recognize vagueness, to identify the emotive pull of a word and to make appropriate allowances for it, and to analyse and elucidate class words and abstractions, are basic to the task of interpretation. Moreover, as different addressees may offer competing interpretations in certain situations, so linguistic skills become important in the process of justifying a particular interpretation. The relationship between interpretation and reasoning will be discussed later, but it is worth noting here that other linguistic skills, such as the abilities to spot (and avoid) the proper meaning fallacy[23] and other false assumptions about language, and to identify various types of ambiguity, are crucial to the development of skill in both interpretation and reasoning.

One aspect of language, namely the special part played by class words and other abstractions in communicating formulations of rules, deserves special mention. Hart puts the matter as follows:

> If it were not possible to communicate general standards of conduct, which multitudes of individuals could understand, without further direction, as requiring from them certain conduct when occasion arose, nothing that we now recognise as law could exist. Hence the law must predominantly, but by no means exclusively, refer to *classes* of person, and to *classes* of acts, things and circumstances; and its successful operation over vast areas of social life depends on a widely diffused capacity to recognise particular acts, things and circumstances as instances of the general classifications which the law makes.[24]

Thus practising lawyers and others who regularly handle general rules need to be skilled in handling class words and other abstract concepts.

Some of the more puzzling questions of legal theory also involve the elucidation of highly abstract concepts such as 'law', 'right', 'duty', 'justice', 'causation', 'fact', 'rule', 'decision' and so on. This kind of analysis is notoriously demanding. In Britain the dominance of analytical jurisprudence within legal theory, and the relatively significant

---

[23] See below, p. 212.
[24] Op. cit., p. 121.

emphasis placed on analytical jurisprudence within legal education, have had as one of their main grounds of justification that the development of this kind of analytical skill is important for legal practice as well as for legal theorizing.[25] It is not relevant here to debate the respective claims of this and other approaches to the study of jurisprudence; but one of the consequences of the dominance of analytical jurisprudence in Britain, and its close associations with analytical philosophy, has been that there is a rich and sophisticated literature readily accessible to those who wish to take advantage of it. The path to mastery of the relevant linguistic skills is not by any means an easy one; but rather than try to duplicate existing introductory works on semantics and clear thinking, we propose merely to give some elementary suggestions about where to begin.

It is worth emphasizing that an important precondition to the kind of command of language required for interpretation is an understanding of the medium. Some people may have a natural facility for handling language in certain kinds of way, but there are too many false assumptions and misconceptions about language in general currency for it to be safe to rely on native wit alone.

The literature on the nature of language is vast, controversial and often confusing. Fortunately, some of the most important points can be made quite simply. In a valuable corrective to misguided attempts prematurely to immerse students in the theoretical literature, Hart wrote as follows:

It is indeed important in jurisprudence to notice certain cardinal features of language, neglect of which has often led to sterile and misleading controversy. Yet it is of the first importance, if these things are to be communicated to lawyers, that they should not be encumbered by any obscure or questionable philosophical theory. This can be done with the use of simple examples, perhaps in the following way.

First: Words are vague; they have only a core of settled meaning, but beyond that a penumbra of borderline cases which is not regimented by any conventions, so that although a motor-car is certainly a 'vehicle' for the purpose of a rule excluding vehicles from a park, there is no conclusive answer as far as linguistic conventions go to the question whether a toy motor-car or a sledge or a bicycle is included in this general term.

Secondly: Words are ambiguous, i.e. have more than one relatively well settled use. A testator leaves his vessels to his son. If the question is whether this includes his flying-boat, it is the *vagueness* of 'vessel' which is the source of the trouble; but if the question is whether the bequest refers to the testator's boats or his drinking-cups, *ambiguity* is responsible.

[25] See, for example, H. L. A. Hart in 105 *U. Penn. L. Rev.* (1957), 953.

Thirdly: We are tempted, when we are faced with words, to look round for just one thing or quality for which the word is supposed to stand. It is often wise to resist this temptation. Perhaps the words stand not merely for one kind of thing but for a range of diverse, though related things. We should not assume whenever we use the expression 'possession' that this must on all occasions refer to the same state of affairs, and the same is true of words like 'crime' and 'law' itself. Moreover, words like 'right' and 'duty' do not directly stand for any states of affairs.

Fourthly: For any account descriptive of any thing or event or state of affairs, it is always possible to substitute either a more specific or a more general description. What we refer to as a Rolls Royce may also be referred to as a vehicle, a motor-car, someone's property, etc. So, too, in answer to the question, 'What did he do?', we may say 'He killed her', or 'He struck her', or 'He moved his arm', or 'He contracted the muscle of his arm'. All of these may be true, but only one of them may be appropriate. What controls the selection of the appropriate description depends on the context and purpose of the inquiry. If we are physiologists we may describe what happened in terms of muscular movements; if we are conducting a criminal investigation when killing is a crime we shall choose the language made appropriate by the legal rule and say he killed her. Plainly the constant possibility of more or less specific description is important to bear in mind when considering the notion of the 'material' facts of the case or in any account of the components of a criminal act.

Fifthly: Obsession with the notion that words must always stand for the same 'qualities' or the same set of qualities whenever they are used has stimulated two contrapuntal tendencies. The first is to insist that words like 'possession' or 'law' *must*, in spite of appearance, stand always for the same common qualities and the diversity is only apparent: this leads to the imposition on the diversity of the facts of a spurious 'constructive' or fictitious unity. The second tendency is to insist that only some one of the range of cases in which a word is used is the proper or 'real' meaning of the word: so that international law is not 'really' law. As against both these tendencies, it is a good thing to repeat that words do not have one true or proper meaning.[26]

A sixth matter, which particularly concerns rules in fixed verbal form, is the fact that communication of the effect of the rule may be obscured by poor grammatical construction. An example of this is syntactic ambiguity; that is to say, within the framework of the sentence, a particular word or expression is capable of affecting two, or possibly more, other parts of the sentence, and this raises inconsistent or incompatible interpretations as to the effect of the rule as a whole.

Syntactic ambiguity is not restricted to the world of rule-communication. There is a generally accepted meaning of the phrase 'standard brown eggs', but there is an ambiguity here which permits two alter-

[26] H. L. A. Hart, 'Dias and Hughes on Jurisprudence', 4 *Jo. Society of Public Teachers of Law* (N.S., 1958), 144-5.

native interpretations, that it means eggs of any shape or size, but of a standard brown colour, or eggs of a standard shape and size, which are also brown in colour. This particular example has been resolved for most purposes in favour of the second interpretation. Where such ambiguity is present, resort is generally had to the context in which the phrase is used; this was the approach the court took which had to decide whether the word 'grave' in the phrase 'grave financial or other hardship' modified not only 'financial' but also 'other hardship'.[27] This type of problem is not uncommon in law, but unlike the use of vague terms (which can be deliberate and sensible), syntactic ambiguity is almost always a defect that can and should be avoided at the formulatory/drafting stage.

Apart from these elementary points, there are of course many other aspects of language that bear upon interpretation. Even at this elementary level, an interpreter requires an understanding of such subjects as definition and other techniques of elucidation, emotive meaning, language functions and common fallacies about language. We were tempted to devote a whole chapter to an elementary exposition of these topics, but given the ready accessibility of a number of excellent introductory works we have decided not to try to cover the same ground and have confined ourselves to making a number of suggestions for further reading.[28]

5 The open texture of rules

To conclude, we propose to deal briefly with two further topics: continuous variation and implied exceptions.

(a) Continuous variation

There is a story of an engineer who was engaged in designing an instrument that could measure length within a margin of error of one-millionth of a centimetre. Shortly after he had solved his problem he stopped to talk to some workmen who were drilling a hole in a pavement to find a gas main; he told them of his achievement. 'You theoreticians can afford your margins of error,' was the response, 'but in our work we have to be *absolutely* accurate.'

Precision and vagueness are relative matters. They are character-

[27] *Rukat* v. *Rakat* [1975] 1 All E.R. 343 (C.A.).
[28] See p. 375 below.

istics of rules as well as of formulations of rules. One of the most difficult problems facing both rule-makers and interpreters is where exactly to draw the line at some point along a continuum. Wherever the line is drawn there is a possibility of almost identical cases falling on different sides of it. The problem is a familiar feature of everyday decision-making: fixing a closing date for applications; deciding borderline cases in an examination or a competition; setting a selling price; deciding where to stop bidding in an auction, and so on. It is, of course, a familiar one to lawyers. It is one kind of question of degree and it is a truism that some of the most difficult questions are questions of degree.

There is a natural tendency to treat the problem of continuous variation as one that necessarily involves *arbitrary* choices. Holmes J., in a famous dissent, put the matter this way:

When a legal distinction is determined, as no one doubts that it may be, between night and day, childhood and maturity, or any other extremes, a point has to be fixed or a line has to be drawn, or gradually picked out by successive decisions, to mark where the change takes place. Looked at by itself without regard to the necessity behind it, the line or point seems arbitrary. It might as well or might nearly as well be a little more to the one side or the other. But when it is seen that a line or point there must be, and that there is no mathematical or logical way of fixing it precisely, the decision of the legislature must be accepted unless we can say that it is very wide of any reasonable mark.[29]

The context of this and other similar statements by Holmes was that of American constitutional litigation in which the Supreme Court was called upon to decide upon the constitutionality of sharp lines drawn by the legislature. Holmes, in pursuance of a policy of judicial restraint in constitutional cases, argued that such statutory provisions should be allowed to stand, provided that the line was drawn within an area where reasonable men might disagree; from this standpoint there is a penumbra of certainty (clearly unreasonable points) and a core of doubt, thus:

| clearly unreasonable | reasonable | clearly unreasonable |

[29] *Louisville Gas Co.* v. *Coleman* 277 U.S. 32, 41 (1928) Holmes J. (dissenting). For two further related dissents by Holmes, see *Schlesinger* v. *Wisconsin* 270 U.S. 230 (1925) and *Weaver* v. *Palmer Bros. Co.* 270 U.S. 402 (1926); extracts from these cases are reprinted and discussed in M. Lerner, *The Mind and Faith of Justice Holmes* (1943), pp. 249-51, 257-61. See also pp. 205-6.

The fact of drawing the line is not arbitrary, argued Holmes, because a line has to be drawn; but, this passage implies, the exact choice of a point where the line is drawn may be arbitrary. This is not very helpful to the person who has to draw the line (the rule-maker, in a broad sense). For him the difficulty is not *whether*, but *where*, a line should be drawn. The root of the difficulty is to settle on a point at which a reasoned answer can be given to the question: 'Why here?' It may be that the best answer in given circumstances is 'A line has to be drawn somewhere and no reason can be advanced for suggesting why any other point is to be preferred.' But detailed examination of the particular problem may suggest reasons, which may be good without being compelling, for preferring one or two points to all others, or, at least, for narrowing the field of choice. Common examples of such reasons would include: 'for the sake of simplicity', 'it's a round number', 'it splits the difference', 'to go beyond this point would open the floodgates',[30] 'it is better to err on the side of leniency than of toughness' (or vice versa), 'there are likely to be fewer borderline cases at point X than at point Y', 'it is better to have a few who feel lucky to be included, than a few who feel unlucky to be excluded'.

In Appendix II there is an exercise concerning a situation in which a committee has to settle on criteria for eligibility for joining a club for bearded men.[31] The notion of a beard had been selected not so much for its entertainment value as for the more serious reason that in this case more than one continuum is involved: days of growth, number of hairs, length of hairs and so on. If tackled properly the problem should provide examples of the following general points.

(i) Many different kinds of *reason* can be advanced for preferring one point to others in a situation in which a point has to be selected somewhere along a continuously varying line; in so far as good

---

[30] See, for example, the famous dictum of Alderson B. in *Winterbottom* v. *Wright* (p. 56 above): 'The only safe rule is to confine the right to recover to those who enter into the contract; if we go one step beyond that, there is no reason why we should not go fifty.' This was quoted with approval by Lord Buckmaster in *Donoghue* v. *Stevenson*, but the subsequent history of the tort of negligence suggests that the difficulty of settling the limits of liability is not necessarily a sufficient reason for not taking the first step and that reasons can be advanced for imposing some limits. When Lord Nottingham asked: 'Where will you stop if you do not stop here?' he received a robust reply: 'Where any visible inconvenience doth appear.' The 'floodgates' argument invoked by Baron Alderson and Lord Nottingham tends to be conservative and is often overstated, but it is not necessarily a bad argument in all contexts.

[31] See p. 262 below.

reasons can be advanced for preferring one point to another, the choice is not *arbitrary*, even though the reasons are not compelling.

(ii)　Many of the reasons depend on *relevant information* being available about the situation, for example the purposes of the club, the likely number of applications, constraints on accommodation and other inhibitions on unlimited membership.

(iii)　Depending on the context, the rule-maker may be well advised to consider re-posing the issue in such a way that a problem of continuous variation is not involved; multiple criteria may be more satisfactory than a single criterion; it may be unnecessary or unwise to lay down any precise criteria in advance of considering particular cases. In general, there is a range of alternative strategies for tackling this kind of problem; reasonably satisfactory solutions to such problems are not necessarily impossible or arbitrary.

(b) Implied exceptions

One aspect of the incompleteness of rules is the possibility that an exception to the rule may be implied by the interpreter. While this may not always be the case, the scope for implying exceptions is often much greater than may appear on the surface; in this respect rules are often less complete than they seem. As we have seen in Chapter 3, it is a familiar feature of English criminal law that certain defences and other exceptions to a statutory provision for a criminal offence may be implied on the basis of general principles of liability in criminal law. Thus even legal rules in fixed verbal form may be subject to exceptions based on rules or principles that may not themselves be in fixed verbal form, or that did not exist at the time of the creation of the rule in question.

It is useful here to distinguish two types of situation. To revert to the familiar example used in relation to vagueness: 'No vehicles allowed in the park.' This example is phrased in the form of an absolute prohibition. It has often been used to illustrate the point that many class words have a core of settled meaning and a penumbra of doubtful cases. The point is also commonly made that cases that fall within the penumbra may be decided on the basis of non-linguistic considerations: thus it would be reasonable to interpret the rule so as to allow invalid chairs into the park, not on the basis of the physical characteristics of such chairs as phenomena, nor on whether an invalid chair would be treated as a 'vehicle' in ordinary usage, but because to admit such chairs could reasonably be interpreted as furthering rather than defeating the purposes of the rule (for example, a policy of providing facilities for quiet recreation). Whether or not it would be accurate to say of such a decision that 'an exception has been made in the case of invalid chairs' is not a question of much moment.

The situation might be different, however, if there were a fire in the pavilion in the centre of the park. The park-keeper, a policeman at the scene and, conceivably at a later date, a court might be called on to decide whether an exception to the rule could be implied in the case of a fire engine or an ambulance entering in the circumstances. The *Buckoke* case and *Johnson* v. *Phillips*[32] indicate that such questions arise in practice and that they can cause difficulty.

It would surely be 'stretching' language to say that a fire engine is not a vehicle, but it would not necessarily be considered unreasonable for authoritative interpreters to imply an *exception* in this kind of case or, alternatively, to *waive* the rule on this particular occasion without changing it for the future. This example brings together and illustrates three points that have all been made earlier: (*a*) that a rule can be open-textured independently of the language of its formulation; (*b*) that a distinction needs to be drawn between 'making an exception' to a rule and 'granting an exemption' under it; (*c*) that the open texture of rules is not necessarily to be considered a defect; or, to put the matter differently, incompleteness is not the same as imperfection.

[32] See pp. 48 and 53 above.

6 The Conditions of Doubt

We have reached a stage at which it is useful to draw together some threads by attempting to answer in general terms the question: under what conditions do doubts arise concerning interpretation of rules? The purpose of this chapter is to present a diagnostic model in the form of a checklist of common conditions of doubt that arise where an interpreter is confronted with a pre-existing rule in fixed verbal form, and is puzzled about the general scope of the rule or about its application to a particular set of circumstances. We shall explore the uses and limitations of this model in this kind of situation and the extent to which it can be applied in other contexts, especially where the rule to be interpreted is not in fixed verbal form.

To say that a person is in the position of a puzzled interpreter typically presupposes four conditions:

(*a*) that the interpreter has a clear conception of his standpoint, situation and role – in other words, he can give reasonably clear answers to the questions: Who am I? What is my position in the process? What am I trying to do?

(*b*) that the potentially relevant rules have been identified, but not necessarily formulated in words;

(*c*) that there is a doubt either about the scope of one (or more) rule(s) or its (their) application to a given fact-situation, or both, or else a doubt about what to do, given that the interpreter is dissatisfied, for one reason or another, with the conclusion suggested by the most obvious interpretation or application of the rule(s).

(*d*) that the interpreter's puzzlement does not relate to his standpoint or role or aims, nor to the validity of the rules in question
unless a question of validity is raised by reference to one or more
other rules.

For purposes of analysis it is convenient to characterize the tasks of
clarifying standpoint, role and objective, and of identifying the potentially relevant rules and determining their validity, as preliminaries to
interpretation, but some or all of them may in practice be intimately
bound up with and difficult to distinguish sharply from the process of
interpretation itself.

Assuming that the preliminaries to interpretation are at least pro-
visionally settled, as with an orderly approach to problem-solving, the
next step is diagnosis, that is the attempt to identify as clearly as
possible the nature and source(s) of the difficulty. One way to approach diagnosis is to establish at what point(s) in the process some
event occurred that may have contributed to the interpreter's doubt.
Let us begin with a standard case involving the following elements: a
single consciously made rule in fixed verbal form; a process analogous
to those involved in the Bad Man in Boston or the *Case of the Legalistic
Child*; and an interpreter who is called upon to perform the role of
impartial adjudicator and who is puzzled about the interpretation or
application of the rule in a particular case. The question for him is:
what exactly is puzzling about this case?

Given the variety of types of rule, and the multiplicity of contexts in
which they are to be found, it is unlikely that a single model can be
devised to fit all rule-processes. However, it is possible to present a
relatively simple picture of typical processes, which would apply to a
wide variety of contexts, non-legal as well as legal. Such a model can
be useful, first to illustrate some of the more common sources of doubt
which arise in interpretation, and secondly as a starting point for
diagnosing puzzlements and doubts about interpretation and application in particular cases. In commenting on this model we shall indicate
some of its limitations and ways in which it can be adjusted to take
account of peculiar or special features in particular contexts.

1 **Some common conditions of doubt: a diagnostic model**[1]

The process can be broken down into four stages as follows:

STAGE I	*STAGE II*	*STAGE III*	*STAGE IV*
Conditions arising before the rule came into existence.	Difficulties and errors arising at the rule-making stage.	Conditions occurring after the creation of the rule.	Special features of the particular case.

Stage I.   Conditions arising prior to the creation of the rule

(1) Erroneous, incomplete or inadequate apprehension of the factual context of the original situation giving rise to the problem.

(2) Incomplete or otherwise unacceptable evaluation of the original situation by the rule-maker.

(3) Inappropriate or unacceptable categorization of the original problem.

(4) Lack of clear policy objectives, or competing or inconsistent or otherwise inadequate policy objectives.

(5) Sheer complexity of the original situation.

(6) The problem was not suitable for dealing with by means of rules.

(7) The existing system of rules, institutions and arrangements made a solution difficult or impossible for this particular problem.

This stage covers events that arise during the process of perceiving and diagnosing problems to the point at which a decision has been taken to use rules as the, or as one, means for resolving the problem. This was discussed at length in Chapter 2, and further examples will be found in later chapters.

Stage II.   The rule-making stage – incomplete, indeterminate or imperfect rules

(8) Doubts about intention.[2]

  (*a*) Rule made inadvertently, or doubtful whether it was intended to make a rule (unintended rule A).

[1] Compare the analysis in F. Bennion, *Statute Law* (1980), Chapters 10-20. The emphasis is different, but the general approach is similar. Bennion's account contains a wealth of concrete examples.

[2] See above, pp. 192ff. Note there is some overlap between doubts relating to intention and some of the other conditions listed.

(*b*) Doubtful whether it was intended to make *this* rule (unintended rule B).

(*c*) Doubtful whether it was intended to use these words (unintended words).

(*d*) Doubt as to what meaning, if any, was intended re these words (meaning).

(*e*) Doubt whether the rule was intended to cover this situation (scope).

(*f*) Doubt as to intended effect of this rule on other rules (effects).

(*g*) Doubt whether these (social, economic, other factual) consequences were intended (purposes).

(*h*) Doubt as to which were the reasons, if any, for making the rule (reasons for rule).

(9) Imperfect or doubtful relationship of the rule(s) to other rules within the same 'system':

(*a*) Uncertain whether this rule repeals, makes an exception to or has other effects on prior rules.

(*b*) Uncertain whether this rule is *ultra vires* or unconstitutional or otherwise invalid because of prior rules.

(*c*) Uncertain whether some general principle (e.g. *mens rea*) applies to this rule.

(*d*) Uncertain whether this rule was *new* or whether it is to be interpreted in the light of its predecessors and of interpretations of them (e.g. are cases interpreting prior statutes authorities for this one?).

(*e*) Uncertain whether past interpretations of other related or analogous rules applicable to this one.

(*f*) Potentially related rules difficult to locate or identify.

(10) Imperfect or doubtful relationship of this rule (or body of rules) to rules of some other 'system'.

(11) The instrument or other means adopted for implementing or furthering the objectives not co-extensive with those objectives (narrower, broader, overlapping, unconnected).[3]

(12) Policy objectives not likely to be furthered in fact by this policy or by this rule as an instrument of the policy.

---

[3] See above, p. 202.

(13) Poor drafting, for example:[4]

  (a) Poor organization.
  (b) Style of drafting inappropriate to the instrument.
  (c) Inappropriate choice of words (e.g. ambiguity; inappropriate vagueness; superfluous words used; undue prolixity; same word used in different sense elsewhere; word used in different sense from ordinary or technical usage).
  (d) Obscure because of complexity.
  (e) Rule is silent about, or does not provide for, certain contingencies ('gaps').
  (f) Intentional obscurity.
  (g) Scope for implying exceptions unclear.
  (h) Internal inconsistency or other logical flaws; contradictory provisions (Catch-22).
  (i) Other faults in drafting (e.g. error of law by draftsman; inappropriate rigidity; potentially related rules overlooked by draftsman).

(14) Deliberate delegation of discretion by use of broad or vague terms or by other means.

(15) The draftsman was presented with an insoluble or almost insoluble drafting problem ('undraftability').

(16) Difficulties occasioned during post-drafting stage (e.g. last-minute amendments, inadequate or misleading or otherwise defective promulgation, or communication of contents of the rule to those affected).

Stage II, the engineering stage, deals both with the process of rule-making and with the product, the rule itself. Some rules are defective because of avoidable error on the part of the draftsman: for example, an unintentional ambiguity or loophole; an unnecessarily labyrinthine statute; a formulation of a rule unnecessarily broader or narrower than its purposes. On the other hand, some rules give rise to choices of interpretation because they are incomplete or imperfect, not because of incompetence on the draftsman's part but for some other reason; for example, there may have been a deliberate delegation of discretion to official interpreters by the rule-maker; or it may have been impracticable for the draftsman to construct a rule coextensive with its policy; doubts may have arisen because of the limitations of language as a

---

[4] For a detailed discussion, see generally F. Bennion, *Statute Law*, op. cit., esp. Chapters 16–18.

medium of communication or just because there are a great many other rules in the system, or because of a lack of clear or consistent policies behind the rule(s).

Other factors that may result in conditions of doubt arising at this stage are connected with the legislative or rule-making process as such. A small number of draftsmen working to an overcrowded schedule is a condition of the British legislative process that does not help good law-making; and political factors in this process may operate as an obstacle to sound law-making, as for example where a statute or other instrument is drafted obscurely in order that its full import may not be apparent to those who might oppose it if they understood it. Similar, but not identical, factors operate in administrative rule-making and in the ways that rules are created or established in complex organizations such as universities, large commercial organizations or trade unions.

Stage III. Events after the creation of the rule

(17) Change in factual context since creation of the rule (e.g. social, economic or technological change).

(18) Change in mores or prevailing values since creation of the rule, resulting in conflict between the rule and newer values.

(19) Change in some values resulting in conflict of values relating to the rule.[5]

(20) Change in meanings of words since creation of the rule.

(21) (a) Past enforcement pattern of this rule (e.g. this rule normally not enforced in this type of case).

 (b) Uncertainty as to weight to be given to the conventions, policies and practices adopted by those charged with implementing the rule.

(22) This rule has been seen to have bad or absurd consequences or effects.

(23) Past authoritative interpretations of this rule in conflict or unsatisfactory.

(24) Subsequent creation of other rules affecting this rule.

[5] For example, although the law's attitude to homosexual behaviour had changed, so that this is now generally lawful when in private (see the Sexual Offences Act 1967), the liberty of the individual to select his own sexual partner creates conflict when this liberty is exercised in the form of advertisements for prospective partners: *Knuller* v. *D.P.P.* [1973] A.C. 435.

This stage covers those events that occur after the original creation of the rule and that give rise to conditions of doubt about its interpretation at a general level, as contrasted with any special features of the particular case. In considering the relationship between rule-makers and interpreters, we suggested that a simple model of interpretation as a part of a process of communication and co-operation failed to take into account not only the point that an interpreter may have different values or objectives from the rule-maker, but also that his overall situation may be different by virtue of events that have taken place since the creation of the rule. Such events can be of various kinds: the original social situation giving rise to the mischief may have changed in one or more respects; advances in technology may have caught the rule-maker unawares; public opinion (or the values of a group concerned with the rule) may have shifted; some defects in the rule may have become apparent; new rules may have been made which are difficult to reconcile with the rule to be interpreted; decisions may have been taken which now function as precedents[6] or otherwise bear on interpretation (as in the policy not to prosecute drivers of fire engines mentioned in *Buckoke*)[7]; and such precedents may themselves be difficult to interpret or to reconcile with each other. It is not intended to deal at length with the relationships between law and change, and the ways in which particular rules and institutions adapt (or survive without adaptation) to changing social conditions. The essential point is that many kinds of event may occur after the creation of a rule, and that these can give rise to doubts in interpretation; the task of diagnosis is to identify how the situation has changed and what difficulties this poses for the interpreter.

Stage IV.   Special features of the present case

(25) Disagreement or uncertainty about what the facts were, or how they should be, categorized.

(26) Decision to invoke the rule dubious (e.g. the decision to prosecute in this case dubious or claimant 'standing on rights' or invoking a forgotten rule or the claim is frivolous or vexatious).

(27) Issues framed inappropriately (e.g. choice of inappropriate charge or cause of action, defective pleadings or inadequate wording of appeal).

[6] See Chapter 8 below.
[7] See p. 48 above.

(28) Unfair or inappropriate procedures followed.

(29) Doubts as to role of this decision-maker or whether this is the right arena for this case.

(30) (*a*) Controversial or eccentric ruling or reasoning by decision-maker at first instance.

      (*b*) Doubt as to whether decision at first instance should be interfered with in this case or this type of case (e.g. appeal court uncertain whether or not to substitute its own judgment as to 'reasonableness' in this kind of case).

(31) This case an example of an extraordinary contingency not provided for by rule-maker.

(32) This case on the borderline of the rule.

(33) Special features of this case which give rise to feelings of sympathy or antipathy (fireside equities).[8]

(34) Embarrassing result in this case (e.g. relations with a foreign government, popular/unpopular accused) or uncertainty as to the consequences of a particular result in this case.

(35) Difference of views between interpreter(s) and others as to one or more of the above.

Stage IV concerns those doubts that may be wholly or partly attributable to special features of the particular case under consideration, such as a judgment by the interpreter that the decision to initiate proceedings was ill-advised,[9] that there was some defect in the procedures that have been adopted, or that there is some extraordinary feature of the facts that gave rise to the present case. This kind of condition may be a troublesome matter for all kinds of interpreters, but it is especially characteristic of the situation of the unhappy interpreter confronted with a rule that more or less clearly indicates a result that he considers undesirable for one reason or another. While it may be open to an authoritative decision-maker to try to mitigate the consequences by such devices as derisory damages or an absolute discharge (or their extra-legal analogues), such problems may be viewed by the unhappy interpreter as sufficiently troublesome to

---

[8] For an explanation and elaboration of this term, see K. Llewellyn, *The Common Law Tradition* (1960), pp. 268–77.

[9] See *Lawrence* v. *M.P.C.* [1972] A.C. 626, which provides an illustration of condition 29 (Viscount Dilhorne's doubt as to the wisdom of the Court of Appeal's decision to give leave to appeal to the House of Lords), and condition 27 (counsel for the appellant's argument that his client was charged under the wrong section of the Theft Act).

justify attempting to interpret or apply the rule in a way that avoids the unwelcome outcome.

Some of the conditions of doubt listed under Stage IV illustrate the fuzziness of the distinctions between interpretation and application, and 'the general' and 'the particular'. For example, condition 31 (extraordinary contingency not provided for by the rule-maker) or 33 (features of the instant case that give rise to feelings of sympathy or antipathy) do not belong clearly to the general or the particular. Each is *potentially* capable of being of wider significance than the particular case, but not necessarily to be treated as such. Indeed, whether or not to treat such features of a case as unique (for practical purposes) or as particular examples of a class, may be one of the choices confronting the interpreter. Thus the distinction between Stage IV and the other stages should not be treated as a rigid one.[10]

2 Uses and limitations of the diagnostic model

Most of the conditions of doubt included in the diagnostic model have been discussed, or at least touched on, in earlier chapters; some will be further elaborated or illustrated in the chapters on cases and legislation. Accordingly, it can be treated as a summary of the main points that are made in this book about the conditions of doubt in interpretation. However, it is also designed to be *used* as an aid to pinpointing, with a fair degree of precision, what is giving rise to puzzlement or difficulty in a particular case. In brief it is a practical tool for diagnosing doubt in interpretation. It may be helpful at this point to give some guidance on the uses and limitations of this tool, even though this involves some repetition.

The purpose of this kind of diagnosis is to tease out the factors which are giving rise to difficulty, in order to arrive at a better understanding of what problems of interpretation are involved and to identify the main starting points for arguments about possible competing interpretations. For identifying the conditions of doubt not only helps to clarify the issues, but also indicates some of the main factors that are relevant to reasoning about them.

The first step, as we have suggested, is to differentiate doubts about interpretation and other doubts which we have referred to as prelimi-

[10] For example, condition 31 may be indistinguishable from condition 12(*e*) in some cases.

naries to interpretation. This is particularly important in situations in which it is not clear whether there are any rules or what the potentially applicable rules are. For identifying and finding rules are not the same as interpreting them. It is even more important to try to separate doubts about the role and objectives of the interpreter, and doubts about what constitutes a correct or appropriate interpretation of a rule in a given context. Because this distinction sometimes breaks down or is difficult to apply in practice, we have included in the model a few factors (especially in Stage IV) which, strictly speaking, bear on preliminaries to interpretation. For example, condition 29 (doubts as to the role of the decision-maker on whether this is the right arena for the case) or 30(*b*) (doubt as to whether the interpretation by a decision-maker at first instance should be upheld on appeal) involve questions about role; in practice – and they frequently cause difficulty in legal contexts – they are quite difficult to disentangle from questions about interpretation *stricto sensu*. The same is true of condition 25 (disagreement or uncertainty about the facts), for it is often the case that the main problem facing an advocate or adjudicator is how to characterize 'the facts' so that they fit the protasis of a pre-existing rule. As a practical matter, the objective is not so much to classify the sources of difficulty as to clarify their nature as best one can.

This leads on to a second point. The model provides a rough checklist rather than a set of mutually exclusive categories. There is, for example, an intimate connection between conditions 32 (this case is on the borderline of the rule) and 12(*c*) (vagueness), and between 12(*e*) (gaps) and 31 (extraordinary contingency not provided for). Often it will not be easy to decide which of two or more conditions fit the particular case most closely or whether it is more appropriate to treat both as being present. This is an area so full of complexities and nuances that rigid distinctions and mutually exclusive categories would introduce a suggestion of precision that is likely to be both artificial and misleading.

In using the model a number of other points need to be borne in mind. Often in a single case several conditions may operate in combination. For example, in the *Case of the Legalistic Child*, Father has first to clarify his role as a preliminary to interpretation[11]; in diagnosing the problem of interpretation he might decide that in addition to making a dubious diagnosis of the original problem (conditions 2, 3 and 4) and making a rule which was both vague (12(*c*)) and not co-

[11] pp. 175–6 above.

extensive with its objectives (9), Mother had been foolish in trying to enforce the rule on this occasion (26), with the result that he has a dilemma as to whether to uphold Mother's authority (29, 34) or to acknowledge that Johnny has found a loophole (12(*e*), 31); underlying this may be a tension between his desire to uphold the 'Rule of Law' and the antipathy aroused by Johnny's obnoxious behaviour (33). Similarly, as we shall see, cases like *Allen* and *Davis* v. *Johnson*[12] involve the combination of several different conditions of doubt in quite complex ways, with no single factor predominating. Thus in *Allen* the ambiguity of 'shall marry' (12(*c*)) was a necessary condition for disagreement – for if the words had not been ambiguous, there would have been no dispute – but the main argument centred round other factors, notably the interpretation of cases interpreting section 57 (23) and the basic rationale for bigamy (4, 17, 18, 24). Some of these factors, notably the original policy and the relevant authorities, were given particular weight, but all of these factors played a part in the arguments.[13]

The model follows the chronological order of a normal sequence of events, but it is worth noting that this is not the only, or necessarily the best, order in which to approach the task of diagnosis. For example, in the situation of the unhappy interpreter, it may well be appropriate to identify at an early stage any features of the case that may be contributing to his dissatisfaction, such as that unfair procedures have been followed. One reason for this is that in such cases there may be other strategies for resolving the problem without resort to interpretation, for strained interpretation is only one of the methods open to an unhappy interpreter in order to achieve the result he desires.

The diagnostic model, then, should be looked at as a flexible aid to sharpening one's awareness of the points causing difficulty in a problem of interpretation. It is important to bear in mind that the list does not claim to be comprehensive, that the categories are not mutually exclusive and that several conditions may co-exist in quite complex ways. The best way to get to grips with the list is to try to apply it to concrete cases. One can do this either by considering examples of problem situations or by analysing the reasoning used by others in disputed cases. The Law Reports provide an excellent source both for learning how to use the model and for testing and refining it; for one of its uses is as a tool for careful analysis of decided cases. Whatever purpose it is being used for, it is important to bear in mind that its

[12] See further, pp. 235 and 323–6 below.
[13] See further, pp. 237–40 below.

primary value is to help answer the question: What precisely is or was puzzling about this case?

The model was specifically designed to fit most easily a situation involving

(a) a single, consciously made rule in fixed verbal form;

(b) a relatively simple process which can be roughly depicted in terms of a sequence of events beginning with the perception of a general problem situation and ending with a particular case, in which certain preliminaries to interpreting (such as determining 'the facts') had been completed; and

(c) an interpreter in the situation of an impartial adjudicator called on to interpret and apply the rule in the present case.

Given the diversity of rules, of contexts of interpretation and of interpreters, it would be unreasonable to expect a single model to fit all conceivable situations. However, we think that this one is sufficiently flexible to be of some help in reasonably straightforward cases even where one or more of the conditions in (a), (b) and (c) above are not present. Provided that it is recognized for what it is, *viz.* a rough illustrative checklist of some common conditions of doubt in interpretation, it can be useful at least as a starting point in a wide variety of contexts.

It would not be appropriate to attempt to present here an elaborate series of alternative models for use in different contexts.[14] But it may help to illustrate some of the uses and limitations of this one, by considering briefly how it might apply to standard cases of rules not in fixed verbal form.

Stages I and II postulated a single actor consciously setting out to diagnose a problem and designing a rule as a means of resolving it. A contrasting picture of the ways some rules come into being is given in William Graham Sumner's account of the growth of folkways, which was discussed in Chapter 5.[15] This emphasized the absence of a determinate rule-maker; to talk of intention, policy, purpose or reason in relation to such rules is problematic, yet it is difficult to make sense of them or to attribute meaning or significance to them without resort to such terms. Thus there may be an added dimension of indeterminacy and obscurity about the contexts out of which some rules not in fixed

---

[14] For a very elaborate model for the interpretation of treaties, see M. McDougal, H. Lasswell and J. Miller, *The Interpretation of Agreements and World Public Order* (1967).

[15] Above, pp. 196–7.

verbal form have emerged. Similarly, in the formulation of such rules, typically no one participant has the status of a draftsman whose formulation is accepted as *the* text of the rule. Accordingly, doubts arising from poor draftsmanship are less likely to occur, but the identity, the level of generality and what constitutes an acceptable formulation of the rule, are correspondingly more likely to be indeterminate.

All of the conditions in Stage III are potentially applicable to rules not in fixed verbal form, but the distinction between events prior and subsequent to the making of the rule breaks down in respect of such rules. Typically, there is not an identifiable moment of time when the rule came into existence; and, in the absence of a frozen text, there is a greater flexibility, and thus more scope for evolution and adaptation. Here again, generalizations need to be treated with caution: texts can evolve and change over time, as well as be subjected to varying interpretations; conversely, some rules not in fixed verbal form can be as rigid and petrified as rules written down on tablets of stone. Nevertheless, the adaptive capacity of flexible rules is worth stressing, for it is important to remember that difficulties for interpreters may have been eliminated as well as created earlier in the process.

All the conditions listed in Stage IV are potentially relevant to interpretation of rules not in fixed verbal form, but it is worth reiterating that the distinction between interpretation and application is particularly inclined to break down in this context.

So far we have concentrated on situations in which problems have been defined fairly narrowly and a limited number of rules has been treated as relevant. But problems and rules cumulate. It is often artificial to the point of being misleading to treat a problem or a rule as an isolated phenomenon. Where rules are themselves part of a large and complex agglomeration or system (which may or may not be 'systematic' in the sense of being orderly), other rules may both generate problems and provide some or all of the means for resolving them. As we have seen, an additional source of doubt in some contexts is how far a particular agglomeration of rules is to be treated as a closed and internally consistent system which is theoretically capable of resolving all its problems internally, and how far co-existing systems of rules are capable of being harmonized. In other contexts involving rules, similar questions may also arise about the weight to be given to claims to logical consistency when these claims conflict, or appear to conflict, with other considerations.

The difficulties and dangers of treating problems and rules in isolation from their broader context, the fact that problems tend to accumulate and that each attempted solution can contribute to the creation of further problems, and the practical constraints which often bar the way to a solution which is direct, simple and neat are all factors which need to be taken into account in a realistic approach to diagnosis of doubt in interpretation. Much of the history of English private law can be read as a story of complex interstitial adjustments within a relatively complex and outwardly static system of rules and remedies. Professor Milsom has neatly summarized the nature of this process and as a warning against naïve rationalism in diagnosis it may be appropriate to let him have the last word:

From time to time, pretending that he belongs in a law school, the medievalist puts on a course with some such title as 'mechanics of legal development'. Part of it goes like this. The law is a reiterated failure to classify life. There have always been categories like tort and contract (the medieval words were trespass and covenant); each cycle begins with fact situations being pinned up under the one or the other without much need for thought. Under each heading, the preoccupations of the formative period dictate more or less clear rules; and the system as a whole acquires mathematical force. But as soon as the force is compelling, the system is out of date. Both the classification itself and the rules within each category formed around yesterday's situations; when today's are pinned up on the same principles, they are subjected to rules and yield results no longer appropriate. The individual lawyer cannot hope to get the rules changed for his client, but he can often try to have his case reclassified. No doubt a promise is a promise: but it may also be or imply a statement, and if the rules of contract do not effectively enforce the promise, the statement may still trigger essentially tortious rules about reliance. This is how *assumpsit* began, not, of course, as the conscious device of a profession suddenly aware that its rules of contract were out of date, but as a back door to justice in a few hard cases. For the front door, the law of contract governing at the time, you needed a document under seal; this once sensible requirement of proof for large transactions was being forced upon small ones by economic and jurisdictional changes, hitting first and worse those who themselves acted on their agreements but had no document with which to attack the other side. It was for such victims that lawyers first sought out a backdoor 'tort theory'. But the inappropriateness of sealing wax for daily business turned it into the main entrance: most agreements were made on the footing that any litigation would be in *assumpsit*, and the document under seal came to be used only for special transactions. And so our first law of contract died its death, and there was conceived that which was to flourish in the late 19th and early 20th centuries....[16]

[16] S. F. C. Milsom, Review of Grant Gilmore, *The Death of Contract*, 84 *Yale Law Journal* (1975), 1585.

7 Reasoning and Interpretation

1 From diagnosis to argument

We have reached a stage where a puzzled interpreter, if he has learned the lessons of earlier chapters, should be in a position to diagnose the source(s) of his puzzlement, at least in any reasonably straightforward case. But diagnosing problems and tackling them are not identical operations. Sometimes, once the nature of a problem has been settled, the solution is straightforward or even self-evident. Sometimes a solution may be arrived at without much understanding on the part of the person(s) involved. Sometimes a problem, once understood, is seen to be insoluble. But more often a solution can be achieved only after a good deal of hard graft.

All these possibilities occur in the context of interpretation. Some problems of interpretation, once diagnosed, need no elaborate apparatus of analysis and reasoning for their resolution. It is small comfort to an official who has to administer a silly rule to recognize clearly that he has been presented with an acute dilemma because someone earlier in the process has made an error or because of some feature of the system that he is not in a position to alter or avoid; the dilemma remains and may not be easily resolved. Perhaps all that he can hope to do is to make the best of a bad job. Similarly the cautious solicitor may feel that an interpretation favourable to his client is so unlikely or so risky that he must advise him not to pursue his chosen course of action (or to plead guilty or to settle), however unhappy the client will be about the result. In particular contexts the factors affecting interpretation and application may point clearly in a single direction.

Even where there is some prospect of establishing a clear or a favourable interpretation, it is a foolish interpreter who expects the problem to resolve itself. A reasoned response to a problem of interpretation typically requires analysis, research, more analysis and the construction of arguments, backed at each stage by that elusive quality, good judgment. In the last four chapters the emphasis has been on the factors which give rise to difficulties in interpretation. Identifying the main conditions of doubt lays the foundation for the next steps, viz. identifying the range of possible or plausible interpretations of the relevant rule or rules, or parts thereof, and constructing arguments in favour of and against each of the main candidates. Whatever the context, a rational approach to interpretation involves constructing and weighing arguments; the process is usefully seen as *dialectical*, in the sense that arguments for and against a proposition, and arguments for and against those arguments, are set against each other, as in a contest. The medieval *disputatio* and arguments on a point of law in adversary proceedings provide an excellent model for dialectical processes, not least because the role of the main protagonists is clear: it is to construct and put forward the strongest arguments on one side and to reveal the weaknesses on the other. It is important to note that reasoning in interpretation is dialectical whether or not the actual process in which the interpreter is involved approximates more closely to an adversarial proceeding, such as a school debate or arguing in court, or to an inquisitorial or investigative enquiry, such as a theologian struggling with an obscure text, a legal scholar trying to resolve a doubtful point or a judge conducting his own investigation into a question of law on which he has to make a ruling. Whenever a serious doubt is involved, perhaps the most important part of the equipment of the skilled interpreter is skill in reasoning, which is part of, but not co-extensive with, skill in persuasion.

Well-developed powers of reasoning, like a good command of language, are an important 'lawyer-like' quality. The two are interdependent aspects of a general ability to think clearly. The purpose of this chapter is to provide a starting point for approaching those aspects of reasoning that are particularly important in interpretation. Just as the differences between problems of interpretation in legal and non-legal contexts can easily be exaggerated, so there may also have been a tendency in juristic literature to dwell too much on the allegedly unique or unusual features of 'legal reasoning'.[1] In our view, an

[1] '*Legal reasoning*' is used here in a narrow sense to cover those kinds of reasoning that

understanding of what is involved in reasoning in general is a more appropriate basis from which to approach the more specialized or peculiar aspects that may be features of reasoning within a particular legal system. And this is the case when approaching reasoning in the broader context of interpretation of rules in general. But carefully selected legal examples can be useful for this purpose, for a number of reasons. First, judicial decisions are among the most elaborately reasoned and public forms of decision-making; the law reports are a rich treasure-house of examples of practical reasoning of more than one kind. Secondly, examples of legal reasoning are useful indicators of what aspects of the subject of reasoning (that is, logic in a broad sense)[2] are especially relevant to problems of interpretation; and thirdly, as every law teacher should know, the adversary process serves as an excellent pedagogical device for developing ability in reasoning and analysis.

We propose to analyse in detail the structure of some possible arguments for each side in the case of *Reg.* v. *Allen*[3] as a preliminary to making a number of basic general points about the nature of reasoning in interpretation, with particular reference to the standpoint of the advocate. In the final section we shall consider how these matters may appear from the standpoints of some other kinds of interpreter. Although nearly all of the examples will be legal, most of the points also apply to interpretation in other contexts.

---

are appropriate to recommending or justifying a conclusion on a question of law in a particular legal system. *Lawyers' reasonings*, a term borrowed from Julius Stone, is used to cover the whole range of types of reasoning appropriate for the various kinds of intellectual tasks typically undertaken by lawyers in their professional capacity. It is part of the thesis of this chapter that even specialized kinds of legal reasoning share many features of practical reasoning in non-legal contexts. Although it is conceded that there may be some unique or unusual features of common law legal reasoning, as contrasted with civil law reasoning on the one hand and non-legal practical reasoning of various kinds on the other, the terms 'legal reasoning' and 'lawyers' reasonings' are not here confined to such features, but cover all the modes of reasoning relevant to the task at hand. No attempt is made here to deal with possible differences between legal reasoning in the common law and in other legal systems.

[2] 'Logic', in the broad sense, refers to the study of reasoning of all kinds, not just deductive or closed-system reasoning (see below, p. 243).

[3] See p. 38 above. At this point the reader is recommended to re-read the case carefully.

2 The structure of argument in Reg. *v.* Allen

The facts in *Allen* can be briefly restated as follows:

In 1853 Allen married W1.
In 1866 W1 died.
In 1867 Allen married W2.
In 1871, still being married to W2, Allen purported to marry W3.
W3 was the niece of W1.

Under the law at that time, marriage to a niece by marriage was void. Accordingly, independently of his marriage to W2, Allen's marriage to W3 would have been void.

The facts are not in dispute. But they were considered to raise a difficult question of law, sufficient to justify reserving the case for consideration by the full Court for Crown Cases Reserved, the predecessor of the Court of Criminal Appeal. It can be inferred from the report, as well as from the judgments in the Irish case of *Reg.* v. *Fanning*,[4] that the instinctive feeling of the judges was that this kind of fact-situation ought to fall within the scope of the offence of bigamy and, judging by opinions expressed by several classes of first-year law students, this would be in line with lay opinion even today. How then did the doubt arise? We suggest that there were two primary and two secondary conditions of doubt in the case. First, the words 'shall marry' were ambiguous: had the words been 'shall go through a form and ceremony of marriage' the problem would never have arisen. Second, the authorities were in conflict; in particular, the Court of Criminal Appeal in Ireland had recently decided, by a majority of 7–4, that the equivalent Irish provision did not cover this kind of case. The Irish court was at that time of high persuasive authority, but a feature of *Fanning* was that the majority judges went out of their way to express regrets at feeling compelled to come to this conclusion. A subsidiary source of difficulty is that there was a doubt about the precise nature of the mischief that the crime of bigamy is designed to prevent. The question, 'Why is bigamy considered to be wrong?' is not as straightforward as it might seem.

This third source of doubt was closely connected with a fourth condition, viz. that a change had taken place in the general situation

---

[4] *Reg.* v. *Fanning* (1866) 10 Cox C.C. 411 is an Irish case decided six years before *Allen* and discussed in detail in the latter case. For citations to all the other cases discussed in *Allen*, see Chapter 1 above.

since the time the original provision was drafted. In 1603, when the
exact wording of the statutory provision was first introduced, making
bigamy a capital felony,[5] the Church had sole jurisdiction to celebrate
valid marriages. Originally bigamy had been considered analogous to
blasphemy and sacrilege as being essentially the desecration of a
solemn religious ceremony. However, when in 1836 provision was
made for celebration of marriages in a secular form,[6] the original
rationale for bigamy lost some of its force. For it seems strange to treat
the deception involved in going through a 'second' marriage ceremony
in a registry office as analogous to blasphemy. Yet other reasons might
be advanced for retaining an offence of bigamy in some form or other:
in the words of Cockburn C.J., it can be the means of 'a most cruel
and wicked deception'; in the case of civil ceremonies there is still an
element of deception, including falsification of the register; in the case
of religious ceremonies, an offence against religion is still involved,
although it is a matter of controversy whether this is an appropriate
sphere for criminal regulation; also the law of bigamy is commonly
seen in more general terms as an important penal instrument for
furthering a general policy of supporting the institution of monogamy.
But, as Glanville Williams has brilliantly argued,[7] these policies are
not identical, and each could be said to be adequately catered for by
other provisions, even if the offence of bigamy was abolished. The
answer to the question 'What's wrong with bigamy?' is not self-
evident.

Against this background, let us look at *Allen* from the standpoint of
counsel on each side preparing their respective arguments.[8] The situation is defined for each of them in almost identical terms: the facts are
given; there is a single question of law which can be expressed in neutral terms as follows: 'What is the meaning of "shall marry" in section
57 of the Offences Against the Person Act 1861?' Their respective roles
within the adversary process are also relatively clearly defined.

The structure of the argument in this kind of case is quite simple:
counsel for each side will advance competing interpretations of the

---

[5] Jac. 1, c. 11. S. 57 of the Offences Against the Person Act 1861 re-enacted with
minor modifications s. 22 of the Offences Against the Person Act 1828.

[6] Marriage Act 1836; see now Marriage Act 1949.

[7] 'Bigamy and the Third Marriage', 13 *Modern Law Review* (1950), 417.

[8] The arguments set out below are a reconstruction of possible arguments, derived
from a number of sources. The actual arguments of counsel as reported in the various
reports of *Allen* concentrated almost exclusively on the case law. See especially 12 Cox
C.C. 193, pp. 194–5

words 'shall marry' and reasons in support of his interpretation and against that of his opponent. *Prima facie* there are three main meanings that could be attached to the critical words:

(*A*) 'shall marry' means 'shall validly marry'; or
(*B*) 'shall marry' means 'shall go through a form and ceremony of marriage recognized by law'; or
(*C*) 'shall marry' means 'shall purportedly enter into a marriage that would have been valid, but for its bigamous character'.

If either *A* or *C* were accepted, Allen would not be guilty of bigamy; if *B* were accepted, then the result would be different. Counsel for Allen has a tactical choice to make: whether to argue for interpretations *A* and *C* in the alternative, or whether to concentrate on one of them. On close examination *A* has very little chance of success. The main arguments relating to it might be stated as follows.

Conclusion A: 'shall marry' means 'shall validly marry'

Pro	Contra
The same word should be construed in the same way in the same statute (*Courtauld* v. *Legh* (1869) L.R. 4 Ex. 126 130 *per* Cleasby B). In the very same section the words 'being married' mean 'being validly married' (*Catherwood* v. *Caslon* (1844) 13 M.&W. 261): therefore 'shall marry' should be interpreted to mean 'shall validly marry'.	This interpretation would lead to an absurdity. For, if the accused is already validly married, the second marriage *cannot* be valid (*Bayard* v. *Morphew* (1815) 2 Phillim. 321). Accordingly no one would ever be guilty of bigamy. It was clearly the intention of the legislature to create some offence. (An application of the maxim *ut res magis valeat quam pereat; Craies on Statute Law* (7th edn, 1971), pp. 103–6).

The absurdity argument is clearly a very strong one. But one effect of accepting it is that section 57 then provides a striking example of the same word being used in two quite different senses within the space of four words in a single statutory provision. However, counsel for Allen would probably be wise to drop any attempts to argue for interpretation *A*. He is accordingly left with alternative *C*; some of the possible arguments for and against this conclusion can be tabulated as follows.

Conclusion C: 'shall marry' means 'shall purportedly enter into a marriage that would have been valid, but for its bigamous character'.

Pro	*Contra*
(*a*) There is strong authority in the case of *Reg.* v. *Fanning* (for citations see Chapter 1) for the proposition that, where the second marriage would have been void independently of its bigamous character, no offence was committed.	(*a*) (i) *Fanning* is an Irish case and so is only of persuasive authority. (ii) *Fanning* is a weak authority because the judges were divided 7–4 and even the majority were reluctant to allow the appeal. (iii) *Fanning* was wrongly decided. The situation in *Fanning* involved deception of both the priest and the woman and so fell within the mischief of bigamy; *Fanning* was based on a misinterpretation of the earlier cases. *Fanning* is also inconsistent with *Brawn's* case (for citations see Chapter 1). (iv) The cases are distinguishable on the facts: *Fanning* concerned a defect in the ceremony; *Allen* concerned a defect in the capacity of one of the parties.
(*b*) (i) The case of *Burt* v. *Burt* (for citations see Chapter 1) supports the proposition. (ii) This case was approved in *Fanning*.	(*b*) *Burt* v. *Burt* is distinguishable on the facts: the *ceremony* in that case was not proved to be capable of producing a valid marriage; the ceremony in this case was capable of producing a valid marriage.
(*c*) (i) In *Reg.* v. *Millis* (for citations see Chapter 1) Tindal C.J. said that the second marriage to constitute bigamy	(*c*) *Millis* was concerned with the validity of the *first* marriage. The statement by Tindal C.J. was merely a

Pro

must mean a marriage of the same kind and obligation as the first. (ii) This dictum was approved in *Fanning*.

(*d*) (i) 'shall marry' is ambiguous. This interpretation is a possible one. (ii) This interpretation is the closest to interpretation *A* (i.e. that 'shall marry' means 'shall validly marry'), which in turn is in accordance with the principle that where possible the same meaning shall be given to the same words in the same Act of Parliament (*re National Savings Bank* (1861) L.R. 1 Ch. App. 547). (iii) Penal statutes must be construed strictly in favour of the accused (for authorities see *Craies*, op. cit., pp. 529 ff.)

(*e*) *Brawn* was disapproved in the more recent case of *Fanning*.

Contra

dictum, based on his own reasoning, and it is not binding.

(*d*) (i) This interpretation defeats the intention of the legislature by leaving part of the mischief unprovided for. (ii) Interpretation *C* is not the *same* as interpretation *A*. Also, the presumption concerning the same words in the same statute is a weak one (for authorities see *Craies*, op. cit., pp. 168-9). (iii) This interpretation is forced and strains the natural meaning of the words.

(*e*) This interpretation is inconsistent with *Brawn*, which has not been questioned since by an English court.

So much for some possible arguments for and against *C*. Now let us look at some arguments for and against interpretation *B*, which is supported by the prosecution.

Conclusion B: 'shall marry' means 'shall go through a form and ceremony of marriage recognized by law'.

Pro

(*a*) *Brawn* supports this interpretation (see further above).

(*b*) *Reg.* v. *Penson* (for citations see Chapter 1) supports this interpretation.

(*c*) (i) This interpretation

Contra

(*a*) See above.

(*b*) *Penson* is distinguishable on the facts.

(*c*) (i) *Heydon's case* does not

Pro

would make the scope of the rule co-extensive with the mischief (*Heydon's case* (1584) 3 Co. Rep. 8, discussed above, p. 160). (ii) The *original mischief* was a desecration of a solemn *religious ceremony*; s. 57 of the 1861 Act merely re-enacted the exact words of the earlier statute. (iii) The mischief rule applies to the time of the original enactment, i.e. 1603. (See authorities cited by *Craies*, op cit., pp. 96–8).

(*d*) Bigamy always involves an act in fraud of the law to give the colour and pretence of marriage where the reality does not exist. This case involved an act in fraud of the law.

(*e*) Bigamy often involves a villainous fraud . . . a cruel and wicked deception.

(*f*) The words 'shall marry' are fully capable of being construed in this way without being forced or strained.

(*g*) This interpretation is restricted to a form and ceremony recognized by law. In *Allen* the ceremony was of this kind. The wider issue is not before the court.

Contra

apply to penal statutes (*A-G.* v. *Sillem* (1864) 2 H. and C. 431, 509 *per* Pollock C.B.). (ii) The scope of the mischief is unclear. By 1861 marriage by civil ceremony had been introduced. Accordingly the rationale of bigamy must have changed. (iii) The relevant date for determining the mischief is 1861.

d) (i) This argument is obscure.
(ii) In any case the argument does not apply to *Allen*, since marriage to a deceased wife's niece cannot exist anyway and W3 would be presumed to know this.

(*e*) This is not necessarily the case. See, for example, *Penson*, where the woman was apparently a party to the proceeding.

(*f*) There is at least one other equally natural interpretation.

(*g*) This interpretation opens the door to convicting people of bigamy who have gone through all sorts of fantastic ceremonies (see *Burt* v. *Burt*).

These will suffice for present purposes. Judged by standards of good advocacy, some of the points are much stronger than others, though much depends on the specific context in which the argument is to be made. Not all of them were used in argument by counsel in the actual case; on the other hand, not all the points made by Cockburn C.J. in his judgment have been included. But this analysis provides a basis for illustrating some basic general propositions about the nature of modes of reasoning typically employed in interpretation of rules.

The following points are intended as a simple general statement of certain cardinal features of the kinds of reasoning used in arriving at or justifying conclusions on points involving the interpretation and application of rules. Like Hart's summary statement about certain cardinal features of language, this is intended merely as a jumping-off point from which to approach some of the literature on reasoning in general and on common law reasoning in particular.

(i) *People are engaged in reasoning when they take certain propositions as the basis for making one or more other propositions; or, in other words, when they take one or more propositions, called the premisses of an argument, and use these to infer another proposition, called the conclusion of the argument.*[9] *In the present context, reasons are premisses in the process of reasoning in which propositions containing one common factor (premisses) are synthesized to produce or support other propositions (conclusions).*

We have neither the space nor the expertise to give an adequate account of the nature of reasoning in general. There is no substitute for studying one or more of the introductory works listed in the suggestions for reading, before moving on to specialized works on legal reasoning. In this respect, one general warning needs to be given about elementary texts on logic and critical thinking.[10] Most of the examples used in such works are examples of reasoning towards *conclusions of fact*, whereas, in the context of interpreting rules, typically the main conclusions are *normative*; that is to say, they take the form of ought-propositions. For example, in *Allen* the main arguments of counsel and of the court were concerned not with the discovery of truth or with explaining facts, but with judgments about what meaning *ought* to be attributed to the disputed words 'shall marry' and

[9] Adapted from J. Hospers, *An Introduction to Philosophical Analysis* (2nd edn 1967, repr. 1970), p. 128.
[10] See p. 375 below.

whether Allen *ought* to be convicted. Much of what is said in elementary discussions of deduction, induction and reasoning by analogy in relation to conclusions of fact can be translated into the context of normative reasoning. But in this kind of reasoning there are specialized features that need to be taken into account.[11]

The following quotation from Runes's *Dictionary of Philosophy* is a fairly typical example of an elementary introduction to reasoning in general:

> *In logic*, Reasoning is the process of inference; it is the process of passing from certain propositions already known or assumed to be true, to another truth distinct from them but following from them; it is a discourse or argument which infers one proposition from another, or from a group of others having some common elements between them. The inference is necessary in the case of deductive reasoning; and contingent, probable or wrong, in the case of inductive, presumptive or deceptive reasoning respectively. There are various types of reasoning, and proper methods for each type. The definition, discussion, development and evaluation of these types and methods form an important branch of logic and its sub-divisions. The details of the application of reasoning to the various sciences, form the subject of methodology. All these types are reducible to one or the other of the two fundamental processes of reasoning, namely deduction and induction. It must be added that the logical study of reasoning is normative: logic does not analyse it simply in its natural development, but with a view to guide it towards coherence, validity or truth.[12]

Two points are worth making about this passage. First, in normative reasoning, some of the premisses and nearly all the main conclusions are normative, and so are not true or false, in the sense of being empirically verifiable or falsifiable. To take a very simple example, the last step in the reasoning of the court in *Allen* could be re-stated in the form of a simple syllogism as follows:

Major premiss: Whosoever being married shall go through a form and ceremony of marriage recognized by law, ought to be convicted of the offence of bigamy.

Minor premiss: Allen, being married, went through a form and ceremony of marriage recognized by law.

Conclusion: Allen ought to be convicted of the offence of bigamy.

Expressed thus, the major premiss and the conclusion are normative; the minor premiss is a proposition of fact. Thus for Runes's

---

[11] See G. Von Wright, *Norm and Action* (1963), preface.

[12] T. Greenwood in D. Runes (ed.), *The Dictionary of Philosophy* (1942), pp. 264–5; see also P. Edwards (ed.), *The Encyclopedia of Philosophy* (1967), *passim*, especially 'induction'.

formulation to be applicable to the context of interpreting rules, the word 'truth' has to be interpreted to be wider than empirical or factual truth.[13]

Secondly, Runes says that all types of reasoning are reducible to *one* of *two* fundamental types, deduction and induction. It is often said that there are at least three types of reasoning to be found in the contexts of arguments on points of law: induction, deduction and reasoning by analogy. There is no necessary contradiction here, for many logicians maintain that reasoning by analogy is one kind of inductive reasoning.[14] It may be useful, at this stage, to consider each of these types specifically in relation to interpretation and application of rules.

Deduction. This is typically from general to particular, as in the above example of syllogistic reasoning in *Allen.*[15] In deduction the conclusion *must* follow from the premisses as a matter of logical necessity; if you accept the premisses, you must also accept the conclusion, as it is logically compelling or *conclusive.* Deduction has a part to play in reasoning in interpretation, but it is important to remember that there is more than one kind of reasoning. A common error is to equate words like 'logical' and 'reasoning' with deductive reasoning and to treat all other modes of reasoning as 'illogical' or 'fallacious'. For our purpose, the important distinction is between *conclusive* and *inconclusive*: reasoning is conclusive where the conclusion follows necessarily from the premisses; this is sometimes referred to as 'closed system reasoning'; it is inconclusive where the premisses *support* but do not *compel* the

---

[13] On the meanings of 'truth' and the distinction between truth and validity see, for example, Hospers, op. cit., Chapter 2; Max Black, *Critical Thinking* (1952), pp. 39–43. In the present context, even if the major premiss is expressed in terms of 'shall be guilty' or the conclusion in terms of 'is guilty' or 'is liable', it is appropriate to treat them as normative.

[14] There are other types of reasoning. Another type, regularly resorted to by Sherlock Holmes and emphasized by C. S. Peirce, and of considerable significance in 'fact-finding' processes in legal contexts, is 'abduction' or 'retroduction', that is to say an inference yielding an explanatory *hypothesis*, rather than supporting a factual generalization (as in induction) or in establishing a particular result (as in deduction). For example, '(i) The surprising fact, C, is observed; (2) but if A were true, C would be a matter of course; (3) hence, there is reason to suspect that A is true.' W. B. Gallie, *Peirce and Pragmatism* (1952), pp. 94–9. We are grateful to the late Dr Robin Haak for drawing our attention to this.

[15] Syllogistic reasoning is only one species of deductive reasoning. There are valid deductive arguments which proceed from general to general, or from particular to particular, or from particular to general. Inductive arguments can proceed from general to particular or from general to general. R. Haak, 'Distinguishing Deductive from so-called Inductive Logic' (unpublished paper, University of Warwick, 1975). S. Mellone, *Elements of Modern Logic* (2nd edn 1948, 1958), pp. 172ff.

conclusion; this is sometimes referred to as 'open system' reasoning.[16]

The place of formal logic in legal reasoning is one of the most problematic topics in Jurisprudence. We propose to attempt no more than to warn the beginner against some elementary pitfalls.

First, it is important to realize that the term 'logic' is used, even by philosophers, in a number of different senses. It is sometimes used as a synonym for reasoning, as in the phrase 'the logic of justification'. It is sometimes used more narrowly to refer to particular kinds of reasoning, notably deductive or closed system reasoning. Terms like 'formal logic', 'symbolic logic', 'mathematical logic' refer to specialized and continually developing fields of study. In everyday discourse words like 'logical' and 'illogical' are often used very loosely to refer to arguments which the speaker considers to be strong or weak, valid or invalid. The first warning to the beginner is to take care how he, and others, use terms like 'logic', 'logical' and 'illogical'.

Secondly, even where 'logic' is confined to reasoning leading to necessary conclusions, very general questions of the kind 'what is the role of logic in legal reasoning?' are ambiguous and misleadingly simple. For example, this question has been variously interpreted to mean: 'To what extent do judges and advocates *explicitly* resort to deduction in justifying their decisions?'; 'To what extent can judgments and other examples of argument towards conclusions of law be *reconstructed* in terms of formal logic?'; 'To what extent is it feasible to resort to deductive-type arguments in legal reasoning?'; or 'To what extent is it *desirable* to do so?'; or even: 'What illumination can be gained by applying the techniques of formal logic to examples of legal reasoning?' All these questions are different, although they are related to each other. They are complex questions; beware of glib answers to them.

Thirdly, there is an unfortunate tendency in juristic controversy to present answers to some of these questions as disagreements between extremists. For instance, it is not uncommon to contrast a view that a legal system is a closed and complete system of rules from which all conclusions on points of law in particular cases can be deduced as a matter of logical necessity (sometimes referred to as 'the slot-machine model'), with the dictum of Mr Justice Holmes that '(T)he life of the law has not been logic, it has been experience',[17] which can be inter-

---

[16] See, for example, E. R. Emmet, *The Use of Reason* (1960), Chapters 4 and 10; and *Learning to Think* (1966), Chapter 2.

[17] O. W. Holmes Jr., *The Common Law* (1881), p. 1.

preted to mean that deductive logic plays no role at all in legal reasoning. Stated in this extreme form, both views are patently absurd. It is encouraging to find that few jurists who have been accused of adopting the slot-machine model have been guilty of any such crudities and that even a cursory reading of Holmes reveals that he was concerned to show that logic is only one of a number of factors in 'determining the rules by which men should be governed' rather than to deny that it had, or should have, any influence in this respect. There are, of course, real differences of opinion, as well as emphasis, among jurists (and between legal traditions) on questions of the kind mentioned above. But the differences are not of an all-or-nothing kind. Indeed, there is probably a higher degree of consensus on some of these matters than might at first sight seem to be the case. For example, within the common law tradition the following conclusion by Guest would probably be widely accepted as relatively uncontroversial:

> Arguments need not be cast in a strictly syllogistic form, provided that they exhibit a logical structure. In the dialectic of the law, logic has an important part to play at a stage when a suggested rule has to be tested in order to discover whether or not its adoption will involve the contradiction of already established legal principles. When a rule is tentatively asserted as an explanation of existing cases, it is not always possible to attend immediately to the logical consequences involved in its enunciation. In *Mersey Docks & Transport Co., Ltd.* v. *Rea, Ltd.*, Scrutton L.J. expressed the opinion that the House of Lords' case of *Elder Dempster & Co., Ltd.* v. *Paterson, Zochonis & Co., Ltd.* had established a principle of 'vicarious immunity' of an agent in English law. An agent, he said, while carrying out a contract, is entitled to any immunity which may be possessed by his principal. In subsequent cases, however, decisions were reached without reference to this principle, and it came to be realized that this rule could not be applied deductively to the facts of these later cases without producing an inconsistent result. Eventually the rule was discarded. In this type of situation logic may be used to detect contradictions and to iron out inconsistencies, to test hypotheses and to discover similarities.[18]

It is worth commenting briefly on one point raised by the last sentence of this quotation: what may be termed arguments about inconsistency. One kind of argument commonly found in reasoning in interpretation is a claim that if a particular interpretation is accepted this will be inconsistent with some other rule. Such arguments need to be treated with caution for a number of reasons. First, it is quite common for some kinds of rules to 'hunt in pairs'.[19] Typically this happens with prescriptions which are both general and vague, such as the maxims

---

[18] A. G. Guest, *Oxford Essays in Jurisprudence* (1961), pp. 195-6.
[19] G. Paton, *Jurisprudence* (4th edn, D. P. Derham, 1972), p. 252; see below, p. 335.

of Equity, some rules of statutory construction or those prescriptions which are designated as 'principles' by Dworkin and as 'guiding standards' by Eckhoff.[20] Such rules indicate reasons which must or may be taken into account in particular cases, but do not dictate any particular result. They are too vague to be contradictories or logically inconsistent with each other, but they may point in different directions. Appeals to such prescriptions should not be treated as examples of arguments about inconsistency.

Secondly, arguments about 'inconsistency' and 'contradiction' may often be more appropriately expressed as arguments about what constitutes an appropriate level of generality for a rule or a concept in a particular context. For example, traditionally a great deal of effort was expended by analytical jurists in trying to elucidate concepts such as 'personality', 'possession' and 'ownership' in terms of consistent principles which transcended particular branches of law. Thus attempts were made to 'reconcile' cases dealing with possession in larceny, trespass, land law, bailment, etc. In English law such quests have often ended in failure because English judges have not attempted to use these concepts consistently at this level of generality. They were more responsive to considerations of policy in particular contexts, than to arguments about consistency at a high level of abstraction. A single example from the law of bigamy illustrates the point. In *R. v. Sarwan Singh*[21] the question arose whether a potentially polygamous marriage is a valid first marriage ('whosoever *being married*') for the purposes of s. 57 of the Offences Against the Person Act. It was argued for the Crown that since such marriages had been recognized for some purposes (e.g. in nullity proceedings) they should be recognized as valid for the purpose of a prosecution for bigamy. The Court rejected this argument. The decision is not an example of logical inconsistency; rather it is an example of the particularistic tendencies of the common law – because polygamous marriages are recognized for some purposes in English law it does not follow that they should be recognized for all purposes. Similarly one aspect of the allegedly more 'logical' approach of civilians is perhaps better expressed in terms of their greater concern

---

[20] R. Dworkin, 'The Model of Rules', 35 *U. Chicago L. Rev.* (1967) 14, reprinted under the title 'Is Law a System of Rules?' in R. Summers (ed.), *Essays in Legal Philosophy* (1968), p. 25 and included in R. Dworkin, *Taking Rights Seriously* (1977); and T. Eckhoff, 'Guiding Standards in Legal Reasoning', 29 *Current Legal Problems* (1976), 205.

[21] [1962] 3 All E.R. 612 (Quarter Sessions), overruled by *R. v. Sagoo* [1975] 2 All E.R. 926 (C.A.); see also Appendix II, section 7.

to develop consistent bodies of principles and concepts at a higher level of abstraction than has been traditional in the common law.

Induction is inconclusive. Typically, inductive reasoning is from particular to general, but the term may be used in a broader sense to encompass all kinds of reasoning in which the premises support, but do not compel, the conclusion. The following is a simple example of induction.

> In case A elements a, b, c, d, and e were present and the plaintiff succeeded.
>
> In case B elements a, b, c d, and e were present and the plaintiff succeeded.
>
> In case C elements a, b, c, d, and e, were present and the plaintiff succeeded.
>
> Conclusion: in all cases in which elements a, b, c, d, and e are present, the plaintiff should succeed.

The cases support the general conclusion, but they do not compel it; one reason why this is so is because there is always a possibility that a new case may turn up and undermine the conclusion. In the world of fact, inductive reasoning is concerned with probabilities; in normative contexts it is more accurate to talk of the relative *strength* or *cogency* of (inconclusive) reasons. Thus to have three cases in support of a proposition is stronger than to have one case in support of it, if they are all decisions of the same court. But one decision of the House of Lords would on its own be stronger than three decisions of the High Court.

Reasoning by Analogy (sometimes called reasoning by example) is typically reasoning from particular to particular. Hospers puts the .matter as follows:

> An analogy is simply a comparison, and an argument from analogy is an argument from comparison. An argument from analogy begins with a comparison between two things, x and y. It then proceeds to argue that these two things are alike in certain respects, A, B, C, and concludes that therefore they are also alike in another respect, D, in which they have not been observed to resemble one another. ... It will be apparent at once that an argument from analogy is never conclusive.[22]

A great deal of attention has been paid to reasoning by analogy in Anglo-American juristic literature because it is widely held that this

is the characteristic mode of common law reasoning. A classic statement is by Edward Levi:

> The basic pattern of legal reasoning is reasoning by example. It is reasoning
> from case to case. It is a three-step process described by the doctrine of
> precedent in which a proposition descriptive of the first case is made into a
> rule of law and then applied to a next similar situation. The steps are these:
> similarity is seen between cases; next the rule of law inherent in the first case
> is announced; then the rule of law is made applicable to the second case. . . .
> The finding of similarity or difference is the key step in the legal process.[23]

Later we shall suggest that this view is, in some respects, an over-
simplification and exaggerates the part played by reasoning by analogy (or example) in legal reasoning. But this kind of reasoning is
important in interpretation, and Levi's account of it is well worth
reading, especially for its vivid account of the way in which common
law concepts and doctrines quietly adapt to new situations and changing needs in the process of application: 'the rules change as the rules
are applied.'[24]

A simple example of reasoning from case to case would take the
following form:

In case x factors A, B and C were present and the result was
judgment for the plaintiff.

In case y (the present case) factors A, B and C are present; therefore
judgment should be for the plaintiff.

In other words, similarities between the *facts* are advanced as reasons
for recommending or justifying the same *results* (particular conclusion).

In case law it is not uncommon for precedents to be cited by
opposing sides in the form of *competing analogies*:

In case x A, B and C were present and the result was judgment for
the plaintiff.

In case y A, B and D were present and the result was judgment for
the defendant.

In case z (the present case) A, B, C and D are present.

Counsel for plaintiff: 'Case z is more like case x than case y, because
of factor C, therefore judgment for plaintiff.'

Counsel for defendant: 'Case z is more like case y than case x
because of factor D, therefore judgment for defendant.'

---

[23] E. Levi, *An Introduction to Legal Reasoning* (1948), p. 1.
[24] Ibid., p. 3.

In such cases the result turns on the relative importance or weight to be attributed to particular elements of similarity or difference, in this example factors C and D.

What is the relationship between reasoning by analogy and induction in the context of reasoning from case to case? The process described by Levi involves three steps. First, a similarity between the present case and a prior case is seen. Second, a rule is formulated for which the prior case is said to stand.[25] The relevant point here is that this stage involves reasoning from particular (a case) to general (a rule) and thus resembles induction; a generalized statement of the material facts of the case becomes the protasis of the rule. As we shall see later, there is often considerable leeway for choice concerning the level of generality at which the protasis is to be formulated.

The third step, according to Levi, is to apply the rule to the present case. This is reasoning from general to particular and so resembles deduction. Sometimes, indeed, this stage can be re-stated in the form of a syllogism.[26] But often reasoning from case to case explicitly involves one less step:

Case x resembles case y in respect of A, B and C.
Therefore case x should be treated like case y.

The explicit reasoning is from particular to particular without a general rule being articulated at any point. Some interpretation of the rule is *implied*, but in an indeterminate way, in that any one of an indeterminate number of rule-formulations of differing levels of generality could be selected.[27]

Reasoning by analogy is typically associated with rules derived from cases and other rules not in fixed verbal form. But much the same kind of process can take place even though a statutory provision is involved, because in a particular case interpretation is often confined

[25] In the context of the doctrine of precedent this is the step of determining a *ratio decidendi* of a case, which is discussed in Chapter 8 below.

[26] See for example the judgment of Pearson L.J. in *Hardy* v. *Motor Insurers Bureau* [1964] 2 Q.B. 745, 763-4.

[27] All or any of factors A, B and C could be crucial or relatively unimportant, and each factor could be categorized at one of an indeterminate number of levels of generality, as for example the facts in *Donoghue* v. *Stevenson* were re-stated in a number of different ways in Chapter 1. Thus reasoning by analogy is closely related to induction, but where the formulation of the general rule is left implicit, there is an extra element of indeterminacy over and above the points that (*a*) reasons of this kind are inconclusive and (*b*) the formulations of rules derived from precedent by judges and others are not frozen; i.e. they are not examples of statements of rules in fixed verbal form.

to elucidating only such aspect of the meaning(s) of doubtful words as are immediately relevant to the case; thus in treating *Burt* v. *Burt* as distinguishable (i.e. different) from *Allen*, Cockburn C.J. left open the question whether in order to establish bigamy the form and ceremony must be one recognized as valid in England, or by local law wherever it happened to have been celebrated, or by some local laws but not others:

> In thus holding, it is not at all necessary to say that forms of marriage unknown to the law, as was the case in *Burt* v. *Burt*, would suffice to bring a case within the operation of the statute. We must not be understood to mean that every fantastic form of marriage to which parties might think proper to resort, or that a marriage ceremony performed by an unauthorised person in an unauthorised place, would be marrying within Sect 57. of 24 and 25 Vict. c. 101.[28]

Thus the court's interpretation did not purport to be a complete exposition (if such were possible) of 'shall marry'; it was sufficient to remove the doubt in *Allen*, but some doubts were left unresolved for the future about the scope of the rule for which *Burt* v. *Burt* was an authority. In a future case, *Allen* and *Burt* v. *Burt* might provide a basis for an argument about competing analogies.

(ii) *Reasoning in interpretation is a species of practical reasoning. The distinction between theoretical and practical reasoning is a subject of controversy among philosophers, but for present purposes it is sufficient to say that practical reasoning is concerned with giving and evaluating reasons for and against acting or deciding in a certain way.*

Reasoning in interpretation shares many of the features of modes of reasoning commonly employed in various kinds of decision-making. In particular, as we have seen, practical reasoning is typically normative; that is, it deals with conclusions about how people *ought* to act or decide as contrasted with, for example, descriptions or explanations in the world of fact. Secondly, in the context of interpretation most or even all of the reasons in an argument may be logically inconclusive, in that they do not support their conclusions as a matter of *logical necessity*. None of the reasons that might be advanced in *Allen* logically compels the choice by the court of one of the conflicting interpretations of 'shall marry'. Some of the reasons are stronger than others, but none requires a particular conclusion. Similarly, the *cumulative effect* of

[28] See p. 43 above.

all the arguments on one side may be very much stronger than the cumulative effect of the opposing arguments, but may nevertheless not be logically compelling. Third, reasoning in interpretation encompasses a variety of kinds of reasons and types of reasoning. Thus in the analysis of possible arguments of counsel in *Allen* are to be found, *inter alia*, arguments appealing to authority (precedents); arguments appealing to considerations of policy; arguments appealing to logical consistency; and arguments appealing to the natural or ordinary meanings of words.

Similarly, as there are different types of reasoning, induction, deduction and analogy, the relationship between the *reasons* advanced in *Allen* may vary also according to the type of *reasoning* employed. Often, in legal interpretation, the three types may be woven together within a single argument in a complex series of intermediate as well as ultimate conclusions; and it is misleading to make statements of the kind 'the basic pattern of legal reasoning is reasoning by example' or 'case law reasoning is inductive and the application of statutes is deductive'.[29] These contain a core of truth, but they are misleading in that they oversimplify.

(iii) *A number of independent reasons may be advanced for or against a conclusion respecting a question of interpretation or application. Some of these reasons may be of differing kinds.*

Two attempts to systematize the kinds of reasons which are appropriate in legal contexts may be briefly mentioned. In *Legal Reasoning and Legal Theory*, Professor Neil MacCormick[30] develops an account of judicial reasoning which starts from the premise that judges are under a duty 'to give only such decisions as can be justified by a good justificatory argument'.[31] The first kind of argument, which should be used in the simplest cases where a clear rule is agreed to be applicable, is by deduction. Where difficulties arise about the rule or its applicability, a judge should resort to 'second-order justification', which is consequentialist in nature. However, it is not sufficient that a proposed justification 'makes sense in the world', that is, is likely to produce beneficial results, it must also 'make sense in the system', a requirement which has two facets. It must be consistent with the system, that is, it

---

[29] See Levi, op. cit., esp. pp. 1–5, 19ff.
[30] D. N. MacCormick, *Legal Reasoning and Legal Theory* (1978).
[31] Ibid., p. 250.

may not contradict any of its valid and binding rules; and the justification must cohere with the recognized principles and analogies which may be derived from the system. It is not possible to do justice to Professor MacCormick's thesis in a short space; but we may observe that it is concerned with reasoning by judges rather than argumentation as a whole, which may involve appeals to sympathy, special pleading, prejudice and other non-rational arguments.

Professor Robert Summers' typology includes 'all basic types of good reasons found in common law cases'.[32] While he identifies five types – substantive, authority, factual, interpretational and critical – Summers concentrates on substantive reasons. These are divided into three subtypes: goal reasons which derive their justificatory force from their predicted beneficial results; rightness reasons which derive their justificatory force from the existence of some norm guiding conduct; and institutional reasons which are goal or rightness reasons tied to specific institutional roles or processes. An example may help to distinguish them. Suppose a consumer sues a retailer for breach of contract for supplying him with completely defective goods, but the retailer refers the court to a contract which the consumer signed before the goods were delivered which contains a clause purporting to divest the consumer of any claim for compensation should the goods turn out to be faulty.[33] A court could strike out the exemption clause by an appeal to some notion of fairness in bargaining – the retailer being in a stronger position than the consumer, and there being effectively little choice between the terms offered by all retailers, it would be unfair to allow the practice of excluding all liability (a rightness reason) – and to the consequences of such clauses being held valid parts of a contract: consumers would suffer financially, safety and production standards might drop, citizens would lose respect for the law (goal reasons). On the other hand, rightness and goal reasons could be invoked to uphold the exemption clause: parties to contracts are entitled to expect courts to enforce their terms when they have been freely entered into, and were courts to strike down terms in contracts *ex post facto*, commercial enterprise would be rendered unpredictable. In addition a court might argue that if such exemption clauses are regarded as unfair or leading to undesirable consequences, it is for Parliament to change the law, not the courts (an institutional reason).

[32] R. S. Summers, 'Two Types of Substantive Reasons: The Core of a Theory of Common-Law Justification', 63 *Cornell Law Review* (1978), 707, 716.
[33] Such a clause would in fact be unlawful; Unfair Contract Terms Act 1977.

There are obvious analogies between Summers' goal reasons and MacCormick's consequentialist arguments,[34] but for the purposes of justifying decisions, Summers gives priority to substantive over authority (precedential) reasons, even in simple cases where MacCormick would argue in favour of reasoning from agreed principles of law.

Both these accounts are of value in illuminating the range of reasons to which judges refer when deciding cases, but their concern with judicial reasoning should not encourage the view that they should be equated with all types of legal reasoning, nor that reasons necessarily make up the entirety of legal argumentation. It may also be noted that all three – MacCormick, Summers and Dworkin – claim to be descriptive, but they disagree on what the reality is. Likewise, although each claims to be prescribing how judges ought to decide cases, their prescriptions vary considerably. Whereas Summers accords priority to substantive reasons, which include goal reasons, Dworkin has argued that decisions should be based on principles, not on policies which prescribe goals. MacCormick, as we have seen, treats consequentialism as the basis of 'second-order justification'.

From the argument for the defence in *Allen* let us select four of the reasons in favour of the conclusion that 'shall marry' means 'shall purportedly enter into a marriage which would have been valid but for its bigamous character':

(a) *Reg.* v. *Fanning* supports the proposition;

(b) *Burt* v. *Burt* supports the proposition;

(c) penal statutes must be construed strictly in favour of the accused;

(d) this interpretation is the one most in harmony with the interpretation given to the words 'being married'.

Some of these reasons were of different kinds and were independent of each other: (a) and (b) were reasons based on precedents – a kind of invocation of authority; (c) was a direct appeal to a general principle of statutory construction; and (d) was an ingenious, and probably weaker argument, based indirectly on the presumption that the same word should be construed in the same sense in the same

[34] As there are between these and Dworkin's policies; see pp. 128–30 above. Dworkin, however, excludes the possibility of appeals to policy as a legitimate ground for deciding cases in adjudication. A close analogy also exists between Summers' rightness reasons and Dworkin's principles. See also the discussion of consequentialist and moralist argument, pp. 135–6 above.

Act. One of the main arguments for the other side was of a different kind again: it was a direct appeal to the policy of the statute. These are only a few examples of the wide range of different kinds of reason which are commonly adduced in support of conclusions in interpretation.

The reasons listed above were independent of each other; that is to say, if any one of them was removed the others still stood. In a famous passage the philosopher John Wisdom put the matter as follows:

> In such cases we notice that the process of argument is not a *chain* of demonstrative reasoning. It is a presenting and re-presenting of those features of the case which *severally co-operate* in favour of the conclusion, in favour of saying what the reasoner wishes said, in favour of calling the situation by the name which he wishes to call it. *The reasons are like the legs of a chair, not the links of a chain.*[35]

The reasons *for* the competing interpretations in *Allen* do not constitute the whole of the argument for each side. For reasons *against* each conclusion are also involved. For example, where Allen was arguing for conclusion *C* (that 'shall marry' means 'shall purportedly enter into a marriage which would have been valid, but for its bigamous character'), one support for this argument was the Irish case *Reg.* v. *Fanning*. Part of the argument for the prosecution consists of reasons why the court should not follow this case. Here again, more than one independent reason could be advanced against following *Fanning*:

(i)   as an Irish case, it is only of persuasive authority;
(ii) it is a weak precedent because the court was divided;
(iii) the facts in *Allen* and *Fanning* are distinguishable;
(iv) *Fanning* was wrongly decided.

This is another example of what Wisdom, later in the same passage, calls '*the cumulative effect of severally inconclusive premisses*'.

Thus Wisdom's striking metaphor of the legs of a chair needs to be modified, especially if arguments of both sides are taken into account. Whereas counsel for *Allen* was erecting legs (arguments (*a*), (*b*), (*c*), (*d*) and (*e*)) in support of his main conclusion (conclusion *C*), counsel for the other side was concerned to destroy or, at least weaken, their

---

[35] J. Wisdom, 'Gods', in *Proceedings of the Aristotelian Society* (1944), pp. 185, 194; reprinted in A. Flew (ed.), *Logic and Language* (First Series, 1960), pp. 187, 195 (*italics* added).

supportive effect. For example, in respect of argument (*a*), this relationship may be depicted thus:

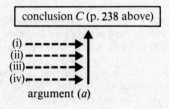

This model will require modification later, but it adequately depicts in simplified form the basic structure of this kind of argument.

Talk of legs of chairs and links in chains in relation to reasoning is, of course, metaphorical. Another metaphor commonly resorted to in this context is that of weighing or balancing. This is the metaphor adopted by the Norwegian jurist, Torstein Eckhoff, in a recent paper which, despite differences in terminology, is very close to the spirit of the analysis presented here. Distinguishing between legal rules, which state relationships between operative facts and legal consequences, and 'guiding standards' which guide reasoning in interpreting rules, Eckhoff writes:

> To know the relevant reasons is not the same as having reached a solution. The weighing of reasons still remains. This weighing is, of course, very easy when all relevant reasons pull in the same direction. But still it is a different process from that of subsuming a set of facts under a rule. And a weighing of reasons which pull in different directions can give rise to considerable doubt and scruples. . . .
>
> Take, for instance, principles of sentencing which I conceive of as typical examples of guiding standards. They supply answers to the question of what must be taken into account when deciding whether an offender should be sentenced and what the sentence should be. They tell us, for instance, that the gravity of the offence and the age and record of the offender must be considered. But they do not determine whether a particular offender should be discharged or imprisoned, or what the length of his prison sentence should be. These questions are left to the judge who has to base his decision on a weighing of the relevant factors.

In dealing with the relations between guiding standards and judicial discretion, Eckhoff continues:

> I am inclined to believe that judges, within certain limits, are free to decide which reasons they will take into account when making evaluations. I do not say that this necessarily must be so, but I hold it to be a quite normal situation in the legal systems with which I am familiar. To be sure, there are guiding

standards to the effect that certain reasons *must* be considered. But in addition to these obligatory reasons there are also arguments which are considered acceptable but not obligatory. There are, in other words, arguments to which a judge *may*, but not must, pay attention.

Secondly, even in cases where only such reasons as the judge must take into account are at stake, will the weighing of pros and cons give some leeway for judicial discretion. Most guiding standards do not say anything about the weight of different reasons. And if anything is said it is, as a rule, only an approximate indication. The normal situation is, in other words, that the weight is not fixed beforehand but is determined by the decision-maker in light of the circumstances of the individual case.[36]

These guiding standards are thus similar to Dworkin's principles, except that Eckhoff does not accept the notion that there is a single right answer.

(iv) The relations between reasons in an argument supporting a conclusion in interpretation can be very complex.

In the last diagram the 'leg' supporting conclusion *C* in *Allen* was depicted as a simple straight arrow. But this is a simplification. A more accurate depiction of the reasoning in respect of the first leg of the arguments of counsel in regard to this conclusion would be something like this:

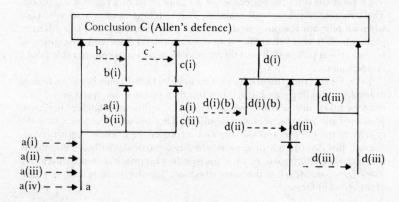

However, even this picture simplifies. For if we were to try to make explicit every proposition and every step in reasoning in counsel's argument, the number of propositions would be greatly increased; indeed such a process of reconstruction is potentially endless. For it is

[36] T. Eckhoff, op. cit., n. 20 pp. 208, 217–18; see further Chapter 8.

characteristic of this kind of reasoning that not every step is meticulously and laboriously spelled out in practice. Legal argument, and everyday practical discourse, can often benefit in a number of ways from an economy of style that leaves a large number of inferences implicit rather than articulated. But it is an endemic weakness of the theoretical literature on legal reasoning that it regularly presents an oversimplified picture of what is an extremely intricate process. A few important steps tend to be selected and presented as the whole. Consider the number of explicit propositions and the number of implicit inferences that could be reconstructed from the judgment of Cockburn C.J. in *Allen* or of Lord Buckmaster in *Donoghue* v. *Stevenson* and ask yourself whether their reasoning is more like a chain, a chair, an intricately woven piece of cloth, a seamless web, a balancing or weighing process, or is best seen, in non-metaphorical terms, as a complex argument.

Professor MacCormick has criticized the use of such metaphors as giving the misleading impression that legal arguments are judged by 'the exact and objective measurements of the honest butcher's scales'.[37] It is an everyday experience in law, as in other contexts such as morals or aesthetics, that preferences can and are expected to be made even though both the kinds of arguments which are or may be appropriate in the context, and the criteria upon which their relevance, cogency and acceptability are to be judged, are in various respects indeterminate. In the dialectical process which typifies legal argumentation, preferences are expressed in terms of one argument being more or less convincing, or stronger, than another; and such preferences are defensible notwithstanding that no exact and objective measurement of them is possible, so long as some criteria exist which are recognized by the disputants. The process of making and expressing choices may be conveniently described as one of balancing or weighing arguments; but we should also recognize the limits of such metaphors and remember that what we are concerned with is complex arguments.

(v) *What constitutes a valid or invalid, a good or bad, a cogent or weak, reason in an argument about interpretation varies from context to context. There are certain special features of reasoning in the context of legal interpretation that are either unique or are given more emphasis than in non-legal contexts; but there are also features that are found in both legal and non-legal contexts.*

[37] *Legal Reasoning and Legal Theory*, op. cit., p. 112.

The story is told that before delivering judgment in *Donoghue* v. *Stevenson* Lord Atkin consulted his children, telling them the facts and asking them what they thought the result should be and whom they thought their 'neighbour' was.[38] If Lord Atkin in his speech had said 'I am in favour of allowing the appeal because my daughter thinks that it is clearly just that the pursuer [plaintiff] should recover', or if he had quoted his children's opinion as authority for the neighbour principle, these would have been two clear examples of reasons that would not have been considered valid within this context. Similarly, if a judge says 'I find the plaintiff irresistibly attractive and accordingly cannot help but decide in her favour' or 'I find for the plaintiff, as he has offered me £100, if I do so', these would generally be considered to be *bad* reasons for his decision.

At the very end of his speech in *Donoghue* v. *Stevenson*, Lord Atkin supports a somewhat narrower formulation of the governing principle, in the following words: 'It is a proposition that I venture to say no one in Scotland or England who was not a lawyer would for one moment doubt. It will be an advantage to make it clear that the law in this matter, as in most others, is in accordance with sound common sense.' Such appeals to common sense are not uncommon in appellate judgments. History does not relate how many people's views Lord Atkin canvassed in order to test out public opinion on the matter, but it is not impossible that his children (and his own feelings) represented most of his sample. It would probably be generally accepted that this particular reason as formulated in the speech was valid (in the sense of permissible), inconclusive, but of some persuasive force, although of a lower status in the hierarchy of legal reasoning than an argument from authority. Lord Atkin based his statement of the neighbour principle[39] largely on an interpretation of two cases, *Heaven* v. *Pender* and *Le Lievre* v. *Gould*.[40] His reasons in support of this proposition are generally accepted to be permissible, inconclusive and not very cogent.

This example usefully illustrates a number of points about judicial reasoning and its relationship to reasoning in non-legal contexts.

First, 'valid' in this context means permissible, but not necessarily conclusive. This applies equally in legal and non-legal contexts relating to interpretation of rules where, as we have seen, reasoning is

[38] E. Cockburn Millar (*neé* Atkin), 'Some Memories of Lord Atkin', 23 *Glim*, 13, 15 (1957).

[39] [1932] A.C. 563, 582.

[40] (1883) 11 Q.B.D. 503; [1893] 1 Q.B. 491.

typically of the open-system type. 'Valid' is commonly used differently in the context of closed-system reasoning, when it is normally confined to reasons that form part of a chain of arguments leading necessarily to a conclusion.

Second, in English law there are certain rules that determine a hierarchy of types of reason in legal contexts. Examples of such rules include the doctrine of precedent and the rule that a provision in an Act of Parliament takes precedence over an inconsistent provision in a statutory instrument or a judicial decision. Thus in legal contexts certain kinds of reasons are conclusive, if clearly applicable, and some are more strongly persuasive than others (for instance, the House of Lords should give more weight to a decision of the Court of Appeal than to a decision of a court of first instance or a decision from another jurisdiction). Thus a distinctive feature of legal reasoning is that there are special rules concerning the validity and weight of certain types of reasons; whereas in other contexts involving interpretation of rules there are few principles or rules beyond the general principles of logic and clear thinking dealing with the validity, cogency or relative priority of different kinds of reasons.

We shall see in later chapters that some of these legal rules, such as the doctrine of precedent and the rules of statutory interpretation, are less determinate than might at first sight appear. Because of this indeterminacy many of the factors affecting reasoning in interpretation apply in much the same way in legal and non-legal contexts.

Thirdly, there are certain conventions of style that may vary from context to context. Thus the difference between saying 'Common sense supports this conclusion' and 'My daughter, who is a very sensible girl, supports this conclusion' may not be very different analytically, but clearly one is stylistically appropriate to the context, and the other is not. Conversely, in an ordinary domestic situation an ingenious and cogent lawyer-like argument by a child to his parents might backfire precisely because it is lawyer-like and hence inappropriate – for Father might respond: 'We don't want any barrack-room lawyers *here*.'

(vi) *Advocacy, in both legal and non-legal contexts, typically involves a combination of rational and non-rational means of persuasion.*

So far in this chapter we have been concerned with analysis of typical modes of *reasoning* in interpretation; but not all argument in this kind of context is purely rational in the sense that it is based solely on appeals to reason, as contrasted with appeals to emotion, to the will, to intuition, to common sense and so on. For example, the task of the advocate is to persuade people to decide or to act in certain ways: and reasoning is only one of a whole range of methods of persuasion. A realistic approach to processes of interpretation needs to give due weight to this fact and to recognize that, from a psychological point of view, it is artificial to draw sharp distinctions between rational and non-rational factors in persuasion and decision-making. The good advocate needs not only to be skilful in rational argument; he also needs some psychological insight.

Appellate judicial processes place more emphasis on procedures designed to maximize rationality than almost any other kind of decision-making: questions of fact are normally separated from questions of law and are treated as settled; the issues are carefully identified and framed in advance; there are fairly elaborate rules defining the validity and force of different types of argument; the ethics of advocacy and the tradition of elaborate, public, reasoned justification for decision are among the factors that are thought to uphold honesty and rationality in argument and decision.[41]

Yet in cases involving a doubt on a question of law, argument by both advocates and judges may consist of a combination of rational and non-rational factors. It is beyond the scope of this work to explore the psychology of decision-making or to enter into the controversy about the degree of rationality that is to be found in judicial processes. But the general point can be illustrated quite simply by a few examples.

As regards advocacy, consider three rules of thumb which almost invariably appear in discussions of the art of appellate advocacy: (*a*) study the particular court; (*b*) 'always go for the jugular vein' (alias, the principle of concentration of fire); (*c*) 'the statement of facts is the heart'.[42]

Each of these standard pieces of advice is based on psychological assumptions about the nature of persuasion. The first is obvious: individuals, including judges, will be more susceptible to persuasion by some arguments than others. The advocate addressing an unfam-

---

[41] See generally S. Toulmin, *The Uses of Argument* (1958); K. Llewellyn, *The Common Law Tradition* (1960); and J. A. C. Brown, *Techniques of Persuasion* (1963).

[42] For references to the art of advocacy, see Appendix II, section 7, question 17, and Appendix III.

iliar court or a varied bench of judges is likely to be at a disadvantage compared with one who is addressing a single judge whom he has encountered often before, for he is in a better position to predict likely reactions to particular lines of argument.

A famous American advocate, John W. Davis, put the second point as follows:

> More often than not there is in every case a cardinal point around which lesser points revolve like planets around the sun, or even as dead moons around a planet; a central fortress which if strongly held will make the loss of all the outworks immaterial. The temptation is always present 'to let no guilty point escape' in the hope that if one hook breaks another may hold.[43]

The psychology of this is also fairly obvious: it is better not to distract attention from your best point; a cumulative argument tends to be more persuasive than a series of disconnected points; and a succinct, forceful argument is likely to be more effective than a long-winded one that includes weak as well as strong points. The importance of this advice will vary according to the context: it is more directly applicable in the United States, where appellate argument is based to a large extent on written briefs, supplemented by oral presentation, than in most other common law jurisdictions where argument is for the most part presented orally in court.

The third rule of thumb is the most interesting, not least because it illustrates the artificiality of rigidly separating fact and value in the context of persuasion. The gist of the advice is that the *manner* in which the facts are presented can have more persuasive force than any abstract argument. Lord Atkin's daughter acknowledges this rather charmingly when she says of her father: 'When he gave us the facts of a case and asked us what we thought about it, his way of presenting the problem was such that there was never any suggestion in our minds that the other side could have a leg to stand on.'[44]

John W. Davis put the matter this way: '[I]t cannot be too often emphasized that in an appellate court the statement of the facts is not merely a part of the argument, it is more often than not the argument itself.'[45]

The judgments of, for example, Lord Atkin and Lord Denning provide ample illustrations of this point, which helps to explain the

---

[43] J. Davis, 'The Argument of an Appeal' (1940), reprinted in *Jurisprudence in Action* (Association of the Bar of the City of New York, 1953), p. 183.

[44] Op. cit., p. 15.

[45] Ibid., p. 181.

phenomenon of common law judges stating the facts more than once during the course of a single judgment. Consider the persuasive force of this famous example:

> Did the accountants owe a duty of care to the plaintiff? . . . They were professional accountants who prepared and put before him these accounts, knowing that he was going to be guided by them in making an investment in the company. On the faith of these accounts he did make the investment whereas if the accounts had been carefully prepared, he would not have made the investment at all. The result is that he has lost his money.[46]

In our experience most law students find this virtually irresistible. It is misleading to suggest that telling a story in a persuasive manner involves a simple appeal to emotion rather than to reason. For it is not difficult to articulate reasons, in the form of implicit principles, why this is an appealing characterization of the situation. But, it is also an error to suggest that appellate advocates and judges *never* resort to direct appeals to emotion: read through the speeches of Lord Buckmaster and Lord Atkin in *Donoghue* v. *Stevenson* and identify the emotive words and phrases used in them.

One final point: we have seen that it is possible to point to clear cases of valid and invalid reasons, reasons that are stronger than others, and of styles of argument that are inappropriate to a particular context; but even in the relatively formal context of legal interpretation in the courtroom, the criteria of validity, of cogency and of appropriateness are vague – this is in an area where the penumbra covers more territory than the core. For this reason advocates, judges and other interpreters are called on to exercise 'good judgment' in choosing which reasons to emphasize and which to play down or drop entirely. Those who seek an easy recipe for this are recommended to turn to *Poor Richard's Almanack*: 'At twenty years of age the will reigns, at thirty, the wit; and at forty, the judgment.'[47]

Postscript: lawyers' reasonings

So far in discussing reasoning and interpretation we have focused almost exclusively on the standpoints of the appellate advocate and the judge in legal proceedings. What of other interpreters? If we look

---

[46] *Candler* v. *Crane, Christmas* [1951] 2 K.B. 164, 176, *per* Denning L.J. (dissenting); and see Appendix II, section 7, question 14.
[47] B. Franklin, *Poor Richard's Almanack* (1741).

at the events and legal arguments in *Allen* from a number of other standpoints, it may help to see how fairly highly structured legal argument relates to the kinds of reasoning that are appropriate at other points in the process.

First, the standpoint of the legislator or other rule-maker: questions about the nature of the mischief and whether there is any need for a separate offence of bigamy have already been touched on. *Allen* revealed a fault in drafting, in the shape of an unnecessary ambiguity, but it also had the effect of eliminating the ambiguity for the future. Part of the reasoning in *Allen* related to what the law *ought to be*; strictly speaking, the kind of reasoning appropriate to this kind of question should be the same, irrespective of the person who is advancing the argument.[48] But in practice the appropriateness of a particular line of argument will be judged in part by contextual factors: in practice arguments concerning what the law ought to be tend to be inhibited by a number of factors in forensic and analogous contexts, such as considerations of relevancy to the issues in the present case, the patience of the court and the constraints of arguing within the framework of existing well-settled doctrine; whereas arguments in a more general legislative context tend to be more free-ranging. Thus one aspect of the arguments in *Allen* overlaps with the kind of reasoning appropriate for deciding what the law of bigamy should be for the future.

Second, the standpoint of the prosecutor at the time of the decision on whether or not to prosecute: clearly interpretation of the relevant rule(s) is only one of a number of factors to be taken into account in deciding whether or not to prosecute a suspected bigamist and, more generally, in deciding on a policy respecting when to prosecute in bigamy cases. We do not know on what grounds the decision to prosecute Allen was taken: that there was a doubt about the law may have come as a surprise to the prosecution; it may have provided a welcome opportunity to seek clarification of the law (a test case, as it were), or the prosecution may have been brought in spite of the doubt. The relevant point here is that legal reasoning in the narrow sense is relevant to, but is only one aspect of, the reasoning appropriate to decisions to prosecute.

Another interesting standpoint for present purposes is that of Allen

---

[48] Dworkin would dispute this. He argues that the question is not what the law *ought* to be, but what it *is*: the duty of courts is to confirm existing rights. Secondly he would argue that where there is doubt as to what those rights are, the only legitimate arguments are those based upon principles; see above pp. 128–31.

himself and his advisers. Consider the position of a friend of Allen, who has some practical legal knowledge, and who is called on to advise him as a friend, without any of the ethical or other professional inhibitions that might affect the approach of a practising lawyer in this situation. Let us first take the decision whether or not to go through the ceremony with Harriet Crouch (W3). The crucial question for Allen at this moment is that of the Bad Man: if I go through this ceremony, what will happen to me? The Law Reports do not tell us whether Harriet knew of Allen's subsisting marriage, why Allen wanted to marry her (or if he really did) and whether either party in fact realized that their marriage would be void anyway (although they were presumed to know the law). Nor do we have enough information from the report to make confident predictions about the likelihoods of detection, or of a decision to prosecute, or of the prosecution being able to adduce sufficient evidence to secure a conviction, or about the kind of sentence to be expected in the kind of case (in 1872) if Allen were to be convicted. Yet all these factors are relevant considerations for advising Allen about the decision whether to go through the ceremony with Harriet; if his decision is reasoned, the appropriate kinds of reasoning will by no means be confined to the factors that potentially formed part of the legal argument.

As to the specifically legal issues, Allen is presumed to know the law. What does this imply? First, that he can confidently predict that his 'marriage' to Harriet would be held to be void. Second, that the law is unclear as to whether going through the ceremony with her would amount to bigamy in law. Suppose that Allen had in fact heard of Fanning's case from friends and, relying on it, had decided to go through the ceremony (after all, he was presumed to know *Fanning*). Does that make the court's decision unjust? Could such a consideration be plausibly woven into counsel's argument on his behalf at an appropriate stage?

Now, let us move to a later point in time: he has been arrested and charged and is due to appear before Baron Martin at the Hampshire Assizes. Perhaps the main questions for Allen (and his legal advisers) are: should he plead guilty or not guilty? If not guilty, what strategy should he adopt? These appear to be questions on which Allen could reasonably expect advice from his professional legal advisers. What kinds of factors should be taken into account in framing advice on these questions? Or, to put the matter differently, what kinds of reason and reasoning would it be appropriate for lawyers to adopt in this context? Clearly it is not identical with the reasoning appropriate to answering the narrow and specific issue of law reserved by Baron Martin. But by this stage in the process the issues have been narrowed and defined more closely, and there is more overlap between arguments of counsel and the reasonings of his advisers.

Thus 'legal reasoning' in the narrow sense of reasoning on a doubtful question of law in the courtroom is only one part of lawyers' reasonings; it occurs in relatively pure forms in certain artificially defined contexts: appellate argument, counsel's opinion on a point of law, law examinations and so on. But it also has a role to play in other contexts as part of other kinds of practical decision-making, such as Allen's decision about whether to go through the ceremony, or whether or not to plead guilty and also, possibly, at the sentencing stage. There is a certain artificiality in isolating reasoning on questions of law in their purest form: not only does this give a false sense of how such reasoning operates in practice, but also there is a real danger that such a separation may also divert attention away from other aspects of lawyers' reasonings, such as reasoning towards conclusions of fact, reasoning about sanctions or reasoning in the process of bargaining; and these may be at least as important in practice and at least as interesting from a theoretical point of view.

8 Interpreting Cases

In ordinary legal usage the word 'case' is ambiguous. We talk of 'reading cases', 'citing cases', 'bringing cases', 'having a good case', 'winning cases', 'submitting no case to answer' and so on. To bring a case against someone means to institute legal proceedings against him; to ask 'have I a good case?' probably means 'have I a good chance of winning in legal proceedings?' When we talk of looking up, citing or reading a case we are talking about a *kind of document*. Similarly in talking of interpreting cases it is helpful to think in terms of interpreting the rather specialized kind of document typically to be found in the Law Reports. For our purpose it is useful to adopt, with slight modification, the following definition:

A case is the written memorandum of a dispute or controversy between persons, telling with varying degrees of completeness and of accuracy, what happened, what each of the parties did about it, what some supposedly impartial judge or other tribunal did in the way of bringing the dispute or controversy to an end, and the avowed reasons of the judge or tribunal for doing what was done.[1]

This definition identifies the principal ingredients with which we are concerned when interpreting cases, viz. a written *report*, of a *dispute*, between *legal persons*, which came before a *court* (or other tribunal). Such a report should tell us (*a*) who the parties were, (*b*) the facts (what allegedly happened), (*c*) the procedural steps (what each of the parties did about it), leading up to (*d*) the *decision* and the *order* of the

---

[1] Adapted from N. Dowling, E. Patterson and R. Powell, *Materials for Legal Method* (2nd edn, 1952), pp. 34-5.

judge or tribunal[2] and (*e*) the reasoned justification, usually referred to as the *judgment* in England or the *opinion* in the United States.

In interpreting cases the first point to bear in mind is that every case that has potential value as a precedent has a dual significance. First, it has a bearing on the particular dispute that came before the court or other tribunal. If the decision and order of the court was final, then from the point of view of the law the matter is closed – it is *res judicata*.[3] Secondly, cases are sources of law in so far as they provide answers to questions of law. When we are interpreting a case we are looking for the answer provided by the case to the question(s) of law before the court. As a matter of strict theory, the question should always be a question as to the scope and meaning of a rule of law and hence be both posed and answered in general terms. Thus in *Allen* the issue of law should not be posed in such terms as 'was Allen guilty?' but as 'what is the meaning of the words "shall marry" in section 57 of the Offences Against the Person Act 1861?'

One outstanding characteristic of rules of law derived from cases is that they are rules not in fixed verbal form. A case can be of precedent value even if no rule was articulated by the court, indeed if no reasons were given for the decision. Furthermore, even if a rule is stated very precisely and explicitly in a judgment, no one is bound by the exact form of words. And just as the answers to the issues raised in the case are not in fixed verbal form, there may well be room for significant differences in the way the issues are formulated.

However, there is a complicating factor. Whereas some cases are sources of law independent of any statutory provisions, other cases are

[2] In this context, when we speak of the judge's decision we mean the conclusion of law at which he arrives having applied the relevant rule(s) to the facts before him. While there may be some doubt as to the precise scope of that conclusion (see below), the decision amounts to a statement of the legal consequences that attach to the facts of the dispute and which create rights, duties, liabilities or obligations in the parties to the dispute. The *order* of the court is the particular implementation of such rights, duties, etc., in concrete form, such as an order to pay so much damages, or granting an injunction, or other form of redress; or an order imposing some penal consequence such as a fine or term of imprisonment.

In addition, it should be observed that the word 'decision' is ambiguous. Apart from the meaning attached to it above, it is also used synonymously with 'judgment', to mean the justification for a particular conclusion of law. See J. Montrose, 'The Language of, and a Notation for, the Doctrine of Precedent', 25 *Northern Ireland Legal Quarterly* (1974), 246-96.

[3] This expression is abbreviated from the maxim *Res judicata pro veritate accipitur*, which means 'a matter adjudicated is received as true'. In law this means that once the decision is final, the dispute cannot be re-litigated by the parties to the dispute: *Re Waring* [1948] 1 Ch. 221.

sources of law because they interpret legislative provisions. Thus *Donoghue* v. *Stevenson* is a precedent that purports to resolve a doubt about a legal rule not based on statute, whereas *Allen* has precedent value as a case interpreting a legislative rule. As a working rule of thumb we can say that, where the issue of law before a court is concerned with interpretation of a rule in fixed verbal form, that issue can always be posed in the form of a question starting 'what is the meaning of (section X of a particular Act, or the words "X" in that Act) ...?'; whereas where the issue of law is related to a non-statutory rule, that is a rule not in fixed verbal form, there is no standard way of posing the issue. Many of the differences of interpretation of *Donoghue* v. *Stevenson* could be expressed by posing the issue of law in that case in different terms. Thus, where the answer to a question of law is a rule not in fixed verbal form, the question of law involved is similarly not in fixed verbal form.

The use of past decisions to assist in the resolution of present problems is an unexceptional feature of the reasoning techniques we employ in both legal and non-legal contexts. In law, resort to precedent, that is to say the use of prior decisions to assist in the resolution of present disputes, has in general reached a considerable degree of refinement, but it has its roots in common human frailties and needs:

> Toward its operation drive all those phases of human make-up which build habit in the individual and institutions in the group: laziness as to the reworking of a problem once solved, the time and energy saved by routine, especially under any pressure of business; the values of routine as a curb on arbitrariness and as a prop of weakness, inexperience and instability; the social values of predictability; the power of whatever exists to produce expectations and the power of expectations to become normative. The force of precedent in the law is heightened by an additional factor: that curious, almost universal, sense of justice which urges that all men are properly to be treated alike in like circumstances. As the social system varies we meet infinite variations as to what men or treatments or circumstances are to be classed as 'like'; but the pressure to accept the views of the time and place remains.[4]

'Precedent' and related notions are not unique to law. People who serve on committees, in administrative agencies and other decision-making bodies may often be faced with a problem which demands a solution but which, for instance, involves issues of conflicting values or competing interests in a borderline case. In such circumstances, in the process of reaching a decision, they may express their reluctance to resolve the conflict in one particular way in the phrase, 'Let's not

[4] K. N. Llewellyn, *Encyclopedia of Social Sciences* (1931), vol. 3, p. 449.

create a precedent'. This phrase contains certain assumptions about problem-solving both for the present and the future. Thus, it is implicit that future decision-makers have some kind of obligation to come to the same conclusion should a similar case arise; that others who observe or rely upon the decisions of the particular body may expect that similar cases in the future will be similarly decided and thus may base their conduct upon such expectations; that the decision-making process is not constituted simply by the *ad hoc* resolution of particular cases, but involves the rational development of general policies or principles through these cases; and that the individual decisions themselves have status as expressions of policy or principle. Such factors provide a basis for demands that precedents be treated as having force or weight, and should not be ignored upon a whim, but departed from only on the basis of rational argument and justification. These four notions, of obligation, expectation of future behaviour, interstitial growth of policy and principle, and the authority of decisions, form the basis of the common law's treatment of precedent.

Systems of law may be unique in having developed rules which govern how courts must (not), may (not) and can (not) deal with prior cases. Whatever those rules may prescribe, they are cumulatively and generally known by the expression, 'a doctrine of precedent'. In a sense, nearly all legal systems have a doctrine of precedent, though its requirements may vary from system to system. Even a legal system which explicitly prohibits the citation of prior cases in court can be said to have a doctrine of precedent in that it has a rule which regulates the use of precedent.[5] The doctrine of precedent is seen at its most formalized in the English common law, a system which is unusual both in regard to the fact that it exhibits a high proportion of rules of law extracted from decided cases, and in its detailed rules which prescribe how the various courts in the judicial hierarchy must, may or can deal with precedent decisions.

1 The doctrine of precedent

According to the English doctrine,[6] a previous decision is to be treated as an authority, if it is analogous to a present dispute before a court, if it was decided by a court which, according to the rules of the

[5] R. Schlesinger, *Comparative Law: Cases and Materials* (1960), pp. 287–322.
[6] See R. Cross, *Precedent in English Law* (3rd edn, 1977).

doctrine, has the status to make decisions which will be deemed to be authoritative, and if the decision has not been abrogated by a statute or a court which has the power to overrule prior decisions. When a court has to deal with a precedent decision, the doctrine prescribes that (*a*) if the precedent is a decision of a court superior to it in the judicial hierarchy, then it *must* follow that precedent in the present case (this is normally called 'being bound by' a precedent); or (*b*) if the precedent is one of its own previous decisions, then, subject to certain exceptions in which it *may* depart from it, it *must* follow the precedent; or (*c*) if the precedent is a decision of a court inferior to it in the judicial hierarchy, then it is not bound to follow the precedent, but may do so if it chooses.

Thus the Court of Appeal must, subject to certain exceptions, follow its own precedents, must follow those of the House of Lords, and may follow those of the High Court but can overrule them. The High Court must follow the precedents of both the Court of Appeal and the House of Lords, and subject to certain exceptions, its own decisions. The House of Lords, being the highest court in the hierarchy, is not bound to follow the decisions of any other court; and until 1966, when it substantially modified the formal terms of the obligation, is normally bound by its own decisions.

Two features of the English doctrine stand out. The first is that despite the existence of an obligation to follow prior cases, the doctrine is permissive in certain crucial respects. For example, the House of Lords' Practice Statement of 1966, by which the modifications to the operation of the doctrine in its Judicial Committee were effected, is quite indeterminate as to the grounds on which the House may depart from one of its previous decisions:

Their Lordships regard the use of precedent as an indispensable foundation upon which to decide what is the law and its application to individual cases. It provides at least some degree of certainty upon which individuals can rely in the conduct of their affairs, as well as a basis for orderly development of legal rules.

Their Lordships nevertheless recognize that too rigid adherence to precedent may lead to injustice in a particular case and also unduly restrict the proper development of the law. They propose, therefore, to modify their present practice and, while treating former decisions of this House as normally binding, to depart from a previous decision when it appears right to do so.

In this connection they will bear in mind the danger of disturbing retrospectively the basis on which contracts, settlements of property and fiscal arrangements have been entered into and also the especial need for certainty as to the criminal law. This announcement is not intended to affect the use of precedent elsewhere than in this House.[7]

Although some considerations are specified as being relevant to the decision whether to depart from a prior case, the House is otherwise at liberty to formulate its own criteria of 'when it appears right to do so'.[8] Similarly the Criminal Division of the Court of Appeal has for some time taken the view that the principle of *stare decisis* does not apply as rigorously to its previous decisions as it does within the Civil Division of the Court of Appeal; but neither has the doctrine, nor in so far as it is the creation of the courts, have the courts of appellate criminal jurisdiction, been more precise about its use.[9]

Nor, at a more general level, does the doctrine in any way specify *when* a previous decision is to be regarded as analogous to the case at hand, or what criteria are to be used by courts to determine the extent, if any, of an analogy between one case and another.

The second feature is that in practice judges routinely follow prior cases even though there is no obligation on them to do so within the terms of the doctrine.[10] It is thus quite common for judges in superior courts to follow decisions of lower courts, that is, decisions which are persuasive only. Indeed, it is usually a matter of some comment when a court does not follow a clear, albeit only a persuasive, authority. That the English judiciary stick closer to precedents than the doctrine requires them to do is well exemplified by the limited use which the House of Lords has made of its liberty under the Practice Statement. Although the House has on a number of occasions considered, or been invited by counsel to consider, overruling one of its decisions on the authority of the Practice Statement, it has invoked it for that purpose in only a very few instances.[11] For example, in *Fitzleet Estates* v. *Cherry*[12] the House stressed the importance of maintaining 'certainty' in the law; a value which it was not prepared to see diminished through

[7] Practice Direction (Judicial Precedent), H.L. [1966] 1 W.L.R. 1234.

[8] For a good discussion of such criteria, and of the use made of the Practice Statement by the House of Lords, see G. Maher, 'Statutory Interpretation and Overruling in the House of Lords' [1981] *Statute Law Review* 85.

[9] See *Taylor* above, p. 45; *Gould* [1968] 2 Q.B. 68 and *Newsome* [1970] 3 All E.R. 455.

[10] Professor Rupert Cross argued that the first rule of precedent is that 'all courts must consider the relevant case law'; but this is not the same as routine acceptance of relevant case law; 'The House of Lords and the Rules of Precedent' in *Law, Morality and Society* (eds. P. Hacker and J. Raz, 1977), p. 145.

[11] One of these was in *Miliangos* v. *George Frank Ltd* [1976] A.C. 443, above, pp. 201–5. See the discussion in Maher, op. cit., Cross, ibid., and *Vestey* v. *I.R.C.* [1980] A.C. 1148.

[12] [1977] 1 W.L.R. 1345.

the reconsideration of precedents. Indeed, in those cases in which the House has rejected reliance on the Practice Statement, the view has been reiterated that it is not sufficient for its use that an earlier decision was wrong; other reasons for departing from it must be adduced.

Although the Judicial Committee of the House of Lords is the supreme judicial authority in our legal system, the Civil Division of the Court of Appeal is generally acknowledged to be the most significant in terms of the influence of its decisions. Its position in the legal system has been described as central, and its responsibility for the stability, consistency and predictability of the system frequently emphasized.[13]

These considerations are thought by many of the judiciary to militate strongly against a liberty to depart from its own decisions being adopted by, or granted to, the Court of Appeal. This explains the emphatic rejection by the House of Lords in *Davis* v. *Johnson* of the efforts of Lord Denning M.R. either to liberate the Civil Division of the Court of Appeal from that aspect of the doctrine of precedent, or to create exceptions in addition to those laid down in *Young* v. *Bristol Aeroplane*. Considering the centrality of the Court of Appeal, *Young* v. *Bristol Aeroplane* may well be regarded as the most important case on the doctrine of precedent. In it, a full Court of Appeal laid down the following proposition and the well-known three exceptions to it:

> The Court of Appeal is bound to follow its own decisions and those of courts of co-ordinate jurisdiction, and the 'full' court is in the same position in this respect as a division of the court consisting of three members. The only exceptions to this rule are: – (1.) The court is entitled and bound to decide which of two conflicting decisions of its own it will follow; (2.) the court is bound to refuse to follow a decision of its own which, though not expressly overruled, cannot, in its opinion, stand with a decision of the House of Lords; (3.) the court is not bound to follow a decision of its own if it is satisfied that the decision was given per incuriam, e.g., where a statute or a rule having statutory effect which would have affected the decision was not brought to the attention of the earlier court.[14]

This rule has been constantly treated as authoritative, and attempts to broaden the scope of the exceptions have for the most part been

---

[13] See e.g. Scarman L.J. in *Farrell* v. *Alexander* [1976] 1 Q.B. 345, 371; quoted with approval by Lord Diplock in *Davis* v. *Johnson*, above, pp. 104–5.

[14] [1944] K.B. 718. This formulation in the headnote of the case was approved by Lord Diplock in *Davis* v. *Johnson*, above, p. 102.

rejected.[15] In *Davis* v. *Johnson*, Lord Diplock treats it as the cornerstone of the doctrine's application to the Court of Appeal, and deprecates in strong language Lord Denning's 'one-man crusade' against *stare decisis*.[16]

There has been argument concerning the status of the doctrine and the values which it is thought to promote. One disagreement is about the juridical basis of the doctrine. Some writers have argued that a court cannot, on its own initiative, declare that it shall be bound by its own previous decisions unless there already exists a rule providing that *that* declaration is itself binding. This logical impossibility, it is argued, extends to a declaration such as the 1966 Practice Statement; for as long as it is operative, there is at least one decision of the House which cannot be departed from, namely the decision mentioned in the Statement not to be absolutely bound by past decisions.

Others have questioned whether the rules of precedent are rules of law or of practice. This question raises some difficult conceptual issues concerning the meaning of the terms involved and the nature of authoritative rules. The thrust of the distinction is that if the rules of precedent are treated as rules of law, then they impose obligations which cannot be modified by the simple device of a Practice Statement, for this does not acknowledge the authority from which such rules emanate. On the other hand, if they are treated as rules of practice only, then they can of course be modified by a Practice Statement in the same way as courts routinely regulate the hearing of cases, the taxation of costs, vacation sittings and so on; but such a Statement could not, it is argued, be effective in a court other than the one which issues it. The argument may be posed as a question: on what basis did the House of Lords in *Davis* v. *Johnson* purport to lay down rules as to how the Court of Appeal should deal with its own previous decisions?

[15] *Morelle* v. *Wakeling* [1955] 2 Q.B. 379. A minor addition to these exceptions was established in *Boys* v. *Chaplin* [1968] 2 Q.B. 1, in which the Court of Appeal decided that in an appeal on a point of substantive law it would not be bound by a previous decision of two Lords Justices on an interlocutory appeal.

[16] In particular Lord Diplock above, p, 103. It is of interest to compare the accounts which Lords Denning and Diplock give of the development and juridical status of the doctrine: Lord Denning emphasizes its value as a prudential prescription which is permissive in many respects and subject to a number of exceptions; Lord Diplock treats it as imposing clear and desirable obligations to which there are limited exceptions. Lord Denning, above, pp. 91-3; Lord Diplock, pp. 102-3. Two discussions of Lord Denning's efforts are H. Carty, 'Precedent and the Court of Appeal', 1 *Legal Studies* (1980), 68 and C. Rickett, 'Precedent in the Court of Appeal', 43 *Modern Law Review* (1980), 136. See now P. Evans (1982) 41 *C.L.J.* 162.

There is disagreement on the way in which these questions concerning the doctrine should be resolved. Most writers accept that the hierarchy of the court structure implies an obligation on inferior courts to follow analogous decisions of superior courts and, apart from the occasional tremor in the Court of Appeal, this obligation is very rarely challenged by judges.[17] There is less agreement on that aspect of the doctrine relating to a court's own precedents. Some regard it as an internal non-binding convention of judicial practice; others treat it as imposing a substantial obligation. Yet others doubt the practical importance of questioning the juridical basis and status of the doctrine: what is clear is that judges do generally acknowledge an obligation to follow their own and superior precedents, that good reasons are required to depart from a previous decision, and that the House of Lords has the power and the authority to specify the extent of the doctrine's application to itself and to inferior courts.

Another aspect of traditional discussions of precedent is exemplified by the fairly common conflict between a judge who takes the view that adherence to precedent is a value which should take priority over the promotion of some other value in a particular case, and a judge in the same case who takes the opposite view. The values claimed for precedent are predictability, stability, efficiency, the elimination of error and of bias, and general coherence between decided cases. These often conflict with values present in the social context within which a dispute arises.[18] No settled criteria exist for determining which set of values to prefer, and it is in difficult cases such as *Farrell* v. *Alexander*[19] and *Davis* v. *Johnson*[20] that Lord Denning and others have raised the question of the desirability of continued adherence to the doctrine with only the limited exceptions of *Young*'s case. In Lord Denning's view, the values which the doctrine represents would in most cases be accorded priority, but the removal of the inhibitions which it imposes would avoid the unhappy consequences of rigidity, inflexibility and substantive injustice which may presently occur. It is impossible to say in general, and as an absolute imperative, whether the values of the system or of

---

[17] In *Broome* v. *Cassell Ltd* [1971] 2 Q.B. 354, Lord Denning argued that a relevant House of Lords judgment was decided *per incuriam* (in ignorance of) a previous decision of the House, and accordingly the Court of Appeal was not bound by it. Lord Hailsham L.C. thought this suggestion 'offensive' and emphatically reasserted the duty of an inferior court to follow decisions of a superior court: [1972] A.C. 1027, 1054.

[18] Above, pp. 145-8.

[19] [1976] Q.B. 345.

[20] Above, pp. 85-95.

the social context should prevail; each has strong claims to be considered in any theory of justification. It is perhaps more appropriate to ask whether a relaxation in the doctrine can be predicted to have beneficial results; but here, too, opinions differ and analogies from other common law jurisdictions, such as the United States of America or Canada, are of limited value. It may also be argued that apart from any instrumental reasons, the doctrine of precedent performs important symbolic functions, in particular concerning the constitutional and political relationship between the courts and the legislature. The claimed consequences of adherence to precedent are that judges decide cases, in particular those involving disputes between citizens and the state, from a position of political neutrality; that the courts declare, but do not make, the law; and that bad law can only be properly changed by Parliament. These tenets of judicial behaviour are, in terms of rhetoric at least, of the first political importance; but whether they accurately reflect the reality of judicial behaviour is a controversial[21] and complex issue, involving a number of factors.

First there are the twin recognitions that notwithstanding that courts are in general not well suited to initiate changes in the law, judges do make law, if only interstitially, and that modern governments have a virtual monopoly over law reform. Then there are the methods of training, selection and appointment of judges and their social background; the historic and prevailing conceptions of the relationship between the constituent elements of the state, including the present understanding and reality of the doctrine of the supremacy of Parliament; and the role of the courts as arbiters of disputes. Each of these is also an issue of considerable complexity, over which writers habitually disagree. It is, however, not possible to make a fully reasoned judgment about the value of the doctrine of precedent without also assuming some position on these other issues. In this sense, the recent reaffirmation by the House of Lords of the value and place of the doctrine within the legal system signifies, at the very least, the continued acceptance of the rhetoric of the traditional role of the courts.[22]

---

[21] See, for example, J. A. G. Griffith, *The Politics of the Judiciary* (1977); and the review of it by W. L. Twining, [1978] *Public Law* 114.

[22] See also the reiteration of the courts' role concerning the interpretation of statutes in *Duport Steel* v. *Sirs* [1980] 1 All E.R. 541; below p. 334.

2 **The practice of precedent**

A distinction needs to be drawn between accounts of the *doctrine* of precedent and descriptions of the *practice* of handling precedent. The doctrine consists of the rules which prescribe how prior cases must, may and can be used; descriptions of practice deal with the techniques which are in fact used by judges and other interpreters in handling the prior cases. The distinction between doctrine and practice is not a sharp one. On the one hand, there are tacit conventions, regularly followed by judges in England, which accord greater respect to prior cases than is required by orthodox formulations of the doctrine. For example, the doctrine of precedent prescribes that a Lord Justice of Appeal *may* overrule, disapprove or not follow a decision of the High Court or he may follow it, as a persuasive authority. In practice a Lord Justice of Appeal will feel under some obligation at least to consider a relevant decision of the High Court and to deviate from it only for some good reason. Similarly the doctrine of precedent does not lay down a formula for extracting rules of law from previous cases, that is, for determining the *ratio decidendi*;[23] indeed English judges have been careful not to make this the subject of a formal rule. Judges in subsequent cases are not bound by the explicit wording used in prior cases; in other words, the *ratio decidendi* is not a rule in fixed verbal form.[24] Nevertheless there is a tacit convention that special attention should be paid to the words used by judges in prior cases and often a passage from a judgment in the prior case is treated as an adequate formulation of the *ratio*. Sometimes judges and other interpreters lay great stress on the particular words used in such judicial formulations; at other times they ignore them entirely or treat them as too wide or too narrow. We shall consider the problem of the *ratio decidendi* further below; the point to be emphasized here is that orthodox formulations of the doctrine of precedent, tacit conventions or rules of practice which are commonly observed in handling cases, and descriptions of the actual techniques used in practice are not always easy to distinguish.

Nevertheless the distinction is an important one. Much of the literature on precedent in England has concentrated on the doctrine but

[23] Below, pp. 286–91.

[24] Rules may come to be formulated in essentially the same terms, and occasionally one particular formulation may become sanctified. One of the clearest examples of this is the celebrated rule in *Rylands* v. *Fletcher* (1866) L.R. 1 Ex. 265; and the rule in *Derry* v. *Peek* (1889) 14 App. Cas. 337 is often similarly treated.

says relatively little about how the techniques are in fact used within the leeways of choice permitted by the doctrine. Too great a concern with the niceties of the doctrine may give a distorted impression of the realities of the practice: on the one hand, the range of techniques available and the ways they are in fact used are more varied and subtle than some orthodox accounts suggest; on the other hand, the respect accorded in practice to certain categories of non-binding precedent may be a more important distinguishing feature of the English approach than the alleged strictness of the doctrine of precedent.

Precedent techniques are techniques of reasoning about how prior cases should be interpreted. They are typically used in the context of justifying a particular result in a case, or in persuading others to come to a particular conclusion, or in supporting formulations of legal doctrine in the process of exposition or in making certain kinds of predictions. It has long been recognized that a variety of techniques is involved in interpreting cases, but it was Karl Llewellyn who first attempted an extensive examination of this aspect of legal reasoning.[25] His somewhat rough and ready list of sixty-four techniques of following and avoiding precedent decisions suggests that even in England the explicit doctrine and tacit conventions of precedent are not necessarily as restrictive an influence on legal developments as is commonly suggested by formalistic discussions of the subject. Within the armoury of techniques available to courts in dealing with precedents, there are many devices for creating law within the framework of authority.

From the standpoint of the advocate, prior cases are potentially favourable, adverse, or neutral, and it is from this standpoint that we can most easily see the way in which these techniques of reasoning are employed. Where the advocate is faced with an adverse precedent he has a number of choices open to him. He may, for example, argue that the precedent was rightly decided but is distinguishable on its facts or on the issue of law it raised.[26] On the other hand, where the cases are analogous, the advocate may use a number of techniques to argue

---

[25] K. Llewellyn, *The Common Law Tradition* (1960), pp. 75-92.

[26] An example of the technique of distinguishing issues of law may be seen in the case in which an advocate is defending a person charged under section 20 of the Offences Against the Person Act, 1861, which makes it an offence to '*inflict*' any grievous bodily harm upon any other person'. This is arguably narrower in scope than section 18 of the Act which makes it an offence to '*cause*' any grievous bodily harm to any person'. Thus, an advocate could challenge a precedent on section 18 on the ground that the issue of law raised by the word 'cause' is different to that raised by the word 'inflict'. See J. Smith and B. Hogan, *Criminal Law* (4th edn, 1978), pp. 370-3.

that the precedent was wrongly decided or is of weak authority by suggesting, for example:

(a) that the precedent involved a faulty interpretation of other prior cases;[27]

(b) that the precedent was a decision given *per incuriam*, that is, in ignorance of a binding statutory or judicial authority;[28]

(c) that the precedent has been subsequently overruled or doubted by other judges:[29]

(d) that the precedent is irreconcilable with prior or subsequent decisions.[30]

These primary techniques are employed quite commonly to avoid prior cases, but in addition there are various secondary techniques for weakening their precedent value, for example, by arguing:

(e) that the deciding court was of low authority;[31]

(f) that the scope of the decision is unclear;[32]

(g) that the reasoning other than from authority is weak;[33]

(h) that the deciding court was particularly influenced by special considerations;[34]

(i) that social conditions have changed;[35]

(j) that the report of the precedent is unreliable;[36]

(k) that the decision has been criticized by academic writers.[37]

This is by no means a comprehensive list, nor are the techniques of equal weight. A precedent can be favourable either in its result or in

---

[27] See Lord Buckmaster in *Donoghue* v. *Stevenson* (Chapter 1 above, p. 56), where he argues that *George* v. *Skivington* is of weak authority because it misinterprets *Langridge* v. *Levy*.

[28] See *Gerard* v. *Worth* [1936] 2 All E.R. 905, which was held to be *per incuriam* in *Lancaster Motor* v. *Bremith* [1941] 2 All E.R. 11.

[29] See Lord Buckmaster in *Donoghue* v. *Stevenson* (Chapter 1 above, p. 56), where he discusses subsequent disapproval of *George* v. *Skivington*.

[30] See the treatment of *Thompson* v. *Milk Marketing Board* [1952] 2 All E.R. 344 in *Eastwood* v. *Harrod* [1968] 2 All E.R. 389.

[31] See Lord Buckmaster's treatment of the American case *Thomas* v. *Winchester* as being of 'no authority', *Donoghue* v. *Stevenson* [1932] A.C. 560, 576.

[32] See Lord Buckmaster (Chapter 1 above, p. 55) where he speaks of *Langridge* v. *Levy* as having been 'variously explained'.

[33] See Lord Buckmaster, id.

[34] See Lord Atkin [1932] A.C. 560, 588, where he treats *Winterbottom* v. *Wright* as a special case because it was decided upon a demurrer.

[35] See Lord Atkin (Chapter 1 above, pp. 56-8), where this factor is implicit.

[36] See *Industrial Properties* v. *A.E.I.* [1977] 2 All E.R. 293.

[37] See Lord Hailsham L.C.'s speech in *Hyam* v. *D.P.P.* [1975] A.C. 55 concerning the criticism of the House of Lords' earlier decision in *D.P.P.* v. *Smith* [1961] A.C. 290.

its reasoning or both, and there are similarly supplementary ways in which additional weight can be attached to a decision, for example by emphasizing the high reputation of the judges in the prior case or the fact of its subsequent approval.

Advocates, however, are not the only participants in the legal process who seek to persuade others to accept a particular line of reasoning. Beside their primary task of justifying their decisions, judges too may try to persuade their colleagues that a particular legal solution to a dispute is the one to be adopted. Where a judge is espousing a currently unpopular result, he must rely heavily on his powers of persuasion, and he may employ a number of rhetorical devices to bolster and protect his case. Some of these devices have been indicated earlier, but we should stress that while some precedent techniques can be isolated, they tend to overlap and fuse into one another and operate cumulatively, so that their effect can best be appreciated by reading a judgment as a whole.

A good example of the cumulation of techniques in dealing with an adverse authority is to be found in the treatment of *Reg.* v. *Fanning* in the reconstruction of the argument for the prosecution in *Allen*'s case presented in Chapter 7. It was possible to argue that (*a*) *Fanning* was only of persuasive authority *and* (*b*) it was of weak persuasive authority because there were four dissentient judges *and* even some of the majority expressed regret in concluding that the appeal should be allowed *and* (*c*) that *Fanning* was wrongly decided (for several reasons) *and* (*d*) that *Allen* and *Fanning* were distinguishable on the facts. It is pertinent to note that in his judgment Cockburn C.J. relied on (*a*), (*b*) and (*c*), but explicitly stated that that although it was open to him to distinguish *Fanning*, he was holding it to be wrongly decided. The effect of this was to open the way for *Allen* to be interpreted relatively broadly, rather than to introduce a fine distinction into the interpretation of 'shall marry'.

Let us now consider the extracts from the speeches of Lords Atkin and Buckmaster in *Donoghue* v. *Stevenson* which are reprinted in Chapter 1. This decision is generally regarded as a landmark in the development of the law of negligence. The potentially relevant precedents at that time were generally considered to stand fairly firmly against the extension of a manufacturer's liability in tort to the ultimate consumer. Nearly all of these precedents were decisions of courts inferior to the House of Lords and so the House was not bound to follow them, but one of the tacit conventions of the doctrine of precedent requires consideration of all relevant precedents irrespective of the place of the deciding court within the hierarchy.[38] Lord Atkin was in favour of allowing the appeal, while Lord Buckmaster supported its dismissal. Yet while they held opposite views as to the outcome of the case, each was able to reconcile his conclusion with the precedents by the use of a number of devices. By looking at this process in respect of their handling of two of the precedents we can see quite vividly a sample of the range and scope of the techniques that operate within the doctrine.

First let us take the case of *Winterbottom* v. *Wright*. This decision tended to support Lord Buckmaster's position, and thus raised no real difficulties for him, but the case was potentially distinguishable from *Donoghue* v. *Stevenson* and so he sought to emphasize the closeness of the analogy between the two cases:

> The case of *Winterbottom* v. *Wright* is, on the other hand, an authority that is closely applicable. Owing to negligence in the construction of a carriage it broke down, and a stranger to the manufacture and sale sought to recover damages for injuries which he alleged were due to negligence in the work, and it was held that he had no cause of action either in tort or arising out of contract. This case seems to me to show that the manufacturer of any article is not liable to a third party injured by negligent construction, for there is nothing in the character of a coach to place it in a special category. It may be noted, also, that in this case Alderson B. said: 'The only safe rule is to confine the right to recover to those who enter into the contract; if we go one step beyond that, there is no reason why we should not go fifty.' [Chap. 1, pp. 55–6.]

Initially, one should notice Lord Buckmaster's clear statement of his intentions with regard to the precedent value of the case. He asserts that it is 'an authority that is closely applicable'. A closer analogy between the two cases is effected by glossing over their factual differences and stating the facts at a higher level of generality. Observe how 'carriages' and 'ginger beer' are now subsumed in the more abstract category of 'articles'. Lastly, Lord Buckmaster's appeal to the 'flood-gates' argument,[39] common to both legal and non-legal contexts, is further reinforcement of his view of the correctness of the case.

What technique(s), then, might we expect Lord Atkin to adopt in order to undermine the precedent value of *Winterbottom* v. *Wright*? He

---

[38] Above, n. 10.

[39] While appeal to this argument may properly warn a judge or other decision-maker of some problematic consequences of his decision, such as an increased volume of litigation or the creation of difficult problems of continuous variation, it may be of doubtful propriety to use factors such as these to deny the merits of a case outright. See also Chapter 5, p. 215.

does not attempt to 'get round' the decision or to overrule it, as he was empowered to do, but chooses the more subtle approach of agreeing with Lord Buckmaster that the case was correctly decided, but arguing that the issue of law raised in *Donoghue* v. *Stevenson* was not an issue in the earlier case.

> It is to be observed that no negligence apart from breach of contract was alleged – in other words, no duty was alleged other than the duty arising out of the contract.... The argument of the defendant was that, on the face of the declaration, the wrong arose merely out of the breach of a contract, and that only a party to the contract could sue.... The actual decision appears to have been manifestly right; no duty to the plaintiff arose out of the contract; and the duty of the defendant under the contract with the Postmaster-General to put the coach in good repair could not have involved such direct relations with the servant of the persons whom the Postmaster-General employed to drive the coach as would give rise to a duty of care owed to such servant. [Chapter 1, p. 57.]

The main point is that, since the plaintiff was not alleging negligence other than in the context of the fulfilment of a contract, then that case can have decided the law only upon that issue, and can have no application to an allegation of negligence as a tort, which is the issue in the present case.[40] By distinguishing the issues in the two cases in this way Lord Atkin is able to dispose of a potentially adverse case while at the same time appearing to respect authority.

George v. *Skivington*, on the other hand, is a decision that appeared to support Lord Atkin's conclusion in *Donoghue* v. *Stevenson*, and in Lord Buckmaster's handling of this case we can see different and more complex techniques. In that case the plaintiff used a shampoo that her husband had bought from the defendant, whose negligent preparation of it caused her hair to fall out. She sued him and won. Lord Buckmaster's main treatment of this case was as follows:

> Of the remaining cases, *George* v. *Skivington* is the one nearest to the present, and without that case, and the statement of Cleasby B. in *Francis* v. *Cockrell* and the dicta of Brett M.R. in *Heaven* v. *Pender*, the appellant would be destitute of authority. *George* v. *Skivington* related to the sale of a noxious hairwash, and a claim made by a person who had not bought it but who had

---

[40] Plaintiffs may plead their case in an area of law which, though it does not seem appropriate to the facts of the case, affords them an additional, or perhaps the only, chance of success. In *De la Bere* v. *Pearson* [1908] 1 K.B. 260 in which the plaintiff, to his detriment, relied upon the financial advice of a newspaper which had invited readers to seek such advice, the action was in contract. While contractual principles did not clearly cover the facts, this was, *at that time*, the only practical course of action available. On the present law, the best course of action would probably be to plead negligence.

suffered from its use, based on its having been negligently compounded, was allowed. It is remarkable that *Langridge* v. *Levy* was used in support of the claim and influenced the judgment of all the parties to the decision. Both Kelly C. B. and Pigott B. stressed the fact that the article had been purchased to the knowledge of the defendant for the use of the plaintiff, as in *Langridge* v. *Levy* and Cleasby B., who realizing that *Langridge* v. *Levy* was decided on the ground of fraud, said: 'Substitute the word "negligence" for "fraud" and the analogy between *Langridge* v. *Levy* and this case is complete.' It is unnecessary to point out too emphatically that such a substitution cannot possibly be made. No action based on fraud can be supported by mere proof of negligence.

I do not propose to follow the fortunes of *George* v. *Skivington*; few cases can have lived so dangerously and lived so long. Lord Sumner, in the case of *Blacker* v. *Lake and Elliot*, closely examines its history and I agree with his analysis. He said that he could not presume to say that it was wrong, but he declined to follow it on the ground, which is I think firm, that it was in conflict with *Winterbottom* v. *Wright*. [Chapter 1, p. 56].

Lord Buckmaster here is dealing with an adverse precedent, and the purpose of this passage is to persuade the reader that *George* v. *Skivington* is a decision that has little authority. This is achieved by a combination of the general tone of the language used and an accumulation of various techniques. The passage, when read as a whole, has an overall persuasive effect that *George* v. *Skivington* was a misguided decision, and while some of this effect cannot be analysed precisely in terms of distinctive precedent techniques, a number of separate points can be identified.

First, Lord Buckmaster suggests that the precedent value of the decision must be low because it is an isolated decision, and it is coupled with and relegated to the rank of mere judicial *dicta*, without which the plaintiff would be 'destitute of authority'. This is reinforced towards the end of the passage, where he draws attention to the fact that it has been disapproved in a subsequent decision. He also seeks to undermine the decision by suggesting that it misapplied or misunderstood the earlier decision in *Langridge* v. *Levy*, and is thus of weak authority. Possibly the main ground on which Lord Buckmaster seeks to distinguish *George* v. *Skivington* is the fact that the defendant knew who the consumer was to be, which, Lord Buckmaster hints, converts the case into a decision on fraud, which has nothing to do with the tort of negligence. In another part of his speech, he says of this case:

It is difficult to appreciate what is the importance of the fact that the vendor knew who was the person for whom the article was purchased unless it be that the case was treated as one of fraud, and that without this element of knowledge it could not be brought within the principle of *Langridge* v. *Levy*. Indeed, this is the only view of the matter which adequately explains the references in the judgments in *George* v. *Skivington* to *Langridge* v. *Levy*.... [[1932] A.C. 571.]

In his treatment of *George* v. *Skivington* on this issue of fraud, Lord Buckmaster is employing a technique similar to that used by Lord Atkin when dealing with *Winterbottom* v. *Wright*, though there are other factors at work in Lord Buckmaster's analysis. Thus he treats the case as dubious authority on the tort of fraud; and *in addition*, in the event of its being seen as a case of negligence, as being wrongly decided on the authority of *Winterbottom* v. *Wright*.

The conflict that existed, in Lord Buckmaster's view, between these two cases introduces a new aspect of precedent technique. Here, the case to be avoided is deemed to be inconsistent with an earlier decision on the basis of the judge's interpretation of that earlier decision. Elsewhere in his speech, Lord Buckmaster accumulates other points against *George* v. *Skivington*, finally purporting to overrule it, suggesting in somewhat emotive terms that it should be buried so securely that its perturbed spirit will no longer vex the law.[41]

The task for Lord Atkin in dealing with *George* v. *Skivington* is a more straightforward one. He adopts, though he does not overemphasize, the decision, and seeks to protect its authority by indicating the dissimilarity between the decision in that case and his own interpretation of *Winterbottom* v. *Wright*:

> I find this [possible conflict] very difficult to understand, for *George* v. *Skivington* was based upon a duty in the manufacturer to take care independently of contract, while *Winterbottom* v. *Wright* was decided on ... a contractual duty to keep in repair. [[1932] A.C. 594.]

The treatment by these two judges of these two cases should give some idea of the techniques that are in regular use in case law reasoning. Through the use of these techniques, Lords Atkin and Buckmaster were able to come to opposite conclusions as to the effect of the case as a whole: 'without that case the appellant would be destitute of authority' (Lord Buckmaster); 'in my opinion several decided cases support the view that in such a case as the present the manufacturer owes a duty to the consumer to be careful' (Lord Atkin); and as to their effect individually: 'with the exception of *George* v. *Skivington*, no case directly involving the principle has ever succeeded in the courts' (Lord Buckmaster); 'Next in this chain of authority comes *George* v. *Skivington*' (Lord Atkin).

[41] [1932] A.C. 560, 576.

One noteworthy feature of Lord Atkin's speech is that in dealing with adverse precedents he made virtually no use of one of the most common techniques, that of distinguishing on the facts. It is important to understand the reason for this. When two cases are distinguished in this way the facts of each are interpreted relatively narrowly and in detail. This will be reflected in the protasis of a rule for which the case may be made to stand; for the more detailed and specific the interpretation of the material facts of the protasis, the narrower the rule. This would have been incompatible with Lord Atkin's objective, which was to establish the basis for a broad rule concerning the duty of care in negligence.

Donoghue v. *Stevenson* and *Allen* are both good illustrations of the point that even the allegedly strict doctrine of precedent in England allows a considerable leeway for varying, sometimes conflicting, interpretations of prior cases. In a number of crucial respects the doctrine is permissive or vague, or both. Thus many cases treated as relevant by interpreters in the context of legal reasoning are of only persuasive authority; the doctrine permits a wide range of techniques for dealing with such cases, that is to say it allows scope for a variety of types of reason to be taken into account both in determining the interpretation to be put on the case and the weight to be attached to it. It is vague both as to the weight to be attached to such reasons and what classes of reason are valid or legitimate. Even where a judge or interpreter is confronted with a potentially 'binding' precedent, the doctrine is vague in certain crucial respects. It lays down no official test for determining what is the binding part of the case. He is permitted to distinguish such cases, but it provides no guidance on the level of generality at which it is to be interpreted, nor what weight to attach to the actual words used in the judgments in the prior case, nor how he is to set about reconciling apparently conflicting 'binding' cases. Indeed, the unhappy interpreter when confronted by a precedent he does not like, may be inhibited from departing from it not so much by the official doctrine of precedent, as by less tangible factors such as his own sense of what is appropriate or the weight of professional opinion.

The room for manoeuvre lies in the nature of legal judgment. Every case is a unique event, and the problem of extending general significance to it involves the identification of elements of that case which are shared by others. This problem is made the more difficult because judges quite often formulate their statements of the facts and of the applicable rule of a particular case several times using different language. Moreover, in many appellate decisions, there will be a multiplicity of judgments, and thus we find that these formulations vary not only within individual judgments but also between them.

To illustrate this fluidity, let us look again at *Donoghue* v. *Stevenson*. Lord Atkin begins his speech by posing the issue in two different ways:

> ... the sole question for determination in this case is legal: Do the averments made by the pursuer in her pleading, if true, disclose a cause of action? I need not restate the particular facts. The question is whether the manufacturer of an article of drink sold by him to a distributor, in circumstances which prevent the distributor or the ultimate purchaser or consumer from discovering by inspection any defect, is under a legal duty to the ultimate purchaser or consumer to take reasonable care that the article is free from defect likely to cause injury to health. [Chapter 1, p. 56.]

The facts as contained in the pleadings were more specific than Lord Atkin characterizes them here, and so we can see that he has implicitly categorized them at more than one level of generality in this one passage alone. Compare now his concluding statement:

> ... if your Lordships accept the view that this pleading discloses a relevant cause of action you will be affirming the proposition that by Scots and English law alike a manufacturer of products, which he sells in such a form as to show that he intends them to reach the ultimate consumer in the form in which they left him with no reasonable possibility of intermediate examination, and with the knowledge that the absence of reasonable care in the preparation or putting up of the products will result in an injury to the consumer's life or property, owes a duty to the consumer to take reasonable care. [Chapter 1, p. 58.]

Notice here that the agent of harm has changed from 'an article of drink' to 'products', and that the nature of the injury has moved from 'injury to health' to 'injury to the consumer's life or property'. In addition, Lord Atkin has introduced the requirement that the manufacturer sell the product in the form in which he intends it to reach the ultimate consumer, and in this formulation of the proposition of law has dropped the 'ultimate purchaser', who appeared in his formulation of the question to be answered.

Even this does not exhaust Lord Atkin's movement up and down various ladders of abstraction.[42] We will conclude this comparison by looking at Lord Buckmaster's statement of the facts and issue in the case.

[42] See the questions and other materials on *Donoghue* v. *Stevenson* in Chapter 1 above; and W. Twining, *Karl Llewellyn and the Realist Movement* (1973), Chapter 10, especially pp. 231-45.

... the facts of this case are simple. On August 26, 1928, the appellant drank a bottle of ginger-beer, manufactured by the respondent which a friend had bought from a retailer and given to her. The bottle contained the decomposed remains of a snail which were not, and could not be, detected until the greater part of the contents of the bottle had been consumed. As a result she alleged, and at this stage her allegations must be accepted as true, that she suffered from shock and severe gastro-enteritis. She accordingly instituted the proceedings against the manufacturer which have given rise to this appeal.

The foundation of her case is that the respondent, as the manufacturer of an article intended for consumption and contained in a receptacle which prevented inspection, owed a duty to her as consumer of the article to take care that there was no noxious element in the goods, that he neglected such duty and is consequently liable for any damage caused by such neglect. [Chapter 1, p. 55.]

The movement between different levels of generality is perhaps more marked here than in the extracts quoted above. Lord Buckmaster states the facts at a low level of generality, including the date on which the injury occurred, but in his formulation of the issue in the case, the bottle has become a 'receptacle' and the decomposed remains of a snail have been abstracted to a 'noxious element'. These extracts illustrate some of the variations that can be encountered within individual judgments and between different judgments.

3 The *ratio decidendi* of a case

When we interpret cases, we ask such questions as 'for what rule(s) of law is this case an authority?' or 'for what proposition(s) of law can this case be made to stand?' Some have answered these questions by maintaining that it is possible to extract from any case, one proposition of law and that this constitutes its *ratio decidendi*. Although there are competing versions of this view, we may characterize it as the 'buried treasure' argument. In this view it is typically assumed (*a*) that every case has one predetermined *ratio decidendi* (at least for each question of law), and (*b*) that the *ratio decidendi* can be *found*, by reading the case, without referring to other cases, and (*c*) that the *ratio decidendi* does not, indeed cannot, change over time. These assumptions do not accord with the realities of the practice of handling precedents in our system. Talk of *finding* the *ratio decidendi* of a case obscures the fact that the process of interpreting cases is not like a hunt for buried treasure, but typically involves an element of choice from a range of possibilities. How unfettered is the choice and how wide the range of possibilities will depend on a variety of factors. One such factor, of crucial importance, relates to (*b*). In reasoning on a point of law we are typically confronted not with a single isolated precedent, but a collection of potentially relevant precedents. Each case has to be read in the context of all the other potentially relevant cases and this is one factor which limits the range of possible interpretations which can be put on it. Any test for determining the *ratio decidendi*, which suggests, explicitly or implicitly, that a case can be interpreted in isolation, without reference to other cases, is unrealistic and misleading. As the courts hand down new decisions, so the range of plausible interpretations of an earlier case may change over time. As we shall see, it is just not true that an interpreter faced with *Donoghue* v. *Stevenson* and its predecessors in 1933 was in the same position as he would be today. For not only have many subsequent cases intervened, but also some of the factors listed in Chapter 6 have contributed to a different climate of opinion affecting arguments about the scope of the duty of care in negligence. Yet a remarkably high proportion of the contributors to the long and rather sterile debate on the problem of the *ratio decidendi* have proceeded on the basis of one or more of these false assumptions or else have defined the term '*ratio decidendi*' in such a way that it ceases to be a central concept in elucidating what is involved in interpreting cases.[43]

Most discussions of precedent, in dealing with this issue, assume the standpoint of the judge if they assume any standpoint at all. But, as we have seen, judges are not the only interpreters of rules, and in the context of rules derived from precedents many of the issues involved in formulating the *ratio* can be shown to be non-contentious or at least less problematical if we adopt the standpoint of the counsellor and the advocate. This is so because what they are typically trying to do in interpreting a case is more easily understood and clearly defined than what a judge may be attempting. Thus a counsellor may be endeavouring to predict a likely judicial or other official response to a particular rule extracted from a precedent, while the advocate seeks to persuade a particular court to reach a particular result on the basis of reasons which support that result; the cases are part of the raw

[43] See esp. A. L. Goodhart, 'Determining the *Ratio Decidendi* of a Case', 40 *Yale Law Journal* (1930), 161 and 'The *Ratio Decidendi* of a Case', 22 *Modern Law Review* (1959), 117; Montrose, '*Ratio Decidendi* and the House of Lords', 20 *Modern Law Review* (1957), 124, 587; Simpson, 'The *Ratio Decidendi* of a Case', 21 *Modern Law Review* (1958), 155 and (1959), 22, 453; J. Stone, *Legal System and Lawyers' Reasonings* (1964), pp. 267–80, and R. Dias, *Jurisprudence* (op. cit.), pp. 63–72.

material from which the advocate's argument is constructed; the roles of the advocate and of the counsellor are relatively clearly defined, and by remarking upon the different formulations of the rule or *ratio* employed from these two perspectives we can see what interpreting cases means in practice.

Let us return to *Donoghue* v. *Stevenson* and examine it, first a few months after the decision in 1932 and then now, from the standpoint of the counsellor advising a client and an advocate arguing his case on a point of law involving negligence. Let us assume that the facts of the present case are that the client had bought a pair of underpants which subsequently turned out to be impregnated with an invisible chemical from which he contracted dermatitis.[44] Because the retailer is bankrupt, the client is contemplating suing the manufacturer, and let us further assume that in 1933 *Donoghue* v. *Stevenson* was the only relevant precedent. The question of law for the counsellor is to predict whether a court would hold that a manufacturer of underwear owed a duty to the ultimate consumer, and so should compensate him if he suffers injury as a result of a defect in the underwear. The answer to this question depends on how widely or narrowly the court is likely to interpret *Donoghue* v. *Stevenson*. At this stage the answer might well be unclear. The case might be interpreted narrowly, applying for instance only to food and drink, or it might be interpreted to include all manufactured goods, or again, to extend the duty of care more widely, along the lines of the 'neighbour' principle. Any of these interpretations stand along with other possibilities as potential formulations of the rule or *ratio* to be extracted from *Donoghue* v. *Stevenson*, and thus the counsellor cannot make a confident prediction. The decision was not unanimous, and if he is cautious, as many solicitors in this position are, he may advise his client that the position is uncertain, and for this reason, among others, that litigation is risky. Thus he might advise writing a solicitor's letter to the manufacturers, but advise retreat if they seem likely to contest an action. Implicit in this advice is a formulation of the *ratio* at a low level of generality.

The cautious counsellor then has interpreted the rule in the precedent as applying only, for example, to articles of food and drink; whereas his more optimistic colleague would have formulated the rule at a higher level of generality, and would thus advise his client that the risk may be worth taking. The situation would be very different

[44] *Grant* v. *Australian Knitting Mills* [1936] A.C. 85.

now, when it would be predicted that the client, assuming he can prove his case, has a good cause of action. This is so because since 1932 a number of decisions have, by eliminating a number of possible formulations of the *ratio* of *Donoghue* v. *Stevenson*, reduced the leeways of interpretation, and thus have to some extent clarified the scope of the rule. This is not to say that all doubts about the scope of the rule have been resolved, nor that there is no leeway for choice, but that the number of possible *rationes* that might have been extracted from the case in 1933 has been reduced by these subsequent decisions, and thus more confident predictions can be made on the basis of the cumulative effect of these decisions. Thus on this analysis the range of possible interpretations of *Donoghue* v. *Stevenson* is not the same now as it was in 1933; whereas on the buried treasure analogy, the *ratio* is the same.

The advocate's main task is to persuade the court to accept a particular result, and this will involve him in persuading the court to accept his interpretation of the law and of the precedents. The advocate for the plaintiff in the hypothetical situation, then, must put to the court an argument that explicitly or implicitly incorporates a *ratio* which at the very least is at a sufficiently high level of generality to cover the facts of his client's case. Possibly he would be better advised to advocate a *ratio* at a somewhat higher level, though it would probably have been poor advocacy to maintain that the 'neighbour' principle represented the *ratio decidendi* of *Donoghue* v. *Stevenson*. Conversely, the defendant's advocate would press for as broad an interpretation of the case as is consistent with success on the part of his client. Like the plaintiff's advocate, he too has a number of possible formulations of the rule, though unlike his opponent they will be of a low level of generality, for example:

(*a*) Scottish manufacturers of ginger-beer in opaque bottles owe a duty of care not to allow dead snails to get into the product;
(*b*) Manufacturers of ginger-beer owe a duty of care not to allow any snails to get into the product; or
(*c*) Manufacturers of articles of food and drink owe a duty of care not to allow any noxious physical foreign body to get into the product.

While each formulation of the *ratio* is consistent with the defendant's success, the advocate would probably have been wise to choose (*c*), on the ground that the court, either intuitively or by looking for a convincing policy reason for selecting a particular category, would hold that (*a*) and (*b*) were too narrow.

This elementary example illustrates the dynamics of interpretation within the adversary process. Typically each side to the action will be pressing an interpretation of relevant precedents that is consistent with the result it is seeking to obtain. Each side may have open to it a number of possible interpretations of a particular precedent that are consistent with the desired result, and good advocacy consists in directing the attention of the court to the most plausible interpretation or perhaps in giving the court a choice of interpretations consistent with that result. Plausibility may be partly a matter of style and intuition, but more importantly it will often be founded on the choice of a way of categorizing the protasis that makes sense in terms of some policy or purpose, whether articulated or not.[45]

If we revert now to the standpoint of the judge, we see that it is his primary task to reach a decision in the particular case before him; and where, as in the hypothetical case envisaged above, there is an important recent precedent, to formulate a *ratio* or rule for which that case is taken to stand, and to apply it to the present case. Often, a judge will seek a relatively narrow formulation of the *ratio* that is consistent with a just resolution of the case at hand. The fulfilment of this task is however somewhat more complex than in the case of the counsellor and advocate.[46] Where a judge is in genuine doubt about which of the possible interpretations of a prior case he is to choose, he has a discretion to exercise that is not governed by any rule of the doctrine of precedent. Typically, the competing interpretations differ in respect of one or more elements that can be presented at different levels of generality. There are no categorical rules to direct judges about the selection of appropriate levels of generality; accordingly there are no general rules for determining the *ratio decidendi* of a case, although there are some guidelines. This is not to say however that judges could not create rules for such occasions, nor that the absence of rules is necessarily to be lamented.

Judges typically seek to adduce reasons for their decisions, and reasons for their particular formulation of the applicable rule; and examination of judicial behaviour reveals the wide variety of reasons that can be employed, of which the following is but a sample: a rule may be supported or otherwise because it has stood the test of time; is

[45] See Chapter 7, especially pp. 259–62.
[46] See Chapter 4, pp. 175–81.

firmly established; is in line with authority; falls within an accepted concept; is consistent with traditional doctrine; serves a useful function; has caused (in)justice; settles a novel case; would prompt a flood of litigation; goes against the weight of precedent; would provide a remedy where none existed before; cannot provide a remedy where none existed before; or flies in the face of common sense. Often judges will overtly appeal to one or other of these reasons, but whether they do or not, the exercise of discretion in choosing one particular formulation of the *ratio* of a prior case involves basically the search for the most persuasive or cogent argument in its favour. While it is difficult to classify these reasons according to their acceptability or to the weight and priority that is to be attached to them, the status, acceptability and permanence of decisions is in this country to a large degree controlled by judicial recognition of and adherence to a great number of constraints that operate on interpreters of precedent cases, and in particular on judges as interpreters.[47]

[47] See K. Llewellyn, op. cit., pp. 19–61, 178–235; and W. Twining, op. cit., pp. 207–10.

9 Legislation

The term 'legislation' can be used to encompass a wide variety of rules in fixed verbal form including Acts of Parliament, subordinate legislation such as statutory instruments and by-laws of local authorities, and rules of European Community law. It can also include rules issued by government agencies which, though not enacted by a formal legislative process, are nevertheless usually regarded as binding by those to whom they are addressed and have become of steadily increasing importance in modern society.

In this chapter we shall concentrate on one type of legislation – statutes. Its aim is to identify the salient features of this process of law-making that contribute to some of the difficulties which may be encountered when handling statutory rules. Chapter 10 will deal more specifically with their interpretation. Although what we shall say directly concerns statutes, many of the features discussed apply to a greater or a lesser extent to the preparation and publication of other forms of legislation, and of other rules in fixed verbal form.

The public general Act is one of the primary instruments by which a government can implement its policies; it is also the single most important source of law in our legal system.

There is hardly any part of our national life or of our personal lives that is not affected by one statute or another. The affairs of local authorities, nationalized industries, public corporations and private commerce are regulated by legislation. The life of the ordinary citizen is affected by various provisions of the statute book from cradle to grave. His birth is registered, his infant welfare protected, his education provided, his employment governed, his income and capital taxed, much of his conduct controlled and his old age sustained according to the terms of one statute or another. Many might think that as a nation we groan under this overpowering burden of legislation and ardently desire to have fewer rather than more laws. Yet the pressure for ever more legislation on behalf of different interests increases as society becomes more complex and people more demanding of each other. With each change in society there comes a demand for further legislation to overcome the tensions which that change creates, even though the change itself may have been caused by legislation, which thus becomes self-proliferating.[1]

Most statutes are enacted after a lengthy process of consultation, in which the proposed Bill will be subject to many pressures and constraints. Some Acts on the other hand are *ad hoc*; responses to demands that the government 'do something' about an emergency or unforeseen difficulty. In such cases a statute may be no more than a cosmetic response to a situation which is perceived as problematic but which has yet to be fully analysed or confronted.

Since the mid-1960s a number of reports have been published which are critical of the present methods of preparation and enactment of Acts of Parliament. These include an important paper on interpretation of statutes by the Law Commissions, two reports on delegated legislation, two reports by the House of Commons Select Committee on Procedure and four reports by the Statute Law Society, an independent body devoted to securing improvements in statute law and furthering education about legislative processes. A new journal, the *Statute Law Review*, was launched in 1980. The passage quoted earlier is taken from *The Preparation of Legislation*, the comprehensive report of a Committee under the chairmanship of Sir David Renton (as he then was), which was published in 1975; but only a few of the major recommendations made by that or the other reports have been implemented. A central weakness of the present system is the fact that, given the complexity and the scale of the tasks of preparing and enacting statutes and of producing and maintaining a satisfactory statute book, the existing institutional arrangements, procedures and resources are quite inadequate. Perhaps the main reason for this is the conspicuous lack of political will to do anything about them.

[1] Report of the Renton Committee, *The Preparation of Legislation* (1975, Cmnd. 6053), para. 7.3 (hereafter cited as *Renton*).

1 The preparation and enactment of statutes

(a) The decision to legislate

Public general Acts are used to regulate a vast range of activities. For example, between 1976 and 1981 statutes were enacted to give powers to meet the water shortage, to give county courts power to grant injunctions in favour of battered wives and partners, to dissolve the Sugar Board, to allow public houses in Scotland to open for longer periods of time, to protect the tenants of tied cottages, to amend the close season for roe deer, to give effect to the international convention for safety at sea, to establish a new law of patents, to give pensioners £10 at Christmas in 1977, to amend various aspects of the criminal law, to give effect to the European Convention on the suppression of terrorism, to consolidate various provisions relating to the interpretation of legislation, to amend section 16 of the Theft Act 1968, to prohibit photography of children for sexual purposes, to establish elections to the European Parliament, to protect authors' royalties when their books are purchased by public libraries, to alter the boundaries of the parliamentary constituencies in Northern Ireland, to provide compensation for parents of children who died from being vaccinated against whooping cough, to regulate the estate agents' industry, to create an independent Republic of Zimbabwe, to amend the law of bail in Scotland, to allow an increase in the cash limits on bingo prizes, to establish a Police Negotiating Board, to give powers to control the importation of bees, to allow council tenants to purchase their houses, to amend the law relating to contempt of court, to amend the law relating to the protection of wildlife and the countryside, to consolidate enactments concerning the Supreme Court of Judicature, to create a new public corporation to run the telecommunications and data processing business of the Post Office, and to redefine British nationality.

These are but thirty of the 326 public general Acts enacted during the period 1976–81. This takes no account of the many other rules having legislative effect concerning their interpretation and implementation which have been promulgated since their enactment. The material origins of these thirty Acts are diverse, as is their intended impact. Some were enacted in response to the recommendations of a specially appointed committee (whooping cough, battered wives and contempt of court), some in response to judicial activity (theft and amendments to the criminal law); some were intended to consolidate existing legislation (interpretation and the Supreme Court of Judicature), some to amend existing legislation (Scottish pub hours, close season for roe deer), some to create new law (estate agents, patents); some were introduced to fulfil Britain's international obligations (suppression of terrorism, safety at sea), some to fulfil our obligations under the Treaty of Rome (elections to the European Parliament); some were governmental responses to sudden events (the 1976 drought); some were instances of long-term government policy (tied cottages, North Sea oil, purchase of council homes and the break up of the Post Office's control over telecommunications). Despite their diversity, these examples are only part of the total legislative output during this five-year period; their significance is that with a few exceptions, they all represent the direct implementation of the government's policy on the matter in question. The exceptions are those measures which are sponsored not by government ministers but by backbench MPs.

Legislation can only be understood in the context of the processes of governmental policy-making, which is the subject of a rich and varied literature. Four salient features will be discussed here.[2]

First, although the final decision concerning the substance of any proposed statute rests with the Cabinet, most proposals will have been widely discussed both within and outside the government. Within the government, those primarily responsible for the proposals will be the relevant Minister(s) and members of the permanent civil service. If the proposals have financial implications, as most do, Treasury officials will have to be consulted. Outside the government there are hundreds of groups representing a vast range of interests and seeking to influence government policy in their favour. When a Bill is proposed they will lobby Ministers and other officials to drop, amend, delay or expedite its proposals according to whether they see them as prejudicial or advantageous to their interests. Sometimes statutes require the co-operation of these groups for their implementation, for example, employers and unions in the case of the Health and Safety at Work, etc. Act concerning safety practices and procedures, or accountants and companies' officials in the case of the preparation of audits under the Companies Acts. Where co-operation cannot be obtained without excessive cost to the government, it may sometimes rely on less formal methods of control, such as voluntary codes of practice.

---

[2] For a fuller discussion of these and other matters raised in this and the following chapter, see D. Miers and A. Page, *Legislation* (1982).

In addition to these groups, many statutes are implemented by the existing personnel of such branches of the executive as the Customs and Excise, the Inland Revenue, the police and local authorities. When representatives of these groups are consulted about legislative proposals, they too have their own interests to protect. Indeed, modern political commentators would say that individual government departments act as pressure groups; they have their own aspirations, values, programmes and priorities and can promote these in concert with or at the expense of other groups (including other governmental departments), with as much vigour, if less publicity, as extra-governmental organizations.

A second feature of the system concerns the way in which policy is made. A diagnostic model of problem-solving[3] may suggest that policy-making and law-making are rational processes involving the identification of goals and values, the selection of policies available for achieving those goals, the prediction of the consequences, good and bad, which may flow from the adoption of each policy, and, finally, the choice of the policy with consequences that most closely match the goals to be secured and which accords with the preferred values. Such a high degree of rationality is rarely achieved in practice. What happens may fit more closely a pattern which has been called incrementalism. Ends and means are often difficult to separate for the purpose of evaluation, and so analysis tends to be confined to a series of well-rehearsed options familiar to all the participants. Often the resulting choice will in practice be close to the existing position; it is as if the test of a good policy is the one upon which all interested parties have least disagreement. A colloquial description of this process is 'muddling through'.[4]

Thirdly, it is a mistake to regard all statutory rules, even those which are expressly intended to further some policy, purely in instrumental terms. Many statutory rules have significant symbolic dimensions which may be just as important to the rule-makers (and to potential interpreters) as their intended instrumental effects, for example, legislation penalizing the possession of certain drugs or making some types of racial or sexual discrimination unlawful.[5] A final point is that many of the difficulties associated with the implementation or

---

[3] Chapter 2 above, pp. 118–19.

[4] A useful discussion is J. Richardson and A. Jordan, *Governing Under Pressure* (1979).

[5] See W. G. Carson, 'Symbolic and Instrumental Dimensions of Early Factory Legislation' in *Crime, Criminology and Public Policy* (ed. R. Hood, 1974).

interpretation of statutes may be attributed to conflicts arising during the preparatory or enacting stages. The provisions in the Housing Act 1980 requiring local authorities to sell council houses to sitting tenants were widely criticized by Labour-controlled councils long before they were enacted, and many of the difficulties which the Conservative government has experienced with their implementation can be attributed to this opposition.

(b) The preparation of a Bill

Notwithstanding that a great number of interests may need to be consulted, and typically their consent secured, before a given aspect of government policy is translated into legislative proposals and thence into a Bill, the critical decision lies with the government, specifically the Cabinet. It alone authorizes the introduction of such proposals into Parliament. The vast proportion of the annual statutory output represents either major commitments made by the party now in government or when it was in opposition, or more routine requests from government departments to extend or modify their powers when they are found to be inadequate to their administrative tasks.

The Cabinet's control over government Bills has for some time been exercised through two of its Committees. The primary tasks of the first are to shape the government's legislative programme within Parliament for its term of office and from year to year. The other is responsible for the implementation of each annual programme, which involves careful planning by the Chief Whip and the Leader of the House of Commons so as to make the best use of the Parliamentary time which is available for legislative business. The Bills themselves are drafted by a small group of lawyers known as Parliamentary Counsel, whose role and position in the process is therefore quite crucial. It is a striking feature of the system of preparation of Bills in this country that it is both highly centralized and conducted by a very small group of people. Established in 1869 within the Treasury Department, the principal task of the Office of Parliamentary Counsel is to draft Bills for the government's legislative programme. The nature of the draftsman's task and his position in the legislative process combine to make his work extraordinarily difficult and demanding. Frequently he has the opportunity to exercise influence on the final product beyond that of a mere technician; similarly he may find himself the subject of a number of conflicting demands and pressures.

In this situation the Office of Parliamentary Counsel appears, at least to outsiders, to have developed a rigorous, arcane and somewhat inflexible craft-tradition. They have an enviable reputation for technical proficiency and, in some of their relatively rare public pronouncements, a less enviable reputation for hubris. There is a seemingly paradoxical situation in which those primarily responsible for a product which is the subject of frequent and sometimes virulent criticism are themselves regularly praised, especially by transatlantic commentators, as representing a model to be emulated. A theme of much recent writing on statute law has been 'criticize the product, but exonerate the producer'.

There are several reasons for this: the draftsman typically acts in response to written instructions; in theory he is meant to act as a channel through which the policy passes to emerge in rule form, but in practice he may exercise considerable influence on the way the policy is to be implemented. Even where, as in the United Kingdom, the draftsman's instructions tend to be detailed and carefully prepared, his role as interpreter of the potential effect of the proposed law on existing and other contemplated legislation, and on the practices and procedures of legal officials and institutions, may bring him into conflict with the policy-maker's needs, for example the need for speed in the preparation of a draft Bill. Moreover, what is required by the policy-maker may not easily be translated into legal provision; and some of the factors in the draftsman's situation stem from the interaction between political objectives and the legal possibilities. Also the draftsman has a number of different audiences, who may have conflicting needs; thus, apart from such MPs as may have assisted in the formulation of the policy behind a particular Bill, an MP, faced with a Bill, wants to know what it is intended to do, and how it may affect those whose interests he represents. These needs may be catered for by one type or arrangement of the clauses of the Bill, but the draftsman must also consider the needs of those who are to implement its substance, for example, public health inspectors, factory inspectors or national insurance commissioners. The needs of judges may be different again.

Political compromise and short-term expediency are also natural obstacles to neat rationalistic law-making. As one commentator has somewhat cynically observed, the draftsman

> ... is the servant and victim of all sorts of external forces beyond his own control - idealistic reformers in a hurry to build Utopia the day after tomor-

row, pragmatic politicians who want to catch the tide of popularity with the showy amendment of some much publicised quirk of the law, wrangling parliamentarians lacerating a Bill with amendments for party purposes.[6]

While this may overstate the position, it does catch the flavour of some of the pressures which are exerted on a draftsman. Thus a Minister needs to consider how to present both to Parliament and to the public the contents of a Bill he is sponsoring; how he proposes to defend it (the more so if it is controversial); how it will be approached in Committee and at the Report stage, and so on. He will know that Parliamentary procedure requires that each clause must be separately put in Committee, and will thus be tempted to prefer a few long clauses to many short ones. Other devices may help him to avoid debate on controversial items.

Parliamentary draftsmen typically have to work at a high level of generality and complexity, and yet are expected to express complicated concepts in simple language. They are required to fit each new Bill or clause into a tangled undergrowth of existing law, a task made more difficult by the inadequate state of the statute book. In the face of these inhibiting factors, it is the more remarkable that the relatively few Parliamentary draftsmen in this country prompt only a small number of complaints.

Apart from their obvious control over the exact wording of a Bill, the draftsmen's central position allows them to exert considerable influence over the way in which proposals for reform of the preparation (and other aspects) of statutes are made. For example, the Renton Committee considered the suggestion that, prior to its first reading, the form and drafting of each Bill should in addition to the existing procedures be scrutinized by a specially constituted Commons committee. The lukewarm response of the then First Parliamentary Counsel to this suggestion was one reason why no recommendation was made.

Another reason is that government does not wish to see its control over Bills diluted. The Cabinet is almost invariably able to ensure the success of its legislative programme, and this is substantially due to its control over three vital aspects of a Bill's progress through Parliament; its timing, its form and the disclosure of its contents. Timing is crucial in a Parliamentary timetable which is heavily overcommitted not only to the debate of public Bills but also to the scrutiny of expenditure and of executive actions. The form of a Bill may be dictated in part by a

[6] Comment, 118 *New Law Journal* (1968), 360.

Minister's desire to forestall critical opposition, or to take advantage of the rules of procedure; the precise content remains a secret until its publication following its first reading. Control over these aspects of the preparation of statutes, in particular over timing, are crucial to success in its legislative programme for any government which commands a workable majority.

(c) The legislative stage

Once a government Bill has received its first reading, usually in the Commons, it then passes through the various debating stages prior to receiving the Royal Assent. However, it is generally acknowledged that Parliament is a legislature in name only. At the turn of the last century, Sir Courtenay Ilbert, a successor to Sir Henry Thring as First Parliamentary Counsel to the Treasury, wrote that the Executive's control over legislation and the relatively minor role that Parliament played in modifying it were relatively well-established features of the constitution.[7] This position is now even more deeply entrenched; Parliament retains its formal control over legislation but exercises very limited substantive control.

In the case of private members' Bills, Parliament is more like a legislature in the full sense. In order to be successful, such a Bill must command the support of a sizeable number of MPs who are prepared to put in considerable effort lobbying other backbenchers and members of the government; it must not generate any serious opposition nor contradict government policy; and it should be drafted by an expert, be allocated sufficient debating time and must not involve the expenditure of public money without government approval. Perhaps the most important factor is the attitude of the government. If it favours the Bill, it can make the services of the Parliamentary draftsman available to its sponsors, as was done with the Domestic Violence and Matrimonial Proceedings Bill, allow some of its own time for debate, or even adopt it as a government measure.[8] Conversely, government opposition will almost inevitably mean that the Bill will be defeated. For these reasons, private members' Bills may be viewed, indirectly at least, as substantively part of a government's policy.

With the exception of private members' Bills, which are quantatively not significant, the legislative stage is entirely dominated by government Bills. Several features of the legislative stage have a par-

---

[7] Sir C. Ilbert, *Legislative Methods and Forms* (1901), pp. 213 and 219.
[8] See Appendix II below, section 9, question 2.

ticular impact on the form and content of a Bill, and may in turn contribute to conditions giving rise to doubts about interpretation.

First, Parliamentary debates are conducted in accordance with a large number of procedural rules, many of which were introduced at the turn of the last century. Their object was to limit debate in various ways and so expedite the government's legislative programme. With the vastly increased quantity and complexity of government Bills, such rules relating to the closure, guillotine motions and the like are now widely regarded as a serious hindrance to even a nominal performance of Parliament's role in reviewing statutory proposals. These rules can be employed so as to avoid debate on controversial clauses; but even without such deliberate manipulation of the clauses of a Bill, the present procedures virtually pre-empt effective debate. Despite many suggestions for radical change, few have been implemented.

Second, the volume of Bills and the pressure of work on MPs renders informed and systematic debate of the substance of a Bill – even without the procedural fetters – a rare event. In fact, the delay in a Bill's progress which can be caused by extensive or critical debate will so seriously dislocate a government's legislative programme that it generally keeps a firm control over the Parliamentary timetable and seeks to limit discussion. Not infrequently, MPs complain about their lack of opportunity to comment upon a Bill, but in the absence of change in the procedures or a significant reduction in government legislation, this is unlikely to be remedied. A suggestion by Sir John Fiennes, a former First Parliamentary Counsel, to the 1970–1 Select Committee on Procedure, that debating time would be relieved if innocuous government Bills were to be given a Second Reading without debate, was not well received by its chairman.[9] This is a neat illustration of the self-defeating desire of MPs to retain control (in theory) over all statutory proposals, which simply contributes to their lack of control (in practice) over very many of them.

Thirdly, although debates seldom have an impact on the content of a Bill unless the government assents to the proposed changes, it does not follow that a Bill once drafted and published remains in that form as it progresses through Parliament; on the contrary, particular clauses in a Bill may be redrafted a dozen or more times as the draftsman seeks to resolve issues which are raised during debate. There is however

---

[9] Second Report of the Select Committee on Procedure, Session 1970–71, H.C. 538, and Minutes of Evidence, H.C. 297, questions 1024–5.

usually very little time in which to draft amendments, and little
opportunity to assimilate them to the structure of the Bill.

2 The intelligibility of statutes

Modern statutes are concerned primarily to determine the structure
and powers of public authorities, and to a lesser extent to regulate the
conduct of citizens and private organizations. A statutory rule both
states the law and communicates it to those affected by it, in particular
to those who have to implement it. Statutes which are addressed
primarily to civil servants or the employees of public bodies are frequently supplemented by a wide range of handbooks, circulars, pamphlets, codes of practice, directives and other documents mostly prepared by the responsible government department. These indicate how
an Act's provisions are to be interpreted and implemented in particular cases. Where a statute confers benefits or imposes liabilities upon
citizens and private organizations, some of these documents may be
made publicly available.

Such documents would be prepared even if the governing statute
was clearly written, for some provisions deliberately leave the determination of individual cases to those implementing it, typically some
administrative agency which is required or given powers to act
'reasonably' or 'as it thinks fit'. In such cases the function of those
documents is to give guidance as to the limits of what is 'reasonable'
or 'fit' in given circumstances. No rule can foreclose all possibilities,
even one that is clearly and precisely drafted; rather the object
is to reduce cases of doubtful application to a minimum. It is however generally agreed that statutory rules are not always especially
intelligible, and that in some instances they defy the efforts of even
the most sympathetic interpreters to make sense of them. The
criticisms that have been made in recent years can be summarized as
follows: there are too many statutes, and their retrieval and clarity are
hampered by the present arrangements for their accumulation and
drafting.

Three issues are implicit in the complaint that there is 'too much'
legislation. The first is concerned with what should be the proper role of
the state in the regulation of behaviour. At one extreme is the conception of a minimal state, one which is limited to the narrow functions of protection against force, theft and fraud, and the enforce-

ment of contracts[10]; at the other is a state which actively seeks to make people better by law, for example, by requiring them to do things for their own good. Some who complain that there is too much legislation mean that the government is too ready to intervene or to meddle in people's affairs when their conduct should be a matter of individual choice, but the relationship between a government's political ideology and the rules which emanate from it is certainly not a simple one. As we saw in Chapter 3, rule density is a familiar feature of our bureaucratic society,[11] and the quantity and complexity of government-inspired rules have been increasing irrespective of the ideological convictions of the governing party. The reasons for this are themselves complex; put very simply, as the modern world becomes more complicated, so do its techniques of control, and bureaucracy itself conduces to the creation of rules. One of the primary purposes of many rules is to control the behaviour of officials by limiting the discretion they exercise, for example, in the conferral of benefits or the imposition of burdens upon the citizen. Moreover, while the particular context of rules affecting such matters as town and country planning and land use, housing, the renting of accommodation, immigration, weights and measures, food and drugs and so on may vary, there will, in a society such as ours, always be rules on these matters. Even where a Conservative government is committed to a policy of dismantling some of the state's apparatus through denationalization, such activity still requires the enactment of rules. It may be that under Nozick's minimal state, there would be 'less law' than exists under the kind of regime prevailing in the United Kingdom; but it should not be forgotten that one version of the Socialist utopia also postulated the withering away of law.

Another issue centres on the appropriateness of statutory intervention in particular contexts. Here it may be argued, for example, that existing statutory controls are adequate and simply require regular or systematic enforcement, or that an Act of Parliament is not suitable to the problem which may be better dealt with by the allocation of financial resources, changes in institutional practices, the introduction of voluntary codes of self-regulation, or other remedies. Whether a government is regarded as unduly interventionist in its use of statutes is a complex question involving the critic's political ideology, value preferences and priorities.

[10] This is the conception argued by R. Nozick in *Anarchy, State and Utopia* (1975).
[11] Above, pp. 147–8.

The third issue raised by the complaint of too many statutes is more directly focused on the institutional arrangements for enacting public general Acts: governments have endeavoured to enact more statutes than the Parliamentary session can comfortably accommodate. It is undoubtedly the case that recent governments have sought to enact a great deal of law, particularly in the first two sessions of a Parliament. The current procedures for enacting Bills were largely devised at the end of the nineteenth century, and since then the quantity and complexity of legislation have greatly expanded, but with relatively minor changes to these procedures. Extended sessions, long sittings, the frequent use of timetable motions and brief intervals between a Bill's stages are all characteristics of an overcrowded programme; but successive governments continue to set goals which require intense management of Parliamentary business. This necessarily puts the draftsman under considerable pressure to comply with the schedule laid down by the Chief Whip. In addition, the government's desire to see its manifesto and departmental initiatives reach the statute book prejudices the chances of other proposals for law reform being acted upon – in particular those of the Law Commissions – some of which are directly concerned with improving the quality of the statute book.

The origins and cogency of the criticisms concerning the retrieval and clarity of statutes vary, and there is considerable disagreement between the critics of the present arrangements and its leading defenders – the draftsmen and other civil servants.

(a) The retrieval of statutes

The term 'statute book' refers to the surviving body of enacted legislation published by authority, not in a single volume but in a number of publications which even the most experienced professional can find difficult to handle. The retrieval of relevant provisions will often be a relatively straightforward task for the user, but there are several factors which can delay or obstruct its completion.

First, there are quite simply many enactments dealing with some subject areas, for example taxation, road traffic, licensing, public health, social services and housing, although some of these areas have been consolidated. Finding one's way around the statute book in areas such as these can be a time-consuming and frustrating experience, but it is often aggravated by the fact that the relevant legislation on any particular topic is quite likely to be found scattered among a number of different statutes, often having nothing in common with one another or with the topic. A primary reason for this is that statutes in this country have never been systematically classified and enacted as part of a comprehensive scheme dealing with each subject area. Until the publication of the first volumes of *Statutes in Force* in 1972, the only official classification was the chronological arrangement followed by its predecessor, *Statutes Revised*, the third and last edition of which was published in 1950. This classification, which is based upon the order in which statutes receive the Royal Assent, is still followed in the official annual volumes, *Public General Acts and Measures*. Under the system adopted in *Statutes in Force*, legislation which is considered to belong to a common category is assembled under a single title, such as agency, agriculture, ancient monuments and memorials, animals, etc., and within each title it is further arranged chronologically. It has taken a decade to publish all 126 titles in the series. When the project was conceived it was the most significant move for many years to improve the organization of the statute book, but with the advances in computer technology it is already technically dated. It should be emphasized, however, that statutes continue to be enacted in the traditional way, that is, without systematic regard for subject groupings. Although in some areas 'principal Acts' exist which are designed to contain the governing legislation on a particular matter, it is the government which is ultimately responsible for the way in which Bills are prepared, and it shows no inclination to adopt such an arrangement on a systematic and comprehensive basis.

Most Commonwealth countries, and others besides, to whom the traditional British method of preparing Bills was exported during the nineteenth century, now maintain statute books which are very much easier to use than our own. One of the key features of this improvement is the publication every ten years or so of a set of revised statutes which incorporate all amendments into one authoritative statement of the law contained in a single statute for each subject. This means that the user often only has to refer to the most recent edition of statutes revised, and only look in one place for the governing legislation on any one subject; any amendments to the provisions with which he is concerned should not be more than ten years old. The ability to produce such regular series of revised statutes in such countries as Canada, Australia, New Zealand and in many American state jurisdictions is based upon a number of considerations which do not obtain in this country, apart from being less affected by entrenched attitudes and inertia: a smaller quantity of legislation, due in part to a shorter legal history and, in some cases, a separation of responsibility for legislation between state and federal government; the use of textual methods of amendment; and, for the most part, the adoption of the principle of one subject, one Act.

The advantage of this system for the user is that he knows that all provisions relating to a given matter, such as theft or divorce, will be found under one heading. The disadvantage for the draftsman and the legislature is that it will result in a larger number of statutes, as amendments have to be separately enacted where they concern separate subjects. An initial difficulty which also had to be tackled by the editors of *Statutes in Force* lies in the choice of categories which are to be used as the basis for organization. Although there are many well-established legal categories, they are neither uncontroversial nor immutable. Individual statutory provisions do not present themselves as members of readily defined groupings, and there may be genuine and profound disagreement as to the appropriateness of choosing one category in preference to another. For example, the Protection of Animals (Cruelty to Dogs) Act 1933 provides that a person convicted of cruelty to a dog may be disqualified from holding or obtaining a dog licence. This could be variously classified under animals, cruelty to animals/dogs, criminal law, licensing, or summary jurisdiction.

In the absence of a comprehensive statutory code agreed upon by the government to which all new enactments can be carefully and systematically assimilated, the primary technique adopted in this country to meet the complaint that statutes are scattered, is consolidation. A consolidating statute is one which re-enacts in one place a number of provisions, previously to be found in a number of statutes, which relate to one subject. Responsibility for preparing consolidation programmes in England has since 1965 been the statutory duty of the Law Commission; the actual drafting of Consolidation Bills is divided according to their complexity between the Office of Parliamentary Counsel and the Commission. Bills which can be drafted speedily are dealt with by the Office's Consolidation Branch, while those which require a longer period of preparation are dealt with by the draftsmen seconded to the Commission from the Office. In Scotland, the Scottish Law Commission and the Lord Advocate's department are jointly responsible for the preparation of Consolidation Bills.

The record of the English law Commission is impressive,[12] but many areas remain to be consolidated, and it is unlikely that the speed at which consolidation has proceeded is likely to increase. There are several reasons for this. First, there is a limited number of draftsmen available to prepare Consolidation Bills. Initially four draftsmen were seconded full time to the Commission from the Office, and a fifth was added shortly afterwards, but it is rare that they are all available for a sustained period of time. Individual draftsmen are frequently re-called to the Office to complete the preparation of programme Bills, and the Commission has other responsibilities for them to perform, such as the preparation of draft law reform and Statute Law (Repeal) Bills. Secondly, consolidation is not always a simple matter of taking sections from existing statutes and re-enacting them verbatim in one Bill. Where the sections have been amended according to what is known as the 'non-textual' method (discussed below), work must initially be done to establish the precise effect of such amendment. In addition, it is sometimes necessary to enact amending legislation before the provisions can be consolidated. In such cases the Commission has to obtain the agreement of the relevant Cabinet Committee to include these occasional amendments in one of the programme Bills. Although such amendments are usually non-contentious, they may nevertheless offer procedural opportunities to the Opposition to delay the Bill, and Ministers are consequently not always inclined to agree to their inclusion.

Thirdly, Consolidation Bills are subject to special Parliamentary procedures. There are three types of Consolidation Bill: those which simply re-enact existing provisions verbatim; those which re-enact existing provisions with corrections and minor improvements under the Consolidation of Enactments (Procedure) Act 1949; and those which include amendments to give effect to recommendations of the Law Commissions. Following their Second Reading, all Consolidation Bills are committed to the Joint Select Committee on Consolidation Bills, whose task is to ensure that the Bill, of whatever type, is properly prepared. One of the reasons why Consolidation Bills are dealt with in this way is to save debating time; but as presently constituted, the

---

[12] The Scottish Law Commission is responsible for the consolidation of enactments relating solely to Scotland, and co-operates with the Law Commission where statutes affecting the whole of Great Britain are under review; see Scottish Law Commission, *Fifteenth Annual Report 1979–80* (1980, Scot. Law Com. No. 61) and the Law Commission, *Fifteenth Annual Report 1979–80* (1981, Law Com. No. 107).

Committee could probably not cope with an increased output from the draftsman without adding to its membership or altering its procedures, both of which changes would have to be approved by Parliament. A fourth obstacle to consolidation, and which can also create difficulties for the user, is the continued presence on the statute book of a large number of statutes which are either 'obsolete, spent, unnecessary or superseded' or are 'no longer of practical utility'. Such legislation may be repealed by Statute Law Revision Bills or by Statute Law (Repeals) Bills respectively, both of which are also the responsibility of the Law Commission.[13]

Accurate retrieval of statutory rules is a problem both for the draftsman and for the user. Recent advances in computer and word-processor technology offer a wide range of opportunities for both groups. Computers have been used in the preparation of *Statutes in Force*, but their potential goes well beyond this. Once all statutory provisions have been stored in a computer's memory, it can be used to speed up the printing of Bills at all stages of their progress through the draftsman's office and the legislature, and as a system of information retrieval for government departments, the publishers of *Statutes in Force*, the Parliamentary draftsmen and professional users. For both draftsmen and users, the value of the computer, as at present perceived, is that it can very quickly search its memory for all statutory provisions relevant to the matter at hand. Where the draftsman is preparing a Bill, it can locate all the occurrences of a particular word or phrase which is to be amended, achieve completeness in repealing or consolidating Bills and assure a consistency in drafting style as between original and new enactments. Coupled with devices such as word-processors, a draftsman can call up and work on individual words and phrases and can quickly see the effect of any changes he makes in the language of a Bill on its other clauses. Speed in the discovery of relevant legislation and substantial alleviation of the problems of physical manipulation of the statute book are among the primary values of such technology for the draftsman and the user. It may not be long before its potential uses are recognized to be very much wider than this.

[13] For a detailed discussion of the history of and present arrangements for enacting proposals for statute law revision and consolidation, see Lord Simon of Glaisdale and J. V. Webb, 'Consolidation and Statute Law Revision' [1975] *Public Law* 285.

(b) **The clarity of statutes**

Two characteristics of the preparation of statutes are frequently alleged to obscure their meaning: the use of the non-textual method of amendment and the complexity of many statutory rules.

(i) METHODS OF AMENDMENT

It is a rare occurrence if a Bill does not amend existing statutory provisions in some way, and some statutes are enacted for the specific purpose of amending the existing law; but whichever is the case, it is clear that the method of amendment employed is of considerable importance to potential users.

There are two main methods of amendment in constant use in United Kingdom Acts, textual and non-textual amendment. Non-textual amendment takes the form of a narrative statement which seeks to explain the effect of the amendment on the original provision. The amendment is indirect; it 'does not in so many words purport to amend the principal law', rather it builds upon the original provision and is cumulative in effect. Textual amendment on the other hand directly amends the original provision by expressly providing for the addition, deletion or substitution of words or phrases. With textual amendment it is possible, though time-consuming, physically to correct the original provision by deleting, adding or substituting the relevant word or phrases. Although this can lead to a very unwieldy and messy annotation of a statutory text, especially where it has been frequently amended, many users often prefer textual amendment, especially where it is necessary to refer to two, and sometimes more, texts to discover the effect of the amendment. You can see in the example below how easy it would be simply to make the necessary corrections to the original provision. This correction can of course be made once the user has understood the effect of the non-textual amendment, but it will take more time and the user may misinterpret its effect.

Section 28 of the Finance Act 1960 deals with the cancellation of tax advantages from certain transactions in securities. Two of the kinds of security to which the section refers are set out in paragraphs (*a*) and (*b*) of section 28 (2):

(2) The circumstances mentioned in the foregoing subsection are that:—

(*a*) in connection with the distribution of profits of a company, or in connection with the sale or purchase of securities being a sale or purchase followed by the purchase or sale of the same or other securities, the person in question, being entitled (by reason of any exemption from tax or by the setting off of losses against profits or income) to recover tax in respect of dividends received by him, receives an abnormal amount by way of dividend; or

(*b*) in connection with the distribution of profits of a company or any such sale or purchase as aforesaid the person in question becomes entitled, in respect of securities held or sold by him, to a deduction in computing profits or gains by reason of a fall in the value of the securities resulting from the payment of a dividend thereon or from any other dealing with any asset of a company; or . . .

These paragraphs were amended by the use of the non-textual method in section 25 (3) of the Finance Act 1962, which is set out below on the left. On the right is the same amendment in textual form.[14]

Non-textual amendment

(3) In section twenty-eight of the Finance Act, 1960 (which provides for the cancellation of tax advantages from certain transactions in securities where the tax advantage is obtained or obtainable in the circumstances set out in subsection (2) of the section),

(a) the reference in paragraph (*a*) of subsection (2) to a person being entitled by reason of any exemption from tax to recover tax in respect of dividends shall include a reference to his being by reason of section twenty (subvention payments) of the Finance Act, 1953, so entitled; and

(b) the reference in paragraph (*b*) of subsection (2) to a person becoming entitled in respect of securities held or sold by him to a deduction in computing profits or gains by reason of a fall in the value of securities shall include a reference to his becoming in respect of any securities formerly held by him (whether sold by him or not) so entitled.

Textual amendment

(3) Subsection (2) of section 28 of the Finance Act 1960, is hereby amended in the following respects

(*a*) by the insertion in paragraph (a), after the word 'income', of the words 'or by reason of section 20 of the Finance Act 1953'; and

(*b*) by the insertion in paragraph (b), after the word 'him', of the words 'or formerly held by him (whether sold by him or not)'.

[14] From the Statute Law Society, *Renton and the Need for Reform* (1979), p. 26.

An important difference between the two is that with the non-textual method it is possible for someone reading the amendment to obtain a rough idea of its effect on the original provision without actually referring to it; whereas with textual amendment, the clause is meaningless without simultaneous reference to the provision it is amending. You can again test this for yourself quite easily with the example above: read the textual amendment without looking at the original provision. All that the amendment tells you is that some new words are being added to the original, but this does not in any way help you to understand what the effect of these additions will be. The non-textual amendment on the other hand does attempt to tell you something of the effect of these additions, although it may not tell you a great deal.

The reason why the non-textual method was adopted in this country was because Sir Henry Thring, the first holder of the position of First Parliamentary Counsel to the Treasury in 1869, saw it as the draftsman's duty, when preparing amending clauses, to provide MPs with a draft which allowed them to get an idea of the legal effect of the amendment for the purpose of debate, without having to look up the original provision. This is called the 'four corners doctrine'. As this method became entrenched, so further amendment of a previously amended provision had to be effected in the same way, which is one of the reasons why it is still in use.

The non-textual method has been the subject of considerable criticism by statute law users, and even by some draftsmen:

> The traditional United Kingdom style, therefore, produced a pottage comprising direct amendments, indirect amendments and provisions incorporating both techniques. The effect at least to one not nurtured from his early years on English statutes, is confusing, particularly so as it rests on a stream of invidious but inevitably inconsistent decisions as to which amendments should properly be effected by one method, which by the other, and which by both.[15]

It was in response to this kind of criticism that the Renton Committee recommended that the practice of textual amendment should be applied as generously as possible. But there are obstacles. In particular, many statutes have already been amended non-textually and are not suitable for the textual method; the textual method would in some instances greatly increase the length of Bills and the time required for the preparation of memoranda explaining the affect of the amendments; and thirdly, as indicated earlier, although the textual method

[15] G. C. Thornton, *Legislative Drafting* (2nd edn, 1979), p. 314.

enables the user to make the appropriate changes on a copy of the amended Act so as to achieve an authoritative statement of the law in one place, such direct substitution can be laborious and, where the affected Act is heavily amended, physically impossible to achieve on the printed page. Nevertheless, efforts are being made to use textual amendment more frequently.

(ii) THE COMPLEXITY OF STATUTORY RULES

It is commonplace to observe that United Kingdom Acts are typically very painstaking and detailed in their formulation of the factual circumstances to which they apply and to the legal consequences which those circumstances attract. The consequence of this drafting style is statutory rules which, it is alleged, are frequently so complicated that they defeat their own purpose – to be understood by those implementing them. Complexity is of itself unobjectionable; it is both naïve and unrealistic to expect all Acts of Parliament to be understood by everyone. This point was well made by the eminent Canadian draftsman, Elmer Driedger:

> There is always the complaint that legislation is complicated. Of course it is, because life is complicated. The bulk of the legislation enacted nowadays is social, economic or financial; the laws they must express and the life situations they must regulate are in themselves complicated, and these laws cannot in any language or in any style be reduced to kindergarten level, any more than can the theory of relativity. One might as well ask why television sets are so complicated. Why do they not make television sets so everyone can understand them? Well, you can't expect to put a colour image on a screen in your living-room with a crystal set. And you can't have crystal set legislation in a television age.[16]

In some instances it may be virtually impossible to devise specific legal provisions to give effect to more general rules or to policies; for example to define what are 'true and fair' accounting procedures for the purposes of the Companies Act 1981, to control the objectionable aspects of chequebook journalism, or to define and protect 'privacy'. Nevertheless, where because of its complexity, a user who is familiar with the subject-matter of a provision cannot, after a reasonable expenditure of intellectual effort and within a reasonable time, make sense of it in relation to a given set of circumstances, it is appropriate to enquire

---

[16] E. Driedger, 'Statutory Drafting and Interpretation', *Proceedings of the Ninth International Symposium on Comparative Law*, University of Ottawa (1971), p. 71; quoted in F. Bennion, *Statute Law* (1980), p. 96.

whether the provisions could not have been drafted in some other way. There are several reasons why this state of affairs has come about.

First, long before the Office of Parliamentary Counsel was created in 1869, a detailed drafting style had become established in the eighteenth and early nineteenth centuries. The reasons for this were partly that the draftsmen were usually Chancery practitioners who simply adopted the detailed style commonly used for drafting private legal texts, and, more significantly, because of the judiciary's reaction to legislation. Because statutes were seen as an appendage to the common law, the courts took the view that they should be interpreted strictly, with each word being given effect. If a set of circumstances did not fall squarely within the words of a section, it was held not to apply to them. Draftsmen came to anticipate this reaction, and assumed a drafting style which sought to ensure that the courts took account of every situation contemplated by the policy. This style involved very detailed specification of the factual circumstances and their legal consequences. This 'excessive individuality' was one of the prime complaints made of statutes during the nineteenth century, but when the Office of Parliamentary Counsel was established, *inter alia* with a view to improving the standard of drafting, the result was that this style became institutionalized in what Sir Harold Kent, a former Parliamentary Counsel, has called 'the Thring technique': 'the single-sentence subsection festooned with exceptions, conditions and provisions'.[17] The judiciary's reaction was to develop further the presumption against statutory changes in the common law and to interpret statutes in a very pedantic way. Not surprisingly, governmental reaction to such interpretation included both frustration that its policies had been rendered ineffective, and distrust of the judiciary's motives, in particular where public law and taxation were involved:

> We find that when an Act comes before a court it is quite often held to mean something which we never intended and we are told that this interpretation is inevitable, in view of well-established rules applicable to the construction of Statutes; it seems to us, however, that these results are arrived at by subtleties and an excessive ingeniousness of argument which are out of place in construing legal documents prepared as Acts of Parliament necessarily are.[18]

---

[17] Sir H. Kent, *In On the Act* (1979), p. 106.

[18] Sir W. Graham-Harrison, 'An Examination of the Main Criticisms of the Statute-Book and of the Possibility of Improvement' [1935] *Jo. of the Society of Public Teachers of Law*, 9, 11. See also R. Stevens, *Law and Politics* (1979), discussing the interpretation of taxing statutes by the House of Lords in *I.R.C.* v. *Duke of Westminster* [1936] A.C. 1: 'The actual conscious or subconscious motives of the law lords in the Westminster case

The judicial failure was originally explained in terms of an 'excessive predilection for common law doctrines'[19] and a consequent hostility to statutes as a source of law. Although we agree with the Law Commissions' criticism that this explanation no longer gives 'a wholly fair impression of the present theory and practice of the British courts',[20] reliance is still placed upon it, even by members of the judiciary, to explain the persistence of the traditional drafting style. For example, Lord Bridge in a recent debate on the English language said:

When Parliament is legislating on many subjects, 90 per cent of the complexity of language which finds its way into the Act of Parliament is really inherent in the legislative process itself. The draftsman is required to embody in statutory terms some highly sophisticated social policy, articulated in great detail and required to be imposed on an already complicated social structure. Above all, the statutory terms must – if language can achieve the object – be proof against judicial misconstruction. Of course, that is an unattainable ideal, but is it any wonder that in these circumstances, in pursuit of his object, the draftsman sacrifices simplicity and lucidity of expression for what he hopes will achieve certainty of meaning?

He continued:

What is the alternative style of legislative prose which can be adopted to avoid such complexity? I think the only style which can be suggested is that Acts of Parliament should confine themselves to broad and simple statements of principle, leaving the elaboration of the details of policy to the courts. But whether that would be a wise move I doubt, for it seems to me that it would carry the danger of imposing on the courts – or allowing to the courts, if you prefer it – a breadth of essentially legislative discretion which the courts are not really well qualified to exercise.[21]

Sir William Dale is a leading advocate of the view that United Kingdom legislation would be greatly improved by the adoption of such a

---

provide a fertile field for speculation, but its effects were clear. The case finally gave the balance of advantage to those with resources sufficient to hire the best legal talent, who might then camouflage the substance of their transaction under some formal disguise. It did not, of course, mean that the taxpayer always won in litigation. It did, however, signal that tax litigation had become an arid, semantic (and often antisocial) vicious circle, and frequently the result of this was a windfall for the taxpayer. Worse still, the attitude that led the judges to examine form rather than substance proved remarkably difficult to undo even when the legislature did intervene' (pp. 207–8). A radically different approach to avoidance schemes is to be found in *Ramsay* v. *I.R.C.* [1981] 2 W.L.R. 449.

[19] The Law Commissions, *The Interpretation of Statutes* (1969, Law Com. No. 21, Scot. Law Com. No. 11), para. 10.

[20] Id.

[21] Lord Bridge, 416 *House of Lords Debates*, cols. 777–8 (28 January 1981).

system, which is commonly associated with the drafting styles to be found in the civil law tradition. By way of example, Dale compares extracts from copyright laws in Great Britain, France and West Germany, which are set out in Chapter 1, section 6 (e). Dale argues that the differences in style mean that the West German and French versions give a 'perhaps general, but firm and intelligible, statement of what copyright is [and] the nature and extent of the right'; whereas the British statute is 'so weakened by qualifications and conditions, so diluted by the introduction of extraneous and particular matters' that its provisions are 'neither brief, nor general, nor firm, not even intelligible'.[22]

There are a number of reasons why it is difficult to assess the strength and acceptability of this argument. Firstly, not all civil law drafting employs general principles unsupported by detailed provisions; French public law displays the same characteristics as are complained of in this country – lack of codification, absence of express repeals and unnecessary complication. Secondly, there are limitations on the value of comparisons of this kind. It is misleading simply to abstract sections from statutes in different legal cultures in order to present one as containing vices to be avoided and the other as illustrating a model to be emulated. Styles of drafting depend *inter alia* upon the historic and prevailing conceptions of the role of and the relationship between the constituent elements of the state, in particular those of the legislature and the judiciary, and the ways in which these roles and relationships are institutionalized and regulated. Accordingly it is usually not possible to transplant legal practices and procedures without amendment into foreign cultures. Thirdly, given the historical background to the present detailed drafting style, it is unlikely that the government, and hence the draftsmen, would be prepared to allow the judiciary the increased discretion which would accompany the use of general principles, in particular in public law.

Two further obstacles are identified by Professor Clarence Smith in a clear and balanced discussion of the differences between English and continental drafting styles: the conservatism both of statute law users and of the draftsmen. Despite their complaints, users 'are inclined to regard the advocates of change as a bunch of irresponsible egg-heads, and worse, would feel uncomfortable . . . if laws were not dressed up as

[22] Sir W. Dale, *Legislative Drafting: A New Approach* (1977), pp. 6–7; and Chapter 1 above, pp. 32–7.

"legal".'[23] The draftsmen on the other hand are so firmly entrenched in the upper levels of the civil service and their practices so firmly established, that they will not change their styles voluntarily; only an order from the Cabinet could achieve this, and that, too, seems unlikely. Even the Renton Committee's innocuous recommendations that statements of principle should be encouraged and that statements of purpose should be used when convenient, have received a muted response from the government. Answering a question put by Lord Renton concerning them, the Lord Chancellor replied that 'Parliamentary Counsel are well aware of these recommendations, and subject to drafting instructions by responsible Ministers, will act upon them.'[24] This reply underlines the point made earlier, that government approval is required for major changes in the practices governing the preparation of legislation, but has not been forthcoming.

Elsewhere in its Report, the Renton Committee recommended that 'in principle the interests of the ultimate users should always have priority over those of the legislators.'[25] Clearly there could be some difficulty in implementing this recommendation, in particular in judging who should be treated as the primary audience. Given that a statute typically has a number of users whose level of comprehension of its legal effect will vary considerably, a choice will have to be made as to which level of comprehension is to be aimed at. The question, who is to exercise this choice, and upon what criteria, is one which has received little attention. Nevertheless the recommendation is a significant departure from the customary view of the relationship between the draftsman and the user.

There are positive steps which could be taken to improve the methods of preparing and enacting legislation and of producing and maintaining the statute book. Some of these concern the resources which are currently allocated to these tasks; consider for example the establishment of the Office of Parliamentary Counsel. It is frankly amazing that the task of drafting some two thousand pages per annum of public general Acts, most of them important and some of them of the first political, social and economic significance, continues to be

---

[23] J. C. Smith, 'Legislative Drafting: English and Continental' [1980] *Statute Law Review* 14, 22.

[24] *Renton*, recommendations 13 and 15; Lord Hailsham L.C., 412 *House of Lords Debates*, cols. 1588-9 (7 August 1980).

[25] *Renton*, recommendations 8 and 19; for the government's response, see 410 *House of Lords Debates*, cols. 1111-14 (18 June 1980).

undertaken by a group of approximately twenty-five people. It is difficult to believe that it is not in the government's interest to make substantial additions to this number. Of course it takes time for a recruit to become a draftsman, between 8–10 years is the traditional cautious estimate, and the limited number of existing Counsel can help to train only a few at a time. But such obstacles are not insurmountable. A larger Office would be able to allocate more draftsmen and more time to each Bill, which would in the short term allow the government's sessional programme to be completed more easily, and Bills to be more carefully drafted and thus more likely to achieve what the government wants. Apart from increasing the size of the Office, Bills could be drafted by those practising and academic lawyers in the UK who already have extensive experience of drafting for other jurisdictions. In the long term more time could be devoted to consolidation and statute law revision, which would in turn make drafting new or amending legislation easier. In addition, many of the suggestions made to the Renton Committee were turned down because their implementation would impose additional burdens on the draftsmen; a larger Office would mean that that objection at least would be removed.

Such an investment in the Office of Parliamentary Counsel is entirely dependent on the government; and it is not surprising that its short-term concern to complete its annual programme is a high priority. But the government also desires its legislation to have the intended impact, and if this does not happen because the draftsmen had to rush the Bill to meet the timetable, one remedy is to increase their numbers. Of course, such benefits as are indicated above would fail to materialize if, by analogy with Parkinson's Law, the government's legislative programme expanded to meet the draftsmen available for its completion. This is a possibility. Historically the Office was established and gradually expanded to meet the increasing demands on government to enact legislation, and in turn the availability of a highly specialized group of draftsmen invited increased legislative activity. But even if there were some expansion in the quantity or complexity of legislation to be enacted, the rules and practices of Parliamentary procedure as presently constituted impose some limits.

Other steps which have been discussed at length in the literature, some of which have been mentioned in this chapter, focus on making the most efficient use of existing procedures, particularly the Parliamentary procedures governing legislative business; on making the product itself more intelligible, for example, through greater use of illustrative examples and explanatory memoranda; and more radically, on the continued existence of the institutional arrangements which have been developed over the past century. For example, there is nothing inherent in the activity of drafting which requires separate institutional arrangements, and a reasonable argument can be made that government drafting could as well be done with the same staff within the Lord Chancellor's Office, which is, through the Statute Law Committee, responsible for the production and maintenance of the statute book. Such a change, like most of the others which have been put forward, requires political will on the part of the government. From the draftsman's point of view, the single most telling factor is the time constraints imposed by the government's legislative programme. This factor falls clearly within the government's control, but no attempts have been made to reduce the programme's content.

Radical improvements in the intelligibility of statutes cannot come about in the absence of change in the system which has been institutionalized for their preparation and enactment. Conflict between different actors in the process of preparation and enactment, excessive traditionalism, government inertia, distrust of reforms, and of technology, political and party reality and vested interest in the *status quo* are all factors which have contributed to the way in which the statute book has developed. Most interpreters will be quite unable to neutralize the operation of these factors in any substantial way, but at least an awareness of their causes and effects should help him to understand why the material with which he is dealing can prove so difficult, and to devise techniques for coping with those difficulties.

10 Interpreting Statutes

All rules can give rise to problems of interpretation; some aspects are shared with literary and other texts, others are special to rules and yet others to particular types of rule. The purpose of this chapter is to bring together the main themes of the book in their application to the interpretation of statutes as one type of legislative rule. Within law some special considerations apply to all statutes, others to particular types of statute; but many of the perennial difficulties and controversies to which statutory interpretation gives rise are to be found in the interpretation of other legislative rules, and of other rules in fixed verbal form, both in legal and non-legal contexts.

Statutory provisions are interpreted by a wide variety of people: judges, magistrates and their clerks, members of tribunals, civil servants, officials in local authorities and other public corporations such as the nationalized industries, trade union officials, architects, chartered surveyors, accountants, barristers, solicitors, students and others. For many of these the application of a statutory provision in a given instance will usually be a routine matter. Where doubts do arise about its scope or meaning, or about its relationship with other provisions, they may often be easily resolved, for example by reference to an authoritative ruling or text, or to some technique of interpretation supplied by the context. This chapter will describe a relatively systematic procedure for identifying conditions of doubt in the interpretation of statutes and for constructing arguments for and against alternative answers[1]; where appropriate, points will be illustrated by reference to *Davis* v. *Johnson*.

[1] The conditions which are presupposed are set out in Chapter 6 above, pp. 218-19.

1 Clarification of standpoint and role

The first stage, as always, is to ask, Who am I? At what stage in the process am I? What am I trying to do? The draftsman of taxing statutes, for example, has the opportunity to formulate the clauses in a Bill so as to forestall or to further particular interpretations. At the same time he is working to the instructions of a government department such as the Treasury or Customs and Excise, and is under pressure to complete the Bill on time. Both factors limit what the draftsman can do. His duty is to prepare a Bill which gives legal effect to government policy and which complies with the Parliamentary rules of public Bill procedure. Ensuring legal effectiveness may entail the subordination of clarity to precision of formulation; this is frequently the case with anti-avoidance provisions. That this priority may prove troublesome subsequently, is not the draftsman's prime consideration. Nevertheless he must be sensitive to the responses of tax-collecting agencies, tax avoiders and the judiciary, and try to formulate the Bill's clauses in such a way that the government's desired interpretation is clear.

For the tax consultant the sections of the Act are a datum, the starting point from which interpretation proceeds, but unlike the draftsman he may regard the government's objectives as a challenge to his ingenuity in achieving the lawful minimization of his client's liability to pay tax. The interpretive techniques he employs are constrained by the attitudes and behaviour of others, notably the Inland Revenue, who have their own policies and practices – for example the selective enforcement of taxing provisions as formulated in their extra-statutory concessions – which may go beyond what the government intended or the judiciary regard as justifiable.[2] Although subject to judicial control, the Revenue is, from the tax consultant's standpoint, more significant by virtue of its power to institute proceedings based on its own interpretations or to settle claims by negotiation.

To understand why there is a problem of interpretation it is sometimes useful to adopt other standpoints: institutional and role-related factors may generate difficulties for the Revenue or the judiciary which are not applicable to a tax consultant. In the following discussion of *Davis* v. *Johnson*, we shall use the standpoint of counsel for Johnson presenting his arguments to the House of Lords.[3]

[2] *Vestey* v *I.R.C.* [1980] A.C. 1148.
[3] Above, pp. 95-8.

2 Identification of the relevant statutory material

The second stage is to identify, locate and assemble an authoritative version of the statutory material relevant to the problem at hand. To some extent this is a matter of systematic search for the relevant provisions and amendments thereto, and for important matters of detail concerning the promulgation of statutes. This kind of research involves library skills of a fairly straightforward kind, although acquiring and exercising them can prove time-consuming and, because of the condition of the statute book,[4] it can be frustrating.

The first step is to discover the original statutory text and then to check whether there have been any amendments to it. Normally both tasks can be carried out by using *Statutes in Force* or Halsbury's *Statutes*. The effect of amendments may be less easy to determine; whether textual or non-textual amendment is used, the reader must be able to reformulate the original rule in such a way as to give precise legal effect to the amendments to it (a process known as conflation).[5] In some cases this may be the source of doubt.

Identifying and, where necessary, reformulating the text are tasks which are normally straightforward, but sometimes occasion difficulty. Apart from the use of the standard referencing services, completing them may involve some ingenuity, such as spotting or establishing connections between separate statutory provisions, conflating lengthy and technical non-textual amendments to an earlier text, using algorithms[6] and other visual devices to help understanding, or creating a doubt which requires resolution through the adoption of a less obvious interpretation. This last alternative may be attractive to the unhappy interpreter, but he may be hard put to it to convince others of its plausibility.[7]

The second step is to discover when the statute came (or comes) into force, to what period of time it applies, and what is its duration.

Commencement. Section 4 of the Interpretation Act 1978 provides:

---

[4] Chapter 9 above, pp. 304-8.

[5] Section 3 of the Domestic Violence and Matrimonial Proceedings Act 1976 textually amended the Matrimonial Homes Act 1967 and section 4 incorporated provisions of that Act by reference; Chapter 1 above, pp. 84-5. The 1976 Act was itself textually amended by section 89 (2) (a) and Schedule 2, para. 53 of the Domestic Proceedings and Magistrates' Courts Act 1978.

[6] See Appendix 1.

[7] See the review by Lord Cross of *Statute Law* by F. A. R. Bennion, [1981] *Statute Law Review*, 122, 124.

An Act or provision of an Act comes into force –
- (a) where provision is made for it to come into force on a particular day, at the beginning of that day;
- (b) where no provision is made for its coming into force, at the beginning of the day on which the Act receives the Royal Assent.

Sometimes an Act will contain a section specifying the day on which it is to come into force. For example the Interpretation Act 1978 which received the Royal Assent on 20 July 1978, provides in section 26 that 'This Act shall come into force on 1st January 1979.' Where the government intends to postpone the commencement of an Act, or parts of it, perhaps because administrative arrangements need to be made for its implementation, the Act will give power to a named authority to specify the commencement day; for example 'This Act shall come into force on such a day as the Secretary of State may by order appoint', and powers may also be given to bring different parts of the Act into force on different days. The Act may go further, requiring the Secretary of State to consult certain groups, or publish codes of practice or guidelines concerning its implementation, before he makes the order.

Commencement Orders take the form of statutory instruments and are published in official and commercial indexes. The postponement of the commencement of Acts is now quite common,[8] and was provided for in the Domestic Violence and Matrimonial Proceedings Act 1976.[9] Although the implementation of this new remedy was a matter of some urgency, substantial changes in the administration of county court business had to be made first. Accordingly, section 5 of the Act, which received the Royal Assent on 26 October 1976, gave powers to the Lord Chancellor to bring it, or parts of it, into force on such days as he chose; but it went on to specify that if any of the Act's provisions were not in force by 1 April 1977, he should make an order bringing them into force.

Time of Application. In the absence of a contrary intention, a statute applies only to circumstances falling within its scope which arise following its commencement. Two occasions when a statute operates

---

[8] On the difficulties which postponed commencement may cause, see the Statute Law Society, *Report of a Working Party on Commencement of Acts of Parliament*, [1980] *Statute Law Review*, 40; and J. Spencer, 'When is a Law not a Law?', 131 *New Law Journal* (1981), 144.

[9] The Commencement Order was in fact made on 25 March 1977, bringing the Act into force on 1 June 1977; Domestic Violence and Matrimonial Proceedings (Commencement) Order 1977, S.I. 1977 No. 559.

with respect to a time prior to its enactment may be distinguished: *retrospective* and *retroactive*.[10] A statute is retrospective in effect when it attaches new consequences to an event which occurred prior to its enactment; for example to indemnify a particular action or to give compensation in respect of a particular injury. A statute is retroactive in effect when it is deemed to have come into force at a time prior to its enactment. Both types are relatively rare; a statute requires express language to have such effect. In addition there is a presumption against making previously lawful acts illegal by either device.

Duration. Once enacted, a statutory provision remains in force until it is repealed by another Act of Parliament or it expires by virtue of a time limit specified in the Act.[11] The principle of desuetude (disuse) is inapplicable to United Kingdom legislation, although Acts of the old Scots Parliament and old treaties in international law may be held to have fallen into desuetude, if long disregarded in practice.[12]

Where a statute is intended to be of temporary effect, provision will be made for it to expire on a specific day, after a specific period of time, or on the occurrence of a specific event. During the last decade a number of statutes were enacted which gave the police extraordinary powers to deal with terrorism and which removed many of the traditional rights and liberties of a person suspected of having committed a 'terrorist' offence. These Acts were all of a 'temporary' nature. For example, section 17 (1) of the Prevention of Terrorism (Temporary Provisions) Act 1976 provides that the substance of the Act 'shall remain in force until an expiry of the period of 12 months beginning with the passing of this Act'. The section goes on to provide that it may be continued in force with the approval of Parliament for further twelve-month periods, and it has in fact been regularly renewed under this power.

3 Identification of the conditions of doubt

The next stage is the identification of the exact word or phrase causing difficulties and of the conditions of doubt which give rise to them. The

---

[10] This follows E. Driedger, 'Statutes, Retroactive Retrospective Reflections', 56 *Canadian Bar Review* (1978), 264.

[11] On rare occasions, a court may hold that an earlier statutory provision has been impliedly repealed by a later one; and difficulties may arise where there is a conflict between a statutory provision and a provision of Community law.

[12] Above, p. 201.

statutory words provide a natural and convenient starting point, and it is usually best to incorporate them into a question indicating the issue which they raise.[13] For example, in *Allen* a single question of law can be formulated in neutral terms as follows: 'What is the meaning of "shall marry" in section 57 of the Offences Against the Person Act 1861?'[14]

Sometimes one may be puzzled by a rule because its style defeats or obscures its substance. This may occur where the rule is unusually long, is subject to a number of qualifications, contains a large number of subordinate clauses, employs negatives or the passive voice, has an unusually complicated syntactical structure, employs words which are archaic, ambiguous, vague, technical, obscure or unfamiliar, or any combination of these.[15]

There are other conditions, too, which may occasion puzzlement. For example, the rule may be perfectly comprehensible in the sense that an interpreter thinks he understands its language, but it somehow appears incongruous when set against the object which it is supposed to secure; or the rule may be comprehensible but rendered puzzling by subsequent judicial or other interpretive action; or again the rule may be comprehensible but appear harsh when applied to the facts of the case at hand.[16] Counsel for Johnson presented the argument in favour of his client largely on the basis that the interpretation sought by Davis would be in conflict with the statutory words and the purposes for which the legislation was enacted. If Davis were granted an injunction, he argued, a mistress would be given the same rights as a married woman, yet there was nothing in the 1976 Act to suggest that so substantial a change in matrimonial law was intended. The 1976 Act was enacted to ease the procedural limitations on the grant of injunctions by county courts, and thus could not be envisaged as also giving an unmarried person the right to exclude from the 'matrimonial home' his or her 'spouse' when in law the 'spouse', like Johnson, had a right to be there by virtue of being a joint tenant, with Davis, of the council flat.[17]

' The condition of doubt to which counsel is referring may be described as the imperfect relationship between the rule at hand and the

---

[13] In criminal appeals to the House of Lords the issue is certified in the form of a question.

[14] For other formulations see Chapter 7 above, pp. 256–7.

[15] Chapter 6 above, pp. 221–2, conditions of doubt nos. 13(c), (d) and (i).

[16] Ibid., conditions of doubt nos. 11, 12, 21, 23 and 33.

[17] Chapter 1 above, pp. 95–6.

existing system of rules; more particularly, it may be said that the interpretation favoured by opposing counsel would be in conflict with a well-established set of rules governing husband and wife.[18] In addition, counsel for Johnson has to cope with the decision of the Court of Appeal granting the injunction and seemingly approving this interpretation, and with other aspects which will be considered below.

A striking feature of *Davis* v. *Johnson* is the variation in the views of the different judges as to the conditions of doubt. It is probably the case that none of them considered the style of section 1 to be problematic; although subsection (1) is a lengthy sentence, it can be readily broken down into a number of reasonably clearly defined occasions on which an injunction may be granted. There was agreement between some of the judges that the difficulty lay in determining the scope of the section, but within this agreement there were different diagnoses of the exact difficulty.

Lord Denning would admit to no doubt about the scope of section 1. He says near the beginning of his judgment, 'To my mind the Act is perfectly clear', and after quoting from the section continues, 'No-one I would have thought could possibly dispute that those plain words by themselves cover this very case'.[19] For him, the doubts were created by what he regarded as the perverse interpretation of the section in the earlier decisions of the Court of Appeal, *B.* v. *B.* and *Cantliff* v. *Jenkins*, whose effect was aggravated by the inhibiting rules of the doctrine of precedent. Past authoritative decisions were the difficulty. In addition, his Lordship took the view that doubts about the mischief which the Act was intended to remedy could have been easily discovered were it not for the rules precluding explicit reliance on Parliamentary proceedings in a court of law. Difficulties were thus created, in Lord Denning's view, by the institutional practices concerning precedent and the interpretation of statutes.[20]

Lords Diplock and Scarman both thought that there were doubts about the scope of section 1, but disagreed as to their exact nature. For Lord Diplock, as for counsel for Johnson, the doubt lay in the seeming conflict between the procedural provisions of section 1 and the existing substantive law relating to the protection of married women and of proprietary interests. In his opinion, the question concerning the scope of section 1 was whether it merely provided a

---

[18] Chapter 6 above, p. 221, conditions of doubt nos. 8(f) and 9(a).
[19] Chapter 1 above, p. 86.
[20] Chapter 6 above, p. 223, conditions of doubt nos. 21(b) and 23.

more expeditious remedy in cases where the unmarried partner already held a proprietary interest, as in *Cantliff* v. *Jenkins* and *Davis* v. *Johnson* (the narrow view), or whether it extended to provide a remedy even to an unmarried partner who held no proprietary rights in the premises named in the injunction, as in *B.* v. *B.* (the wider view).

Lord Scarman approached the issue somewhat differently. He agreed that it was 'highly unlikely that Parliament could have intended by the sidewind of subsection (2) to have introduced radical changes into the law of property', but took the view that as the Act was concerned with *personal* rights (injunctions are personal remedies), it was not necessary to construe the section so as to imply such an effect upon property law. The difficulty arose not because the section was obscure or because it conflicted with existing property rights but because the Lords Justices in the earlier appeals *B.* v. *B.* and *Cantliff* v. *Jenkins* has misperceived the nature of the remedies being provided in the Act. Had they recognized that it was to do with personal rights they would like Lord Scarman have found 'nothing illogical or surprising in Parliament legislating to over-ride a property right, if it be thought to be socially necessary'.[21]

Their Lordships were agreed that Lord Denning's creation of a fourth exception to the rule that the Court of Appeal is bound by its own decisions and his explicit references to Hansard added to the difficulties in the case; and Lord Diplock and Viscount Dilhorne in particular disapproved in unequivocal terms these novel techniques of interpretation.[22]

4 The construction of arguments

In the interpretation of statutes, as for rules in fixed verbal form generally, the text of the rule(s) is a natural starting point. The question arises: how far is it helpful and permissible to look beyond the text to other material as aids to interpretation?

In many areas, in particular of public administration, such as education, immigration, employment, social security, value added tax, housing and planning, there exists what may be called a specialist 'subculture' of rules, practices, conventions and procedures concern-

[21] Chapter 1 above, p. 109.
[22] The conditions of doubt in *Davis* v. *Johnson* can be summarized as including nos. 8(e), (f), and (g), 9(a) and (e), 11, 21(b), 23 and 33.

ing the interpretation of the governing statutory provisions.[23] Familiarity with this kind of context will almost always be of help to an administrative official, either directly or by analogy, and will also form an essential part of the context for other interpreters. Whether these aids are permissible depends ultimately upon the courts, when an individual or private organization challenges a ruling based upon them. Even where judicial control is limited to the form of an administrative decision rather than extending to its substance, judicial attitudes to interpretation and to the use of such aids will, for most administrators, constitute a *model* of what is permissible.[24]

Statutes tend to differ from non-legal rules in three ways: there are rules which govern the interpretation of statutes; there is a wide range of types of material which is potentially relevant to interpretation of a statutory text; and there are some rules which govern the use of such material by requiring, permitting or prohibiting consideration of it by certain interpreters and, in some instances, by giving authoritative status to arguments based upon it. In non-legal contexts there tend to be few or no rules in fixed verbal form, there is usually little or no legislative 'furniture' which can be used as aids to interpretation, and it is even less likely that there will be rules regulating the use of such aids. But as with the doctrine of precedent, the rules governing interpretation of statutes and the use of aids tend, for the most part, to be permissive and vague, so that the difference between legal and non-legal rules in fixed verbal form is not as great, in this respect, as might at first sight seem to be the case. The first step at this stage is for the interpreter to identify and assemble the raw material from which he will draw arguments to support or undermine alternative interpretations.

Beyond such factors as the time at his disposal, the availability of the material and the optimal use of his resources, there are no limits on the kinds of raw material which he might identify as being useful. The fact that some of it cannot be explicitly referred to in judicial settings is for these purposes irrelevant; they may still help to suggest good arguments. Of course the kinds of material which are admissible in courtooms, and which may be authoritative there – such as prior judicial decisions on the words in issue – are very likely to be treated

[23] See, for example, C. Harlow, 'Discretion, Social Security and Computers', 44 *Modern Law Review* (1981), 546.

[24] A valuable insight into a government department's reactions to judicial interpretation is provided by Civil Service Department, *Legal Entitlements and Administrative Practices* (1979, Chairman Mr R. Wilding).

as authoritative in other contexts, such as in communications between solicitors who have no intention of going to court. But it would be quite wrong to infer from the standard treatments of statutory interpretation, which deal with the explicit authoritative status of particular kinds of argument and the sources from which they are drawn, that material which is not admissible in a courtroom is without value in preparing arguments to be presented there or in some other context. The following discussion describes briefly three sources from which arguments for and against alternative interpretations may be drawn; statutory material, judicial decisions and other extrinsic material, and indicates the acceptability of these in a courtroom.

(a) **Statutory material**

(i) INTERNAL

Frequently the scope or meaning of a rule is qualified by other rules in the same statute. Such qualifications may extend or limit the rule, provide for specific applications of an otherwise general rule, specify how a particular rule is to be implemented, state exceptions, or attach a specific meaning to a word or phrase. Qualifications of the last sort are generally contained in an interpretation or definition section, while some of these others appear in Schedules at the end of the statute, or may be promulgated separately as a statutory instrument. In addition, all statutes contain a long title which indicates the object of the enactment, while older statutes contain lengthier preambles explaining not only what the Act is intended to do, but also why. Such statements of institutionalized intent are rare now, but arguably could be profitably revived.[25]

Draftsmen use express words where they intend one provision to be qualified by another, but its interpretation may nevertheless be affected by other rules not specifically referred to. Many doubts about interpretation have arisen because of the uncertain relationship between one provision and another in the same statute[26]; but it is also a common kind of reasoning to compare the wording of particular

---

[25] Chapter 5 above, pp. 192–200; and *Renton*, paras. 11.6–11.8.

[26] And because of the uncertain usage of the same word in the same or different sections: so in section 57 of the Offences Against the Person Act, the word 'marry' is used in different senses in the opening words of the provision (see Chapter 7 above, p. 237); and because of the uncertain usage of a word within an area of law, e.g. 'custody' of children in family law: see Mrs Justice Booth, 'Child Legislation', *Statute Law Review* (forthcoming).

sections so as to advance or support a preferred interpretation. For example, in *Davis* v. *Johnson*, counsel argued as follows: at the time of Davis's application for an injunction restraining Johnson from occupying the council flat, she was in fact living in the Chiswick Women's Refuge; thus she and Johnson were not then 'living with each other in the same household' and accordingly, on a literal construction of the section, she was not entitled to an injunction. This interpretation is supported by a comparison of the words in section 4 of the Act which deals with injunctions restricting occupation of the matrimonial home by a husband or wife. Here the Act speaks of a person who is 'entitled ... to occupy a dwelling house. ...' This section does not require the party applying for an injunction to be at that time in occupation; it is necessary only that he or she had a right to occupy. Davis had a right to occupy, because she was a joint tenant with Johnson, but section 1 requires them to be living with each other in the same household at the time of the application. If it was intended that the remedy provided by section 1 should be available in the same circumstances as in section 4, which is what Davis's counsel is asserting, then why did the draftsman not use the same words?[27]

(ii) EXTERNAL

To a limited extent the interpretation of statutes is regulated by statute, the most important being the Interpretation Act 1978. However, the traditional approach to judicial interpretation, which has been endorsed by the Law Commission, the Renton Committee and by the government, is that it is the function of the judiciary to interpret with the minimum of direction from Parliament how they should set about their task.

The question of the extent to which statutory interpretation should be the subject of precise and general rules is raised in a quite specific way in relation to what can and cannot be achieved by an Interpretation Act. The enactment in a single place of a number of standardized definitions and conventions can, it is felt, help the draftsmen and those users who are familiar with the provisions. It can also reduce the length of some statutes and other instruments. Thus even the relatively modest provisions of the Northern Ireland Interpretation Act 1954 had the effect, according to one authority, that without it, 'the annual volumes of the Northern Ireland Statutes would, upon a conservative

[27] Chapter 1 above, p. 98. See Lord Denning's response, p. 88.

estimate, be approximately one-third larger than they are'.[28] But in common law countries the role of Interpretation Acts has tended to be a limited one, generally confined to such matters as ways of expressing number and gender, or providing certain common form provisions, but generally not attempting to provide a wide-ranging legislative dictionary of uniform stipulative definitions which would be binding on draftsmen and interpreters. This tribute to the flexibility of language and to the dangers of generalization is characteristic of the traditions of the common law. But it is a largely unexplored question whether this almost total rejection of a legislative dictionary is not itself an example of over-generalization. The Interpretation Act 1978 consolidated a number of definitions contained in the repealed Interpretation Act 1889 and elsewhere, but some regarded it as a missed opportunity. On the other hand, the draftsman of the Northern Ireland Act concluded that the 1978 Act 'probably does as much as can be done in an Interpretation Act to shorten and simplify Acts'.[29]

A noteworthy but unsuccessful attempt to change the traditional relationship between Parliament and the judiciary was Lord Scarman's sponsorship of Interpretation of Legislation Bills in the 1979–80 and 1980–81 sessions of Parliament. Both were based on the Law Commissions' draft Bill published in 1969,[30] the 1980 Bill being a verbatim reproduction, the 1981 version incorporating some amendments to accommodate the criticisms made of the earlier version. The Bills, which would have authorized explicit reliance on a variety of sources presently excluded by the courts, notably policy documents prepared by official agencies upon which Acts are based, were controversial and encountered considerable opposition.[31] The principal objections were that they confused the constitutional division of function between the courts and Parliament; that they would create further difficulties for the government draftsmen who would be drafting Bills knowing that other texts not prepared by them would be construed with the statutory text to produce an interpretation of it; that they

[28] W. A. Leitch and A. G. Donaldson, 'The Interpretation Act – Ten Years Later', 16 *Northern Ireland Legal Quarterly* (1965), 215, 237.

[29] W. A. Leitch, 'Interpretation and the Interpretation Act 1978', [1980] *Statute Law Review*, 5, 13.

[30] Law Commissions, *The Interpretation of Statutes* (1969, Law Com. No. 21, Scots Law Com. No.11).

[31] See generally 405 *House of Lords Debates*, cols. 276–306 (13 February 1980), 418 *House of Lords Debates*, cols. 64–83 (9 March 1981) and 1341–7 (26 March 1981); and F. A. R. Bennion, 'Another reverse for the Law Commissions' Interpretation Bill', 131 *New Law Journal* (1981), 840.

would admit references to texts whose relevance, reliability and availability was very variable; and lastly, that the attendant costs for
lawyers, government departments and ultimately their clients would
be significantly increased, as interpreters would in effect have to equip
themselves with these texts and to read them in case they shed some
light upon alternative interpretations. Although the 1981 Bill was,
because of the amendments to it, more favourably received, this pragmatic objection was still influential in defeating it.

Apart from the Interpretation Act 1978, support for alternative
interpretations may always be obtained from statutes *in pari materia*,
that is statutes which deal with the same classes of persons, things and
activities as that in issue. Counsel in *Davis* v. *Johnson* placed considerable reliance on provisions in the Matrimonial Homes Act 1967 as
amended, and judicial interpretations of it, to show that since some of
the remedies available to a married woman had been limited where
they were in conflict with the husband's property rights, it could not
possibly be the case that Parliament had intended just such a conflict
in the case of an unmarried woman to be resolved in her favour. The
weight which may be placed upon such analogies or disanalogies
varies from case to case, and it is difficult to generalize about it.

(iii) THE LAW OF THE EUROPEAN COMMUNITIES

The European Economic Community is the most important of the
three communities which constitute the European Communities,[32]
and its Treaty, and the Regulations and Directives made under it
have had an increasingly significant impact upon United Kingdom
statutory provisions. Community law forms part of a legal system
which is *sui generis*, from which premise three important consequences
for our legal system flow[33]: first, Community Regulations are directly
applicable, that is, they form part of the law of a member state without
any intervening act on the part of the domestic legislature being either
necessary or indeed permissible. Secondly, in certain circumstances
Treaty provisions and regulations are directly effective, that is, they
confer rights upon individuals which national courts are obliged to
uphold; and thirdly, in cases of conflict between Community law and
national law, the necessity of ensuring uniform application of Community law requires that precedence be given to the former over the

[32] The other two are the European Coal and Steel Community and the European
Atomic Energy Community.

[33] This is based on D. Miers and A. Page, *Legislation* (1982), Chapter 1.

latter. These consequences are recognized in sections 2 (1) and 3 of the European Communities Act 1972, and clearly impose new obligations and interpretive requirements on judges in the United Kingdom.

The primary functions of the interpretation of Community law are that it should seek to further the objectives of the Community as a whole, and of the scheme of the particular Treaty provisions under review. These functions are institutionalized in the European Court, which has a prerogative to formulate authoritative and binding interpretations of Community law so as to achieve uniformity in its application by member states. Although all techniques of interpretation are evident in the judgments of the European Court, including formalism, teleological and schematic techniques lie at the centre of its approach to interpretation, and these are intended to be preferred by national courts as well when they are interpreting Community law.[34] Lord Denning has responded to this challenge in characteristic style:

... when we come to matters with a European element, the treaty is like an incoming tide. It flows into the estuaries and up the rivers. It cannot be held back. Parliament has decreed that the treaty is henceforward to be part of our law. It is equal in force to any statute ... What then are the principles of interpretation to be applied? Beyond doubt the English courts must follow the same principles as the European Court. Otherwise there would be differences between the countries of the nine. That would never do. All the courts of all nine countries should interpret the treaty in the same way. They should all apply the same principles. It is enjoined on the English courts by s. 3 of the European Communities Act 1972 ... What a task is thus set before us! The treaty is quite unlike any of the enactments to which we have become accustomed ...

It lays down general principles. It expresses its aims and purposes. All in sentences of moderate length and commendable style. But it lacks precision. It uses words and phrases without defining what they mean. An English lawyer would look for an interpretation clause, but he would look in vain. There is none. All the way through the treaty there are gaps and lacunae. These have to be filled in by the judges, or by regulations and directives. It is the European way.

Likewise the regulations and directives. They are enacted by the Council of Ministers sitting in Brussels for everyone to obey. They are quite unlike our statutory instruments. They have to give the reasons on which they are based ...

Seeing these differences, what are the English courts to do when they are faced with a problem of interpretation? They must follow the European pattern. No longer must they examine the words in meticulous detail. No

[34] See H. Kutscher, 'Methods of Interpretation as seen by a judge at the Court of Justice', in *Reports of the Judicial and Academic Conference of the Court of Justice of the European Communities* (1976); and A. Bredimas, *Methods of Interpretation and Community Law* (1978).

longer must they argue about the precise grammatical sense. They must look to the purpose or intent. To quote the words of the European Court in the *Da Costa* case; they must limit themselves to deducing from 'the wording and the spirit of the treaty the meaning of the Community rules ...' They must not confine themselves to the English text. They must consider, if need be, all the authentic texts, of which there are now eight ... They must divine the spirit of the treaty and gain inspiration from it. If they find a gap, they must fill it as best they can. They must do what the framers of the instrument would have done if they had thought about it. So we must do the same.[35]

Lord Denning's efforts to extend these principles to the interpretation of statutes which incorporate international conventions have been less successful. It is frequently argued that judges should adopt Community or continental styles of interpretation, that is styles which stress the purpose of an enactment, in preference to the more traditional approaches, when interpreting any statute; but as we shall see, this is a controversial matter.

(b) Judicial decisions

A judicial decision on the words in issue, or on the same or similar words in a statute *in pari materia*, will in many cases constitute an authoritative and final interpretation. In judicial contexts, decisions on statutes *in pari materia* are held to be not as persuasive as those directly on the statute in question. We have seen that counsel for Johnson relied on judicial decisions, particularly *Tarr* v. *Tarr*, concerning a statute *in pari materia*, and he also relied on the Court of Appeal decisions in *B.* v. *B.* and *Cantliff* v. *Jenkins* which were directly in point.

The judicial interpretation of statutes is a subject which has received a very great deal of attention; more perhaps than it deserves if we recall Cross's observation that 'the vast majority of statutes never come before the courts for interpretation'.[36] Those which do are largely concerned with private obligations between natural or legal persons, and with the public obligations which citizens owe to the state, or the state, through its executive agencies, owes to the citizen. Legislation which is addressed to the internal regulation of government or of public bodies is seldom the object of judicial interpretation. On the other hand, it is estimated that over fifty per cent of cases in the High Court and above involve a question of statutory

[35] *Bulmer* v. *Bollinger* [1974] 2 All E.R. 1226, 1231 and 1237-8. Lord Denning has not been entirely consistent; *McCarthy's* v. *Smith* [1980] 3 W.L.R. 929. See also Lord Diplock's remarks in *Henn* [1980] 2 W.L.R. 597, 635-7.

[36] Sir R. Cross, *Statutory Interpretation* (1977), p. 1; and Chapter 4 above, pp. 176-7.

interpretation, so it is a subject of some importance for the judiciary. Many writers – and some judges – now argue that there is a recognizably 'right' way for judges to approach interpretation; we consider this in the next section.

JUDICIAL INTERPRETATION OF STATUTES

The judicial function in the interpretation of statutes was emphatically reasserted by the House of Lords in *Duport Steel* v. *Sirs*. Lord Scarman said:

.... in the field of statute law the judge must be obedient to the will of Parliament as expressed in its enactments. In this field Parliament makes and unmakes the law, the judge's duty is to interpret and to apply the law, not to change it to meet the judge's idea of what justice requires. Interpretation does, of course, imply in the interpreter a power of choice where differing constructions are possible. But our law requires the judge to choose the construction which in his judgment best meets the legislative purpose of the enactment.[37]

This is a constitutional and political point of the first importance, reflecting the traditional conception of the division of functions between Parliament and the courts. Although the judiciary have developed recognizably distinct approaches to the interpretation of fiscal,[38] criminal, consolidating,[39] and some constitutional[40] statutes, descriptions of judicial interpretation have traditionally stressed the conspicious failure of the judiciary to develop systematic and coherent methodological principles to match the treatment accorded to areas of substantive law. 'There are', wrote Professor Cross, 'no binding judicial decisions on the subject of statutory interpretation generally as opposed to the interpretation of particular statutes; all that there is is a welter of judicial *dicta* which vary considerably in weight, age and uniformity.'[41]

Some of these *dicta* support certain recognizable presumptions and canons of interpretation, such as: an Act is to be looked at as a whole; statutory words are to be read according to their meaning as popularly

---

[37] [1980] 1 All E.R. 529, 551.

[38] This view has been challenged by Mr Justice Vinelott, 'Interpretation of Fiscal Statutes', *Statute Law Review* (forthcoming), who draws in particular on the remarks of Lord Wilberforce in *Ramsay* v. *I.R.C.* [1981] 2 W.L.R. 449.

[39] Difficulties may arise here depending on the *type* of consolidation; see Chapter 9 above, pp. 307–8 and *Maunsell* v. *Olins* [1975] A.C. 373, discussing condition of doubt 9 (d).

[40] The interpretation of constitutional provisions is of course of much greater importance in countries such as the United States.

[41] Op. cit., p. 42.

understood at the time the Act became law; an Act is presumed not to alter existing law beyond that necessarily required by the Act; where two rules in a statute conflict, the latter takes precedence; in ordinary usage 'and' is used conjunctively, 'or' disjunctively; any interpretation of a provision which would render nugatory (or more obscure) any other provision of an Act will normally be rejected; and an Act is to be interpreted so as not to disturb vested property rights. Some of the prescriptions such as the famous triumvirate of the Literal Rule, the Golden Rule and the Mischief Rule have taken the form of broad general principles; yet others are quite narrow and specific, such as the *eiusdem generis* rule which provides that 'the general word which follows particular and specific words of the same nature as itself takes its meaning from them and is presumed to be restricted to the same genus as those words'.[42]

A commonly remarked feature of most, but not all, of these principles of interpretation is that they are of little practical assistance in settling doubts about interpretation in particular cases. This is partly due to vagueness, but also because in many cases where one principle appears to support one interpretation there is another principle, often of equal status, which can be invoked in favour of an interpretation which would lead to a different result. Neither is systematic analysis encouraged by an uncritical acceptance of the view that literalism, or exegetical interpretation, is generally a bad thing while a purposive approach is a good thing.[43] Literalism is frequently portrayed as promoting systemic values at the expense of social values, which are to be discovered and promoted by a purposive approach; but, as we saw earlier, this conception is an oversimplification of what is involved in interpretive tasks. For some interpreters, the method of interpretation is as good as the results it achieves; but one is not necessarily easier than the other.

Following some judicial *dicta*, notably those of Lord Simon in *Maunsell* v. *Olins*[44] and of Lord Diplock in that case and in *Carter* v. *Bradbeer*[45] and *Fothergill* v. *Monarch Airlines*,[46] academic writers now argue that the triumvirate of rules of interpretation have fused into one, which is to give effect to the purpose of the statute.[47] Judicial

---

[42] Maxwell, *Interpretation of Statutes* (1969), p. 297; and see *Quazi* v. *Quazi* [1979] 3 W.L.R. 633.

[43] Chapter 4 above, pp. 183-6.

[44] [1975] A.C. 373.   [45] [1975] 1 W.L.R. 1204.   [46] [1980] 3 W.L.R. 809.

[47] E.g., D. Lloyd, *Introduction to Jurisprudence* (4th edn, 1979), p. 865; E. Driedger, *The Construction of Statutes* (1974), p. 67 and Cross, op. cit., pp. 42-3.

interpretation has been analysed as comprising two stages. In the first the judge reads the statute in its legal and factual context so as to acquire a general idea of the legislature's intention and purpose. At this stage he may look at any material he chooses. His next task is to read the particular statutory words in issue in their primary and natural meaning, and if this produces an absurd result which the legislature cannot reasonably be supposed to have intended, he may invoke an alternative interpretation which does. In the performance of this second task, there are limits on the kinds of material upon which he may explicitly and authoritatively rely.

This is the kind of analysis which Professor Cross put forward as constituting the 'rules of English statutory interpretation'[48]; but care should be taken not to impose a greater degree of rigidity at a higher level of generality than is warranted by English judicial doctrine or practice. As with precedent, the judges have given themselves a good deal of leeway as to what are considered to be legitimate techniques of interpretation. First, the *dicta* which are relied upon to support this analysis are no more than that, although they are clearly intended by their authors to be attempts to systematize methodological principles. As has been said many times of the rules of statutory interpretation, they 'are not rules in the ordinary sense of having some binding force. They are our servants not our masters ... in each case we must look at all relevant circumstances and decide as a matter of judgment what weight we attach to any particular rules.'[49] Secondly, although *dicta* of the House of Lords are generally persuasive, it is only a few of its members who have attempted to systematize judicial approaches to interpretation. Thirdly, judicial practice does not, for the most part, explicitly reflect this structured procedure. In most cases involving statutory interpretation courts resolve their doubts by reference primarily to the legal context of which the statute is part – company, family, tax law – and in particular to any prior decisions. References to the 'intention of Parliament' and 'the purpose of the statute' are reasonably frequent, though used in various senses, and there are occasional references to presumptions or canons of interpretation. On the other hand there are usually very few explicit references to what are or what ought to be the methodological principles guiding interpretation; nor is it easy to discern whether the judges are implicitly following some procedure. Lastly, there is a constitutional point.

[48] Op. cit., p. 43.
[49] Lord Reid in *Maunsell* v. *Olins* [1975] A.C. 373, 382.

Although interpretation is a function for the judiciary, they could not, like Parliament has done with the Interpretation Act, lay down binding rules of general application; for example, it is difficult to imagine judges attempting overtly to establish a principle that all statutes are 'to receive such fair, large, and liberal construction and interpretation as will best ensure the attainment of the object of the Act and of such provisions according to its true intent, meaning and spirit'.[50]

As we noted in connection with Community law, suggestions have been made that what are loosely called Continental or civil law techniques of interpretation should be generally adopted by English judges. This is a matter of some controversy.[51] First, there is no agreed description of what these techniques of interpretation specifically entail beyond a general acceptance that they involve appeals to the purposes for which the statute being interpreted was enacted to serve. Secondly, explicit adoption of a statute's purpose runs counter to the judiciary's traditional conception of its role as upholding the 'rule of law', which permits it to declare unlawful the interpretation placed upon a statutory provision by a member of the executive who *is* endeavouring to serve its purposes. Thirdly, the analogy with the European Court is not complete; for unlike the courts here, it has administrative and constitutional functions and owes its primary allegiance to the Treaties and to their realization. The European Court is partial in a way unknown to English judges. Moreover its judgment in a case, which is delivered after submissions have been made by the parties, the European Commission and the Advocate-General, is specifically focused upon the questions referred to it by the court of the member state, and which are framed and answered in terms of general propositions of Community law. Although the European Court does not engage in the kind of discursive reasoning typical in this country, English courts do not necessarily find its judgments determinative on the questions raised.[52] Finally, styles of interpretation bear some relationship to styles of drafting, and in so far as the characteristics of Continental or civil law interpretation are attributable to the characteristics of the enactments to be found

[50] Section 5(j) of the New Zealand Acts Interpretation Act 1924. See the commentary of the Law Commissions, op. cit., para. 33.

[51] See S. Herman, 'A Study of the English Reaction to Continental Interpretive Techniques', 1 *Legal Studies* (1981), 165 and Lord Wilberforce in *James Buchanan* v. *Babco Forwarding and Shipping* [1977] 3 W.L.R. 907, 912.

[52] E.g. *Jenkins* v. *Kingsgate (Clothing Productions) No. 2* (1981) Industrial Relations Law Reports 388.

in that tradition, they cannot readily be transferred without some modification.[53]

The pragmatism of English judges makes discussion of the proposition that they ought *in general* to adopt a purposive approach to interpretation a little unrealistic. As we have noted, the judiciary have given themselves considerable leeway as to what are to be regarded as legitimate techniques of interpretation. Thus formalism can be seen as playing a role in the interpretation of texts and in the relationship between the courts and Parliament which is analogous to that performed by the doctrine of precedent. But like appeals to precedent, formalism may also be a sign of laziness, lack of thought, evasion or small-mindedness. The adoption of a purposive approach on the other hand, encourages explicit consideration of the objects and scheme of the statute, and of the extent to which these will be given effect by the interpretations proposed in a given case.

The trends which have been identified in recent judicial practice suggest that a sharp distinction between literal and purposive interpretation may now be regarded as misleading. It encourages the view that the judiciary approach the task of interpretation by asking themselves first, are the words of the Act plain and unambiguous, and secondly, if they are not, how can they be interpreted so as to give effect to the intention and purpose of Parliament? Glanville Williams has argued that a better description of current practice is reflected[54] in the questions: What was the statute trying to do? Will the proposed interpretation effectuate that object? Is the proposed interpretation ruled out by the language of the statute? Thus literalist and purposive interpretations may be seen to represent varying emphases on how these questions are to be answered; in particular, on how far a judge is prepared to go in deciding whether a proposed interpretation is or is not sustained by the language of the statute. In short, context, language and purpose are all relevant, but there are still no settled priority rules for weighing these factors.

(c) Other extrinsic material

Apart from statutory and judicial material, support for alternative interpretations may be found in academic writings, annotations and

---

[53] Chapter 9 above, pp. 315–16; and see *Phonogram* v. *Lane* [1981] 3 All E.R. 182.

[54] 'The Meaning of Literal Interpretation' 131 *New Law Journal* (1981), 1128 and 1149. See also Vinelott J., op. cit., n. 38.

other commentaries on the Act. Other kinds of material which may be of value are those reports prepared by official bodies upon which the statute was based, the explanatory notes which accompany Bills through Parliament, and the vast range of circulars, pamphlets and leaflets which are prepared by or on behalf of government agencies. The quality and helpfulness of these materials vary considerably. In areas such as health and safety at work, social security, national insurance and public health, departmental directives concerning the implementation and interpretation of provisions will, as we have noted, frequently be treated as authoritative by many official interpreters. On the other hand, reports of Royal Commissions, the Law Commissions and similar bodies, may or may not be helpful, depending on such factors as the presence in the report of a draft Bill with accompanying explanations of its legal effects and the qualitative proximity of such a Bill to the statute which was enacted. Sometimes the interpreter may have little to go on which is of much help beyond the text of the statute; in others he may be in danger of being inundated. Sometimes 'aids' raise more doubts than they resolve.

Three questions need to be distinguished: (*a*) What kinds of explanatory material should be officially provided by the rule-maker and in what form? (*b*) What kinds of material should be officially excluded as aids to interpretation in formal legal argument? (*c*) What weight should be given to each kind of aid which is admissible? It is not proposed to attempt a comprehensive answer to these questions here.

The first question has for the most part not been extensively discussed in print. Although the Law Commissions did recommend the use of specially prepared explanatory and illustrative material in appropriate cases, this has not been acted upon by the government, nor does there appear to be much enthusiasm for the kind of *travaux préparatoires* which accompany the Communities' legislation. On the other hand, the question of the admissibility of certain types of material in formal legal argument has been the subject of considerable judicial and other attention. On the basis of a number of recent decisions of the House of Lords,[55] the following propositions concerning policy documents of different kinds may be formulated:

(i) the reports of Royal Commissions, the Law Commissions, the Criminal Law Revision Committee, the Law Reform Com-

---

[55] *Black-Clawson International* v. *Papierwerke Waldhof-Aschaffenburg* [1975] A.C. 591; *Fothergill* v. *Monarch Airlines* [1980] 3 W.L.R. 809; *James Buchanan & Co.* v. *Babco Forwarding and Shipping*, op. cit., and *Davis* v. *Johnson*, Chapter 1 above, pp. 106-7.

mittee, Parliamentary Select Committees and departmental enquiries and working parties may be cited and relied upon where
there is an ambiguity in a section, in order to clarify the purpose
of the enactment but not the meaning of individual words;
(ii) the reports of Parliamentary proceedings (Hansard) and other
explanatory notes prepared to accompany a Bill through its
legislative stages are not normally admissible;
(iii) international treaties and conventions which are incorporated
into domestic law (that is, enacted by statute), and the *travaux
préparatoires* which preceded them, may be referred to where the
words of a section are ambiguous, in order to ascertain their
meaning; although the weight to be attached to *travaux préparatoires*
may vary from case to case and should only be relied upon where
they are accessible and indicate a clear intention on the part of
the rule-makers.

There are a number of reasons why the courts permit only limited,
and in the case of Parliamentary proceedings, no formal access to these
materials. Hansard is excluded partly because it is generally agreed
that what is said in the passion or lethargy of Parliamentary debate is
unlikely to be a reliable guide to the legislators' intentions, and partly
because there is a Parliamentary rule of privilege which forbids counsel
from citing it in court without prior permission from the relevant
House: it is therefore thought inappropriate for judges to cite it.[56] In
the case of the other kinds of materials, while it is not suggested that
they are irrelevant or unhelpful as background to understanding an
Act, their relevance to the meaning of individual words will vary
considerably, depending on the closeness between an original set of
recommendations, whether accompanied by a draft Bill or not, and
the Act.[57] Where a statute enacts such a Bill verbatim, a further
objection to using it as evidence of the meaning of particular words,
and which indeed applies to all these extrinsic materials, is a constitutional one: it is Parliament that makes the law in the form of public
general Acts, not a commission appointed by one of the branches of

[56] Chapter 1 above, pp. 111–12. In *Hadmor Productions* Lord Denning in fact used the
comments of an Opposition spokesman on the Employment Bill 1980 (Lord Wedder-
burn) to reinforce what he understood to be the Government's intentions. In *R. v. Local
Commissioner for Administration* [1979] Q.B. 287, Lord Denning demonstrated another
way of quoting Hansard: reading verbatim reports of debates in textbooks.

[57] Sir George Baker, one of the members of the Court of Appeal in *Davis* v. *Johnson*,
gave evidence to the Commons' Select Committee in his former capacity as President
of the Family Division of the High Court.

the executive; it is the function of the courts to give authoritative interpretations of what Parliament has enacted, not any other agency. The final objection, and which was in part responsible for the defeat of the Interpretation of Legislation Bills, is that the costs of obtaining legal advice and of litigation would be increased.

One of the considerations which motivated the Law Commissions' recommendations was the achievement of a more rational mode of interpretation in which account would be taken of 'the interaction between the form of a communication and the rules by which it is to be interpreted'.[58] Another was clarification of the status of these extrinsic materials in formal legal argument. The latter has more or less been achieved as a result of cases like *Davis* v. *Johnson*, but the former consideration remains controversial. Both Interpretation of Legislation Bills would have given authoritative status to all the kinds of material mentioned above with the exception of Hansard, which was explicitly excluded, and would have introduced the statutory principle that 'a construction which would promote the general legislative purpose underlying the provision is to be preferred to a construction which would not'.[59] This principle draws its inspiration from similar provisions in New Zealand[60] and Canada, and would give statutory recognition to a particular kind of relationship between the courts and the legislature – one of co-operation. But, as we have seen, even for the judiciary this is not the only role which they assume, or which is always considered to be appropriate.[61] In addition there are difficulties with the notions of purpose and intent which would persist even if formal access to evidence of them were permitted. In the event, the most influential objection to the Law Commissions' Report was, as Lord Hailsham L.C. said, that it 'got across the departments and aroused the antagonism of the Parliamentary draftsmen'.[62]

The third issue is what weight should be attached to those materials which are admissible? The short answer is that it is neither possible nor desirable, in most cases, to be specific. The persuasiveness of an argument drawn, for example, from a Law Reform Committee Report, will depend on many factors: the terms and scope of its inquiry,

[58] Law Commissions, op. cit., para. 5.
[59] Interpretation of Legislation Bill 1981, clause 2(a) and see Chapter 5 above, pp. 200–5.
[60] Quoted above, p. 337, and fn. 50. Such a provision was introduced in Australia in 1981: see Appendix II, section 9, question 9.
[61] Chapter 4 above, pp. 182–3.
[62] 405 *House of Lords Debates*, col. 300 (13 February 1980).

the depth of its research, the nature of its recommendations, the existence of other views on the recommendations, the relationship between them and the Act, and so on. As we have observed, 'weight' is a metaphor, and we do not suggest that it is possible to assign a quantitative value to a particular source or to the arguments drawn from it. Occasionally the legislature may specify the degree of persuasiveness. For example, in the Carriage by Air Act 1961, which enacts the Warsaw Convention 1929 as amended by the Hague Protocol of 1955 into domestic law, it is provided that in the event of a conflict between the English and French texts of the Convention, the French shall prevail.[63] But this is rare; and even if it were possible for the courts to develop priority rules for distinguishing between arguments, they would probably not wish to do so.

From the point of view of the interpreter, the formal position about the admissibility of certain kinds of aid should not be given too much weight. For almost any purpose it is of paramount importance to understand what the statute is about: for instance, in the area of commercial transactions, he will benefit from some knowledge of commercial dealing in general, the characteristics, problems, customs and usages of the particular trade he is concerned with, the legislator's perception of the situation he was trying to deal with, the strategy and tactics of the particular body of statutory material, and so on. Such background knowledge is almost invariably of great importance in any difficult case. How the interpreter can best acquire it must depend on his experience, opportunities, time and general situation. The only sensible thing to do is to make intelligent use of all available aids to understanding the problem, even if some of them may not be overtly employed in legal reasoning and justification. There are no formal limits on aids to diagnosis and, as we have emphasized in earlier chapters, diagnosis is the first step in a rational approach to interpretation.

Epilogue: towards a theory of legislative interpretation?

In a brilliant article entitled 'How to Read the Civil Rights Act', Ronald Dworkin argues that in dealing with problems of interpreting statutes in hard cases, judges need a 'theory of legislation', that is, 'a theory of how to determine what legal rights and duties [the legislature] has

---

[63] This was the statute in issue in *Fothergill* v. *Monarch Airlines*, op. cit.

established when it enacts a particular set of sentences'.[64] Anglo-American writers who have advocated literal or liberal approaches to interpretation could be said to be advancing prescriptive theories of legislative interpretation. Sir Rupert Cross, in his attempt to combine the literal and liberal approaches in a single principle, was not merely expounding rules of interpretation; he also claimed that this is the correct way for judges and others to approach the task.[65] Similarly, though sometimes on a grander scale, civilian writers tend to conceive the primary function of the legal scientist in this area as being the development of prescriptive theories of interpretation. The same might also be said of some writers on international law[66] and on European Community law.[67]

Recently, increasing attention has also been paid to legislation from a sociological perspective and there have been calls for the development of sociological theories of legislation, dealing with how legislative rules are made, with their implementation, impact and other aspects of how they operate in practice, and with interpretation of legislation seen as a form of behaviour.[68] There has been a substantial number of detailed studies on the creation and emergence of norms in general and of particular statutes; there is a developed, though controversial, body of 'impact studies', but there have been relatively few detailed sociological studies of interpretation. It is probably also true to say that general sociological theories of legislation are still in their infancy.[69]

The purpose of this book has been to provide a broader approach than traditional works on 'legal method' to the art of interpreting rules, first, by viewing the handling of rules as a basic human art and, secondly, by emphasizing the importance of understanding the nature and context of interpretation as a foundation for developing the rele-

[64] R. Dworkin, 'How to Read the Civil Rights Act', *New York Review of Books*, 20 December 1979, p. 37.

[65] Op. cit., pp. 1-2, 42-3.

[66] For example, M. McDougal, H. Lasswell and J. Miller, *The Interpretation of Agreements and World Public Order* (1967).

[67] See the reference to Kutscher and Bredimas, op. cit. Continental writers such as Jhering and Gény have argued elaborate, though conflicting, prescriptive theories for the interpretation of codes of law. See Lenhoff, 'On Interpretative Theories: A Comparative Study in Legislation', 27 *Texas Law Review* (1949), 312 and Herman, op. cit.

[68] See R. Tomasic, 'The Sociology of Legislation' in *Legislation and Society in Australia* (1980, ed. R. Tomasic), p. 19 and the same author's unpublished paper presented to a Conference on Theories of Legislation (the Institute for the Sociology of Law in Europe), Oxford, September 1981.

[69] See Suggestions for Further Reading below, p. 378.

vant general skills. We have examined the nature of rules in general, rules as responses to problems, how and why problems of interpretation arise, what is involved in reasoning about competing interpretations in legal and other contexts, and the special factors that have to be taken into account in interpreting cases and statutes in common law jurisdictions, especially England and Wales. Three general themes have been given special emphasis: that the main conditions that give rise to problems of interpretation in legal contexts also arise in many non-legal contexts; that what constitutes an appropriate interpretation is relative to the standpoint, situation, role and objectives of the particular interpreter; and that in order to understand and interpret any rule it needs to be looked at in the context of the situation and problems which led to its creation and of the processes in which it operates in practice. This emphasis on the situation of interpreters and the background of rules to be interpreted, together with a greater emphasis on problems than on rules, justifies calling our general approach 'contextual'. This leaves open the questions whether we have advanced a theory of interpretation, if so what kind, and if not, why not? It may be appropriate to finish by addressing these questions.

It should be clear that no attempt has been made here to present an empirical theory of legislation of the kind advocated by Tomasic and others. The focus has been on the art of interpretation rather than on describing and explaining the behaviour of rule-makers and interpreters. Nevertheless, we have drawn, directly and indirectly, on the work of Alfred Schutz, R.G. Collingwood and Karl Llewellyn, as well as on recent sociological and other writings on law. Some of the ingredients of the context of interpretation as we have depicted it will be familiar to sociologists of law: the pervasiveness and variety of rules; the relativity of social problems and their definitions; the significance of process, standpoint, role and purpose in interpretation; the uses and limitations of naïve instrumentalism and of simple rationalistic models; the notions that rules come into existence in a variety of ways; that they are often instruments of power, but yet they can be the products of negotiation, compromise or incremental growth rather than conscious rational creation; that their significance may be expressive, symbolic, instrumental or aspirational, or a combination of these; that rules are not self-enforcing, and do not necessarily or even often have direct impact on behaviour or attitudes in a simple relation of cause and effect; that the creation and interpretation of rules may take place in a context where conflict or consensus or something in between predominates; that individuals and groups are often subject to multiple systems of rules, but that to talk of 'systems' often involves fiction or hyperbole; that it is difficult to avoid talking of rules as if they were things, yet such 'reifying' talk often serves to obscure an underlying indeterminacy and complexity in the real world. Some of these ideas are familiar and are elaborated with great sophistication in the sociological literature; others await further development. Thus this book has not attempted to develop a sociological theory of legislation, but it has drawn on relevant sociological literature and we hope that, in turn, it may provide one possible jumping-off point for further exploration of that literature.

What of a prescriptive theory of interpretation? If by this is meant a recommended set of rules or procedures which it is claimed will yield right or correct answers in particular cases, then it is clear that no such theory is advanced here. We do not believe that there is one right answer in hard cases or that problems of interpretation can be solved primarily by rules. However, some general advice has been offered to interpreters: clarify your standpoint and objectives; consider the nature and characteristics of the material to be interpreted; diagnose the conditions that have given rise to the puzzlement or problem; identify the range of plausible or possible interpretations in this context, and consider what arguments might be advanced for and against each alternative; differentiate problems of interpretation from problems of locating or identifying potentially applicable rules and, in particular, do not conflate puzzlements about rules and about roles.

We have also suggested a general intellectual procedure for approaching statutes, subordinate legislation, and similar instruments. This can be succinctly restated as follows: after clarifying your standpoint and objectives and assembling a 'package' of relevant material, find your way round the instrument as a whole (if necessary with the aid of an algorithm); then anchor the problem of interpretation precisely in a specific word or words in the text; consider the word(s) in the context of the clause, the section and the instrument as a whole, including the general design that can be extracted from within its four corners; articulate the competing meanings of the words to be interpreted and consider these in the context of the instrument itself, of evidence of its general background and its purposes, and of analogous or otherwise relevant rules. Eliminate possible interpretations that would produce absurd results at a general level (e.g. that 'shall marry' means 'shall validly marry')[70] and, perhaps, in this particular case. Then diagnose carefully the condition(s) giving rise to the present doubt, and from these proceed to construct arguments for and against each of the competing interpretations. Following such advice should often narrow the range of possibilities, sometimes to a point where there is only one serious alternative. It points in a general direction, but it does not amount to a fully developed theory either of interpretation in general or of judicial interpretation in particular.

Why have we not gone further? This question needs to be answered at a number of different, though related, levels. One reason is simply a matter of the objectives of this book: it is intended as an introduction to its subject; to echo I.A. Richards, the main aim has been to help to understand some of the difficulties in the way of interpreting rules rather than to provide a recipe, if such were possible. This in part represents a reaction against over-generalized recipes – facile prescriptions based on too little diagnosis; but it also stems from a concern to bring out the pervasiveness of problems of interpretation in the everyday world of affairs in contrast with the tendency to emphasize the unique features of legal interpretation. Our concern has been to emphasize the generality of problems and the particularity of appropriate solutions.

Nearly all of the theories mentioned in the opening paragraph of this Epilogue are narrowly focused theories of *legal* interpretation, whereas our concern has been broader in that we have tried to explore at least some connections between interpreting rules in legal and non-legal contexts, without claiming to deal with all types of interpretation. The contrast is even greater because most standard legal theories are either explicitly or implicitly theories of *judicial* interpretation, whereas we have been concerned to emphasize the problems of a wide range of different participants in legal and other processes. Thus, although this is intended as an introduction, it is rather more broadly focused than most jurisprudential treatments of the subject. But, it might be objected, surely judicial interpretation is the central case of legal interpretation and, as such, ought to be the primary concern of lawyers and law students? It is undoubtedly true that judicial interpretation has special claims to our attention, not only because of the authority and finality of judicial decisions, but also because how judges have interpreted or will interpret particular legal rules has a direct bearing on the concerns of other actors, including the good citizen,

[70] See above, p. 237.

the bad man, the expositor, the cautious solicitor, the advocate, the administrator, and the agent of enforcement – whether official or otherwise. Actual and potential judicial interpretations cast a long shadow even on those legal questions which rarely, if ever, come before the courts. Nevertheless the centrality of judges has been greatly exaggerated in the past, with the result that other factors have been overlooked or neglected. Judicial rulings and reasonings are only part of a variety of relevant factors, the relative importance of which depends on the particular context of interpretation.

There is another reason for not concentrating exclusively on judicial interpretation. Questions of role and objectives are intimately related to the activity of interpreting, but it is important for clarity of thought to differentiate between puzzlements about the former (Who am I? What am I trying to do?) and genuine puzzlements about interpretation, attributable to one or more conditions of doubt, such as ambiguity of wording, indeterminacy of purpose, or changes in circumstances since the creation of the rule. It happens that 'the proper role of the judge' is one of the most intractable issues of jurisprudence; accordingly for purposes of exposition some difficulties of interpretation are more easily understood if one adopts a less problematic standpoint, such as that of the advocate or the bad man. This point was stressed in relation to the *ratio decidendi* because much of the traditional debate, in our view, has its roots in puzzlements about the proper role of judges rather than in what is involved in reading cases intelligently. The same considerations apply to other aspects of legal interpretation, because interpretation is typically part of some broader activity.

It follows from the above that a rounded prescriptive theory of judicial interpretation involves a theory of adjudication or, at the very least, a clear conception of judicial roles. Here we agree with Dworkin, as we do on the point that in difficult cases the resolution of doubts in interpretation (and particular justifications for such resolutions) often, if not always, presupposes some theory of political morality. We would go further and suggest that a theory of legislative interpretation also requires an adequate way of classifying types of statutes (and other documents), at least to the extent that the very different kinds of attitudes, techniques and other interpretive baggage that, for instance, are associated with written constitutions, commercial codes, taxing statutes and international conventions – what we have referred to as the specialist subcultures – are adequately differentiated. We have not attempted to develop a theory of adjudication, a theory of political morality or a taxonomy of legislation in this book; accordingly a rounded theory of judicial interpretation is beyond its scope.

Is a prescriptive theory of judicial interpretation or of interpretation in general, either feasible or desirable? The following quotation from I. A. Richards might be taken as suggesting scepticism about feasibility: 'Neither this book *nor any other* ... can give a recipe for discovering what the page *really* says.' Is this scepticism of one right answer or of more than that? Here analogies with literature are illuminating, at least up to a point.[71] Debates as to whether there is a correct or best way of interpreting a novel or a poem (or the Bible or a musical score) may throw some light on the question, Is there a correct way of interpreting legal rules? At the very least they suggest that this is a perennially controversial area: there are rigorists and liberals in theology and literature as well as law; recent conflicts between structuralists, historicists and others may serve to remind us that pluralism in literature is a widely subscribed option, but one that has not gone unchallenged. There is, too, a view with a respectable ancestry that accepts no single theory of literary interpretation as paramount, yet implies that this does not necessarily involve commitment to the extreme relativist position that there are no standards of criticism. Our view of legal interpretation is rather like that. It might be termed moderate relativism: we are sceptical of the claim that there is one right answer to every problem of interpretation, but that does not imply that there are never clear cases or better answers; we are sceptical of the notion that legal interpretation can best be studied through the doctrine of precedent and the rules of interpretation, rather than through analysis of problems set in the context of relevant processes, roles, standpoints and techniques, and of the nature of the materials and texts to be interpreted. Finally, we are sceptical of the idea that it is either feasible or desirable to develop a prescriptive theory of interpretation that will be *determinative* of all or even a significant number of seriously contested questions; but that is not to say that nothing can be done to elucidate the nature of some of the more common problems nor to give some general guidance as to how to set about tackling them. In that limited sense this book has tried to lay a foundation for such a theory.

---

[71] See K. S. Abraham, 'Statutory Interpretation and Literary Theory: Some Common Concerns of an Unlikely Pair' [1979] *Rutgers Law Review*, 676.

Appendix I Algorithms and the Structure of Complex Rules

Many rules, especially legal rules, are very complicated, involving exceptions, qualifications, provisos and so on. In these cases, the reader may be in doubt as to the relationship between the various parts of the rule, and it may help to rewrite the rule in diagrammatic form. The first part of section 20 (1) of the Powers of Criminal Courts Act 1973 reads:

> No court shall pass a sentence of imprisonment on a person of or over twenty-one years of age on whom such a sentence has not previously been passed by a court in any part of the United Kingdom unless the court is of opinion that no other method of dealing with him is appropriate...

At first sight, this may seem a little confusing because of its negatives; the structure of the rule obscures an immediate understanding of what the rule is designed to cover. We can rewrite the section in a schematic form, thus:

No court shall pass a
sentence of
imprisonment on a
person ...

... of or over twenty-
one years of age on
whom such a sentence
has not previously been
passed by a court in
any part of the United
Kingdom ...

... unless the court
is of opinion that no
other method of
dealing with him is
appropriate....

The advantages of this type of presentation over conventional prose style are that it is clearer to the reader, it should be more easily understood, and it provides a simple checklist of the conditions under which the provision operates. To assist our understanding of the structure of complex rules we can employ another type of diagrammatic presentation of rules, the algorithm. An algorithm is a precise set of instructions for solving a well-defined problem.[1] It takes the form of a structured series of questions with answers providing instructions for total or partial (when more questions need to be answered) resolution of the problem. Here is the rule in the example above stated in algorithmic form:

Algorithm designed to instruct a court of its powers of imprisonment of a person over the age of twenty-one who has not previously served a prison sentence

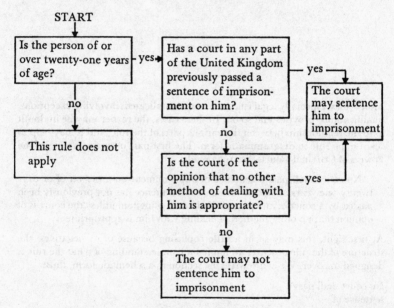

An algorithm comprises a sequence of questions to which the answer is either 'yes' or 'no', each answer automatically taking the reader to the next question relevant to his case. Either of these answers may take the reader outside the ambit of the rule, or provide a solution to his specific case, in which event there is no need to proceed further. Indeed, in such a case, if the algorithm has been constructed properly it should be impossible to proceed further. This last statement indicates a fundamental attribute of the algorithm: it eliminates choice for the reader of a rule. Provided he can answer the questions, the reader of a rule in algorithmic form should always reach the

[1] This is adopted from B. Lewis and P. Woolfenden, *Algorithms and Logical Trees* (1969).

conclusion appropriate in his case. It follows from this also that the reader may not need to read the whole rule, which might otherwise be a source of confusion for him, for the process of questions and answers should mean that he reads only those parts that are applicable to his case. These attributes of the algorithm follow from the fact that in the algorithm the rule is broken down into a series of questions to which the reader *can* only answer 'yes' or 'no'. This allows us to state one basic rule for algorithm construction:

(i) *To each question there can only be one 'yes' and one 'no'.* Each 'yes' or 'no' takes the reader automatically to the next relevant question, but this also means that only one question can follow on each answer. In other words, following each answer, the reader has no choice as to the next question. This leads to a second basic rule:

(ii) *There can be only be one question following each answer.* The rule above is subject to variation where an answer leads to a conclusion (usually called an 'outcome'). In that event, of course, that part of the algorithm is complete, and no more questions need or can be asked.

The function of an algorithm is to present rules in a visually more comprehensible form than conventional prose. An algorithm will not resolve all doubts that may arise as to the interpretation of a rule. In the example used above, if the reader does not know what is meant by 'a sentence of imprisonment', converting the rule into algorithmic form will not help him to resolve his doubt, though in some cases the conversion may help him to identify more closely the locus of his doubt. An algorithm only affects the arrangement of the parts of a rule, and because it cannot resolve doubts arising as to the interpretation of words employed in the rule, or as to the rule's policy, it is defined as a precise set of instructions for resolving a *well-defined* problem.

Algorithms can be used both by those who wish to discover the effect of a rule in a particular case and by those teaching and learning about the interpretation of rules. House purchase, claims for redundancy payment or unemployment benefit, income tax etc. bring the layman into contact with complex rules of law, and here the clarity of the algorithm can help him to establish quickly whether the provisions of a particular rule apply to his case, while its structure may eliminate possible error by saving him the trouble of having to understand the whole provision when only a part of it is applicable.[2] Algorithms may also help lawyers to familiarize themselves with the effect of recently published legislative rules; although by virtue of their professional expertise in rule-handling, as a class, they perhaps have less need of assistance.

Algorithms can be a useful educational technique for imparting and acquiring an understanding of the interrelationship of the parts of a rule; and they are adaptable, so that it is possible to move from simple to more difficult

[2] See, for example, the Consumer Association's Journal, *Which?*; in particular *Money Which?*, September 1972, p. 156, on controlled and regulated tenancies; June 1973, p. 105, on how to appeal against a rates assessment; and September 1973, p. 59, on how married women may find their national insurance class; and the example in Chapter 1, p. 32. For further examples see 'Sentencing and the Advocate', 142 *Justice of the Peace* (1978), 367; 'Determination of Mode of Trial and Penalties under the Criminal Law Act 1977', 128 *New Law Journal* (1978), 637; 'Tax Treatment of Severance Payments', 127 *New Law Journal* (1977), 1153.

Algorithm designed to show the main requisites for liability in defamation

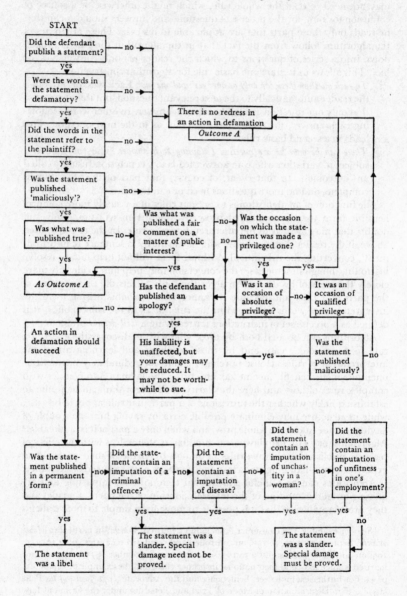

exercises.[3] They can also be used to organize into manageable form large quantities of data or other material,[4] for example evidence to be presented at a lengthy trial or rules of particular areas of law such as property law, tax law, civil and criminal procedure and to show the individual elements of rules not in fixed verbal form, such as, in the example on p. 352, the requisites of defamation. This algorithm is a *simplified* statement of the requisites of defamation; for detail the reader is referred to a standard textbook.

We do not wish to exaggerate the claims made for algorithms in the context of rule-handling.[5] Their more obvious limitations are that they become cumbersome when applied to lengthy rules, that they can take a long time to construct, and that their utility wanes as one becomes familiar with particular rules. Algorithms are a tool for promoting skill in the handling of complex rules and, as such, may be dispensed with at times. In addition, the legal examples given in this appendix to illustrate what use may be made of algorithms and how they are constructed have primarily been isolated sections from statutes. It goes without saying that this is an artificial way of reading statutory rules, which are normally part of a much wider range of provisions, and which need to be read in the light of them. Thus, the algorithms are to varying degrees incomplete, in that they do not explicitly take account of other relevant rules, and an interpreter who is seeking to present a comprehensive statement of a rule would have to account for them, either by including their text in his algorithm, or by referring to them in some other way.

The process of reasoning in algorithms is not unlike a commonsense approach to problem-solving, in that one seeks to eliminate possibilities by adopting some coherent plan; but perhaps the most important aspect of the acquisition of proficiency in reducing a rule from prose to algorithmic form is the intellectual discipline that is involved. Before you can present a rule in this way you must be in a position to understand the interrelationship of the different parts of the rule, and we conclude this brief discussion with an algorithm (on page 354) designed to assist algorithm-writers to evaluate their algorithms, and some exercises in constructing an algorithm. Further information on algorithms may be obtained from *The Algorithm Writer's Guide* (Longmans, 1972) by D. M. Wheatley and A. W. Unwin; *Psychology of Reasoning* (Batsford, 1972) by P. Wason and P. Johnson-Laird; and *Algorithms* by I. Horabin and B. Lewis (ed. D. Langdon, Educational Technology Publications, New Jersey, 1978).

[3] See for example, the Association of Law Teachers, *Bulletin* no. 20, October/November 1973, pp. 5-13; and *Legal Studies in Curriculum Social Work Education* (C.C.E.T.S.W.), paper no. 4, p. 44 and appendix D (July 1974).

[4] Compare J. H. Wigmore's technique for analysing masses of evidence: *Science of Judicial Proof* (1937).

[5] The limitations and the uses of algorithms are well exemplified in *Algorithms for the Social Services Nos. 1, 2 and 3* (which deals with provisions from the Children and Young Persons Act 1969 and the Mental Health Act 1959), published by the Local Government Training Board.

Algorithm designed to help algorithm-writers evaluate their algorithms

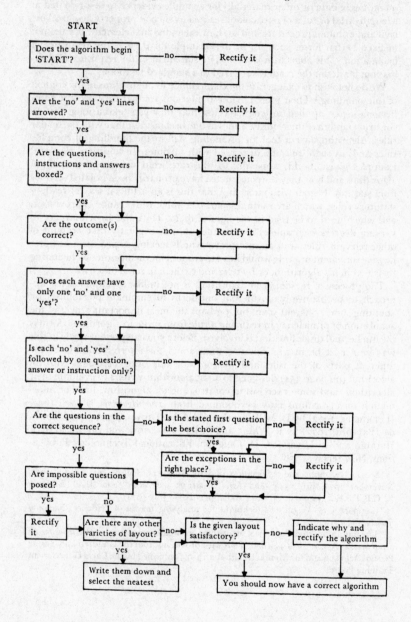

EXERCISES

1. The requirements in law for committing a person in custody to the Crown Court with a view to imposing a sentence of borstal training are stated as follows:[6]

> Where a person is convicted by a magistrates' court of an offence punishable on summary conviction with imprisonment, then, if on the day of the conviction he is not less than fifteen but under twenty-one years old and is a person who, under subsections (2) and (4) of section one of the Criminal Justice Act 1961, may be committed for a sentence of borstal training, the court may commit him in custody or on bail to the Crown Court for sentence in accordance with the provisions of section twenty of the Criminal Justice Act 1948.
>
> A person committed in custody under subsection (1) of this section shall be committed;
> (a) if the court has been notified by the Secretary of State that a remand centre is available for reception, from that court, of persons of the class or description of the person committed, to a remand centre;
> (b) if the court has not been so notified, to a prison.

Construct an algorithm to inform a magistrates' court of its powers to commit a person in custody to the Crown Court for borstal training.

2. Construct an algorithm designed to show the circumstances in which a county court judge may grant an injunction under section 1 of the Domestic Violence and Matrimonial Proceedings Act 1976 (above, p. 83).

3. Construct an algorithm designed to show when benefits are payable by the General Executive Council of the T. & G.W.U. in the event of a union member being killed as a result of an accident at work (Chapter 1, section 6(a)).

[6] Magistrates' Court Act 1952, section 28 (as substituted by the Criminal Justice Act 1961, s. 1(5) and Sched. IV, V and VI and amended by the Criminal Justice Act 1967, Sched. 6, and the Courts Act 1971, s. 56 and Sched. 9).

Appendix II Exercises

Note

These exercises are designed to bring out and develop points dealt with in the text and to give practice in using some basic skills in rule-handling. Some require only a few minutes to complete, others will take much longer; a few involve use of a law library. We have devised a substantial number of questions in order to give teachers, students and other readers an element of choice.

1 Exercises on Bigamy (Chapter 1)

Read the following cases and answer the questions: *Tolson* (1899) 23 Q.B.D. 168; *Gould* [1968] 2 Q.B. 65; *Newsome* [1970] 2 Q.B. 711; *Sarwan Singh* [1962] 3 All E.R. 301; and *Sagoo* [1975] 2 All E.R. 926.

QUESTIONS

1. D, a married man, goes through a form and ceremony of marriage with his girlfriend P, who believes him to be single. Unknown to D, his wife (W) is killed in a car accident as he and P are exchanging their marriage vows. Does D commit bigamy?

Would your answer be different if:

  (a) unknown to D, when he and W married 10 years ago, W lied about her age, and was in fact $15\frac{1}{2}$ years old; or

  (b) unknown to P, D is in fact a woman who has a very masculine appearance, is undergoing hormone treatment to develop her masculinity and proposes to undergo a sex-change operation; or

  (c) the marriage between D and W was potentially polygamous, as they had been married in a country where polygamy is lawful and D had a wife by a former marriage; or

(d) unknown to P, the whole ceremony through which she was going was a hoax arranged between D and a friend of his who is a defrocked priest; or

(e) D had not seen W for seven years, mainly because for the last six years he has been prospecting in the Australian outback.

2. The cases *Taylor, Gould* and *Newsome* discuss the application of the doctrine of precedent in the Criminal Division of the Court of Appeal. Formulate a series of propositions summarizing what the cases say about this matter.

3. On what grounds did the court in *Sagoo* overrule *Sarwan Singh*?

4. In the light of the cases you have read, redraft section 57 of the Offences Against the Person Act 1861 to reflect the present law.

5. What is the function of bigamy, and how is it used?

6. What social information would you find (a) necessary, (b) useful to you as chairman of a committee which has been asked to look at, and consider possible changes in, the law of bigamy?

2 Exercises on Chapter 2

1. Reread the materials on standpoint and role in Chapter 1, section 11. Construct a replacement for the Johnny exercise set in some context other than that of the home and designed to illustrate the main factors to be considered when diagnosing a problem of interpretation from the standpoint of the final adjudicator. Provide a commentary in note form, explaining all the points raised by the exercise. What difference(s) are attributable to the change of context?

2. Take a recent copy of a non-tabloid newspaper such as *The Times, Guardian, Daily Telegraph, Financial Times, Observer* or *Sunday Times*, and read *all of it* with the following questions in mind:

(a) How many passages deal directly with legal matters?

(b) How many passages would be more easily understood by a person with a basic grounding in law?

(c) What branches of law would one expect regularly to feature or to be directly relevant to each main section (e.g. the sports pages, the arts section, the business section, the advertisements)?

(d) Which features more prominently in your copy of the newspaper: legislation; case law; 'non-legal' rules?

(e) Identify examples of: rule density; conflicting systems of rules; legalism; deviations between what the relevant rules prescribe and actual results in particular cases.

(f) Identify examples of Summers' five basic techniques of law.

(g) Identify examples of 'problems' either created by law or to which law is expected to provide a complete solution.

3. The government is concerned about the increasing number of injuries (and fatalities) caused by 'glue-sniffing' among young people. Suppose you were the Minister whose department has been charged with the responsibility for preparing a report on the subject, together with proposals for some kind of

legislative control. What kind of information would you require to prepare your report and how would you set about discovering it? What groups and individuals are likely to be instrumental in the formulation of policy objectives? What considerations would you take into account when determining whether to introduce legislation or not? Assuming you did decide to use legislation, what possible strategies are available to you to control the incidence of 'glue-sniffing' and what legal techniques would be most appropriate for implementing them? What general conclusions would you draw concerning the proper steps to be taken in inquiries of this sort?

3 Exercises on Chapter 3

1. Identify and write down ten examples each of rules in fixed verbal form and rules not in fixed verbal form. In what ways does the absence of a fixed verbal form affect the formulation of a rule?

2. Give one or more examples of: (*a*) an entirely purposeless rule; (*b*) a rule the main purpose of which was to uphold a moral principle regardless of the consequences; (*c*) a rule with several partly competing or conflicting purposes; (*d*) a rule which outlived its original purposes, but which none the less continued to serve a useful function.

3. Analyse the following rules in terms of their protasis and apodosis:
   (*a*) Rules 3, 5 and 9 of the school rules in Chapter 1, section 4(b)(i);
   (*b*) Section 57 of the Offences Against the Person Act 1861 (Chapter 1, section 7(a));
   (*c*) Section 6(1) of the Land Compensation Act 1961 (Chapter 1, section 6(c)).

4. Distinguish between a prescriptive and a descriptive proposition. Which of the following propositions are descriptive and which prescriptive?
   (*a*) No. 4 of the school rules in Chapter 1, section 4(b)(i);
   (*b*) 'I think the judge will decide in our favour.'
   (*c*) 'If you move your pawn there, you will be checkmated.'
   (*d*) A textbook statement of the law of bigamy.

5. Distinguish between an exception to and an exemption from a rule. Are the following examples of exceptions or exemptions?
   (*a*) Rule 7 of the school rules in Chapter 1, section 4(b)(i);
   (*b*) The general amnesty declared a few years ago on illegally held firearms, so that their owners would give them up to the police without fear of prosecution.

6. List as many synonyms or near-synonyms for the word 'rule' as you can; for example, principles, conventions.

7. List as many *species* of the *genus* 'rule' as you can; for example, moral rules. Sporting rules would be *species*, but rules of football would count as a *sub-species* for this purpose.

8. Aeroplane-hijacking has been a major problem in recent years.
   (*a*) Assume that only one of the law's five basic techniques (Chapter 3,

p. 157 is to be used to deal with this problem. Which of the five do you think would be most likely to be most effective and why?

(*b*) Assume that any of the other five may also be used, in addition to the one chosen under (*a*) above. Which ones would you use, and explain how and why.

Your answers to (*a*) and (*b*) should reflect considerable thought about the main features of the law's five basic techniques and about how these features determine the utility and limits of each technique.

9. Study the existing law dealing with the consumption of alcohol. Explain how each of the five basic techniques in Summers' theory comes into play in the operation of the present overall programme.

10. Distinguish between the function(s), and the use(s), of a rule.

11. What is the function of the rules of inheritance in Arusha society, and how are they used? (see Chapter 1, section 5).

12. Assemble and diagnose five examples of legalisms, using the diagnosis of the *Case of the Legalistic Child* as a model. How do your examples help to elucidate the concepts of 'legalism' and 'formalism'? What difference, if any, is there between a 'lawyerlike' and a 'legalistic' argument?

4 Exercises on Chapter 4

1. Distinguish between a question of fact, a question of law, and a question of mixed law and fact. Are the following questions to do with *Reg.* v. *Allen* questions of fact or questions of law:

(*a*) Whether Allen went through a second ceremony of marriage;

(*b*) Whether Allen, in his second 'marriage', 'married' a person who was within the prohibited degree of consanguinity;

(*c*) Whether Allen, being married, married?

2. List 100 transitive verbs which can be used with the word 'rule', and divide them into sub-categories.

3. What is the relationship of the following activities to that of interpretation:

(*a*) Deciphering the Rosetta Stone.

(*b*) Reading a play by Shakespeare.

(*c*) Complaining about shoddy service in a restaurant.

(*d*) Disciplining a student for an alleged breach of university regulations.

(*e*) Marking examination scripts.

(*f*) Making a will.

(*g*) Mending a broken T.V. set.

4. What is meant by the application, and the interpretation, of a rule? What are the differences between them?

5. Does application of a rule necessarily presuppose that some interpretation has been put on it?

6. Identify some of those who might be required, or wish, to interpret the following rules:

(*a*) The school rules in Chapter 1, section 4(b)(i).

(*b*) The rule in *Buckoke* v. *G.L.C.* (Chapter 1, section 8).

(*c*) The rule in *Donoghue* v. *Stevenson* (Chapter 1, section 9).

(*d*) Section 57 of the Offences Against the Person Act 1861 (Chapter 1, section 7).

Would all those you have identified necessarily be likely to interpret the rule in a spirit of co-operation with the rule-maker? If not, how might that affect their interpretation of it?

5 Exercises on Chapter 5

1. Study in outline the law relating to obscenity in this country.

(*a*) Identify as many reasons as you can think of for having rules about obscenity.

(*b*) Identify as many problems as you can discover that have arisen in respect of the administration of these laws, and diagnose why these problems have arisen.

(*c*) One of the conditions of doubt about the law relating to indecent displays is that what constitutes an indecent display depends upon each individual's response, which is neither easily measurable nor consistent. Would it be an improvement to identify in the relevant legislation, for example, (i) various parts of the body that it shall be deemed indecent to display, or (ii) those circumstances under which it would be indecent to display any particular part of the body? Can you think of any other devices for deciding what is 'indecent' or 'obscene'?

(*d*) Suppose that a country with a much stricter attitude to the public display of the body than is the case in Britain, were to legislate, *inter alia*, that it would be indecent 'to leave the leg uncovered in public at any point above a line drawn two inches from above the kneecap'. What difficulties might arise in the administration of this rule? In particular, how would you advise the country's rule-makers to deal with the following cases:

   (i) Doctors' examinations of patients at road accidents and the like.

   (ii) Marathon-runners.

   (iii) People sunbathing in swimming trunks in their back gardens which are overlooked by an office block?

2. Fill in the 'game' chart on page 361 very approximately, making provisos in footnotes if you wish. Answer in terms of standard cases. The five categories of answer to be used on the chart are:

√	nearly always, or always
a	to a greater extent
b	to a lesser extent
X	never, or only exceptionally
$\frac{1}{2}$	about half and half

A. Duplicate bridge	E. Professional football
B. Patience	F. Boxing
C. Mountaineering	G. Advocacy
D. Roulette	H. Bargaining or negotiating

I. War   J. 'Scorer's discretion' (see Hart, *The Concept of Law*, pp. 138-42)

	A	B	C	D	E	F	G	H	I	J
Equipment e.g. ball	✓									
Teams or Sides	✓									
Governed by established rules	✓									
Scoring (points, goals, etc.)	✓									
Physical exertion	×									
A large element of chance	b									
A large element of skill or strength	a									
Purpose: enjoyment by participants	✓									
Purpose: enjoyment by spectators	b									
Referee, umpire or judge	✓									
Special clothing	×									
Do you usually think of it as a game?	yes									

(a) Can you find any criteria of 'game' which are (a) necessary, (b) sufficient, (c) jointly sufficient?

(b) Construct a similar chart for 'rule', selecting your own suggested criteria and examples.

6 Exercises on Chapter 6

1. Using the diagnostic model set out on pp. 220-6, identify the conditions of doubt which arose in the following problems contained in Chapter 1.
    (a) Section 2(b).
    (b) Section 3, question 3.
    (c) Section 4(b)(ii), question 2.
    (d) Section 4(c)(i), questions 1-4.
    (e) Section 8, question 1.
    (f) Section 10, question 4.

2. Read Professor L. Fuller's allegory, 'The Case of the Speluncean Explorers', 62 *Harvard Law Review* (1948-9), 616 and diagnose the conditions of doubt which arose according to each of the judges in the Supreme Court of Newgarth.

3. The best way to use and to test the value of the diagnostic model is to take any random series of cases involving one or more disputed points of legislative interpretation and to diagnose the conditions of doubt involved in each case. We recommend the following cases as illustrating a broad variety of the conditions of doubt listed in Chapter 6: *Hereford and Worcester C.C.* v. *Newman* [1975] 2 All E.R. 613; *Fisher* v. *Bell* [1961] 1 Q.B. 394; *Dockers' Labour Club* v. *Race Relations Board* [1976] A.C. 285; *Sakhuja* v. *Allen* [1973] A.C. 172; *Re X* [1975] 1 All E.R. 697; *R.* v. *Arrowsmith* [1975] 1 All E.R. 472; *Farrell* v. *Alexander* [1977] A.C. 59; *Knuller* v. *D.P.P.* [1973] A.C. 435; *Miliangos* v. *George Frank* [1976] A.C. 443; *R.* v. *Collins* [1973] 1 Q.B. 100.

4. Take any five of the following cases from [1977] 1 All E.R. and diagnose the conditions of doubt in each case: *Ravenseft Properties* v. *D-G. of Fair Trading*; *Maynard* v. *Osmond*; *Re D.*; *Cummings* v. *Granger*; *Re F.*; *Paul* v. *Constance*; *Fougère* v. *Phoenix Motor Co.*; *Starr* v. *N.C.B.*; and *Spackman* v. *S. of State for the Environment*.

5. A club for bearded men was set up in 1960 in a small town at a time when sporting a beard was interpreted symbolically as a reflection of certain social values. For some years there were no precise criteria of membership. Now two things have occurred: first, beards have lost much of their symbolic force in the town and many more people have beards; second, membership of the club carries with it certain privileges with regard to the purchase of cheap tickets on charter flights abroad. There has been a sudden rise in applications for membership and there is a feeling that criteria for membership should be made much more precise. You have been asked to draft rules embodying such criteria.
    (a) What are the difficulties in devising fair and workable criteria?
    (b) What other facts are relevant to you as draftsman?
    (c) Draft the rules and give reasons for your choices.

6. (a) When is a tea-break 'too long'? (see *R.* v. *Industrial Injuries Commissioner, ex parte A.E.U.* (No. 2) [1966] 2 Q.B. 31).
    (b) How many prostitutes constitute a brothel? (see *Donovan* v. *Gavin* [1965] 3 W.L.R. 352).

7 Exercises on Chapter 7

1. Which do you think were (*a*) the strongest, and (*b*) the weakest, arguments advanced by each side in *Allen?*

2. Using the approach adopted at pp. 237–41 analyse the main arguments which might have been advanced for each side in (*a*) *Buckoke* v. *G.L.C.*; (*b*) *R.* v. *Taylor*; (*c*) *R.* v. *Gould.*

3. Give an example of a conclusion which is valid, but not true, and of a conclusion which is true, but not valid.

4. Distinguish (*a*) 'open' and 'closed' systems of thinking; (*b*) predictability from logical necessity; (*c*) descriptive and normative statements.

5. Distinguish, giving legal examples, deduction, induction and reasoning by analogy.

6. 'In fact the fallacy of "Argument by Analogy" is that it is never possible to argue by analogy' (Emmet). Does this mean that one of the most important forms of legal reasoning is fallacious?

7. 'The reasoning may take this form: A falls more appropriately in B than in C. It does so because A is more like D which is of B than it is like E which is of C. Since A is in B and B is in G (legal concept), then A is in G. But perhaps C is in G also. If so, then B is in a decisively different segment of G, because B is like H which is in G and has a different result than C' (Levi). Is it possible to fit either Lord Atkin's or Lord Buckmaster's reasoning in *Donoghue* v. *Stevenson* into this form?

8. Read pp. 56–7 of J. Stone, *Legal System and Lawyers' Reasonings* (1964) and find five examples from case law of competing analogies.

9. 'Does this mean that in all those numerous instances of doubt and uncertainty which arise in the application of legal rules, courts really have a completely free choice in the matter and arrive at merely arbitrary decisions? Anyone who studies the elaborately reasoned judgments of English courts must be surprised if not shocked to hear these carefully considered conclusions stigmatized as arbitrary. These are certainly no more, and indeed usually a good deal less, arbitrary than the decisions which we take in other non-legal affairs of daily life' (D. Lloyd.)

Give an example of an arbitrary and a non-arbitrary decision in (*a*) a legal, and (*b*) a non-legal, context. What exactly is meant by 'arbitrary' in these contexts?

10. 'Scientific thought concerns itself with analysing and classifying the elements of given fact-situations and determining their relations to one another for the purpose of acquiring ability to predict the relations between these elements if recurring in a future situation. This procedure involves the same basic thought processes which are involved in the procedure of judicial thinking – the isolation of identities, their formulation in general propositions, and the application of these propositions to specific situations. Here, however, the resemblance ends' (Dickinson).

(*a*) In what ways do scientific and judicial thinking differ?

(*b*) Is there only one mode of reasoning characteristic of each type of thinking?

11. Restate in your own words, as persuasively as you can:

(a) The case for Johnny in the broom episode.

(b) The case for the prosecution in *Allen*.

Identify the propositions which make up the argument in each instance.

12. Give examples of (a) clearly good reasons; (b) clearly bad reasons; (c) reasons about which there might reasonably be disagreement as to whether they were good or bad, valid or invalid, cogent or weak, in relation to a particular result in (i) the case of Johnny, and (ii) *Allen*.

13. State the facts (a) in *Donoghue* v. *Stevenson*, (b) in some extra-legal dispute with which you are familiar, in a manner which illustrates the axiom: 'the statement of facts is the heart'.

14. Read Lord Denning's judgments in the following cases: *Heinz* v. *Berry* [1970] 1 All E.R. 1074; *Dutton* v. *Bognor Regis U.D.C.* [1972] 1 Q.B. 373; *Miller* v. *Jackson* [1977] Q.B. 966 and *Lim Poh Choo* v. *Camden and Islington A.H.A.* [1979] 1 All E.R. 332. Do you agree that these contain 'persuasive' statements of the facts of each case? To what techniques does Lord Denning resort in order to make his judgments persuasive?

15.* Read Professor Summers' article concerning legal reasoning which was referred to in Chapter 7, p. 252. Now read the decisions of the Court of Appeal and of the House of Lords in *Farrell* v. *Alexander* [1976] Q.B. 345; [1977] A.C. 59; and

(a) analyse the reasons given in the judgments in terms of Summers' five types;

(b) are there any other arguments used by the judges which do not readily fall within Summers' typology?

16. Carry out the same exercise as in question 15 using the judgments of Lords Denning, Diplock and Scarman in *Davis* v. *Johnson* set out in Chapter 1.

17. In *The Common Law Tradition*, Karl Llewellyn reiterated what he regarded as the 'Seven ABCs of Appellate Argument':

First, and negatively, *the Insufficiency of Technical Law: it is plainly not enough to bring in a technically perfect case on 'the law'* under the authorities and *some* of the accepted correct techniques for their use and interpretation of 'development'. Unless the judgment you are appealing from is incompetent, there is an equally perfect technical case to be made on the other side, and if your opponent is any good, he will make it . . .

Second, the Trickiness of Classification: a 'technically' perfect case is of itself equally unreliable in regard to the interpretation or classification of the facts. For rarely indeed do the raw facts of even a commercial transaction fit cleanly into any legal pattern; or even the 'trial facts' as they emerge from conflicting testimony. No matter what the state of the law may be, if the essential pattern of the facts is not seen by the court as fitting *cleanly* under the rule you contend for, your case is still in jeopardy. This is of course the reason for the commercial counsellor's concern with 'freezing' the transaction by a well drawn document which does fit cleanly into known and highly certain legal rules . . .

Per contra, and *third*, the *Necessity of a Sound Case 'in Law'*: *Without a technically perfect case on the law*, under the relevant authorities and some one or more of the thoroughly correct procedures of their use and interpretation, *you have no business to expect to win* your case. Occasionally a court may under the utter need for getting a decent result go into deliberate large-scale creative effort; but few courts like to ...

Fourth, the Twofold Sense and Reason: the real and vital central job is to satisfy the court that sense and decency and justice require (a) the rule which you contend for in this *type* of situation; and (b) the result that you contend for, as between these parties. *You* must make your whole case, on law and facts, make *sense*, appeal as being *obvious* sense, inescapable sense, sense in simple terms of life and justice. If that is done, the technically sound case on the law then gets rid of all further difficulty: it shows the court that its duty to the Law not only does not conflict with its duty to Justice but urges to decision along the exact same line.

... It is a question of making the facts talk. For of course it is the facts, not the advocate's expressed opinions, which must do the talking. The court is interested not in listening to any lawyer rant, but in seeing, or better, in discovering, from and in the facts, where sense and justice lie.

This leads to interesting corollaries:

Fifth, the Statement of Facts is the Heart: It is trite that it is in the statement of the facts that the advocate has his first, best, and most precious access to the court's attention. The court does not know the facts, and it wants to. It is trite, among good advocates, that the statement of the facts can, and should, in the very process of statement, frame the legal issue, and can, and should, simultaneously produce the conviction that there is only one sound outcome.

Sixth, Simplicity: It is as yet less generally perceived as a conscious matter that the *pattern of the facts* as stated must be a *simple* pattern, with its lines of simplicity never lost under detail; else attention wanders, or (which is as bad) the effect is drowned in the court's effort to follow the presentation or to organize the material for itself ...

Seventh, The Principle of Concentration of Fire: Even three points, or two, can prove troublesome as dividers of attention unless a way can be found to make them sub-points of a single simple line of attack which gains re-inforcement and cumulative power from each sub-point as the latter is developed ...

To which Llewellyn added two further points:

The function of the oral presentation is, if that be do-able, to catch and rivet attention, to focus the issue into a single challenging question, to make the facts create ineluctable conviction as to where right lies, and to fit that conviction into a persuasive, even compelling legal frame. The brief can develop the frame; but the oral argument must get the case set into the desired frame, and for keeps.

If a brief has made the case for what is right, and has made clear the reason of the rightness, and has found and tailored and displayed the garment of law to clothe the right decision fittingly, then it is not only unwise but indecent not to furnish also in that brief a page or two of text which gathers this all together, which cleans up its relation to the law to date, which puts into clean words the soundly guiding rule to serve the future, and which shows that rule's happy application to the case in hand. What is wanted is a passage which can be quoted verbatim by the court, a passage which so clearly and rightly states and crystallizes the background and the result that it is *recognized* on sight as doing the needed work and as practically demanding to be lifted into the opinion.

(*The Common Law Tradition* (1964), pp. 237–46.)

(*a*) To what extent did counsel in (i) *Allen*; (ii) *Davis* v. *Johnson*; and (iii) *Lawrence* v. *M.P.C.* [1972] A.C. 627, observe these precepts?

(*b*) Choose a variety of cases from different areas of law and analyse counsel's arguments in terms of Llewellyn's advice.

(*c*) To what extent is this advice to advocates applicable to arguments about questions of fact, of policy, and of what the law ought to be?

8 Exercises on Chapter 8

1. Examine any ten cases reported in the past five years in which there have been dissenting judgments and examine the techniques used in each case by any two judges who disagreed with each other in arriving at divergent interpretation of the same precedents.

2. In Chapter 8, we analysed the way in which Lord Buckmaster and Lord Atkin handled the two precedents, *Winterbottom* v. *Wright* and *George* v. *Skivington*. Now read the whole of their speeches in the law reports and, using this analysis as a model, compare their handling of *Langridge* v. *Levy*, *McPherson* v. *Buick*, and *Francis* v. *Cockrell*.

3. Consider the following facts: Over a period of two years John Doe invested heavily in the Rio Bravo Nickel Co., which subsequently went bankrupt. He was encouraged to invest on the strength of optimistic reports prepared by the company's accountants, which were described by an independent expert witness as 'defective and deficient' and as presenting the position of the company at that time as 'wholly contrary to the actual position'. John is thinking of taking action against the accountants. Assuming that the year is 1934 and that *Donoghue* v. *Stevenson* is the only relevant precedent, construct an argument from the standpoint of:

(*a*) a cautious solicitor acting for John

(*b*) an optimistic solicitor acting for John

(*c*) the accountant's barrister

(*d*) John's barrister

(*e*) a judge in the mould of Lord Buckmaster

(*f*) a judge in the mould of Lord Atkin

Would your argument be any different today?

4. Identify the range of meanings of the following expressions: *ratio decidendi*; *obiter dictum*; a binding decision; decision; reason-for deciding; material to the decision; the facts of a case.

5. Can a case have more than one *ratio decidendi*?

6. Must every case have at least one *ratio decidendi*?

7. Was the 'neighbour principle' a necessary part of Lord Atkin's decision in *Donoghue* v. *Stevenson?*

8. Is the 'neighbour principle' an *obiter dictum?* Are there any examples of *obiter dicta* in the extracts from Lord Buckmaster's speech?

9. What facts did Lord Atkin treat as material in *Donoghue* v. *Stevenson (a)* expressly (*b*) impliedly?

10. Can the *ratio decidendi* of a case be changed by subsequent cases?

11. Can there be (*a*) a *ratio decidendi*, (*b*) a reason, which is not a rule?

Donoghue *v.* Stevenson

(You should read the whole case before attempting these exercises.)

1. *Procedure*
    (*a*) From reading the report, what do you understand to have happened in the action before the case reached the House of Lords?
    (*b*) Which was settled first in this case – the issues of fact or the issues of law?
    (*c*) The appeal was allowed. Was this the end of the matter? If not, what further possible steps might have followed?
    (*d*) The issues of fact had not been finally settled before the case reached the House of Lords. How did Lord Buckmaster and Lord Atkin know what the facts were?

2. *Rules*
    (*a*) State the rule or rules of law which Lord Buckmaster thought applied to this case. Were they (or was it) in fixed verbal form? How do you know?
    (*b*) What do you think that Lord Atkin meant by a general principle? Is it different from a rule?
    (*c*) Can you analyse the neighbour principle in terms of its protasis and apodosis? If not, why not?
    (*d*) [The case] 'was a clear instance of the court's taking account of the new conditions of mass production and complex marketing of goods wherein there are many intermediaries between manufacturer and consumer, and by a conscious work of judicial legislation, imposing on manufacturers certain minimum standards of care in favour of the consumer' (Street).
        (i) What evidence is to be found in the speeches of Lords Atkin and Buckmaster that they took into account 'new conditions of mass production', etc.?
        (ii) Which of the cases discussed in the speeches involved problems arising out of the advent of mass production?
        (iii) How new were these 'new conditions'?
        (iv) Why should mass production create a need to change the legal rules governing the relations between manufacturer and consumer?

3 *Reasoning*

   (*a*) Is it fair to say of Lord Atkin's speech in *Donoghue* v. *Stevenson*: 'He came to the conclusion early on that the plaintiff should win and thereafter all his efforts were directed to manipulating the authorities so that they fitted in with the conclusion'?

     If this is fair comment, does it involve a serious criticism of Lord Atkin's behaviour?

     How free was Lord Atkin to *manipulate* the authorities?

   (*b*) What is a 'source' of law? What 'sources' were considered binding on them by Lord Atkin and Lord Buckmaster?

   (*c*) Comment on the passage at [1932] A.C. 567 beginning 'Now the Common Law must be sought ... the appellant's case.'

   (*d*) Comment on the paragraph at [1932] A.C. 576, 'One further case mentioned ... on this view the case does not advance the matter.' Are American decisions a 'source' of law in English courts? What does Lord Buckmaster mean by 'authority' and by 'the source of the law'? Does Lord Atkin's attitude to American cases as possible 'sources' of law differ from Lord Buckmaster's?

   (*e*) At [1932] A.C. 573 Lord Buckmaster says that Brett M.R. laid down 'unnecessarily the larger principle which he entertained'. What does this mean? Do you consider Lord Atkin's 'neighbour' generalization (ibid., p. 580) was 'unnecessary'? If so, is Lord Atkin being hypocritical in the passage commencing 'I venture to say ... unduly restricted' (ibid., pp. 583-4)?

   (*f*) Why does Lord Buckmaster say that the *dicta* of Brett M.R. 'are *rightly* relied on'? ([1932] A.C. 571). What does this mean?

   (*g*) 'In my view, therefore, the *authorities* are against the appellant's contention, and *apart from authority* it is difficult to see how any common law proposition can be formulated to support her claim' ([1932] A.C. 577). Comment.

   (*h*) Alderson B.: 'The only safe rule is to confine the right to recover to those who enter into the contract; if we go one step beyond that, there is no reason why we should not go fifty' (*Winterbottom* v. *Wright* (1842) 10 M. & W. 109, 115). Do you agree?

   (*i*) What does Cardozo J. mean when he says in *MacPherson* v. *Buick* (1916) 217 N.Y. 382: 'Precedents drawn from the days of travel by stagecoach do not fit the conditions of travel today'? What implications might this have for the doctrine of precedent?

   (*j*) 'The majority [in *Donoghue* v. *Stevenson*] did appeal to social convenience and policy as one of the justifications for their decision: "the categories of negligence are never closed". This is an argument which has always been somewhat suspect in England.' Heuston: 20 *Modern Law Review* (1957), 1, 4-5. Comment.

   (*k*) 'Even if [the neighbour principle] is regarded as *dictum*, the carefully considered and often approved utterances of a Law Lord are in no way to be equated to the (perhaps ill-reported) remarks of a puisine judge made at nisi prius. There are *dicta* and *dicta*.' Heuston, ibid., p. 8. Comment.

(*l*) Is the *ratio decidendi* of *Donoghue* v. *Stevenson* the same today as it was in 1933?

9 Exercises on Chapters 9 and 10

1. Choose (*a*) a government Bill, and (*b*) a private member's Bill, and follow their progress through Parliament. Using the Parliamentary debates, and any other material you can discover, try to answer the following questions:
   (*a*) for what reasons was the Bill introduced?
   (*b*) were any particular individuals or groups influential in pressing for the Bill to be enacted?
   (*c*) what differentiates a Bill's Parliamentary stages?
   (*d*) what obstacles lay in the path of the private member's Bill?
   (*e*) how many amendments were moved by the Opposition and by government backbenchers at the Committee stage, and how many were finally accepted by the government?
   (*f*) what were the primary objectives of the Bill?
   (*g*) for what reasons (if any) was the Bill opposed?
   (*h*) how effective was the opposition (if any)?
   (*i*) were any timetable motions used on the government Bill?
   (*j*) what factors do you think will affect the impact of the Bill should it become law?

2. Compare the drafting of Section 1 of the private member's Domestic Violence Bill with that of the 1976 Act (Chapter 1, section 12(*c*) and (*d*)). Do you think that the problems in *B.* v. *B.*, *Cantliff* v. *Jenkins* and *Davis* v. *Johnson* would have arisen if the Private Member's Bill had been enacted verbatim?

3. Compare the drafting styles to be found in the Larceny Act 1916 and the Theft Act 1968. In particular, compare the sections relating to burglary, notice the single use of the word 'building' in the Theft Act, and the use of a number of synonyms for it in the earlier statute. Can you think of any reasons why this substitution might have been made? Do you see any changes in the arrangement and structure of these provisions in the later version? Why do you think these changes may have been made?

4. Compare s. 14 of the Sale of Goods Act 1979 with s. 2-314 of the Uniform Commercial Code. Which of these two do you find easier to read? Give reasons for your answer. Identify as many differences as you can between the two in respect of the terminology, the arrangement, and the detail used in each. By whom, and for whom, do you think these two provisions were drafted?

5. An Act requires that farmers should license 'all cattle, sheep, horses, pigs, goats, asses, and other farmyard animals and cats kept in farmyards for mice and rat catching'. The question arises whether the words 'other farmyard animals' cover a sheepdog who is kept in a farmyard. (N.B. Sheepdogs are at present exempt from needing licences under the Acts dealing with licensing of dogs.) Discuss.

6. Consider the possible problems of interpretation which may arise in connection with the following fictitious draft Bill:

The Outdoor Entertainments Bill:

cl. 1 Any person who engages in the management and performance of any entertainment musical or other dramatic diversion or any show designed to amuse or distract members of the public outdoors shall require an entertainments licence.

cl. 2 An Entertainments Licence may be granted by the local authority.

cl. 3 Any person who, being an entertainer as described in section 1, carries on any theatrical or comic performance without having previously obtained a licence shall be guilty of an offence and be liable on conviction:

    (*a*) to a fine, or

    (*b*) to be refused a license upon such occasion as he may apply for an Entertainments Licence.

cl. 4 In this Act, 'outdoors' means any place which is not covered by a roof or other covering; and 'entertainment' includes any activity which members of the public find entertaining.

Redraft the Outdoor Entertainments Bill so as to take account of your criticisms.

    7. Here is the basic definition of theft as stated in the Theft Act 1968:

    1 A person is guilty of theft if he dishonestly appropriates property belonging to another with the intention of permanently depriving the other of it; and 'thief' and 'steal' shall be construed accordingly.

The partial definition of the word 'dishonestly' as used in that definition reads:

    2(1) A person's appropriation of property belonging to another is not to be regarded as dishonest:

    (*a*) if he appropriates the property in the belief that he has in law the right to deprive the other of it, on behalf of himself or of a third person; or

    (*b*) if he appropriates the property in the belief that he would have the other's consent if the other knew of the appropriation and the circumstances of it; or

    (*c*) (except where the property came to him as trustee or personal representative) if he appropriates the property in the belief that the person to whom the property belongs cannot be discovered by taking reasonable steps.

    2 A person's appropriation of property belonging to another may be dishonest notwithstanding that he is willing to pay for the property.

A cashier in a supermarket takes £5 one Saturday morning because he is broke, and wants to take his girlfriend out that evening. He knows that he is not permitted to borrow money from the till; however, he does intend to repay the money on Monday, and because he does not start work until the afternoon he can cash a cheque at the bank on his way to work. He has £50 in the bank.

In law, the cashier has appropriated property belonging to another with the intention of permanently depriving the other of it (he has that intention because although he intends to repay, he cannot obviously replace the *exact* notes taken, and thus intends to deprive the owner of those notes permanently); but it is arguable whether it can properly be said that he is dishonest. Construct an argument from the point of view (*a*) of the prosecution and (*b*) of the cashier, as to whether or not he was dishonest.

8. Read the decisions of the Court of Appeal and of the House of Lords in
Lawrence v. *M.P.C.* [1971] 1 Q.B. 373; [1972] A.C. 627.
  (*a*) Describe the tactics used by appellants' counsel concerning the interpretation of the Theft Act.
  (*b*) The following factors appear in counsel's argument:
    (*a*) the merits of the case
    (*b*) the correctness of the charge made against his client
    (*c*) the possible redundancy of section 15
    (*d*) the general legal principle involved
    (*e*) the intention of the legislature
    (*f*) the layman's idea of theft.
    Would you say he relies upon all these equally? Can you identify one
    particular ground upon which special reliance is placed?
  (*c*) How does Viscount Dilhorne deal with the points raised by counsel?
  Does he deal with them all? What would you say is the principal ground
  on which he rejects the applicant's argument?
  9. The following provision was inserted in the Acts Interpretation Act 1901
of Australia by the Statute Law Revision Act 1981:

Regard to be had to purpose or object of Act

  15AA. (1) In the interpretation of a provision of an Act, a construction
that would promote the purpose or object underlying the Act (whether that
purpose or object is expressly stated in the Act or not) shall be preferred to
a construction that would not promote that purpose or object.

Consider critically the desirability of adopting such a provision into the law of
England and Wales.

Appendix III Suggestions for Further Reading

The following is a selective bibliography of writings which provide possible starting points for exploring in more detail some of the more general themes and particular topics touched on in the text.

General

We know of no single work which covers exactly the same ground as the present one, but the following have points of contact in a number of places. Max Black, *Critical Thinking* (Prentice-Hall, 1952), E.R. Emmet, *The Use of Reason* (Longman, 1960) and *Learning to Philosophise* (Longman, 1960; Pelican, 1968) are useful general introductions to the more analytical aspects of the study of rules and their interpretation. Mary Douglas (ed.), *Rules and Meanings* (Penguin, 1973) provides a useful conspectus of some of the relevant sociological and anthropological literature. James B. White, *The Legal Imagination* (Little, Brown, 1973) contains a great deal of material, non-legal and legal, which could be used to illustrate and expand many of the themes in this book; so does R. Summers and Charles G. Howard, *Law, Its Nature, Functions and Limits* (Prentice-Hall, 2nd edn, 1972). C.K. Allen, *Law in the Making* (Oxford University Press, 7th edn, 1964) still remains the best general introduction to legal interpretation in England.

For readers with no prior legal background, Glanville Williams, *Learning the Law* (Stevens, 10th edn, 1981), John Farrar, *Introduction to Legal Method* (Sweet and Maxwell, 1977), Lon Fuller, *Anatomy of the Law* (Pelican, 1971), and Phil Harris, *Introduction to Law* (Weidenfeld and Nicolson, 1980) are useful starting points. Another is D. Derham, F.K.H. Maher and Louis Waller, *An Introduction to Law* (Law Book Co. of Australia, 2nd edn, 1980). Karl Llewellyn's *The Bramble Bush* (Oceana, 2nd edn, 1951) is very different in conception and style, but was also directed to beginning law students in the United States. Our own approach has been influenced by Llewellyn (even the legalistic child grew out of one of his examples). Chapters 1–5 of *The Bramble Bush* are directly relevant.

Some aspects of legal interpretation are dealt with in standard works on Jurisprudence. Some of the more general issues are raised in Lon Fuller's entertaining article, 'The Case of Speluncean Explorers', 62 *Harvard Law Review* (1949), 616. This has been reprinted in several anthologies, including R. Henson (ed.), *Landmarks of the Law* (Harper and Row, 1960), which contains several other classic essays concerned with interpretation. Introductory works include Dennis Lloyd, *The Idea of Law* (Penguin, 1970), R.W.M. Dias, *Jurisprudence* (Butterworth, 4th edn, 1976) and Michael Zander, *The Law-Making Process* (Weidenfeld and Nicolson, 1980). Dennis Lloyd, *Introduction to Jurisprudence* (Stevens, 4th edn, 1979) is also useful, especially Chapters 4, 7 and 11. Julius Stone's *Legal System and Lawyers' Reasonings* (Stevens, 1964) is more difficult, but is particularly useful as a bibliographical guide to the literature up to 1964.

Four important works which in different ways add some historical perspective and may serve as correctives to facile rationalism are Peter Stein's *Regulae Juris* (Edinburgh University Press, 1966), S.F.C. Milsom, *Historical Foundations of the Common Law* (Butterworth, 2nd edn, 1981), K.C. Davis, *Discretionary Justice* (University of Illinois, 1971), D. Hay *et al.*, *Albion's Fatal Tree* (Allen Lane, 1975).

Chapters 1–2

Both of the authors have regularly used additional materials to supplement Chapter 1 in our own teaching, but these vary according to the objectives and nature of the course. For further details, see the authors' 'Notes for Teachers'.

On problems, see John Dewey's *How We Think* (Harrap, 1909) and *Logic: The Theory of Enquiry* (Holt, Rinehart and Winston, reprinted 1966), Clarence Morris, *How Lawyers Think* (1938), E.R. Emmet, *The Use of Reason* (op. cit.) and G. Polya, *How to Solve It* (Princeton, 2nd edn, 1957). On 'social problems' see P. Worsley *et al.*, *Problems of Modern Society* (Penguin, 1972) and the literature cited there. On domestic violence see M.D.A. Freeman, *Violence in the Home* (Saxon House, 1979), Erin Pizzey, *Scream Quietly or the Neighbours will Hear* (Pelican, revised edn, 1979). On 'moral panics' (p. 119) see Stuart Hall, *Policing the Crisis* (Macmillan, 1978), which deals with official and press responses to an alleged increase in the incidence of mugging. On the contrast between the way lawyers and their clients perceive and define 'problems', see Z. Bankowski and G. Mungham, *Images of Law* (Routledge, 1976), pp. 32 ff. For a useful account of the constraints on rational policy-making as a response to problems, see J.J. Richardson and A.G. Jordan, *Governing Under Pressure* (Martin Robertson, 1979).

Chapter 3

The philosophical and sociological literature on rules is vast and rapidly expanding. The following is a selection of standard theoretical writings: helpful general discussions of the nature of rules are to be found in the following philosophical works: Max Black, *Models and Metaphors* (Cornell, 1962); Newton Garver, 'Rules' in P. Edwards (ed.), *Encyclopaedia of Philosophy*; D. Schwayder, *The Stratification of Behaviour* (Routledge, 1965); K. Baier, *The Moral Point of View* (Cornell, 1955; Random House, 1965); there is a good discussion of 'Duties and Rules' in Dias, *Jurisprudence* (op. cit., Chapter 8); also worth consulting are D. Emmett, *Rules, Roles and Relations* (Macmillan, 1966) and R.S. Downie, *Roles and Values* (Methuen, 1971). Rather more advanced are G. Von Wright, *Norm and Action* (Routledge, 1963); D. Lewis, *Convention* (Harvard, 1969); G. Gottlieb, *The Logic of Choice* (Allen and Unwin, 1968); Edna Ullmann-Margalit, *The Emergence of Norms* (Oxford, 1977); Peter Collett (ed.), *Social Rules and Social Behaviour* (Blackwell, 1977), A. Ross, *Directives and Norms* (Routledge, 1968) and F. Waismann, *The Principles of Linguistic Philosophy* (Macmillan, 1965), especially Chapters 1, 2 and 7. See also Judith Shklar, *Legalism* (Harvard University Press, 1964). On the distinctions between rules, habits, commands and predictions, see especially Hart, *The Concept of Law* (op. cit.), *passim*, and the defence and refinement of Hart's views in D.N. MacCormick, *H.L.A. Hart* (Arnold, 1981); on rules and principles see R. Dworkin, 'The Model of Rules', 35 *University of Chicago Law Review* (1967), 14 and references cited there. On analysis of duty, right etc., see W. Hohfeld, *Fundamental Legal Conceptions* (Yale University Press, 1964) and standard jurisprudence texts such as Dias and Stone. On attitudes to rules see, for example, Jean Piaget, *The Moral Judgment of the Child* and J.L. Tapp and F.J. Levine, 'Legal Socialization: Strategies for an Ethical Legality', 27 *Stanford Law Review* (1972), 1 and works cited there. On justified departures from legal rules see M. Kadish and S. Kadish, *Discretion to Disobey* (Stanford, 1973). On the functions of rules and the law-jobs theory, see K. Llewellyn, *Jurisprudence* (Chicago, 1962), Chapter 14; K. Llewellyn, 'The Normative, the Legal and the Law Jobs', 49 *Yale Law Journal* (1940), 1355 and K. Llewellyn and E.A. Hoebel, *The Cheyenne Way* (University of Oklahoma, 1941), especially Chapters 10 and 11. In considering the law-jobs theory it is useful to take account of R. Merton, *On Theoretical Sociology* (Free Press, 1967), Lewis A. Coser, *The Functions of Social Conflict* (Routledge, 1972) and Alan Hunt, *The Sociological Movement in Law* (Macmillan, 1978). See further, William Twining, *Karl Llewellyn and the Realist Movement* (Weidenfeld and Nicolson, 1973), Chapter 9 and Appendix B and C.

On interpreting 'reality' see Mary Douglas (ed.), *Rules and Meanings* (op. cit.) and Peter Berger and Thomas Luckman, *The Social Construction of Reality* (Allen Lane, 1967).

Chapters 4-6

On the standard legal literature on interpretation see R. Dias, *Bibliography of Jurisprudence* (Butterworth, 3rd edn, 1979) and the sections on Chapters 7 and 8 below. On the relationship between rule-makers and interpreters see, *inter alios*, L. Fuller, 'The Case of the Speluncean Explorers', op. cit.; L. Jaffé, *English and American Judges as Law-makers* (1969); R. Megarry's *Miscellany at Law* (Stevens, 1955) and *A Second Miscellany-at-Law* (1973) are rich treasuries of concrete, and often amusing, examples of many of the points made in Chapters 4-6.

The main themes in Chapter 5 take Hart's *The Concept of Law* as their starting point. For a contrasting approach see particularly L. Fuller, *The Morality of Law* (Yale University Press, 1969). On language and the law see especially Glanville Williams, 'Language and the Law', 61 *Law Quarterly Review* (1945), 71, 179, 293, 384 and 62 *L.Q.R.* (1946), 387 and Lloyd, *Introduction to Jurisprudence* (op. cit.) and references there.

In addition to the works by Max Black and E.R. Emmet cited above (p. 372), the following general introductions to semantics and clear thinking are recommended: R. Thouless, *Straight and Crooked Thinking* (Pan, 1974); L. Susan Stebbing, *Thinking to Some Purpose* (Penguin, 1939); S. Ullman, *Words and Their Use* (Muller, 1961); Stewart Chase, *The Tyranny of Words* (Methuen, 6th edn, 1947); J. Wilson, *Thinking With Concepts* (Cambridge, 1971) and Antony Flew, *Thinking About Thinking* (Fontana, 1975). At some stage during his education every law student ought to read J.L. Austin, *How To Do Things With Words* (Oxford, 1962). On the conditions of doubt see F. Bennion, *Statute Law* (Oyez, 1980).

On the 'intention' of the legislature, see Dias, *Bibliography of Jurisprudence*, op. cit.; and on the development of rules in response to novel or exceptional circumstances, Lon Fuller, 'Reason and Fact in Case Law', 59 *Harvard Law Review* (1946), 376 and 'Human Purpose and Natural Law', 3 *Natural Law Forum* (1958), 68 and Ian McNeil, 'The Many Futures of Contracts', 47 *Southern California Law Review* (1974), 691.

Chapter 7

Useful introductions to reasoning in general include the works by Black, Flew and Emmet cited above and R. Hospers, *Introduction to Philosophical Analysis* (Routledge, 2nd edn, 1969); Peter Alexander, *An Introduction to Logic* (Allen and Unwin, 1969); S. Mellone, *Elements of Modern Logic* (2nd edn, 1958); Part I of M. Cohen and E. Nagel, *An Introduction to Logic and Scientific Method* (Routledge, 1961), reprinted as *An Introduction to Logic* (Routledge, 1963); and N. Rescher, *Dialectics* (State University of New York, 1977).

On practical reasoning see S. Toulmin, *The Uses of Argument* (Cambridge, 1964), D. Gauthier, *Practical Reasoning* (Oxford, 1963). Especially relevant for lawyers is the work of Chaim Perelman. The *locus classicus* is C. Perelman and L. Olbrechts-Tyteca, *The New Rhetoric: A Treatise on Argumentation* (University of Notre Dame Press, 1969). The reader may find it easier to start with Perelman's *The Idea of Justice and the Problem of Argument* (Routledge, 1963). J. Raz (ed.), *Practical Reasoning* (Oxford U.P., 1978) contains useful essays, some of whose themes are explored in greater detail in the more difficult *Practical Reason and Norms* (Hutchinson, 1975).

R. Summers, 'Two Types of Substantive Reasons', 63 *Cornell Law Review* (1978), 707–88 contains the elements of a comprehensive account of judicial reasoning; a more sustained discussion is D. N. MacCormick's *Legal Reasoning and Legal Theory* (Clarendon Press, 1978). R. Dworkin's controversial thesis is to be found in *Taking Rights Seriously* (Duckworth, 1978).

On Advocacy, in addition to the works cited in the footnotes, see D. Napley, *The Technique of Persuasion* (Sweet and Maxwell, 2nd edn, 1975), R. Du Cann, *The Art of the Advocate* (Penguin, 1964), E. A. Parry, *The Seven Lamps of Advocacy* (Allen and Unwin, 1923).

Chapter 8

In the British literature on the interpretation of cases, discussion has centred very largely on the rules of precedent; see, for example, R. M. W. Dias, *Jurisprudence*, op. cit.; P. J. Fitzgerald (ed.), *Salmond on Jurisprudence* (Sweet & Maxwell, 12th edn, 1966) and C. K. Allen, *Law in the Making*, op. cit. *Precedent in English Law* by Sir R. Cross (Oxford U.P., 3rd edn, 1977) is the leading exposition of the doctrine as it is understood in Great Britain. A more thoughtful account of the theory of precedent is R. Wasserstrom, *The Judicial Decision* (Stamford U.P., 1961).

As should be clear from the text, we are generally more in sympathy with the analysis adopted by K. N. Llewellyn in *The Common Law Tradition* (Little, Brown, 1960). Other classic works by American writers such as *The Nature of the Judicial Process* by B. Cardozo (Yale University Press, 1921) and O. W. Holmes, 'The Path of the Law', 10 *Harvard Law Review* (1897), 457 are recommended. *The Judge* by Lord Devlin (Oxford U. P., 1981) and two books by Lord Denning M.R., *The Discipline of Law* and *The Due Process of Law* (Butterworths, 1979 and 1980), give some idea as to how judges conceive their role; more critical are L. Jaffé, *English and American Judges as Law-Makers*, op. cit.; M. D. A. Freeman, *The Legal Structure* (Longman, 1974) and J. A. G. Griffith, *The Politics of the Judiciary* (Fontana, 1977). A comprehensive account of the House of Lords as a judicial body is R. B. Stevens' important *Law and Politics* (Weidenfeld and Nicolson, 1979).

On the constraints which operate on judges as interpreters, the reader is again referred to K. N. Llewellyn, *The Common Law Tradition* (op. cit.). See further, J. Frank, *Courts on Trial* (Atheneum, 1949) and B. Laskin, *The Institutional Character of the Judge* (Hebrew University of Jerusalem, 1972). See also M. Zander, *The Law-Making Process*, op. cit., and J. Farrar, *Introduction to Legal Method*, op. cit.

Chapters 9 and 10

For a systematic description of the preparation, enactment, interpretation and impact of legislation, see D. Miers and A. Page, *Legislation* (Sweet and Maxwell, 1982).

The Government and Politics of Britain by J. P. Mackintosh (Hutchinson, 4th edn, 1977), and *The Legislative Process in Great Britain* by S. A. Walkland (Allen and Unwin, 1968) are excellent introductions to the political literature. J. Richardson and A. Jordan, *Governing Under Pressure*, op. cit., is more detailed on policy-making, while J. A. G. Griffith and T. C. Hartley, *Government and Law* (Weidenfeld and Nicolson, 2nd edn, 1981) is recommended for those who wish to pursue in more detail the relationship between legislative process and the enactment of legislation; for a more specialized approach to a particular source of legislation, see J. A. G. Griffith, *Parliamentary Scrutiny of Government Bills* (Allen and Unwin, 1974). A useful case-study is M. J. Barnett, *The Politics of Legislation: The Rent Act 1957* (Weidenfeld and Nicolson, 1969).

A specifically legal account of the preparation and interpretation of legislation is F. Bennion, *Statute Law*, op. cit.; other more specialized accounts of drafting are E. Driedger, *The Composition of Legislation* (Dept. of Justice, Ottawa, 1976): R. Dickerson, *The Fundamentals of Legal Drafting* (Little, Brown, 1965) and G. C. Thornton, *Legislative Drafting* (Butterworth, 2nd edn, 1979). *In on the Act* by Sir H. Kent (Macmillan, 1979) contains the memoirs of a former Parliamentary Counsel, and provides a rare and valuable, though somewhat dated, account of the Office of Parliamentary Counsel.

There are several publications which are critical of the present arrangements for the preparation of Bills. Among these are: the report of the Renton Committee, *The Preparation of Legislation* (Cmnd. 6053, 1975); Sir W. Dale, *Legislative Drafting: A New Approach* (Butterworth, 1977); and four reports of the Statute Law Society: *Statute Law Deficiencies* (1970), *Statute Law: The Key to Clarity* (1972), *Statute Law: A Radical Simplification* (1974) and *Renton and the Need for Reform* (1979), all published by Sweet and Maxwell.

Similarly, there is a great deal of material which describes and analyses the interpretation of statutes. The standard texts, however, vary between fairly technical accounts of the application of the so-called 'rules' of interpretation, such as Maxwell on *The Interpretation of Statutes* (Sweet and Maxwell, 12th edn, 1969) and *Craies on Statute Law* (Sweet and Maxwell, 7th edn. 1971) on the one hand, and the more general jurisprudential treatment to be found in such books as R. M. W. Dias, *Jurisprudence*, op. cit., and *Salmond on Jurisprudence*, op. cit., on the other. Sir R. Cross, *Statutory Interpretation* (Butterworth, 1976) gives a clear exposition of judicial approaches to interpretation. More critical accounts are to be found in the Law Commission's excellent paper, *The Interpretation of Statutes* (1969, Law Com. No. 21, H. C. Paper 256), in J. Willis, 'Statute Interpretation in a Nutshell', 16 *Canadian Bar Review* (1938), 1, with whose functional approach we are more in sympathy, and in J. Stone, *Legal System and Lawyers' Reasoning*, op. cit. The *Statute Law Review* (Sweet and Maxwell) is a valuable periodical containing material relating to the preparation, interpretation and teaching of legislation.

Legislation and Society in Australia, edited by R. Tomasic (Allen and Unwin, 1980), contains a useful summary of the principal contributions to theoretical and empirical studies of the creation, implementation and impact of legislation; in particular in Chapters 1-4. Some of the expanding literature which we recommend are: J. W. Hurst, *Law and Social Process in United States History* (New York, Da Capo Press, 1972); M. Feeley, 'The Concept of Laws in Social Science', 10 *Law and Society Review* (1976) 497; R. B. Ferguson, 'Legal Ideology and Commercial Interest', 4 *British Journal of Law and Society* (1977), 18; and K. Renner, *The Institutions of Private Law and Their Social Functions* (Routledge and Kegan Paul, 1976).

Index